SPECIAL EDUCATION, MULTICULTURAL EDUCATION, AND SCHOOL REFORM

ABOUT THE AUTHORS

Cheryl A. Utley is currently an Associate Research Professor in the Schiefelbusch Institute of Life Span Studies, The Juniper Gardens Children's Project, University of Kansas, Kansas City, Kansas. Her graduate degrees are from the University of Arizona and the University of Wisconsin-Madison. Dr. Utley is a researcher, teacher educator, and scholar. Her specific areas of interest include multicultural education and teacher education, assessment, observational learning, and effective instructional practices (e.g., peer-mediated instruction).

Festus E. Obiakor is currently a Professor of Special Education in the Department of Exceptional Education, University of Wisconsin-Milwaukee. His graduate degrees are from Texas Christian University and New Mexico State University. Dr. Obiakor is a teacher, scholar, consultant, and poet–his specific areas of interests include self-concept, multicultural education, comparative/international education, retention of at-risk students and educational reform/program evaluation. He is author of *The Eight-Step Multicultural Approach: Learning and Teaching with a Smile*.

On the cover: Joycelyn Strickland, a fourth grade teacher, is pictured with a second and fourth grade high-achieving multicultural learners in her classroom at Benjamin Banneker Elementary Science & Technology Magnet School, Kansas City Kansas Unified School District (USD) #500, located in Kansas City, Kansas.

SPECIAL EDUCATION, MULTICULTURAL EDUCATION, AND SCHOOL REFORM

Components of Quality Education for Learners with Mild Disabilities

Edited by

CHERYL A. UTLEY

The Juniper Gardens Children's Project
University of Kansas
Kansas City, Kansas

and

FESTUS E. OBIAKOR

University of Wisconsin-Milwaukee
Milwaukee, Wisconsin

Charles C Thomas
PUBLISHER • LTD.
SPRINGFIELD • ILLINOIS • U.S.A.

Published and Distributed Throughout the World by

CHARLES C THOMAS • PUBLISHER, LTD.
2600 South First Street
Springfield, Illinois 62704

©2001 by CHARLES C THOMAS • PUBLISHER, LTD.

ISBN 0-398-07118-7 (hard)
ISBN 0-398-07119-5 (paper)

Library of Congress Catalog Card Number: 00-060773

With THOMAS BOOKS *careful attention is given to all details of manufacturing
and design. it is the Publisher's desire to present books that are satisfactory as to their
physical qualities and artistic possibilities and appropriate for their particular use.*
THOMAS BOOKS *will be true to those laws of quality that assure a good name
and good will.*

*Printed in the United States of America
CS-R-3*

Library of Congress Cataloging-in-Publication Data
Special education, multicultural education, and school reform : components
of quality
eduction for learners with mild disabilities / edited by Cheryl A. Utley and
Festus E. Obiakor.
    p. cm.
   Includes bibliographical references and index.
   ISBN 0-398-07118-7 -- ISBN 0-398-07119-5 (pbk.)
   1. Multicultural education. 2. Children of minorities--Education.
  3. Handicapped children--Education. I. Utley, Cheryl Anita Rose.
  II. Obiakor, Festus, E.

LC1099 .S64 2000
370.117--dc21   00-060773

To my mother, Bertie M. Utley; to my sister, Beverly Briter-amos, and immediate family members for their support and encouragement throughout my professional career. To Soka Gakkai International (SGI) President Daisaku Ikeda for his efforts in promoting peace, culture, and education throughout the world.

To my wife, Pauline; to my children, Charles, Gina, and Kristen; and to Mama and all my family members in Nigeria for their unconditional love and kindness. To my well-wishers and friends, thanks for hanging in there with me!

CONTRIBUTORS

Dale P. Blesz
Department of Reading & Special Education
Southwest Missouri State University
Springfield, Missouri

Ellen A. Brantlinger
Department of Special Education
Indiana University
Bloomington, Indiana

William J. Carter, Jr.
Department of Special Education
University of Kansas Medical Center
Kansas City, Kansas

Vivian C. Correa
Department of Special Education
University of Florida
Gainesville, Florida

Martha J. Coutinho
Department of Human Development & Learning
East Tennessee State University
Johnson City, Tennessee

Vera I. Daniels
Department of Special Education
Southern University and A & M College–Baton Rouge
Baton Rouge, Louisiana

Ingrid L. Draper
Urban Special Education Leadership Collaborative
Education Development Center, Inc.
Newton, Massachusetts

Edgar G. Epps
Department of Urban Studies
University of Wisconsin-Milwaukee
Milwaukee, Wisconsin

Bridgie Alexis Ford
Department of Counseling and Special Education
University of Akron
Akron, Ohio

Kathleen C. Harris
College of Education
Arizona State University West
Phoenix, Arizona

Simon Kim
Division of Educational Psychology, Research, and Evaluation
University of Missouri-St.Louis
St. Louis, Missouri

Sue Ann Kline
Department of Special Education
University of Kansas Medical Center
Kansas City, Kansas

J. Ruth Nelson
National Center on Educational Outcomes
University of Minnesota
Minneapolis, Minnesota

Ann Nevin
College of Education
Arizona State University West
Phoenix, Arizona

Festus E. Obiakor
Department of Exceptional Education
University of Wisconsin-Milwaukee
Milwaukee, Wisconsin

Alba A. Ortiz
Department of Special Education
University of Texas-Austin
Austin, Texas

Donald P. Oswald
Department of Psychiatry
Virginia Commonwealth University
Richmond, Virginia

Cynthia Reynolds
Department of Counseling and Special Education
University of Akron
Akron, Ohio

Zaline Roy-Campbell
Department of Education Theory and Practice
State University of New York (SUNY)–Albany
Albany, New York

Robert Rueda
Department of Educational Psychology
University of Southern California
Los Angeles, California

Richard L. Simpson
Department of Special Education
University of Kansas Medical Center
Kansas City, Kansas

Brenda Smith Myles
Department of Special Education
University of Kansas Medical Center
Kansas City, Kansas

Ellen Teelucksingh
National Center on Educational Outcomes
University of Minnesota
Minneapolis, Minnesota

Martha L. Thurlow
National Center on Educational Outcomes
University of Minnesota
Minneapolis, Minnesota

Cheryl A. Utley
Juniper Gardens Children's Project
Schiefelbusch Institute for Life Span Studies
University of Kansas
Kansas City, Kansas

FOREWORD

Schools are experiencing dramatic demographic shifts and are now serving an increasing number of students who are multicultural; in fact, in many urban school districts, multicultural learners are already the majority student enrollment. Unfortunately, though, there is abundant evidence that general and special educators are not prepared to respond to this changing student population as evidenced by widespread academic underachievement, high retention and dropout rates, and disproportionate representation of multicultural learners in remedial and special education programs. Too many students, in both general and special education, experience instructional programs and services which are inconsistent with their linguistic, cultural, socioeconomic and other background characteristics and which emphasize low-level, basic skills with insufficient attention paid to developing higher order thinking, problem-solving skills, and creativity. These educational practices can have long-term, negative consequences for students in terms of their self esteem and their academic, social, and economic outcomes. The very programs designed to improve student performance, in actuality, maintain their low performance, a situation which has stimulated a plethora of standard-based school reform efforts.

While the rhetoric suggests that educational reform movements are to include all students, the reality is that school improvement activities are developed and implemented without specific attention to the needs of multicultural learners. Reform efforts have met with limited success because policymakers, researchers, teacher educators, and general and special educators do not understand how important variables such as language, culture, poverty, and/or disability influence the teaching-learning process and student outcomes. Consequently, multicultural learners are not provided with what they need to be academically successful–high expectations and a challenging curriculum presented in ways that are compatible with their background characteristics so they can meet high academic standards.

The challenge for educational reformers, then, is to ensure that all students have equal access to quality education and it is precisely this challenge that is addressed by Cheryl A. Utley, Festus E. Obiakor, and their contributors in their cutting edge book, *Special Education, Multicultural Education and School Reform: Components of Quality Edu-*

cation for Learners with Mild Disabilities. The authors have done an outstanding job of helping educators understand the importance of integrating the philosophy and knowledge base of multicultural education into educational programs and services. The information presented in this text can contribute significantly to building a shared knowledge base relative to multicultural education among general and special educators. Such a knowledge base is fundamental not only to ensuring that educators understand multicultural learners, but it is the foundation for designing comprehensive educational programs and services which meet the needs of multicultural learners in all of the programs in which they are served.

The authors address essential elements of school reform and improvement, including establishing positive school climates for multicultural learners, ensuring that teachers use instructional programming options known to be effective for multicultural populations, and designing multicultural special education programs which address students' linguistic and cultural characteristics *and* their disability-related needs simultaneously. Among the authors' most important messages are the following:

- *All* educators must understand the interrelationships among language, culture, socioeconomic status and values and the ways in which these influence academic and social behaviors of students.
- Multicultural education must be aimed at increasing respect for diversity, decreasing prejudice, improving interethnic group relations, understanding intraindividual and interindividual differences, and resolving cultural incompatibilities between students' styles of learning and behavior and educators' styles of instruction.
- Teaching is a cross-cultural encounter. Consequently, a fundamental component of creating a supportive and accepting learning environment for multicultural learners is helping general and special educators acquire the skills they need to assess the unique academic and social characteristics of multicultural learners, including those with mild disabilities, and to accommodate student diversity in the teaching-learning process. Teacher education programs, at the preservice and inservice levels, must thus infuse multicultural knowledge and skills into their curricula.
- Improving educational outcomes for multicultural learners cannot happen without restructuring general and special education in response to the changing student demography and the individual and specific needs of multicultural learners.
- Among the most important elements of successful school reform are inclusion, multiculturalism, consultation, teamwork, cooperation, partnership, and empowerment. A key reform strategy is building collaborative relationships among stakeholders, including teachers, students, administrators, and families.

As we advance in this new millennium, we must find ways to effectively serve students who have been historically ill-served by the public school education system.

This text provides an excellent resource for designing programs and services to ensure that multicultural learners are able to achieve their maximum potential in general and special education programs. When multicultural education is successful, everyone, students and teachers alike, learn to understand and value their own cultural identities, have opportunities to experience other cultures and learn to interact successfully cross-culturally, and they learn the value of working together to create a society which accepts, respects, and values diversity. The messages in this text can serve as cornerstones of standards-based reform and school improvement. They are keys to successful multicultural education.

Alba A. Ortiz, Ph.D. Professor,
Department of Special Education
Director, Office of Bilingual Education
H.E. Hartfelder/The Southland Corporation
Regents Chair in Educational Leadership
College of Education
The University of Texas at Austin
Austin, Texas
March 2000

PREFACE

General and special educators are consistently challenged to respond to school re-form programs. Because of current demographic changes and shifts in powers and paradigms, it has become imperative for the fields of multicultural education and special education to address issues of reform. As a result, one critical question de-serves our immediate attention. How can an equitable and culturally responsible ed-ucation be provided for multicultural learners with mild disabilities in inclusive classroom settings? This book addresses this issue and bridges gaps between the school reform movement in special education and multicultural education.

Our premier concern is that the school reform movement has ignored education-al challenges and dilemmas facing multicultural learners with mild disabilities, their families, and teachers. Many special education advocacy groups, researchers, and scholars have had similar concerns in spite of traditional reform programs. We be-lieve the school reform movement in special education is caught up in a "rat race" and in its half-hearted pursuit for "equality and equity." It has become increasingly apparent that general and special educators have ignored and overlooked the cogni-tive, behavioral, and affective needs of multicultural learners with mild disabilities.

This book acknowledges the complexities of different cultures within the family, community, and society. Not only does it recognize multiethnic or global relation-ships between multicultural groups, it also recognizes cultures, ethnicities, symbols, languages, values, and learning and behavioral styles of different groups of individu-als. We state unequivocally that a multicultural education framework is multidimen-sional and aims at increasing respect for diversity, reducing prejudice, improving interethnic group relations, understanding intraindividual and interindividual differ-ences, and resolving cultural incompatibilities between students' learning and be-havioral styles. Realizing one's learning potential through scholarship and achievement are important components of quality education for multicultural learn-ers with and without disabilities. We challenge researchers and scholars to translate re-search into practice so that general and special education practitioners and policymakers can make decisions and recommendations that provide an effective ed-ucation for multicultural learners.

We are glad that leading researchers and scholars in the fields of multicultural education and special education were instrumental in putting this visionary book together. Chapter One describes the effects of race, culture, and poverty on multicultural learners with disabilities. Chapter Two challenges the underlying assumptions and rationale for serving multicultural learners in special education settings. In Chapter Three, trends in the disproportionate representation of multicultural learners with mild disabilities are examined. Chapter Four presents cultural and linguistic diversity as a central component for understanding multicultural learners with disabilities. Chapters Five, Six, and Seven discuss the multidimensional problems and prospects facing multicultural learners with learning disabilities, emotional/behavioral disorders, and gifts and talents. In each of these chapters, we examine contemporary perspectives related to issues of definition, assessment, and intervention in order to better understand and provide solutions for educating multicultural learners and their families. In Chapter Eight, the role of multicultural education in a results-based education system is evaluated. Chapter Nine explains collaborative consultative endeavors that enhance multicultural learning. In Chapter Ten, a culturally responsible teacher education program is discussed in terms of standards, knowledge bases, and skills. Chapter Eleven addresses the restructuring of public schools to form school and community partnerships. And, Chapter Twelve summarizes new directions for the field of multicultural special education. On the whole, this book brings contemporary issues, concerns, and perspectives related to multicultural learners to the school reform debate. As a result, researchers and scholars will find it useful. In addition, it will be an important text for undergraduate and graduate courses in multicultural special education.

We would like to express our deepest appreciation to the contributors for their commitment to school reform for multicultural learners and for sharing their ideas in this book. We are very grateful to Drs. Alba A. Ortiz and Edgar G. Epps for their scholarly contributions in the Foreword and Summary Comments. We would like to acknowledge Dr. Charles R. Greenwood, Director of the Juniper Gardens Children's Project, for his support in this venture. We are especially grateful to Bernadine Roberts and Mary Williard, members of the Juniper Gardens Children's Project Support Staff for their assistance in this project.

Cheryl A. Utley
Festus E. Obiakor

CONTENTS

SPECIAL EDUCATION, MULTICULTURAL EDUCATION, AND SCHOOL REFORM

Chapter 1

MULTICULTURAL EDUCATION AND SPECIAL EDUCATION: INFUSION FOR BETTER SCHOOLING

CHERYL A. UTLEY AND FESTUS E. OBIAKOR

The current public school system is based upon the democratic philosophy of equal educational opportunities for all children. It is on this premise that children of all cultures, languages, genders, or exceptionalities are educated. School reform movements, public policies, court cases, and legislative mandates have been enacted to provide maximum opportunities for students whose race, nationality, gender or language are different from the majority culture (Obiakor, 1994; Obiakor & Utley, 1997, 1998). Despite these efforts, equal educational opportunities for students of diverse cultural, ethnic, linguistic, and socioeconomic backgrounds seem to be deferred dreams. The historic educational reality of these students is that their education mostly occurs in urban environments with little commitment to individuality, respect for differences, equal opportunity for all, freedom of discourse, and opportunities for upward mobility (Banks, 1999; Kozol, 1991;

West, 1993). The results have been more labels and more categories that fail to recognize and value the multiple skills, capabilities, competencies, and intelligences of students (Artiles & Trent, 1994; Gardner, 1993; Gould, 1981; Hilliard, 1995; Obiakor & Algozzine, 1995).

In addressing the issues of underachievement and school reform, multicultural education has become one of the focal points in the increasingly intense conflict over racial and ethnic equality (Olneck, 1993; Rodriguez, 1999). In the United States, the majority of arguments on the educational equality for multicultural learners focuses on the distribution of monies and resources, rewards, and achievement outcomes among different groups of individuals (Kozol, 1991). However, the issue of whether groups enjoy equal respect, status, dignity, and honor in schools is just as important as knowing whether resources are distributed equally among

3

schools (Trueba, 1993). Questions about access or opportunity to appropriate services and the similarities and differences between race and disability must also be brought to bear as well as questions regarding the conditions under which separate and inclusive educational programs for students with disabilities entail discrimination. Other critical questions remain unanswered. Are the procedural rights of multicultural learners with mild disabilities respected? Does belonging to cultural or linguistic groups imply a disability? Are multicultural learners with mild disabilities protected against the stigma of exclusion, lowered expectations, misclassifications, misdiagnoses, and poor instructional programs? Are multicultural learners with mild disabilities treated as responsible citizens with full potential to participate in this society?

Increasingly, general and special educators are interested in implementing inclusive education programs for multicultural children with mild disabilities. However, if general and special education programs are to be properly implemented, educators must understand, appreciate, and fully value the cultural diversity that exists among students. As Banks (1994) indicated, "teachers are human beings who bring their cultural perspective, values, hopes, and dreams to the classroom. They also bring their prejudices, stereotypes, and misconceptions to the classroom. The teachers' values and perspectives mediate and interact with the teacher and influence the way that messages are communicated and perceived by the students" (p. 159).

Apparently, while cultural diversity in the student population is increasing, the composition of the teaching or professional force is decreasing (American Association of Colleges for Teacher Education, 1994; Ewing, 1995; Obiakor, 1993; Zeichner, 1992). For instance, Zeichner described the dilemma when he explained:

Because the demographic composition of the teaching corps is unlikely to change significantly, even under the most optimistic scenario, and because alternative routes will most likely continue to supplement rather than replace general campus-based programs, the problem of educating teachers for diversity, in most instances, will continue to be one of educating White, monolingual, and mostly female teacher education students during preservice teacher education in college and university settings to teach diverse learners effectively. (p. 1)

Teacher-student differences will be compounded by the presence of many students who come from families residing in poverty communities and from families who do not speak English (Hildago, Bright, Sui, Swap, & Epstein, 1995). In addition, factors such as immigrant status and acculturation (Trueba, 1989, 1993), second language and dialectal differences (Brice-Heath, 1989; Sugai, Maheady, & Skouge, 1989; Tharp & Gallimore, 1988), and incompatible instructional practices (Franklin, 1992) have profound primary and secondary effects on children's learning and social adjustment. As Hanna (1994) pointed out:

Student-teacher and student-student misunderstandings and confrontations, are, of course, common; cultural diversity complicates (and may increase and/or magnify) some types of academic and social problems because of the clash of attitudes, values, and behavior. Such cross-cultural misunderstandings and different behavior patterns reinforce existing prejudices against minorities and majorities. Misunderstandings and dislikes of different behaviors may also alienate individuals and groups and foster the inability to develop trust and rapport. (p. 73)

We believe multicultural education and special education are complementary and these relationships are fundamental to the innovative schooling process of multicultural learners with and without mild disabilities. A plethora of innovative school policies and educational programs has been implemented in classrooms to address individual needs and goals of students with mild disabilities. These initiatives have focused on (a) school restructuring, (b) modifications in the general education curriculum, and (c) measurement of student outcomes. The school reform movement, however, has yet to address the impact of poverty, cultural, linguistic, and social factors on educational outcomes of multicultural learners with mild disabilities or to provide these students with equitable educational services (Garcia & Dominguez, 1997; Obiakor, Algozzine, & Ford, 1994).

Our purpose, then, in this chapter is to integrate the philosophy of multicultural education in the field of special education. First, we present demographic trends to reflect the rapidly increasing racial/ethnic diversity in classrooms, schools, and communities and the challenges that face general and special educators. Second, we focus on pertinent issues such as poverty, race, and the disproportionate representation of multicultural learners in educational programs because they directly affect the categorization of these students as learning disabled (LD), behaviorally disordered (BD), and mildly mentally retarded (MMR). Third, we discuss the meaning of culture and the underlying assumptions of cultural diversity and disability paradigms. And lastly, we discuss multiculturalism and multicultural education and the infusion of this philosophy in special education.

DEMOGRAPHIC TRENDS IN UNITED STATES SCHOOLS

Immigration patterns and the geographic distribution of families in the United States have changed from a monocultural society to a pluralistic and diverse one (Aponte & Crouch, 2000; U.S. Bureau of the Census, 1991). Demographic trends have shown that the number of racial/ethnic categories in the United States have expanded rapidly and to a significant degree. Spickard, Fong, and Ewalt (1996) reported that:

The racial categories in the 1940 census were White and non-White (by the latter, the census takers meant mainly African Americans). During the next three censuses, the number of categories slowly increased, exploding in the 1980 and 1990 censuses. There were 43 racial categories and subcategories on the 1990 census forms, including White; Black; American Indian, Eskimo, or Aleut; Asian or Pacific Islander; with 11 Asian subcategories and four Pacific Islander subcategories; other race; and a Hispanic origin grid with 15 subcategories that included Mexico, Puerto Rican, Cuban, and other Hispanic. The multiplication of racial categories stems in part from the growing numbers of immigrants, particularly from Asia and Latin America, and their descendants. In 1990, the U.S. population was 76 percent White, 12 percent African American, 9 percent Hispanic, and 3 percent Asian. (p. 15)

More recent statistics provided by *America's Children: Key National Indicators of Well-Being* (1999), substantiates earlier statistics showing that trends in racial and ethnic diversity among children has grown dramatically in the United States. By the year 1998, 65 percent of United States children were White, non-Hispanic; 15 percent were Black, non-Hispanic; 15 percent were Hispanic; 4 percent were Asian/Pacific Islander; and 1 percent were American Indian/Alaska Native. The number of Hispanic children has increased faster than that of any other racial and ethnic group, growing from 9 percent of the child population in 1980 to 15 percent in 1998. By the year

2020, it is projected that more than 1 in 5 children in the United States will be of Hispanic origin. The percentage of Hispanic children will outnumber the percentage of Black-non-Hispanic. The percentage of children who are Hispanic will have increased from 15 percent in 1998 to 22 percent in 2020, while the percentage of children who are Black, will remain fairly stable. The percentage of Asian/Pacific Islander children doubled from 2 to 4 percent of all United States children between 1980 and 1998. Their percentage is projected to continue to increase to 6 percent in the year 2020. By the year 2050, conservative demographic projections are 52 percent White, 16 percent African American, 22 percent Hispanic, and 10 percent Asian (The New Face of America, 1993).

Trends in Poverty and Race Statistics

General and special educators are challenged to provide equitable educational outcomes for children living in poverty or adverse environmental circumstances. Sherman (1997) remarked that "poverty matters profoundly to the 14.5 million United States children—more than one in every five—who live below the poverty line" (p. 1). As shown in Table 1.1, serious health and education problems impact the lives of children residing in poverty (Children's Defense Fund, 1997). Poverty and race are important societal factors that affect the lives of many multicultural children in distinct ways. Huston (1991) wrote:

> Race is the most striking and disturbing distinction between families whose poverty is persistent and those for whom it is transitory. Black children have a much higher risk of living in chronic poverty than do white children. The average black child in the Panel Study on Income Dynamics spent 5.5 years in poverty; the average nonblack child spent 0.9 years in poverty. Many chronically poor children also live in single-mother families. Mothers who are either unmarried or in their teen years at the end of the child's birth and who are poorly educated have children who are at risk for long-term poverty. (p. 9)

The poverty rate is a widely used indicator of economic disadvantage which measures the proportion of a population whose cash income is below the official poverty line. The young child poverty rate is defined as the percentage of children under age six who live in families with a combined income below the federal poverty line. During much of the last two decades, children in the United States began to experience higher rates of poverty in urban, suburban, and rural areas. In addition, the child poverty rate "continues to exceed the rate for older children, ages 6 though 17, and is more than double the rate for adults, ages 18 through 64, and the elderly, ages 65 and above" (National Center for Children in Poverty, 1999, p. 1). In the document, *Changing America: Indicators of Social and Economic Well-Being by Race and Hispanic Origin* (Council of Economic Advisors for the President's Initiative on Race, 1998), trends in poverty rates for racial and ethnic groups saw some fluctuations. For example, in the 1960s and 1970s, child poverty rates for all ethnic and racial groups declined sharply. In 1985, 20% of all children lived in families with incomes below the official poverty level; 41% of all African American and 37% of all Hispanic children lived in poverty (U.S. Department of Education, 1988). By 1988, the rate had dropped to approximately 19.5% for all children; among children under age 3, it was 23.3% (Children's Defense Fund, 1989; Rainwater & Smeeding). There has been, however, a modest increase in relative child poverty since 1988. From 1989 to 1992, the rates of child poverty increased from 19.6% to 21.9%.

Table 1.1
CHILDREN'S BAD OUTCOMES BY FAMILY INCOME

Outcome	Low-Income Children's Higher Risk
Health	
Death in childhood	1.5 to 3 times more likely
Stunted growth	2.7 times more likely
Iron deficiency as preschoolers	3 to 4 times more likely
Partly or completely deaf	1.5 to 2 times more likely
Partly or completely blind	1.2 to 1.8 times more likely
Serious physical or mental disabilities	about 2 times more likely
Fatal accidental injuries	2 to 3 times more likely
Pneumonia	1.6 times more likely
Education	
Average IQ scores at age 5	9 test points lower
Average achievement scores for ages 3 and older	11 to 25 percentiles lower
Learning disabilities	1.3 times more likely
In special education	2 or 3 percentage points more likely
Below usual grade for child's age	2 percentage points more likely for each year of childhood spent in poverty
Dropping out from ages 16 to 24	2 times more likely than middle-income youths; 11 times more likely than wealthy youths

Source: Sherman, A. (1998). *Poverty matters: The cost of child poverty in America.* Washington, DC: Children's Defense Fund.

For children under the age of six, the rates of child poverty increased to 22.5% to 25.0% (Rainwater & Smeeding, 1995). For African American young children, the child poverty rate is 40 percent and for Hispanic children, the child poverty rate increased more rapidly than for other groups and is 38 percent.

Immigrant and refugee families and children are a large and increasing core of American society, communities, and schools (Harrison, Wilson, Pine, Chan, & Buriel, 1990; Spickard, Fong, & Ewalt, 1996). Many immigrant and refugee families and children live in poverty because they are unable to find permanent employment or jobs that pay high wages. As a consequence, their financial resources tend to be limited making it difficult for them to provide adequate diet, health care, housing arrangements, and living conditions for their children (Chan, 1980; Drachman, 1996). Currently, many legal immigrants and refugees receive benefits such as Assistance for Families of Dependent Children (AFDC), Medicaid, and food stamps provided they meet the same eligibility requirements as United States citizens. According to the Center for the Future of Children (1995), many children in immigrant households receive AFDC and are United States born.

Impact of Poverty and Environmental Risk Factors on Students with MMR and LD

The effects of various combinations of environmental risk factors in the United States already have a tremendous impact on the lives of students with mild disabilities. Environmental risk factors that are associated with higher rates of mental health (e.g., childhood depression) and behavioral disorders in children are poverty, minority ethnic status, parental psychopathology, physical or other maltreatment, a teenage parent, premature birth or low birth weight, parental divorce, and serious childhood illness (Fujiura & Yamaki, 2000; Rueda & Forness, 1994; Shalala, 1999; Tuma, 1989). A few years ago, Krauss and Hauser-Cram (1992) predicted that four trends will have significant implications for service delivery providers. These trends are (a) an increase in the number of children living in poverty; (b) an increase in children afflicted with human immunodeficiency virus (HIV) infection and disabilities caused by maternal substance abuse; (c) the disproportionate increase of minority and non-English speaking families within the general population; and (d) the increase in the employment rate of women with young children.

Several studies have focused on the interface between poverty, environmental risk factors, and the disabling conditions associated with MMR (Baumeister, Kupstas, Klindworth, & Zanthos, 1991; Hodapp, Burack, & Zigler, 1990; Yeargin-Allsopp, Drews, Decoufle, & Murphy, 1995), childhood depression (Rueda & Forness, 1994), and LD (Gottlieb, Alter, Gottlieb, & Wishner, 1994). Socioeconomic status (SES), in conjunction with a number of related multiple risk factors (Sameroff, Seifer, & Zax, 1982; Sameroff, Seifer, Barocas, Zax, & Greenspan, 1987), are important determinants of socioemotional and cognitive competence in multicultural families with members with MMR. For instance, in research studies of African-American families with members with MMR, Sameroff et al. (1987) concluded that cumulative environmental risk factors associated with poverty influence child developmental outcomes. These environmental risk factors include (a) history of maternal MR; (b) high maternal anxiety; (c) parental perspectives on

attitudes, beliefs, and values as related to their child's development; (d) limited positive maternal interactions with their child; (e) head of household in an unskilled occupation; (f) minimal maternal education; (g) minority status; (h) reduced family support; (i) stressful life events; and (j) large family size. The number and combination of these environmental risk variables rather than the nature of any one specific risk factor places multicultural families and children at a greater risk for failure in school and society. It is well-documented that MMR is strongly linked to social, cultural, and economic factors that place multicultural families and children at risk for numerous prenatal, perinatal, and developmental disability problems (Parker, Greer, & Zuckerman, 1988), language (Barnard & Morisset, 1995), and mental health (Sameroff & Seiffer, 1995). For example, African American children experience less healthy development than their Caucasian counterparts in all phases of the life cycle. In the initial stage of life, African American babies born in impoverished environments and in low SES families are more likely to die than Caucasian babies born in affluent communities. Factors such as increased rates of low birth weight and HIV infection threaten the health and development of African American babies. In addition, developmental delay and learning and behavior disorders, which constitute the vast majority of special education enrollment in schools, are often the result of compromised health, economic, and social environments during infancy and early childhood, rather than genetic or other physical anomalies (Barnard & Morissett; Simeonsson, 1994).

The relationship between poverty and MMR is complex and persons diagnosed with this disability are associated with SES related contingencies (e.g., substandard housing, poor nutrition, and non-existent health care). According to Baumeister, Kupstas, Klindworth, and Zanthos (1991), MMR is also referred to as the "new morbidity" and results from a "transaction of environmental, behavioral, and biological forces, which act in concert, producing long-lasting effects which are cumulative . . ." (p. 43). These researchers described five major classes of variables which create a synergistic effect that is very powerful. These five classes of variables are:

1. Predisposing variables, such as demographic characteristics, genetic endowment, and behavioral characteristics.
2. Catalytic variables including acute and chronic poverty and its multidimensional effects.
3. Resource variables including access to appropriate education, health care, nutrition, or counseling.
4. Proximal variables which directly create conditions, such as low birth weight, intrauterine growth retardation, or

preterm birth, but are the result of the previous three types of variables.
5. Outcome variables which include adverse conditions such as developmental disabilities, and chronic health problems.

As a nation, America is feeling the devastating consequences of disproportionate placements and services for multicultural children than ever before. The living conditions of African Americans, Hispanics, American Indians, and Asian/Pacific Islanders place them at greater risk for biomedical, neurological, and health problems. The conditions that produce complications of pregnancy and delivery, prematurity, and low birth weight, and the learning and emotional problems must be taken into serious consideration as placement options and services are examined by the multidisciplinary team.

Impact of Poverty and Race on the Issue of Disproportionate Representation

The issue of disproportionality of multicultural learners in special education continues to be very controversial and problematic (Dunn, 1968; Landesman & Ramey, 1989; Morrow, 1994; Oswald, Coutinho, Best, & Singh, 1999; Utley & Mortweet, 1999). Since the 1960s, researchers, educators, and policymakers have expressed concerns about the disparities in the participation rates of multicultural learners in special education (Artiles & Trent, 1994; Dew, 1984; Dunn, 1968; Lipsky & Gartner, 1997; Meadmore, 1993; Ortiz & Yates, 1984; Tucker, 1980). In the *Twentieth Annual Report to Congress on the Implementation of the Individuals with Disabilities Education Act* (U.S. Department of Education, 1998), Congress found that between "1980 and 1990, the rate of increase in the number of White Americans was 6 percent, while the rates of increase for racial and ethnic minorities were much higher: 53 percent for Hispanics, 13.2

percent for African Americans, and 107.8 for Asians" (p. II–19).

Young children, just as older children and adolescents, are negatively affected by poverty (Brooks-Gunn, Duncan, & Aber, 1997). In studying the characteristics of these students, Gottlieb, Alter, Gottlieb, and Wishner (1994) reiterated that:

Children in special education are poor, with more than 90% being on some form of public assistance. About 70% are male, and 95% are members from a minority group. The 95% figure is best interpreted in relation to the fact that 93% of the entire school population in the 165 schools is minority . . . students in special education come from families where both the mother and father are seldom present . . . information obtained from a compilation of computerized records generated at the school building when a child enters school, only 10% to 25% of children in special education live at home with both parents; the majority of students live with their mother only. About 5% are cared for by older siblings. . . . Approximately 85% had attended at least one other school prior to being referred to special education . . . Finally children with LD are an immigrant population, with 19% being foreign born and 44% coming from households where English is not the primary language spoken by the parents. . . . (p. 457)

Many factors (e.g., geographic location, the combination of large classes, limited resources, inexperienced teachers, and the lack of family and community support) have a direct bearing on the quality of educational opportunities available to multicultural learners in urban school districts. Gottlieb, Alter, and Gottlieb (1999) reported that in the New York City school system, there is a 0.90 correlation between the percentage of students in 635 elementary schools who participate in free or reduced-price lunch programs and the percentage of children in those schools whose standardized reading test scores fall into the lowest quartile. In addition, a –0.94 correlation exists between the percentage of children in the lunch program and the percentage of children whose standardized reading scores fall into the fourth quartile. Despite the accomplishments of the civil rights movement, general education school reform initiatives, and federal legislation, the disproportionate representation of multicultural learners in special education may be viewed as one of many variables influencing the identification and placement of these students in classes for students with LD and EBD (Coutinho & Repp, 1999; Ford, Obiakor, & Patton, 1995; Obiakor & Ford, 1995).

The influence of predictor variables (e.g., housing, income, poverty, gender, age, students' behavioral and academic histories) on the disproportionate representation of multicultural learners categorized at LD has been studied by Artiles, Aguirre-Munoz, and Abedi (1998). These researchers examined a large sample of eighth graders residing in urban, suburban, and rural geographical areas from the National Education Longitudinal Study (NELS) database (Ingels, Abraham, Karr, Spencer, & Frankel, 1990). Using discriminant analyses, these authors compared two disability status groups in order to identify which variables influenced educational placement and significantly discriminated between them. The best predictors that distinguished the educational placement of Hispanics with LD and non-LD were (a) family structure/rules, (b) family size, and (c) math achievement. For African American students with LD and non-LD, (a) perceptions of social status, (b) family structure/ rules, and (c) family size influenced educational placement. For White students with LD and non-LD, (a) perceptions of academic standing, (b) family structure/rules, (c) perception of social status, and (d) family size determined placement in special education.

The conclusions resulting from this large body of research have yielded patterns of variability in the disproportionate representation among African-American, Hispanic, American Indian, and Asian/Pacific Islander students with MMR (Gollnick & Chinn, 1994; Harry, 1994), LD (Gottlieb et al., 1994; Ortiz & Maldonado-Colon, 1986) and BD (Anderson & Webb-Johnson, 1995; National Mental Health Association, 1993; Oswald, Coutinho, Best, & Singh, 1999; U.S. Department of Education, 1992). It is important to note, however, that the use of different definitions and technical methods does not mitigate the fact that the issue of disproportionality continues to be problematic in today's schools. Implications for research suggest that poverty and race are variables that place students at high risk for educational failure and poor outcomes because of inappropriate identification, placement, and services (Gottlieb et al., 1994, 1999).

Impact of Cultural Diversity and Disability Paradigms on Students

Ethnic and cultural definitions of, and meanings attached to, disability are central to the understanding of issues confronting multicultural children and youth with disabilities and the provision of services (Brookins, 1993; Hoernicke, Kallam, & Tablada, 1994; Keogh, Gallimore, & Weisner, 1997). Ford (1992) noted that many special educators have not given priority to acknowledging "individual differences relating to cultural backgrounds and attitudes, world views, values and beliefs, interests, culturally conditioned learning styles, personality, verbal and nonverbal language patterns and behavioral and response mechanisms" (p. 108). As a consequence, a lack of valuing of cultural differences in student achievement and social behaviors has resulted in (a) the ethnocentric presumption of biological determinism and racial superiority (Gould, 1981; Hilliard, 1995); (b) lowered expectations toward multicultural learners with mild disabilities (Obiakor, 1999; Obiakor & Schwenn, 1995); and (c) the use of poor instructional techniques and behavior management procedures (Ford, Obiakor, & Patton, 1995; Obiakor & Algozzine, 1995). It is, therefore, important that general and special educators understand the interrelationship between culture, values, and language and the meaningful ways in which these three variables influence academic and social behaviors of students with mild disabilities.

Culturally defined belief systems and expectations are linked to the ways in which people utilize community services. For example, Hispanic families with children with MMR, are more likely than their White counterparts to keep their child at home than in an institution or a community setting for habilitation (Zuniga, 1998). Traditional views about disabilities from the Asian American perspectives are often highly varied and do not necessarily connote the same meaning of clinical descriptions and definitions of Western terminology (Chan, 1992; Smith & Ryan, 1987) (see Tables 1.2 to 1.5).

The relationship between culture and disability differs along a continuum of assumptions about the world, its people, and the ways they learn (McDermott & Varenne, 1995). Artiles and Trent (1994) argued that "both constructs are directly related to the fundamental notion of 'difference,' and both are socially construed; however, they have distinct cultural roots" (p. 424). The three distinct ways of thinking or approaches about the nature of culture and disability are (a) the deprivation approach, (b) the difference approach, and (c) the culture-as-disability approach. However, before we discuss these paradigms, an understanding of the term, "culture" is imperative to prevent a false analogy between cultural diversity and disability.

Culture: A Conceptual Definition

Culture denotes a complex integrated system of beliefs, values, and behaviors common to a large group of people and may include adaptive responses, a shared language and folklore, ideas and thinking patterns, and communication styles (Cushner, McClelland, & Safford, 1996). As members of a cultural group, people interact with the dominant society and become aware of different ways of behaving, different expectations, and they may change their thinking individually or collectively (Shade, 1989, 1997). Apparently, the knowledge of cultural group characteristics, learning styles (i.e., communication, linguistic, and response styles) and modalities explain human behavior (Shade, Kelly, & Oberg, 1997). A couple of years ago, Shade and New (1991) suggested that culture "induces different approaches to how individuals use their minds by providing a set of rules that become preferred

Table 1.2
CHARACTERISTICS OF AFRICAN AMERICAN FAMILIES
WITH MEMBERS WITH DISABILITIES

African American World View/Beliefs/Values

- Collective orientation and group effort within the larger community
- Greater respect for elderly and their role in the family
- More oriented to the situation than time
- Kinship and extended family bonds are strong.
- Strong religious and spiritual orientation
- Authoritarian child rearing practices
- Households are designated as a female single head of household status.
- Values of loyalty, assertiveness, and independence are emphasized.
- Communication style: Speak with affect; direct eye contact (prolonged) when speaking, but less when listening; interrupt (mm taking) when can; quick responding; affect, emotional, and interpersonal

African American Viewpoints on Disability

- Disability is interpreted as bad luck or misfortune
- Disability is attributed to punishment for disobeying God, the work of the devil and evil spirits.
- Young African American children are taught to view people with disabilities as they view non-disabled people.
- African American families and communities incorporate individuals with disabilities into all aspects of their lives.
- Young African American children are taught not to stare at people with disabilities.

Implications for Professionals

- Poverty is not an indication of dysfunction; many low-income families provide stable, loving environments for their children (Willis, 1992).
- Students' needs should be addressed using a family-focused approach to intervention in which strong family support systems are used to achieve specific goals.
- African American children learning needs and strengths should be based on observations made by teachers and parents than on scores from standardized tests.
- Misdiagnosis in speech production may occur if the presence of an articulation disorder is based entirely on the results of formal articulation tests (Cole & Taylor, 1990).
- Professionals need to make sure that at least two family members understand teacher suggestions, provide school materials, and follow-up on family progress.
- African American children learn best when teaching strategies are highly affective and emphasize interpersonal interaction, encouragement, and praise.

Note: The term multicultural learners is used interchangeably with constructs such as culturally and linguistically diverse, children of color, language minority students, multicultural learners, and minority children. Other variables and terms associated with multicultural learners include socioeconomic status, (SES), race, ethnicity, and language. Each of these terms has different connotations in the research literature and there is presently no general consensus how to define and differentiate these terms. Multicultural learners are very heterogeneous and generalizations about each group should be avoided.
Source: Adapted from Roseberry-McKibbin, C. (1995). *Multicultural students with special language needs: Practical strategies for assessment and intervention.* Oceanside, CA: Academic Communication Associates.

Table 1.3

CHARACTERISTICS OF HISPANIC AMERICAN FAMILIES WITH DISABILITIES

Hispanic World View/Beliefs/Values

- Collective orientation and collective group identity are fundamental Hispanic values with an emphasis on the group rather than individualism and competition.
- Values of Interdependence, solidarity, loyalty and reciprocity among family members are stressed.
- Cooperation within the family is valued more than individual achievement
- The Catholic Church plays an important role in family life.
- Relaxed and flexible attitude toward time than persons from other cultural groups
- Emphasis on interpersonal relationships than on factors related to time
- Tendency toward more patriarchal family structure. The welfare of the family is the responsibility of the father and he is seen as the authority figure.
- Children are taught to respect the elderly, taught to listen, obey, and not to challenge authority.
- Emphasis is on the extended family member structure

Hispanic Views on Disability

- Family and friends may indulge children with disabilities, therefore, children are not expected to participate in interventions (National Coalition of Hispanic Health and Human Services Organizations, 1988).
- Families have more difficulty accepting 'invisible" disabilities such as !earning disabilities or reading disorders than disabilities that are visible (Cheng & Langdon, 1993).
- Families believe in a healing process called, 'curanderismo,' that occurs when folk practices (and not health care) are used (Langdon & Cheng, 1992).
- Visible disabilities such as cleft palate and cerebral palsy are associated with external causes such as witchcraft with parents believing that they are being punished (Zuniga, 1998).
- Families value vitality and health and may hide a child with a disability from professionals to prevent treatment (Anderson & Fenichel, 1989).
- Families seek out the Catholic Church and spiritualism to heal and dispel evil spirits (Zuniga, 1998).

Implications for Professionals

- Hispanic families may refuse to speak Spanish in the school environment.
- Hispanic families may be prefer to remain uninvolved in the decision-making process, thus relying on school personnel.
- Hispanic children may be more comfortable with cooperative, group learning activities than individualistic, competitive learning situations.
- Professionals should use formal titles with Hispanic adults to show respect (Anderson & Fenichel, 1989; Roseberry-McKibbin, 1995).
- Hispanic parents may not openly disagree with school personnel because of their respect for professionals.
- Professionals must acknowledge the family's culture in order to win their trust and confidence.
- School personnel must accurately define and differentiate between the terms language disorders and learning disability.
- Hispanic families are more receptive to professionals who use a humanistic orientation rather than a task orientation manner to intervention.

Table 1.4
CHARACTERISTICS OF ASIAN/PACIFIC ISLANDER FAMILIES
WITH MEMBERS WITH DISABILITIES

Asian/Pacific Islander World Views/Beliefs/Values

- Revere and appease the ancestors or the spirits of the deceased
- Restraint is internalized according to family values; feelings of guilt or shame can act as a powerful means of social control.
- Harmony is the basic rule guiding interaction with others; behavior should be based on role expectation; self-expression or feelings that may cause conflict are not encouraged but are restrained to maintain harmonious relations.
- Family members have clearly defined roles, and the individual acts in accordance with role expectation Parent-child relationships are bound tightly and continue through the whole life; individualism is thought of as selfish or not considerate of other family members.
- The child's behavior is the reflection of the family's dignity and "face;" filial piety and deference to elders are stressed; child's rights are not emphasized; children's obligations to the family also are emphasized by their parts or elders (Cartledge, Lee, & Feng, 1995).

Asian/Pacific Islander Views on Disability

- Asian/Pacific Islander parents believe that children with disabilities have visible signs of the disability. Disabilities such as learning disability and stuttering are signs that their children are not trying hard enough. Parents do not believe that special education, rehabilitation, and therapy are needed as interventions for their children (Bebout & Arthur, 1992; Roseberry-McKibbin, 1995).
- Asian/Pacific Islander parents believe that physical disabilities require special education or rehabilitation services.
- Some Asian/Pacific Islander families believe that birth defects are the effects of sins committed by their ancestors.
- Asian/Pacific Islander students with physical disabilities may be viewed by parents as a punishment for their sins and they may choose to isolate their children from society. Healing practices may include visitation to temples and shrines.
- Asian/Pacific Islander parents are resistant to outwardly seeking medical services and assistance from the school system for their children with disabilities because they feel the responsibility for treatment is with the family.
- Asian/Pacific Islander families may not be familiar with Western medical practices and select health practices such as acupuncture, herbs, and massage as treatment for their children with disabilities.

Implications for Professionals

- Professionals must establish a rapport with the family prior to discussions about their children with disabilities.
- Respect is shown by how you dress for home visits. Informal dress is viewed as a sign of disrespect.
- Open discussions about children with disabilities is viewed as being disgraceful by Asian/Pacific Islander families.
- Respect is shown by addressing the older members of the family first–Asian/Pacific Islander families may exchange gifts for professional services.
- Language barriers may exist in communicating with Asian/Pacific Islander families. Asian speakers' English language patterns include a variety of languages and dialects spoken by this population.

Table 1.5
CHARACTERISTICS OF AMERICAN INDIAN FAMILIES
WITH MEMBERS WITH DISABILITIES

American Indian World Views/Beliefs/Values

- Extended family and family ties are emphasized more than monetary and materialistic values. The extended family provides support during difficult times.
- Extended family provides care for the children and nursing care for the elderly family members. Family members support siblings, distant kin, and elderly parents.
- Conflict between family members and generations may occur because of certain beliefs held by the older members.
- Caring for children is the responsibility of family or tribal members; babysitters are prohibited. Parent-child relationships are close knit with an emphasize on affection.
- American Indian children are taught respect for the elderly and authoritarian figures.
- American Indian families downplay their achievements and do not brag about their talents and accomplishments; they strive to be cooperative rather than individualistic.
- Tribal customs emphasize harmony between individuals, society, and nature.
- Punctuality and time are not viewed as important as establishing harmonious human relationships.

American Indian Views on Disability

- Health diseases that are more prevalent among American Indian families include otitis media, bacterial meningitis, fetal alcohol syndrome (FAS), cleft lip and palate, diabetes, gastrointestinal disease, malignant neoplasms, and tuberculosis (Roseberry-McKibbin, 1995; Stewart, 1992).
- Health care needs of children with disabilities may go unattended because they do not qualify for residential health care services if they reside in urban areas.
- American Indian children with disabilities may be viewed as the Great Spirit's gift. Other American Indian family members believe that disabilities result from witchcraft or moral transgressions (Anderson & Fenichel, 1989).
- American Indian children are accepted because American Indian members believe that these individuals have an important role to play in the community.
- American Indian family members are reluctant to use services provided by speech language pathologists.

Implications for Professionals

- Professionals must build a trusting relationship with family members before discussing concerns related to children with disabilities (Roseberry-McKibbin, 1995).
- Because the extended family is emphasized within American Indian culture, professionals should address all family members and not just the parents of children with disabilities. Professional should include all family members in the rehabilitation and intervention process.
- Professionals should consult with the tribal members before selecting an intervention or treatment.
- Traditional American Indian approaches may be preferred over urban medical care practices. Keeping records developmental milestones and case histories of children are not viewed as being important because children should be allowed to grow individually and according to their own pace
- American Indian families concept of time is different from the concept of time within the public school system. It is important for professionals to be flexible in scheduling conferences.
- Professionals must acknowledge American Indian customs and culturally-relevant materials that influence learning subject matter. For example, it is the cultural norm for American Indian children to learn concepts when multi-sensory and whole language activities are used in the classroom (Goldstein & Hammergren, 1994).
- Professionals should develop interventions that utilize the learning strengths (e.g., visual modality) of American Indian children (Swisher & Deyhle, 1989).

methods of acquiring knowledge" (p. 321). In the same vein, Banks (1994) identified six major components of culture, namely (see Figure 1):

1. *Values and Behavioral Styles:* These are abstract, generalized principles of behavior to which members of society attach a high worth or regard.
2. *Languages and Dialects:* These make up ways in which people reflect the world they live in.
3. *Non-verbal Communications:* These are the ways in which people look at each other.
4. *Cultural Cognitiveness:* This entails an awareness of the unique and distinct characteristics of their cultural thinking.
5. *Perspectives, World Views, Frames of Reference:* This entails endorsements of particular views about events that occur more frequently within groups.
6. *Identification:* This entails how individuals feel about their cultural group and internalize the group's values and standards.

A mistaken view of culture is reflected in the phrase, "a culture of poverty." Although poverty has a long-standing impact on a child's development and experiences, the term culture should not be equated with poverty or SES. Equating culture and poverty is a false analogy! That is, better educated persons or professional households do not have more culture than do poor uneducated people. It is noteworthy to recognize that an individual's status as poverty may change over time, either improving or worsening.

The Deprivation Approach

This approach was advocated by researchers from 1965 to 1980 to explain school failure in multicultural children. The belief was that multicultural children failed in school because of impoverishing experiences in the home. An underlying assumption of this approach is that members of various cultural groups develop differently enough so that members can be shown to be measurably distinct on various developmental milestones (McDermott & Varenne, 1995). This approach, based upon psychometrics and the measure of intelligence, looks at individuals who perform poorly on tests as examples of what the people of that group have not yet developed (e.g., levels of abstraction, syllogistic reasoning, and linguistic behavior).

The Difference Approach

This approach is based upon the underlying assumption that members in different cultural groups develop equivalently and are aware of the abilities needed to develop and survive in society. As an explanation of school failure, this approach suggests that multicultural children who are taught by teachers from a more dominant cultural background suffer from miscommunication and alienation and, as a result, give up on school. In comparing the deprivation approach and the difference theory, McDermott and Varenne (1995) wrote:

> Against a flood of deprivationist thinking in the 1960s, the difference stand took shape to honor the lives of those who had been left out of the system and who were in turn being blamed for their failings. Where the deprivationist saw poverty in the language of black children, sociolinguists (e.g., William Labov, Roger Shuy) saw only a different dialect, grammatically as complex as any other language and lacking nothing but the respect of mainstream speakers of English. Where the deprivationists saw cognitive delays in the behavior of inner-city children, ethnographic psychologists (e.g., Michael Cole) showed how thinking was invariably complex once it was studied in relation to ongoing social situations. Where the deprivationists saw immorality and the breakdown of the family among the poor, anthropologists (e.g., Elliot Liebow, Carol Stack) found

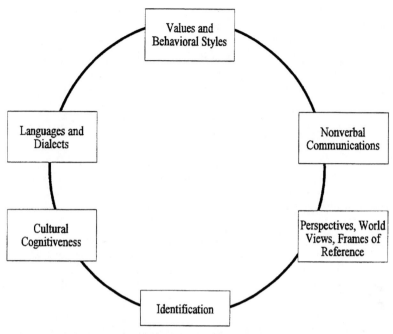

Figure 1.1. Elements and components of culture. Source: Banks, J.A. (1994). *Multiethnic education: Theory and practice* (3rd ed.). Needham Heights, MA: Allyn & Bacon.

caring behavior set against a breakdown in the opportunities available in the job market. Where deprivationists saw mayhem in classrooms, ethnographers (e.g., Frederick Erickson, Peg Griffin, Ray McDermott, Hugh Mehan) looked closely and saw tremendous order, some of it oppositional but an order nonetheless. (p. 35)

The Culture-as-Disability Approach

This approach takes the position that every culture teaches people what to aspire to and hope for and eliminates those individuals who are to be noticed, handled, mistreated, and remediated as failures (McDermott & Varenne, 1995). The term, "culture," takes on a new meaning, one that refers to an organization of hopes and dreams and how the world should be. Thus, each person possesses qualities that qualify him or her to be treated differently in society. The underlying assumption of this approach is that mainstream society develops a set of tasks and a theory of cognitive development which people of different backgrounds might be differentiated, measured, classified, remediated, and excluded. This theory is also embedded in wider-scale institutions and political agendas that permit industrialized countries, governments, and technologically advanced nations to isolate individuals for public scrutiny and control. There are ethnographic accounts of the schooling process of teachers, students, and administrators disabling each other. Examples of the culture-as-disability paradigm are the management of biological disorders (e.g., alcoholism, autism, and schizophrenia) and the handling of disorders in which aggressive behaviors and social interactions are negative (e.g., behaviorally disordered). The field of LD is no exception!

Critics such as Coles (1987) and Kronick (1988) suggested that the category of LD was created to justify the poor performance of students in school and to provide services for students who are failing academically. Trueba's (1989) observations support the notion that disabilities are an attribute of schools. He remarked that "children seeming 'unpreparedness' for mainstream schooling is only a measure of the rigidity and ignorance of our school system, which creates handicaps out of social and cultural differences" (p. 70). Classroom instruction is perceived by multicultural learners as being rigidly managed, fast-paced, and meaningless. These students feel that teachers do not understand their cultural knowledge and experiences. In addition, some multicultural learners cannot adjust to a new educational system that is based upon rules and regulations that are foreign to them and are not a part of their daily routines. Because of poor performance, they are penalized by being officially labeled as incompetent and disabled. In other words, children who are culturally and linguistically different from the mainstream are prime candidates for the label, "learning disabled."

The responsiveness of psychologists and service providers to the needs of multicultural learners with disabilities is a critical factor in the delivery of services in schools and the mental health system. Service providers must have appropriate knowledge and skills about the needs of multicultural learners in order to conduct psychological assessments and provide psychological services (American Psychological Association, 1993). These abilities include (a) recognizing diversity; (b) valuing the role that culture and ethnicity/race play in the social, psychological, and economic development of ethnic and culturally diverse populations; (c) understanding that SES and political factors significantly impact the psychosocial, political, and economic development of ethnic and culturally diverse groups; (d) helping clients to maintain and resolve their own sociocultural identification; and (e) understanding the interaction of culture and gender on behaviors and needs.

In this chapter, we vehemently argue that constructs such as "culturally deprived," and "culturally disadvantaged" imply a deficit-orientation and the absence of cultural genuineness and competence. These terms imply that there is a "good" culture or a "bad" culture. Individuals within each cultural group (i.e., intragroup) reflect differences in values, beliefs, attitudes, behaviors, and adaptations made in order to survive and to make transitions from one environmental setting to another. These adaptations to the dominant culture vary according to factors such as length of residence in the dominant culture, motivation to assimilate or maintain group identity, and societal conditions (Garcia & Dominguez, 1997). For multicultural groups to survive in their communities and maintain their identities, they must have developed sociocultural attributes, values, attitudes, and coping behaviors that are very different from the dominant culture. In addition, the ecological factors (e.g., demographic, social, economic, and educational) within each cultural group must be taken into consideration when examining differences among cultural groups. We believe societal characteristics, adaptations, skills, and behaviors of cultural groups to assimilate into society are transmitted from cultural groups to future generations.

MULTICULTURALISM AND SPECIAL EDUCATION

Multiculturalism acknowledges the complexities of culture in society. It is not limited to understanding multiethnic or multinational relationships between diverse groups, but recognizes behavioral styles, culture, symbols, languages, values, and ancestry of different people (Banks, 1977; Banks & Banks, 1997; Fu, 1993; Gay, 1992; 1994, Penderson, 1991). For instance, Gay (1994) maintains that multiculturalism supports the notion of *e pluribus unum*–making one cohesive culture and unified nation out of all of the different peoples and influences that comprise the United States. The focus becomes the relationship between the individual and the pluralistic society where ethnic groups value their own cultural identities while sharing common elements within the dominant culture (Banks, 1993; Banks & Banks, 1993; Trotter, 1993).

The translation of multiculturalism from an ideological approach to concrete school policies, curricula, and teaching practices is referred to as "multicultural education." According to Nieto (2000), multicultural education is:

A process of comprehensive and basic education for all students that challenges and rejects racism and other forms of discrimination in schools and society and accepts and affirms the pluralism (ethnic, racial, linguistic, religious, economic, gender, and among others) that students, their communities, and teachers represent. Multicultural education permeates the curriculum and instructional strategies used in schools, as well as the interactions among teachers, students and parents, and the very way that schools conceptualize the nature of teaching and learning. Because it uses critical pedagogy as its underlying philosophy and focuses on knowledge, reflection, and action (praxis) as the basis for social change, multicultural education promotes the democratic principles of social justice. (p. 305)

What are the assumptions on which to base a multicultural education program? According to Baruth and Manning (1992), there are several underlying assumptions associated with multicultural education, namely:

1. Cultural diversity is a positive, enriching element in a society because it provides individuals with increased opportunities to experience other cultures and thus to become more fulfilled as human beings. Cultural diversity should be viewed as a strength with the potential of helping people better understand their own culture.

2. Multicultural education is for all students. Everyone can benefit from a better understanding of cultural differences and of their own cultural background.

3. Teaching is a cross-cultural encounter. Culture plays a significant role in teaching/learning situations. Socioeconomic status, ethnicity, gender, and language have a powerful and dynamic effect upon one's outlook and attitude towards school.

4. Multicultural education should permeate the total school curriculum, rather than taking a "one-course" approach or a teaching unit approach. The school must be genuinely multicultural: The curriculum, the composition of the administration, faculty, and staff, expectations that reflect an understanding of culturally different groups, attitudes toward school success, and learning styles must be a part of the school.

5. The education system has not served all students equally well. Members of different minority groups have not fared well in the U.S. school system.

6. Schools will continue to experience and reflect increasing cultural diversity due to influxes of immigrants and refugees and due to the high birthrates of some culturally diverse groups. American society continues to grow diverse.

7. It is the responsibility of elementary and secondary schools to implement appropriate multicultural education programs that contribute to better understandings of cultural differences, show the dangers of stereotyping, and reduce racism, sexism, and classism. Since the U.S. educational system is characterized by cultural diversity, elementary and secondary schools are the best transmitters of understanding and respect for cultural diversity. (pp. 150–151)

Within a multicultural education framework, the reality is that cultural and linguistic characteristics co-exist and interact with disability-related factors. For special education programs to be effective, they must address the interfacing influence of these variables on the academic performance and social interactions of multicultural learners with mild disabilities. Effective programs are, therefore, based upon the same principles of multicultural education and special education.

INFUSION OF MULTICULTURAL EDUCATION INTO SPECIAL EDUCATION

Contemporary viewpoints and trends in special education suggest that understanding multicultural education in the context of special education is essential as a component of educational programs for students with disabilities (Grant & Sleeter, 1998). Professionals are interested in understanding the nature of the relationship between multicultural issues and special education and in determining ways to effectively provide services for students who have been historically underserved, neglected, or mistreated in the public school system (Ford, Obiakor, & Patton, 1995; Utley, 1995).

The disciplines of multicultural education and special education share several common features. For example, multicultural learners with disabilities face quadruple jeopardy due to a combination of factors, such as poverty, language, culture, and/or disabling condition and these students are vulnerable to inappropriate placements in special education (Grossman, 1995, 1998; Harry, 1992; Utley, 1995). Environmental influences operative in multicultural education are also present in special education and are contributing factors to the academic and social problems of these children referred for special education. In the legislative arena, the Civil Rights Movement, legislation, and litigation are integral parts of establishing a foundation for equitable education for multicultural learners with and without mild, moderate, and severe disabilities. With regard to expectations, multicultural children often have stereotypical expectations from teachers, peers, and society (Obiakor, 1999). Additional commonalities between multicultural education and special education are visible in (a) local, state, and federal policies; (b) cultural pluralism, diversity, and values; (c) teacher expectations, achievement, and socialization; (d) teacher education; and (e) parent-teacher relationships (Baca & Cervantes, 1998; Hardman, Drew, & Egan, 1999).

The merger between the disciplines of multicultural education and special education presents a set of particular challenges to both fields of study and requires a critical analysis of factors that make infusing multicultural education into special education a constructive and progressive teacher education program (Ball & Harry, 1993). General and special educators and other service delivery providers are concerned with diagnosing individual differences in intelligence, achievement, adaptive behaviors, and information-processing abilities. Theorists from other disciplines such as anthropology and social psychology (e.g., Brislin, 1990; Garcia, 1978, 1994; Mead, 1977; Ogbu, 1978, 1988, 1995) are concerned about recognizing cultural aspects, including (a) ways of life of people; (b) cultural continuity (e.g., ideas transmitted from generation to generation); (c) identifiable childhood experiences resulting in internalized values; (d) socialization of children into adults; (e) consistent patterns and practices; (f) cultural patterns that are maintained despite mistakes and slipups in the system; and (g) a feeling of helplessness and loss of empowerment that results when cultural patterns are changed. This distinction between individual differences and culture in designing educational programs for multicultural learners with and without mild disabilities is very real and important. Is it then any wonder that the over representation of students from multicultural or low-SES backgrounds has become an important issue in special education?

Because of the changing demographic trends in schools, and communities, it is essential that educators shift their paradigm of excluding cultural, ethnic, and linguistic factors in the definition, assessment, classification, placement, and educational programming of students with disabilities. The focus should be on valuing and including cultural and linguistic factors to (a) create supportive learning environments in general and special education classes; (b) provide instructional strategies and materials that are culturally and linguistically appropriate; and (c) develop programs that have a significant impact on student performance (Byrd, 1995; Ewing, 1995; Garcia & Malkin, 1993; Utley,

Delquadri, Obiakor, & Mims, 2000). For instance, with regard to relevant cultural characteristics that affect learning, the majority of standardized tests do not include standardized and normative information on multicultural groups. Because of cultural and language differences, pinpointing academic strengths, multiple intelligences, and weaknesses of multicultural learners may be difficult (Atkinson, Morten, & Sue, 1993; Baca & Cervantes, 1998; Cartledge, Lee, & Feng, 1995; Chan, 1980; Franklin, 1992; Ortiz & Garcia, 1990; Spring, 1994; Sue, 1995; Sue & Sue, 1990; Wright, 1995). Therefore, these students may be misidentified, misassessed, misdiagnosed, and disproportionately placed and misinstructed in general and special education classes (e.g., Algozzine & Obiakor, 1995; Ford, Obiakor, & Patton, 1995; Heller, Holtzman, & Messick, 1982; Obiakor, 1994, 1999). In previous research, Garcia (1992) and Ortiz, Garcia, Wheeler, and Maldonado-Colon (1986) confirmed that without such an understanding, professionals will continue to have difficulty distinguishing between learning and social problems that reflect cultural and language characteristics and those that are the result of a disability.

CONCLUSION

In this chapter, we have argued convincingly that a comprehensive school reform agenda that infuses multicultural education into special education is warranted. This agenda will emphasize the relationship between poverty and environmental factors, and cultural, social, and linguistic facets of children's development, learning processes, and socialization. From this framework, cultural diversity would be recognized as a vital element in the process of education throughout the total life span of students with and without mild disabilities. In addition, collab-

oration amongst teachers, students, administrators, and families would be a key to school success. Crucial elements in the educational process would consist of (a) relationships with the home and school, (b) providing appropriate training for school personnel, (c) developing school curriculum programs that foster diversity, and (d) implementing effective instructional programs.

This chapter sets the stage for many of the issues addressed throughout this book. We have identified significant issues related to poverty, race, and culture in the field of special education. However, when we look at the implementation of educational programs for multicultural learners with mild disabilities, there is a grave concern that these students are not receiving appropriate educational services in inclusive and least restrictive environments. Many of them continue to be identified using psychological assessment tools that lack validity and reliability. They also continue to struggle in special education settings that ignore their visible talents, capabilities, and competencies. In view of the current situation, it is unclear as to whether or not the school reform movement has changed, or in some cases, will change the plight of multicultural learn-

ers with and without mild disabilities. In spite of these dismal circumstances, the plight of these students with disabilities in the school reform movement cannot be ignored. We believe that general and special educators must foster a pluralistic society through multicultural education in their least restrictive classrooms. Educators from preschool to university levels cannot afford to ignore the (a) historical backgrounds of multicultural learners, (b) languages and symbols that multicultural learners bring to class, (c) social and behavioral patterns of multicultural learners, and (d) events that have molded the cultural identities of multicultural group members.

REFERENCES

Algozzine, B., & Obiakor, F.E. (1995). African American quandaries in school programs. *Scholar and Education, 17*, 75–87.

American Association of Colleges and Teacher Education (1994). *Teacher education pipeline III: Schools, colleges, departments of education enrollments by race, ethnicity, and gender.* Washington, DC: Author.

American Psychological Association (1993). Guidelines for providers of psychological services to ethnic, linguistic, and culturally diverse populations. *American Psychologist, 48*, 45–48.

Anderson, M., & Webb-Johnson, G. (1995). Cultural contexts, the seriously emotionally disturbed classification, and African-American learners. In B.A. Ford, F.E. Obiakor, & J.M. Patton (Eds.), *Effective education of African-American exceptional learners: New perspectives* (pp. 151–187). Austin, TX: Pro-Ed.

Anderson, P.P., & Fenichel, E.S. (1989). *Serving culturally diverse families of infants and toddlers with disabilities.* Washington, DC: National Center for Clinical Infant Programs.

Aponte, J.F., & Crouch, R.T. (2000). The changing ethnic profile of the United States in the twenty-first century. In J.F. Aponte & J. Wohl (Eds.), *Psychological intervention and cultural diversity* (2nd ed.) (pp. 1–17). Needham Heights, MA: Allyn & Bacon.

Artiles, A.J., Aguirre-Munoz, Z., & Abedi, J. (1998). Predicting placement in learning disabilities programs: Do predictors vary by ethnic group? *Exceptional Children, 64*, 543–559.

Artiles, A.J., & Trent, S.C. (1994). Over representation of minority students in special education: A continuing debate. *The Journal of Special Education, 27*, 410–437.

Atkinson, D.R., Morten, G., & Sue, D.W. (1993). *Counseling American minorities: A cross-cultural perspective* (4th ed.). Madison, WI: WCB Brown & Benchmark.

Baca, L., & Cervantes, H.T. (1998). *The bilingual special education interface* (3rd ed.). Columbus, OH: Merrill.

Ball, E.W., & Harry, B. (1993). Multicultural education and special education: Parallels, divergences, and intersections. *The Educational Forum, 57*, 430–437.

Banks, J.A. (1993). *Teaching strategies for ethnic studies.* Needham Heights, MA: Allyn & Bacon.

Banks, J.A. (1994). *Multiethnic education: Theory and practice* (3rd ed.). Needham Heights, MA: Allyn & Bacon. Bloomington, IN: Phi Delta Kappa Educational Foundation.

Banks, J.A. (1994). *Multiethnic education: Theory and practice.* Needham Heights, MA: Allyn & Bacon.

Banks, J.A. (1999). *An introduction to multicultural education* (2nd ed.). Needham Heights, MA: Allyn & Bacon.

Banks, J.A., & Banks, C.A. (1993). *Multicultural education: Issues and perspectives* (2nd ed.). Needham Heights, MA: Allyn & Bacon.

Banks, J.A., & Banks, C.A. (1995). *Handbook of research on multicultural education.* New York: Macmillan.

Barnard, K.E., & Morissett,C.E. (1995). Preventive health and developmental care for children. Relationships as a primary factor in service delivery with at-risk populations. In H.E. Fitzgerald, B.M. Lester, & B. Zuckerman (Eds.), *Children of poverty: Research, health, and poverty issues* (pp. 167–195). New York: Garland.

Baruth, L.G., & Manning, M.L. (1992). *Multicultural education of children and. adolescents.* Needham Heights, MA: Allyn & Bacon.

Baumeister, A.A., Kupstas, F.D., Klindworth, L.M., & Zanthos, P.W. (1991). *Guide to state planning for the prevention of mental retardation and related disabilities associated with socioeconomic conditions.* Washington, DC: The President's Committee on Mental Retardation.

Bebout, L., & Arthur, B. (1992). Cross-cultural attitudes about speech disorders. *Journal of Speech and Hearing Research, 35* (2), 45–52.

Brice-Heath, S. (1989). Oral and literate traditions among Black Americans living in poverty. *American Psychologist, 44,* 367–373.

Brislin, R.W. (1990). *Applied cross-cultural psychology.* Newbury Park, CA: Sage.

Brookins, G.S. (1993). Culture, ethnicity, and bicultural competence: Implications for children with chronic illness and disability. *Pediatrics, 91,* 1056–1062.

Brooks-Gunn, J., Duncan, G.J., & Aber, J.L. (1997). *Neighborhood poverty: Context and consequences for children* (Vol. 1). New York: Russell Sage Foundation.

Byrd, H.B. (1995). Curricular and pedagogical procedures for African American learners with academic and cognitive disabilities. In B.A. Ford, F.E. Obiakor, & J.M. Patton (Eds.), *Effective education of African-American exceptional learners: New perspectives* (pp. 123–150). Austin, TX: Pro-Ed.

Carlson, E., Hirschorn, R.R., Ryaboy, S., & Zhao, M. (1996). *Factors associated with disability prevalence in difference racial/ethnic groups* (Report to the Office of Special Education Programs, U.S. Department of Special Education, Contract No. HS9 203500). Washington, DC: U.S. Department of Special Education.

Cartledge, G., Lee, J.W., & Feng, H. (1995). Cultural diversity: Multicultural factors in teaching social skills. In G. Cartledge & J.F. Milburn (Eds.), *Teaching social skills to children and youth* (pp. 328–355). Needham Heights, MA: Allyn & Bacon.

Center for the Future of Children. (1995). Immigrant children and their families: Issues for research and policy. In the David and Lucille Packard Foundation, *Critical issues for children and youth* (Vol. 5, No. 2) (pp. 72–89). Los Altos, CA: Author.

Chan, K.S. (1980). *Limited English speaking, handicapped and poor: Triple threat in children* (ERIC Document Reproduction Service No. ED 247 686).

Chan, S. (1992). Families with Asian roots. In E.W. Lynch & M.J. Hanson (Eds.), *Developing cross cultural competence: A guide for working with young, children and their families* (pp. 259–300). Baltimore, MD: Paul H. Brookes.

Cheng, L.L., & Langdon, H.W. (1993). *Best practices in working with second language learners with possible language/learning problems: A collaborative approach between the clinician, school staff and the student's family.* Paper presented at University of Pacific Summer Colloquium, Stockton, CA.

Children's Defense Fund (1989, December). Poverty drops slightly in 1988 but continues to rise for young children and young families. *Children's Defense Fund Reports, 11,* 1 & 4.

Children's Defense Fund (1998). *Poverty matters: The cost of child poverty in America.* Washington, DC: Author.

Chinn, P.C., & Hughes, S. (1987). Representation of minority students in special education classes. *Remedial and Special Education, 8,* 41–46.

Cole, L., & Taylor, O. (1990). Performance of working class African-American children on three tests of articulation. *Language, Speech, and Hearing Services in Schools, 21,* 171–176.

Coles, G.S. (1987). Excerpts from the Learning Mystique: A critical look at learning disabilities. *Journal of Learning Disabilities, 22,* 267–273.

Council of Economic Advisors for the President's Initiative on Race (1998). *Changing America: Indicators of Social and Economic Well-Being by Race and Hispanic Origin.* Online at http://www.whitehouse.gov/WH/EOP/CEA/html/publications.html.

Coutinho, M.J., & Repp, A.C. (1999). *Inclusion: The integration of students with disabilities.* Belmont, CA: Wadsworth.

Cushner, K., McClelland, A., & Safford, P. (1996). *Human diversity in education: An integrative approach* (2nd ed.). New York: McGraw-Hill.

Dew, N. (1984). The exceptional bilingual child: Demography. In P.C. Chinn (Ed.), *Education of culturally and linguistically different exceptional children* (pp. 1–42). Reston, VA: The Council for Exceptional Children.

Drachman, D. (1996). Immigration statuses and their influence on service provision, access, and use. In P.L. Ewalt, E.M. Freeman, S.A. Kirk, & D.L. Poole (Eds.), *Multicultural issues in social work* (pp. 117–133). Washington, DC: National Association of Social Workers.

Dunn, L.M. (1968). Special education for the mildly retarded. Is much of it justifiable? *Exceptional Children, 34,* 5–22.

Ewing, N.J. (1995). Restructured teacher education for inclusiveness: A dream deferred for African-American children. In B.A. Ford, F.E. Obiakor, & J.M. Patton (Eds.), *Effective education of African American exceptional learners: New perspectives* (pp. 189–207). Austin, TX: Pro-Ed.

Federal Interagency Forum on Child and Family Statistics (1999). *America's children: Key national indicators of well-being.* Washington, DC: Author.

Finn, J.D. (1982). Patterns in special education placement as revealed by OCR surveys. In K.A. Heller, W.H. Holtzman, & S. Messick (Eds.), *Placing children in special education: A strategy for equity* (pp. 322–381). Washington, DC: National Academy Press.

Ford, B.A. (1992). Multicultural education training for special educators working with African American youth. *Exceptional Children, 59,* 107–114.

Ford, B.A., Obiakor, F.E., & Patton, J.M. (1995). *Effective education of African American exceptional learners: New perspectives.* Austin, TX: Pro-Ed.

Ford, D.Y. (1998). The underrepresentation of minority students in gifted education: Problems and promises in recruitment and retention. *The Journal of Special Education, 32,* 4–14.

Franklin, M.E. (1992). Culturally sensitive instructional practices for African-American learners with disabilities. *Exceptional Children, 59,* 115–122.

Fu, V.R. (1993). Culture, schooling, and education in a democracy. In C. Treppte, V.R. Fu, & A.J. Stremmel (Eds.), *Multiculturalism in early childhood programs* (pp. 38–51). Urbana, IL: ERIC Clearing House on Elementary and Early Childhood Education.

Fujiura, G.T., & Ymaki, K. (2000). Trends in the demography of childhood poverty and disability. *Exceptional Children, 66,* 187–199.

Garcia, R.L. (1978). *Fostering a pluralistic society through multiethnic education.* Bloomington, IN: Phi Delta Kappa Educational Foundation.

Garcia, R.L. (1992). Educating for human rights: A curriculum blueprint. In C. Diaz (Ed.), *Multicultural education for the 21st century* (pp. 166–178). Washington, DC: National Education Association Publication.

Garcia, R.L. (1994). *Understanding and meeting the challenge of student cultural diversity.* Boston, MA: Houghton Mifflin.

Garcia, S.B., & Malkin, D.H. (1993). Toward defining programs and services for culturally and linguistically diverse learners in special education. *Teaching Exceptional Children 26,* 52–58.

Garcia, S.B., & Dominguez, L. (1997). Cultural contexts that influence learning and academic performance. *Child and Adolescent Psychiatric Clinics of North America, 6,* 621–655.

Gardner, H. (1993). *Multiple intelligences: The theory of practice.* New York: Basic Books.

Gay, G. (1992). Effective teaching practices for multicultural classrooms. In C. Diaz (Ed.), *Multicultural education for the 21st century* (pp. 38–56). Washington, DC: National Education Association.

Gay, G. (1994). *At the essence of learning: Multicultural education.* West Lafayette, IN: Kappa Delta Pi.

Goldstein, N.L., & Hammergren, K.M. (1994, November). *Language intervention in mathematics for Native American LD students.* Paper presented at the annual meeting of the American Speech-Language-Hearing Association, New Orleans, LA.

Gollinick, D., & Chinn, P.C. (1994). *Multicultural education in a pluralistic society* (4th ed.). Columbus, OH: Merrill.

Gottlieb, J., Alter, M., & Gottlieb, B.W. (1999). General education placement for special education students in urban schools. In M.J. Coutinho & A.C. Repp (Eds.), *Inclusion: The integration of students with disabilities* (pp. 91–110). Belmont, CA: Wadsworth.

Gottlieb, J., Alter, M., Gottlieb, B.W., & Wishner, J. (1994). Special education in urban America: It's not justifiable for many. *The Journal of Special Education, 27,* 453–465.

Gould, S.J. (1981). *The mismeasure of man.* New York: Norton.

Grant, C.A., & Sleeter, C.E. (1998). *Turning on learning: Five approaches for multicultural teaching plans for race, class, gender, and disability* (2nd ed.). Upper Saddle River, NJ: Merrill.

Grossman, H. (1995). *Teaching, in a diverse society.* Needham Heights, MA: Allyn & Bacon.

Grossman, H. (1998). *Ending discrimination in special education.* Springfield, IL: Charles C Thomas.

Hanna, J.L. (1994). Issues in supporting school diversity: Academics, social relations, and the arts. *Anthropology & Education Quarterly, 25,* 66–85.

Hardman, M.L., Drew, C.J., & Egan, M.W.(1999). *Human exceptionality* (3rd ed.). Needham Heights, MA: Allyn & Bacon.

Harrison, A., Wilson, M., Pine, C., Chan, S., & Buriel, R. (1990). Family ecologies of ethnic minority children. *Child Development, 61,* 347–362.

Harry, B. (1992). *Cultural diversity, families, and the special education system.* New York: Teachers College Press.

Harry, B. (1994). *The disproportionate representation of minority students in special education: Theories and recommendations.* Alexandria, VA: National Association of State Directors of Special Education.

Heller, K.A., Holtzman, W.H., & Messick, S. (1982). *Placing children in special education: A strategy for equity.* Washington, DC: National Academy Press.

Hildago, N.M., Bright, J.A., Sui, S.F., Swap, S.M. & Epstein, J.L. (1995). Research on families, schools, and communities: A multicultural perspective. In J.A. Banks & C.A. Banks (Eds.), *Handbook of research on multicultural education* (pp. 498–524). New York: Macmillan.

Hilliard, A.G. (1995). Culture, assessment, and valid teaching for the African-American student. In B.A. Ford, F.E. Obiakor, & J.M. Patton (Eds.), *Effective education of exceptional African American learners: New perspectives* (pp. ix–xvi). Austin, TX: Pro-Ed.

Hodapp, R.M., Burack, J.A., & Zigler, E. (1990). *Issues in the developmental approach to mental retardation.* New York: Cambridge University Press.

Hoernicke, P.A., Kallam, M., & Tablada, T. (1994). Behavioral disorders in Hispanic American cultures. In R.L. Peterson & S. Ishii-Jordan (Eds.), *Multicultural issues in the education of students with behavioral disorders* (pp. 115–125). Cambridge, MA: Brookline Books.

Huston, A.C. (1991). *Children in poverty: Child development and public policy.* New York: Cambridge University Press.

Ingels, S.J., Abraham, S.Y., Karr, R., Spencer, B.D., & Frankel, M.R. (1990). *NELS: 88 Base Year Student Component Data File User's Manual.* Washington, DC: National Center for Education Statistics.

Keogh, B., Gallimore, R., & Weisner, T. (1997). A sociocultural perspective on learning and learning disabilities. *Learning Disabilities Research & Practice, 12,* 107–113.

Kozol, J. (1991). *Savage inequalities: Children in America's schools.* New York: Crown.

Krauss, M.W., & Hauser-Cram, P. (1992). Policy and program development for infants and toddlers with disabilities. In L. Rowitz (Ed.), *Mental retardation in the year 2000* (pp. 184–196). New York: Springer-Verlag.

Kronick, D. (1988). *New approaches to learning disabilities: Cognitive and metacognitive.* Philadelphia, PA: Grune & Stratton.

Landesman, S. & Ramey, C. T. (1989). Developmental psychology and mental retardation: Integrating scientific principles with treatment practices. *American Psychologist, 44,* 409–415.

Langdon, H.W., & Cheng, L.L. (1992). *Hispanic children and adults with communication disorders:* Assessment and intervention. Gaithersburg, MD: Aspen.

Lipsky, D.K. & Gartner, A. (1997). *Inclusion and school reform: Transforming America's classrooms.* Baltimore, MD: Paul H. Brookes.

MacMillan, D.L., & Reschly, D.J. (1998). Overrepresentation of minority students: The case for greater specificity or reconsideration of the variables examined. *The Journal of Special Education, 32,* 15–24.

McAdoo, H.P., & McAdoo, J.L. (1985). *Black children.* Beverly Hills, CA: Sage Publications.

McDermott, R., & Varenne, H. (1995). Culture as disability. *Anthropology & Education Quarterly, 26,* 324–348.

Mead, M. (1977). Applied anthropology: The state of the art. In A.F.C. Wallace, J.L. Angel, R. Fox, S. McChendon, R. Sady, & R. Shorer (Eds.), *Perspectives on anthropology.* Washington, DC: American Anthropological Association.

Meadmore, D. (1993). Divide and rule: A study of two dividing practices in Queensland Schools: In R. Slee (Ed.), *Is there a desk with my name on it? The politics of integration* (pp. 27–38). London, England: Falmer Press.

Morrow, R.D. (1994). Immigration, refugee and generational status as related to behavioral disorders. In R.L. Peterson & S. Ishii-Jordan (Eds.), *Multicultural issues in the education of students with behavioral disorders* (pp. 196–207). Cambridge, MA: Brookline Books.

National Center for Children in Poverty (1999). *Young children in poverty: A statistical update.* New York: The Joseph L. Mailman School of Public Health of Columbia University.

National Center for Education Statistics (1997). *Statistical analyses report: Profiles of students with disabilities as identified in NELS: 88* (Technical Report No. 97-254). Washington, DC: U.S. Department of Education.

National Coalition of Hispanic Health and Human Services Organization (1988). *Delivering preventive health care to Hispanics: A manual for providers.* Washington, DC: Author.

National Conference of Christians and Jews, Asian American Journalists Association, & Association of Asian Pacific American Journalist Association (1991). *Asian American handbook.* Chicago, IL: Author.

National Mental Health Association (1993). *All system.* Washington, DC: Author.

Nazzaro, J.N. (1991). *Special problems of exceptional minority children.* In culturally diverse exceptional children in school. Washington, DC: National Institute of Education. (ERIC Document Reproduction Services No. 199 993).

Nieto, S. (2000). *Affirming diversity: The sociopolitical context of multicultural education* (3rd ed.). White Plains, NY: Longman.

Obiakor, F.E. (1993). Multiculturalism: Critical issues facing teacher education programs. In *Bueno Center for Multicultural Education Monograph Series* (Vol. 9). Boulder, CO: University of Colorado.

Obiakor, F.E. (1994). *The eight-step multicultural approach: Learning and teaching with a smile.* Dubuque, IA: Kendall/Hunt.

Obiakor, F.E. (1999, Fall). Teacher expectations of minority exceptional learners: Impact on "accuracy" of self-concepts. *Exceptional Children, 66,* 39–53.

Obiakor, F.E., & Algozzine, B. (1995). *Managing problem behaviors: Perspectives for general and special educators.* Dubuque, IA: Kendall/Hunt.

Obiakor, F.E., Algozzine, B., & Ford, B.A. (1993). Urban education, the general education initiative, and service delivery to African-American students. *Urban Education, 28,* 313–327.

Obiakor, F.E., Algozzine, B., & Ford, B.A. (1994). Education reform and service delivery to African American students. In S.B. Garcia (Ed.), *Addressing cultural and linguistic diversity in special education: Issues and trends* (pp. 1–9). Reston, VA: Council for Exceptional Children.

Obiakor, F.E., & Ford, B.A. (1995). *Restructuring and reforming: "Rat race" for excellence or failure?* Paper presented at the 73rd Annual International Convention of the Council for Exceptional Children, Indianapolis, IN.

Obiakor, F.E., & Schwenn, J.O. (1995). Enhancing the self-concepts of culturally diverse students: The role of the counselor. In A.F. Rotatori, J.O. Schwenn, & F.W. Litton (Eds.), *Advances in special education* (Vol. 9) (pp. 191–205). Greenwich, CT: JAI Press.

Obiakor, F.E., & Utley, C.A. (1997). Rethinking preservice preparation for teachers in the learning disabilities field: Workable multicultural strategies. *Learning Disabilities Research & Practice, 12* (2), 100–106.

Obiakor, F.E., & Utley, C.A. (1998). What do reform and restructuring mean for culturally diverse learner? In B.A. Ford (Ed.), *Compendium: Writings on effective practices for culturally and linguistically diverse exceptional learners* (pp. 88–98). Reston, VA: The Council for Exceptional Children.

Ogbu, J.U. (1978). *Minority education and caste.* San Francisco, CA: Academic Press.

Ogbu, J.U. (1988). Human intelligence testing: A cultural-ecological perspective. *National Forum: The Phi Kappa Phi Journal, 68,* 23–29.

Ogbu, J.U. (1995). Understanding cultural diversity and learning. In J.A. Banks & C.A. Banks (Eds.), *Handbook of research on multicultural education* (pp. 582–593). New York: Macmillan.

Olneck, M.R. (1993). Terms of inclusion: Has multiculturalism redefined equality in American education. *American Journal of Education, 101,* 234–260.

Ortiz, A.A., & Garcia, S.B. (1990). Using language assessment data for language and instructional planning for exceptional bilingual students. In A.L. Carrasquillo & R.E. Baecher (Eds.), *Teaching the bilingual special education student* (pp. 25–47). Norwood, NJ: Ablex.

Ortiz, A.A., Garcia, S.B.,Wheeler, D., & Maldonado-Colon, E. (1986). *Characteristics of limited English proficient students served in programs for the speech and language handicapped: Implications for policy and practice, and research.* Austin, TX: The University of Texas, Handicapped Minority Research Institute on Language Proficiency.

Ortiz, A.A., & Maldonado-Colon, E. (1986). Recognizing learning disabilities in bilingual children. *Journal of Reading, Writing, and Learning Disabilities International, 2,* 43–56.

Ortiz, A.A., & Yates, J.R. (1984). Linguistically and culturally diverse handicapped students. In R.S. Podemski, B.M. Price, T.E.C. Smith, & G.E. Marsh II (Eds.), *Comprehensive administration of special education* (pp. 114–141). Rockville, MD: Aspen.

Oswald, D.P., Coutinho, M.J., Best, A.M., & Singh, N.N. (1999). Ethnic representation in special education: the influence of school-related economic and demographic variables. *The Journal of Special Education, 32,* 194–206.

Parker, S., Greer, S., & Zuckerman, B. (1988). Double jeopardy: The impact of poverty on early child development. *Pediatric Clinics of North American, 35,* 1–14.

Pederson, P.B. (1991). Multiculturalism as a generic approach to counseling. *Journal of Counseling and Development, 70,* 6–12.

Rainwater, L., & Smeeding, T.M. (1995). U.S. doing poorly—compared to others. *News and Issues, 5,* 4–5.

Reschly, D.J. (1991). The effects of placement litigation on psychological and education classification. *Diagnostique, 17,* 6–20.

Robertson, P., & Kushner, M.I. (1994). An update of participation rates of culturally and linguistically diverse students in special education: The need for a research and policy agenda. *The Bilingual Special Education Perspective, 14,* 1–16.

Rodriguez, F. (1999). *Affirming equity: A framework for teachers & schools* (3rd ed.). Dubuque, IA: Kendall/Hunt.

Roseberry-McKibbin, C. (1995). *Multicultural students with special language needs: Practical suggestions for assessment and intervention.* Oceanside, CA: Academic Communication Associates.

Rueda, R.S., & Forness, S.R. (1994). Childhood depression: Ethnic and cultural issues in special education. In R.L. Peterson & S.I. Jordan (Eds.), *Multicultural issues in the education of students with behavioral disorders* (pp. 40–62). Cambridge, MA: Brookline Books.

Sameroff, A.J., & Seifer, R. (1995). Accumulation of environmental risk and child mental health. In H.E. Fitzgerald, B.M. Lester, & B. Zuckerman (Eds.), *Children of poverty: Research, health, and poverty issues* (pp. 233–257). New York: Garland.

Sameroff, A.J., Seifer, R., Barocas, R., Zax, M., & Greenspan, S. (1987). IQ scores of 4-year-old children. Social-environmental risk factors. *Pediatrics, 79,* 343–350.

Sameroff, A.J., Seifer, R., & Zax, M. (1982). Early development of children at risk for emotional disorders. In *Monographs of the Society for Research in Child Development* (Vol. 47). Chicago, IL: University of Chicago.

Serwatka, T.S., Deering, S., & Grant, P. (1995). Disproportionate representation of African Americans in emotionally handicapped classes. *Journal of Black Studies, 25,* 492–506.

Shade, B.J. (1989). *Culture, style, and the educative process.* Springfield, IL: Charles C Thomas.

Shade, B.J. (1997). *Culture, style, and the educative process: Making schools work for racially diverse students* (2nd ed.). Springfield, IL: Charles C Thomas.

Shade, B.J., Kelley, C., & Oberg, M. (1997). *Creating culturally responsive classrooms.* Washington, DC: American Psychological Association.

Shade, B.J., & New, C.A. (1991). Cultural influences on learning: Teaching implications. In J.A. Banks & C. McGee Banks (Eds.), *Multicultural education: Issues and perspectives* (pp. 317–329). Needham Heights, MA: Allyn & Bacon.

Shalala, D.E. (1999). *Mental health: A report of the surgeon general.* Online at http://www.surgeon-general.gov/library/mentalhealth/home.html.

Sherman, A. (1998). *Poverty matters: The cost of child poverty in America.* Washington, DC: Children's Defense Fund.

Simeonsson, R.J. (1994). *Risk resilience and prevention: Promoting the well-being of all children.* Baltimore, MD: Paul H. Brookes.

Smith, M.J., & Ryan, A.S. (1987). Chinese-American families of children with developmental disabilities: An exploratory study of reactions to service providers. *Mental Retardation, 25,* 345–350.

Spickard, P.R., Fong, R., & Ewalt, P.L. (1996). Undermining the very basis of racism—its categories. In P.L. Ewalt, E.M. Freeman, S.A. Kirk, & D.L. Poole (Eds.), *Multicultural issues in social work* (pp. 14–20). Washington, DC: National Association of Social Workers.

Spring, J. (1994). *Deculturalization and the struggle for equality: A brief history of the education of dominated cultures in the United States.* New York: McGraw-Hill.

Stewart, J.L. (1992). Native American populations. *American Speech Hearing Association, 34,* 40–42.

Sue, D.W. (1995). Toward a theory of multicultural counseling and therapy. In J.A. Banks & C.A. Banks (Eds.), *Handbook of research on multicultural education* (pp. 647–662). New York: Macmillan.

Sue, D.W., & Sue, D. (1990). *Counseling the culturally different: Theory and practice.* New York: John Wiley & Sons.

Sugai, G., Maheady, L., & Skouge, J. (1989). Best assessment practices for students with behavior disorders: Accommodation to cultural diversity and individual differences. *Behavioral Disorders, 14,* 263–278.

Swisher, K., & Deyhle, D. (1989). The styles of learning are different, but the teaching is just the same: Suggestions for teachers of American Indian youth. *Journal of American Indian Education* [Special Issue], pp. 1–14.

Tharp, R., & Gallimore, R. (1988). *Rousing minds to life: Teaching. learning and schooling in social context.* Cambridge, England: Cambridge University Press.

Theodorson, G.A., & Theodorson, A.G. (1969). *A modem dictionary of sociology.* New York: Barnes and Noble.

Trotter, T.V. (1993). Counseling with young multicultural clients. In A. Vernon (Ed.), *Counseling children and adolescents* (pp. 137–155). Denver, CO: Love.

Trueba, H.T. (1989). *Raising silent voices: Educating the linguistic minorities for the 21st century.* New York: Newbury House.

Trueba, H.T. (1993). Many groups, one people: The meaning and significance of multicultural education in modem America. *Bilingual Research Journal, 6,* 91–116.

Tucker, J. (1980). Ethnic proportions in classes for the learning disabled: Issues in non-biased assessment. *The Journal of Special Education, 86,* 351–360.

Tuma, J.M. (1989). Mental health services for children: The state of the art. *American Psychologist, 44,* 188–199.

U.S. Bureau of the Census (1991). *Statistical abstract of the United States: 1991.* Washington, DC: U.S. Government Printing Office.

U.S. Department of Education (1988). *Youth indicators 1988: Trends in the well-being of American youth.* Washington, DC: Author.

U.S. Department of Education (1992). *Fourteenth annual report to Congress on the implementation of the Individuals with Disabilities Education Act.* Washington, DC: Government Printing Office.

U.S. Department of Education (1998). *Twentieth annual report to Congress on the implementation of the Individuals with Disabilities Education Act.* Washington, DC: Government Printing Office.

U.S. Department of Education, Office of Special Education. (1992). *How well are youth with disabilities really doing? A comparison of youth with disabilities and youth in general. A Report from the National Longitudinal Transition Study of Special Education Students.* Menlo Park, CA: SRI International.

U.S. Department of Education, Office of Civil Rights (1987). *The 1986 Elementary and secondary school civil rights survey: National summaries.* Washington, DC: DBS Corporation.

Utley, C.A. (1995). Culturally and linguistically diverse students with mild disabilities. In C.A. Grant (Ed.), *Educating for diversity: An anthology of multicultural voices* (pp. 301–324). Needham Heights, MA: Allyn & Bacon.

Utley, C.A., Delquadri, J.C., Obiakor, F.E., Mims, V. (2000, Winter). General and special educator's perceptions of teaching strategies for culturally and linguistically diverse students. *Teacher Education and Special Education, 23,* 4–50.

Utley, C.A., & Mortweet, S.L. (1999). The challenge of diversity. In M.J. Coutinho & A.C. Repp (Eds.), *Inclusion: The integration of students with disabilities* (pp. 59–90). Belmont, CA: Wadsworth.

Wagner, M., Newman, L., D'Amico, R., Jay, D., Butler-Nalin, P., Marder, C., & Cox, R. (1991).

Youth with disabilities: How are they doing? Washington, DC: Office of Special Education Programs.

West, C. (1993). *Race matters.* New York: Vintage Books.

Willis, W. (1992). Families with African American roots. In E.W. Lynch & M.J. Hanson (Eds.), *Developing cross-cultural competence: A guide for working with young children and their families* (pp. 121–150). Baltimore, MD: Paul H. Brookes.

Wilson, L.C. (1994, November). *Language development as perceived by reservation-based Navajo families.* Paper presented at the annual meeting of the American Speech-Language-Hearing Association, New Orleans, LA.

Wright, J.V. (1995). Multicultural issues and attention-deficit disorders. *Learning Disabilities Research & Practice, 10,* 153–159.

Yeargin-Allsopp, M., Drews, C.D., Decoufl, S.D., & Murphy, C.C. (1995). Mild mental retardation in black and white children in metropolitan Atlanta: A case-control study. *American Journal of Public Health, 85,* 324–328.

Zeichner, K.M. (1992). *Educating teachers for cultural diversity.* East Lansing, MI: Michigan State University, National Center for Research on Teacher Learning.

Zuniga, M.E. (1998). Families with Latino roots. In E.W. Lynch & M.J. Hanson (Eds.), *Developing cross-cultural competence: A guide for working with young children and their families* (2nd ed.) (pp. 209–250). Baltimore, MD: Paul H. Brookes.

Chapter 2

DISPELLING MYTHS AND STEREOTYPES CONFRONTING MULTICULTURAL LEARNERS WITH MILD DISABILITIES: PERSPECTIVES FOR SCHOOL REFORM

ELLEN A. BRANTLINGER AND ZALINE ROY-CAMPBELL

In this chapter, we focus on the myths and stereotypes confronting multicultural students who have been identified as having mild disabilities. Our discussion on the effects of poverty, race, and culture on children's physical, cognitive, social, emotional, and language development includes an overview of the controversies surrounding the mild disabilities classification (i.e., learning disabled, mildly mentally retarded, emotionally disturbed) and separated instructional arrangements commonly used with them.

In spite of federal mandates to keep classified children in mainstream classrooms to the greatest extent possible, the number of children receiving special services has increased steadily over recent decades (Tomasi & Weinberg, 1999). Children from low-income families are especially likely to be classified as mildly disabled and to be placed in special classes (Brantlinger, 1993; Hilliard, 1992a;

Obiakor, 1992; Tomlinson, 1999). Because of the strong correlation between social class and minority ethnicity, children of color and those with limited English proficiency also are disproportionately classified as disabled and overrepresented in special education classrooms (Artiles & Trent, 1994; Gollnick & Chinn, 1990; Harry, 1994; Kunjufu, 1986; Oswald, Coutinho, Best, & Singh, 1999; Patton, 1998; Robertson, Kushner, Starks, & Drescher, 1994). Special education status is not the only indicator of "lack of adjustment" and second rate standing in school for students of color or those with limited English proficiency. In the United States, regardless of their actual achievement, students from lower socioeconomic or minority segments of society are assigned to lower tracks (Oakes & Guiton, 1995; Wells & Serna, 1996) and generally have a range of negative educational experiences and outcomes (Adams & Singh,

30

1998; Delpit, 1995; Ladson-Billings, 1992; Welch & Hodges, 1997; Zisman & Wilson, 1992). The same situation is true in England (Barton, 1997; Gilborn, 1995; Gilborn & Gipps, 1996; Tomlinson, 1999) and Australia (Slee, 1996).

In terms of the absence of multicultural learners at the upper end of tracking, Ford (1992) referred to how little scholarly attention has been devoted to this issue. Discrimination and differential outcomes continue to appear at the twelfth grade level. For example, African Americans run into bias and fare less well at post-secondary educational levels whether as students or faculty (Bell, 1994; Cose, 1993; Emihovich, 1999; Foster, 1999; Futrell, 1999; Latham, Gitomer, & Ziomek, 1999; Lawrence-Lightfoot, 1994; McCarthy, 1993; Welch & Hodges, 1997; West, 1994). In spite of stated federal priorities, access to universities by minority and low-income students has declined and financial aid has gone increasingly to middle-class students who could manage without it (Orfield, 1992). The segregation of students into low-income schools or special education and low track classrooms mirrors the ghettoed existence of families—both are relegated to the sidelines of mainstream life. More adults of color and those with limited English proficiency have incomes below the poverty level; they are disproportionately poor (Comer, 1988; Conley, 1999). The "underclass," as the poor recently have been dubbed (Kornblum, 1984; Wilson, 1987), is not a small minority; about 30% of United States families are economically disadvantaged (Nelson, 1995). It is important to note that when special education was taking root in American schools, the general rationale for separate programming was that differences among students were pathologies that could be identified, treated, and remedied by specially trained personnel. Presently, more skeptical views about the meaning of classification and purpose and results of special education are held by both professionals and the recipients of services. In order to dispel myths and confront stereotypes about poor and minority children, many of whom have been carelessly classified as mildly disabled, deconstruction of the personal pathology and individual deficit models is a central undertaking of this chapter.

Some special educators (e.g., Fuchs & Fuchs, 1994; Gresham & Forness, 1996; Kauffman & Hallahan, 1995; MacMillan, Semmel & Gerber, 1994) have insisted that separate special education programming is needed to meet the unique needs of students with disabilities. In contrast, Allington and McGill-Franzen (1992) view special education as a separate system that is expensive and that does not have educational benefits that improve the life chances of recipients. In terms of being "special," teaching in special education settings has not been unique but rather remarkably similar to instruction in regular classes (Cline & Billingsley, 1991; Troyna & Vincent, 1996). Most importantly, students who actually receive services often evaluate them as not helpful and resent disability labels and segregation (Allen, 1999; Brantlinger, 1994; Jones, 1972; Warner, Thrapp, & Walsh, 1973). Students also express resentment about low tracks or ability groups (Elbaum, Schumm, & Vaughn, 1997). This finding is consistent with the fact that up to 50% of students receiving special education services drop out of school prior to graduation (deBettencourt, Zigmond, & Thornton, 1989; Wolman, Bruininks, & Thurlow, 1989). Concern about negative attitudes of mainstream children and teachers has led some who claim to be in favor of inclusion to feel that a separate special education system is necessary (e.g., Sabornie, Marshall, & Ellis, 1990; Schumm & Vaughn, 1995; Zigmond & Baker, 1990). Others (e.g., Brantlinger, 1997; Patton, 1998; Stainback & Stainback, 1996; Taylor, 1995) have questioned the value of segregation and advocate inclusion even with less-than-ideal conditions in regular education. They have stressed that the first priority for advocates of students with learning and behavioral differences should be to reform mainstream schools and classrooms so that they better accommodate pupil diversity.

Inclusion advocates challenge the medical model which posits pathology in individuals and contend that disability is a social construct that results from arbitrary and inflexible school arrangements (Algozzine, Ysseldyke, & McGue, 1995; Carrier, 1986; Coles, 1987; Gartner & Lipsky, 1987; Skrtic, 1991; Sleeter, 1986; Tomlinson, 1982, 1996, 1999; Varenne & McDermott, 1998). Concern has been expressed about the ethics of eliminating low-achievers from schools testing pool due to pressures of high-stakes accountability testing (Haladyna, Nolan, & Haas, 1991; McGill-Franzen & Allington, 1993; Mehan, 1992). Conflict of opinion about the education of students identified as disabled within special education professional ranks is similar to general educators' worry about the impact of other school arrange-

ments on low-achievers (Fine, 1991; Goodlad, 1983; Oakes & Lipton, 1992; Page, 1991). Classified children have no monopoly on problems in school. Personnel interact with all low-achievers in less positive and educationally constructive ways than they do with high-achievers (McCaslin & Good, 1996; Parker, Gottlieb, Gottlieb, Davis & Kunzweiller, 1989). Nevertheless, when children are put in low status placements, their school careers become even more problematic (McDermott & Varenne, 1995; Mehan, 1995; Moran, 1984; Richardson, 1994; Tobias, 1989). Stigmatizing placements carry far-reaching symbolic meanings for students, teachers, and parents (Allen, 1999; Brantlinger, 1993; Corbett, 1997; Franklin, 1994). Such labels as "gifted and talented, at-risk, learning disabled, and emotionally disturbed" have profoundly political implications (Christensen, 1996; Giroux, 1989). Because both classified and non-classified low-achievers suffer in school, the point of this chapter is that general and special educators must rethink how they educate all children.

CAUSES OF DIFFERENTIAL SCHOOL OUTCOMES

After citing the persistent findings about links between social status and school outcomes, it is necessary to explore reasons for the connections. By definition, poor children come to school from unequal financial circumstances, but educators must challenge the assumption that "flaws" in children or families are totally, or even primarily, responsible for unequal educational outcomes (Brantlinger & Guskin, 1987, 1992). Several theories about differential success rates point to middle class advantage in schooling. Bourdieu and Passeron (1977) claimed that affluent people have the attributes or the cultural capital preferred in educational institutions while

the cultural traits of other classes are devalued. In *The Hidden Injuries of Class,* Sennett and Cobb (1972) referred to an anthropological idea, pseudo-speciation, in which a tribe's inner solidarity and cohesion are so strong that they believe their customs form the standards for others. This theory accounts for White, middle-class school personnels' lack of understanding and tolerance for outsiders' ways. It is consistent with current suggestions for multicultural and equitable schooling put forth by a number of prominent scholars (Banks, 1997; Foster, 1997; Grant, 1990; Ladson-Billings, 1992, 1994; Meier, 1993; Obiakor, 1994; Osborne, 1996; Sleeter, 1995;

Spindler & Spindler, 1994; Weinstein, Madison & Kuklinski, 1995; Wells, Hirshberg, Lipton & Oakes, 1995).

Achievement disparities can also be explained by the ample documentation that human and material school resources are vastly different for poor and monied constituencies (Burton, 1999; Gamoran & Berends, 1987; Jencks, 1972; Kozol, 1991; Sapon-Shevin, 1993; Sexton, 1961). For example, Kozol reported that New York City spent about $7,000 for each pupil while wealthy New York suburbs spent $15,000. At the time, the difference in outlay for 12 years of schooling in the respective districts amounted to approximately $100,000 per child. In terms of annual funding for a class of 36, Kozol calculated that based on a per-pupil expenditure of $5,585 in New York City and $11,372 in Manhasset (suburb), there was an annual difference of over $200,000 per class.

A philosophy of local control holds firm in school funding formulas. This means that along with advantaged living conditions, middle-class children have advantaged school circumstances. The impact of school expenditures on school experiences and outcomes must be acknowledged. Middle-class parents insist on the best schooling for their own children (Brantlinger, Madj-Jabbari, & Guskin, 1996; Brantlinger & Madj-Jabbari, 1998; Wildman, 1996). Low-income parents are rarely in powerful enough positions to make demands or have their wishes met (Brantlinger, 1985a, 1985b, 1985c, 1987; Harry, 1992; Lareau, 1989; Useem, 1992). Then, too, they may be so resigned to disparities in life circumstances that inequities in schooling do not seem unusual or unexpected and so they do not stand up for equal rights. With their disproportionate political and professional clout, middle-class people could make changes in school funding formulas if they were interested, or, more aptly put, if it were in their own interest. State and federal controls already govern a number of aspects of education (Kantor & Lowe, 1995). Truly democratic leaders (and voters) could choose to ensure financial equity among schools. Nevertheless, although affluent parents wax eloquently about democratic ideals, they still want school advantages for their own children (Bingham, Haubrich, White, & Zipp, 1990; Brantlinger et al., 1996). They perceive their offspring and other children of their class to be significantly different from low-income children. The perceived distinctions become the rationale for specialized and segregated education (neighborhood suburban schools, high tracks) (Brantlinger & Majd-Jabbari, 1998). Sieber (1982) found that high-income parents who moved into renovated (gentrified) brownstones in an urban area confronted local school authorities with demands for advanced classes for their children which, in effect, created an advantaged school within a school and a two-tier system. In Ontario, Olson (1983) observed how funds meant to develop bilingual programs to improve relations between English and French speaking people subsequently were used to establish French immersion programs limited to advanced students; that is, elitist programs that benefit middle-class children.

Middle-class people are comfortable with cultural deprivation hypotheses that blame the victims of oppression (Ryan, 1971). Ray and Mickelson (1990) cited United States Secretary of Labor Cavazos' espousal of the "defective worker philosophy" in his claim that trade and budget problems cannot be resolved without overcoming educational problems. Indeed, the host of national initiatives that raise school accountability demands (e.g., *A Nation at Risk, America 2000*) are based on the faulty logic that the economy is in trouble due to ill-prepared workers (Berliner & Biddle, 1995). There is ample evidence of the glut of unemployed or underemployed workers with college degrees.

Although rhetorically committed to equal opportunity, schools contribute little toward equalizing the life chances of students. Indeed, they generate inequalities and stigmatize even average performance (Roth, 1992). The contest structure of schools–the supposed vehicle for social mobility–is not only not antithetical to prevailing American ideologies but is valued precisely because it legitimates inequality (Brantlinger et al., 1996; Conforti, 1992; Connell, 1993). Supposedly a meritocracy, school is symbolically violent because it teaches students that societal ranking systems are scientific, fair, and neutral (Delamont, 1989). As previously discussed, both the competitive structure and stratified outcomes of schools are products of powerful people's desires and actions. And, as the generous eras of former U.S. Presidents Roosevelt, Kennedy, and Johnson wane, there is diminished support for desegregation (Kozol, 1991). Ray and Mickelson (1990) claimed that the local policy paralysis in democratic restructuring reflects capitalists' inability to see how they contribute to an array of contradictions in the social fabric. This unwillingness to undertake critical analyses of corporate restructuring is evidence of affluent people's self-interest.

Affluent constituencies and professionals *talk* about kinder, gentler circumstances. Many books about poverty and racial isolation have made best seller lists (Edelman, 1987; Kotlowitz, 1991, 1998; Kozol, 1991; Wilson, 1987). Reading about problems and thinking or expressing socially sensitive feelings, however, may be cathartic thus serve to relieve readers of obligation to take action. Simple awareness of problems does not solve them. Such inaction on the part of powerful people is consistent with Freire's (1973) judgment that oppressed people cannot trust dominant groups to change conditions for them, but must take action in their own behalf.

Given the embeddedness of privilege and deprivation in schooling–the intertwining of dominant culture and institutional structures–making schools equal would not be easy. The phrase "money speaks" is readily translated into "the voices of the wealthy–White people–are heard and controlling." Another saying "power corrupts" applies to those who determine policy which directs disproportionate public funds to their own class. Whether consciously or not, advantaged people repeatedly develop stratifying systems that prevent a redistribution of advantage.

THE DEVELOPMENT OF DEVIANCE OUT OF DIFFERENCE

School practices are influential in how children and adults perceive themselves, others, and the world around them. Certain children have learned–been taught by formal and hidden curricula–that they are not as smart and deserving as others. Technical labels seem scientifically correct and so are impervious to criticism. Yet, classification is a practice of power that produces effects deeply inscribed on the oppressed (Howe, 1996; Ladwig & Gore, 1994). Tinney (1983) wrote of interconnections between such

"isms" as sexism and racism. He distinguished three (overlapping) levels of oppression: *institutional* bias that prevents equal benefits in schools and other institutions; *individual* prejudice and stereotyping; *collective* discrimination of norms and values that legitimize oppression. For example, White English is the standard of correct grammar applied by teachers and employers. Symbolism in language has a host of negative denotations and connotations (Dyson, 1993). The word before "Black" refers to sin, evil, fear, crime, dirt, depression, and death (Morrison, 1993). Corson (1992) and Gilbert (1992) identified how language–within and outside the classroom–locate individuals in disadvantageous positions in school and society.

When the damaging effects of biased circumstances for some ethnic or racial groups are proclaimed, others often counter that, with the exception of Native Americans, United States citizens have all been immigrants or descendants of immigrants whose personal ambitions, talents, or hard work allowed them to succeed. To explain the persistence of achievement discrepancies for African Americans, Ogbu (1995) postulated that differences exist in various immigrant groups' cultural models of what it means to be a minority. He distinguished between the adaptations of voluntary and involuntary immigrants by pointing to a status mobility frame of reference, "making it" optimism, learned survival strategies, available role models, degree of trust or distrust of White Americans and their institutions, high self-image and positive collective identity, and continuity of culture and language. Similarly, West (1994) looked to the historical roots of Black slavery and White supremacy to explain why the present United States society is stratified along racial lines.

Whether racist acts are deliberate by Whites and whether Whites are conscious of their own racism is disputed (Danforth, 1996; Hooks, 1994; Scheurich, 1993; Scheurich & Young, 1997). Extending a colonial metaphor to race relations, M. Harris (1992) argued that difference is not only historically institutionalized and purposefully managed; that refutation of positive aspects of African Americans history and culture purposefully miseducates African Americans and marks them as outsiders. Asante (1991) concurred that the Eurocentric canons that dominate United States institutions systematically distance and culturally dislocate African American children and others who

are underrepresented, misrepresented, silenced, and marginalized.

Although she would be unlikely to disagree with M. Harris' analysis and conclusions, V. Harris (1992) emphasized that, since the Civil War, education has served as a signifier for social mobility for Blacks. She cited DuBois' classic example of double-consciousness: African Americans disdain the same society they fervently seek to join. Harris set off the emancipatory from the oppressive functions of schooling. School is liberating when it reconstructs society or allows marginalized individuals to participate in institutions. It is oppressive when it inculcates ideologies that denigrate groups, misrepresent or omit their history, or limit access to enabling knowledge. One problem in correcting these denigrations and omissions, is the continuing underrepresentation of Black teachers (Futrell, 1999; King, 1993). Even well-intentioned White teachers seem unaware of their own subtle racism and how they are implicated in systems that stratify (Britzman, 1997; Weiss, 1995; Wright, 1994).

In reaction to systemic miseducation in White-dominated public schools, the enrollment of African Americans in independent Black institutions (IBIs) has increased (Benson, 1991). Traditionally, Black parents selected private schools for their children because they felt they had higher academic standards, better discipline, Black role models, safer environments, a religious emphasis, or because they somewhat insulated children from society's racism (Lomotey & Brookins, 1988). Shujaa (1992) noted a desire among Black parents to have their children in schools which build "an African-centered cultural base" and "counter Eurocentric hegemony" (p. 149). It is sadly ironic that the rationale for *Brown v. Board of Education* (1954)–that racial integration is essential to Black children's positive self esteem–turned out not to eliminate bias and inequities so that now many Black parents believe segregation is necessary for their children to achieve academically and socially and have pride in themselves and their heritage. Unfortunately, educators, parents, and the public are unaware of the nature and extent of discrimination in public schools and/or have made insufficient efforts to eradicate it.

THE IMPACT OF RACE, ETHNICITY, AND SOCIAL CLASS ON STUDENT CHARACTERISTICS

One intention of our overview of the power relations that influence the nature of schooling was to build a framework for analyzing dimensions of child development. Several aspects of student characteristics are relevant to this chapter: physical growth, school/individual cognitive style congruence, student and teacher views of each other, stereotyping, perceptions of school, and self-perception. Themes of importance of context in shaping cognition and the damaging effects of class and racial bias and domination will continue to frame and permeate our discussions.

Physical Development

Poor children and their parents are likely to suffer from impoverished conditions (Polakow, 1992). Good nutrition and shelter are essential to healthy physical and mental growth. Yet, children of families with limited funds may be deprived of such nourishment. Without a health care system that meets the needs of all citizens, poor people are denied access to good medical care (Associated Press, 1999). Gaps in medical attention are particularly damaging during the prenatal months. Babies from impoverished families stand a greater risk of low birth weight, birth complications, and infant mortality. They often are not inoculated against disease. In *Savage Inequalities,* Kozol (1991) documented how because of economic constraints, poor people have no choice but to live in proximity to toxic waste dumps or in dwellings with high lead or asbestos content. These toxins take a toll on optimal child development.

The influence of poverty, race, and culture on physical development, however, takes surprising twists and turns. People in wealthy countries have higher rates of cancer and heart disease due to the overabundance of animal fats and sugars in their diets. Wealthy children may settle into poor habits of exercise, such as being driven, rather than walking or biking. In contrast, those who lack the cultural attributes to compete in the Eurocentric or middle class-oriented academic parts of school may turn to sports—investing in their physical competence instead. In the end, the physical development of all humans is tied to the health of the environment. According to Pinar and Bowers (1992), United States citizens face a serious ecological crisis that they have not adequately addressed. An examination of life-styles would reveal that wealthy people use more than their share of natural resources, hence pollute more. Postmodern and postcolonial analyses challenge assumptions about the validity of westernization, industrialization, and material progress. To stop the distortion of human development by material overconsumption and misuse, it may be better to look to the poor as models of environmentally sane living. This pursuit may lead to valuing philosophies that respect a balance between humans and nature similar to the outlook of Native Americans, whose views previously were seen as primitive and backwards (Deloria, 1984).

Identity Formation

In analyzing identity construction, many have studied how race, class, and gender weave complex sets of subjectivities that are situated in individuals' cultural and historical world and are influenced by schooling (Cochran-Smith, 1995; Nader, 1996; Weis, 1990; Weis & Fine, 1996; Zane, 1994). Self-image, self-definition, and self-esteem—all parts of identity building—are interrelated concepts that many educators believe hold the key to differential school performance. By engaging students, parents, and teachers in autobiographical story-telling or observing the dynamics of classrooms, scholars have been able to note the many ways that families, communities, and schools shape children's evolving views of themselves and society (Ayers, 1990; Brantlinger, 1993; Carter, 1993; Deyle & Swisher, 1997; Finders, 1997; Fivush, 1991; Gudmundsdottir, 1990; Henry, 1995; Paley, 1990; Schoem, 1989). For instance, Schoem's collection of life stories of Black, Jewish, and Latino college students shows the influence of ethnicity in students' outlooks concerning schooling.

Pelham and Swann (1989) detailed the cognitive and affective components of self-views which develop in school contexts and concluded that some students suffer permanent loss of confidence and esteem. They claimed that some students turn to drugs as an escape or form of self-destructive behavior that arises from self hate. Others reject school as a self-definer and choose gang affiliation to gain positive self-identity. Economic stress also accounts for depression-loneliness and delinquency-drug use (Lempers & Clark-Lempers, 1990). From a different standpoint, it has been noted that participation in gang and drug cultures may be an avenue to positive self-esteem and financial success for some adolescents (Bourgois, 1995; Okundaye, 1999). It certainly can be considered a playing out of the American free enterprise system. Chief Executive Officers (CEOs) in large international corporations constantly engage in entrepreneurships that are antisocial and that cause a great deal of suffering. Little attention is directed at their actions under unregulated capitalism, whereas small-time dealers are scorned and heavily penalized for their acts.

Cognitive Competence

Similarities in cognitive styles exist among those who share linguistic and cultural environments (Hilliard, 1992b; Reyner, 1992; Shade, 1982). Ovando and Collier (1998) drew from an extensive literature review to illuminate cognitive attributes (reflective and impulsive tempo, internal and external locus of control) and recommend using teaching strategies that accommodate individual differences. Similarly, in warning of a potential clash between home and school cultures, Delpit (1992) acknowledged the impossibility of creating perfect "culturally matched" learning situations for each ethnic group. There are a myriad of cultural and language styles. Because of diaspora, differences exist within groups and there is an overlap between groups on cognitive dimensions. Teachers can attempt to understand students' ethnicity as well as their own. In examining cultural traits, however, general and special educators must proceed cautiously so as not to perpetuate damaging myths and stereotypes (Robinson, 1994). To understand low achievement in certain students, insight might be gained from looking at cognitive competence in others.

In *Competitive Ethos and Democratic Education,* Nicholls (1989) wrote that success in the U.S. society is likely to be defined as superiority over others. Interpersonal competition exacerbates egotism in some and diminishes any sense of accomplishment among others. Many children learn to see themselves as failures and take little pleasure from their explorations, learning, and lesser accomplishments in school. They close down in school. Nicholls suggested that even for children who excel a sense of superiority and entitlement

creates problems in school and in postschool life. Brantlinger (1993) found that middle-class students assumed they were brighter and harder-working than low-income students, hence thought their better grades and higher participation rates in school activities were due to their own efforts and talents. Unfortunately, many low-income students held the same disabling views as their affluent schoolmates. Weiss (1990) contended that White adolescents personalize accounts of identity and do not name skin color as a privileging force in their lives and warned that this depoliticization of consciousness means that struggles around race, class, and gender emerge more powerfully outside of schooling. Addressing children's concepts of justice and power, Palonsky (1987) concluded that the image of children as innocents must be challenged.

Stereotypes and Bias

Categorization of humans, including stereotyping (expectations of individuals based on their group membership), is a pervasive characteristic of social cognition (Smith & Zarate,1990; Zarate & Smith, 1990). Mental associations that link social class, academic prowess, and worthiness are prevalent among children and adults (Brantlinger, 1993; Eder, 1995). In spite of the deluge of attention directed at teacher expectancies, Garibaldi (1992) maintained that teachers still are not immune to negative self-fulfilling prophecies about ethnic minority students. In an earlier study of this genre, Fuchs (1973)

traced how eager, compassionate first-year teachers gradually learned to blame children and parents for school failures. Brantlinger (1985a; 1993) found that low-income parents and youth were aware that middle-class teachers were biased against members of their social class; affluent students and their parents confirmed the truth of the low-income people's impressions (Brantlinger et al., 1996). Relatedly, Good, Slavings, Harel, and Emerson (1987) observed teachers' biased expectations cause differential feedback which results in some students becoming intellectually passive in classrooms.

Affect and Social Climate

At least until the recent spate of violence in schools, a common social construct has been that school has a therapeutic or at least a neutral impact. Evidence is accruing about

how school causes or contributes to problematic attitudes and behaviors (Brandau & Collins, 1994; Brantlinger, 1991; Comer, 1991; Elias, 1989; Finders, 1997; Fine, 1991;

Fordham & Ogbu, 1986; Shimahara, 1983). Limited access to a coveted competitive best leads to the stress of failure (Lightfoot, 1987) and disconnection from academic life (Strahan, 1988, 1989). The ubiquitous recent school initiatives that overemphasize academic success (Berliner & Biddle, 1995) may exacerbate stress-related problems and alienation among some students (Merton, 1994) and teachers (Little, 1996).

Interview studies by Brantlinger and colleagues (1985a, 1985b, 1985c, 1987, 1993, 1996, 1998) focused on the relations between social class in affiliation and social constructs of self and other. After attending class in homogeneous elementary schools, secondary students in class-mixed schools were suspicious of schoolmates from other schools (i.e., other social classes). They interpreted classmates' actions from a within-class perspective and their views were distorted by myths allowed to flourish because of so little early contact. One distortion of reality by both high-and low-income students was the view that low-income adolescents were aggressive. In describing actual conflicts, students repeatedly told of behaviors which in gender relations have been called "borderwork" (Thorne, 1986). While walking in corridors, high-status youths often pushed peers into low-income schoolmates. The pushers then scuttled off as the low-income students retaliated against the student who bumped into them. If a teacher witnessed the ensuing fight, the low-income student was inevitably assumed to be at fault and was punished. High-income adolescents admitted that they were rarely penalized for infractions. In spite of the evidence of aggression by high-income adolescents, both groups felt low-income youth were "short-fused," "on edge," and ready to fight. They were called "rednecks" and "bullies." At the same time, low-income youth expressed anger at teachers and high-income students, complaining about rejection, ostracism, and powerlessness in school. Feeling vulnerable and on the defensive, they intentionally incorporated a violent (powerful) image into their persona by dress and demeanor. In contrast, in spite of their name-calling, bullying, and aggression, high-income adolescents felt themselves to be well-behaved and innocent of wrongdoing. Low-income students echoed this attitude by calling high-income schoolmates "good kids" and "respectable."

Shimahara (1983) noted that themes underlying segregation include "feeling comfortable" with one's own kind. Shrum, Cheek, and Hunter (1988) observed increasing homophily in race relations at the middle school level, caused by adolescents' divisive and exclusive cliques that were stress-producing to members and alienating to others. In looking at race relations, Zisman and Wilson (1992) showed how free-forming peer groups intersect with, and reinforce, formal classroom grouping patterns and school organization. In spite of the evidence that schools are sites of struggles among peers, educators seem reluctant to confront cruel relations of middle-class students (Brantlinger, 1993; Eder, 1995; Finders, 1997).

Aspirations and Values

In spite of common misperceptions about the influence of aspirations on educational and vocational attainment, values related to achievement have been found to be fairly uniform for all classes and races (Seginer, 1983). Other affective factors do influence educational outcomes, namely hopes and expectations. Low-income families do not have the confidence that their children's school careers will be positive and are aware of the discrepancy between funds needed for postsecondary education and their own financial resources (Brantlinger, 1985c). Noting the dynamic, multileveled nature of thought, Fordham and Ogbu (1986) and Garibaldi (1992) showed how African American students have high aspirations for school attainment, but worry about losing their cultural identity if they strive to achieve. MacLeod (1987) documented how minority youth often echo dominant messages in spite of being shut out from dominant pathways to success. Fine (1991), and Ray and Mickelson (1990) argued that non-college-bound students' school behaviors and outcomes are realistic responses to an unstable and unpromising labor market in the U.S.

In contrast to the abundance of attention directed at the motives and values of poor people, middle-class children and parents are held up as role models. Some high-income children, however, do what they have to do in school to succeed—"play the game," but with a good deal of cynicism. Or, school competition pressures them to achieve as a mark of status and a way to access wealth. High achievement can be a sign of conformity and insecurity. Higher aims of education, such as to gain knowledge to improve societal conditions, are ignored. The unnamed motives of successful people protects the legitimation of inequities. It is too easy for the credentialed, professional class (Troyna & Vincent, 1996) to focus on those who do not succeed and to attribute their problems to inadequate motives or inferior family values (Wright, 1993). The reasons for the success of high-income children have rarely come under the scrutiny of empirical study.

LANGUAGE PROFICIENCY, LANGUAGE POLITICS

In addressing language proficiency and style, we examine the role it plays in social perceptions and identity formation as well as in achievement. Twenty-five years ago, sociolinguist Labov (1973) illustrated how Black English was rule-governed, complex, and functional for communication, different from but not inferior to White English. Nevertheless, some forms of White English are still used as the "standard" to which other versions of English are compared. Gee (1989) distinguished secondary discourses (ways of believing, writing, and speaking) connected with institutions such as schools and universities from primary discourses learned at home. It was argued that middle-class families' primary discourse is similar to secondary discourse, which facilitates school success; there is a cultural and linguistic match. Black home discourse is like Black church discourse, and very different from school discourse. Moreover, Gee contended it is difficult to learn secondary discourse, if one has not been born into it. Yet, Delpit (1992) reminded readers that Black leaders have used the language of dominant discourse in their fight for liberation. She maintained that minorities can transcend circumstances into which they were born by learning discourses that allow access to prestigious and powerful societal institutions. Even if knowing dominant discourse is a ticket to success in dominant institutions, many researchers (Apple, 1996; Bourdieu, 1984; Corson, 1992; Cummins, 1989) argued that discourse should be expanded or decentered to include invisible and silenced voices. Documenting the richness of Black English, its life, voice, clarity, and connection to a Black value system, Jordan (1988) stressed that its use should be encouraged and preserved. Language is culture expressed in sound (Ovando, 1990).

Two of the most virulent controversies in education have surfaced in California over bilingual education and the Ebonics movement. Both have similar grounding: that education should acknowledge and incorporate children's home language and culture. Advocates for these movements are concerned with the continuation of diverse language and cultural styles and the possibility that integrating home language and culture into schooling will improve the educational outcomes of minority students. Most supporters would stress that standard English literacy is a primary goal, but the enhancement of other language skills and cultural styles is also beneficial. Both movements are entangled in general struggles about whether the United States is truly pluralistic or whether assimilation to a European-American culture is necessary for a cohesive national identity (see Harper, Braithwaite & LaGrange, 1998; Mitchell, Destino, Karam & Colon-Muniz; Taylor, 1998; Wright, 1993).

In response to the attack on bilingual education, Crawford (1999) contended that, as the numbers of Asian and Latin American immigrants increased, language politics have become a convenient surrogate for racial politics. There is a sense that bilingualism is divisive to national unity. Ovando and Collier (1998) argued that linguistic diversity does not threaten the dominant use of English in the United States. Regardless of difference of opinion about bilingual education, based on the equal protection clause of the constitution, the *Lau v. Nichols* (1974) Supreme Court decision established the legal precedent that equal opportunity does not translate into the same education for all. This litigation means that children with limited English proficiencies must be provided with additional services, such as a bilingual education, for equal opportunity to occur.

Although supported by law and litigation, Crawford (1999) observed that many of the problems of establishing bilingual programs stem from the fact that the Bilingual Education Act of 1968 was enacted with few precise guidelines, thus provided an ambiguous framework for language policy. He further contended that administrators dislike special programs because they require recruiting teachers with new skills, modifying schedules, and implementing curricular changes. Nevertheless, Ovando (1999) cited the cumulative body of knowledge from linguistics and cognitive psychology that native language support in high-quality classrooms produces good results. Hakuta and Snow (1986) believed that the rush to immerse very young children in English is inappropriate. They argued that language proficiency is complex, skills learned in one language transfer to another, reading is best taught in the native language, and children are enhanced cognitively by bilingualism. Lucas, Henze, and Donato (1990) delineated the key features of effective schooling for language minority students: (a) value is placed on diverse cultures so speaking a language other than English is treated as an advantage rather than a liability; (b) expectations of language minority students are high and teachers challenge students with complex questions and difficult work; (c) staff development is designed explicitly to help serve language minority students more effectively; and (d) parents are involved and empowered.

RECOMMENDATIONS FOR PRACTICE

Based on the aforementioned details, we suggest constructive ways to encourage the success and full participation of a broad range of diverse students in America's public schools. First, general and special educators must interrogate myths, assumptions, and stereotypes. They must also identify accurate causes of conditions for poor people and people of color. The legacy of blaming the victim allows a continuation of paternalism and an inability to bring existing resources to bear on problems (Kirst & McLaughlin, 1989; Wright, 1993). They must also assume responsibility for students' school success and dispel myths that attribute deficiencies to learners. The cultural deprivation hypothesis must finally be laid to rest.

To combat privilege and oppression, there must be an awareness of the ways they are manifested in schools and society. Lather's (1991) cry for openly ideological research is applicable to political analysis and action. Researchers claim objectivity and neutrality when they focus on technical aspects of education, but this maintains status quo power relations (Brantlinger, 1997). Lather noted that whether people are aware of it or not, professional work is grounded in values. Personal integrity and communicative clarity require an explicit rendering of values and goals. Keedy (1992) used the phrase "creative insubordination" for the tactics of principals who work against the grain of common-biased practice to enable the success of poor children and children of color. Yet, it is appalling that in a supposed democracy, people should feel the need to be covert in attacking disparities. Activists such as Myles Horton (1998) and the late Dr. Martin Luther King, Jr. who were not afraid to disturb powerful constituencies, should be models for others who pursue transformative agendas.

Second, general and special educators must acknowledge the strengths of human diversity and pluralism. Students of color will make up about 46% of the nation's population by 2020 (Banks, 1997). Greene (1993) stressed the need to heed multiple voices that have been silenced and of making them part of the ongoing conversation. Views of intelligence and learning must be broadened and other human characteristics rewarded (Mehan, Hubbard, & Villaneueva, 1994; Meier, 1993). A true democracy hinges on open expression of ideas and urges participation on the part of its constituencies and guards against silencing voices. The organization of school, which is typically authoritarian, hierarchical, and departmentalized, must be restructured so that it becomes a model of democracy and so students learn to be active agents in determining policy and day-to-day practices.

Third, general and special educators must emphasize common customs, needs, and goals and seek a comprehensive inclusion. Everyone must cherish his or her culture but not be closed to others. For instance, identity politics carried to the extreme have resulted in the tribal atrocities of the former Yugoslavia and Rwanda, and outrageous lynchings of many African Americans in many parts of the United States. Multicultural education that allows students to affirm their own culture's value while remaining members of a common community are most worthwhile. Transformative curriculum seeks commonality through a consensus of values and provides the skills and knowledge to take part in civic events of a democratic country (Banks, 1992). Greene (1993) liked Dewey's idea of school as a "great community" that reaches toward social connectedness.

Fourth, general and special educators must encourage the representation of heterogeneous constituencies. Teachers, who are largely middle-class and White, view curriculum from a Eurocentric position (Banks, 1997). Increasing representation of faculty, staff, and administrators can be accomplished through affirmative action, creative credentialing and responsive teacher education. Diverse student bodies can be brought together through community planning, neighborhood desegregation, detracking, and inclusion of children with disabilities in general education classes.

Fifth, general and special educators must reduce asymmetrical home/school power relations. They must redirect focus from "dysfunctional families" to dysfunctional schools (Comer, 1991) and communities. Schools must collaborate with community-based organizations to address student and family resources and needs (Herrington & Lazar, 1999; Jones, 1992).

Sixth, general and special educators must tie curriculum to the life experiences of children. Public school personnel should recognize and discuss students' out-of-school experiences even if they are problematic and depressing (Brantlinger, 1992). It is counterproductive to pretend that realities such as a weak economy, shortage of lucrative jobs, interpersonal cruelty, and pervasive bias do not affect students. Authentic relations require honest communication.

And seventh, general and special educators must engage students in real problem solving. Adults convey to students that they—middle-class, White people—have societal situations figured out and under control. In fact, humans face serious problems for which there are few ready solutions. Children must be inducted into society with a sense that they will be called upon to find solutions for environmental and social problems. The importance of individual initiative, social responsibility, and a community perspective must be acknowledged (Gutmann, 1996).

CONCLUSION

In this chapter, we have addressed a variety of prejudices and discriminatory practices that impede the school success of multicultural students, those with limited English proficiencies, and those whose families are impoverished. The continuing overrepresentation of students from these backgrounds in segregated, stigmatizing, and demeaning school and societal settings is a phenomenon that general and special education professionals and all citizens concerned about social justice and democratic practices must address. Instead of looking downward at the victims of oppression, it is imperative that we turn the gaze instead at professional practice and upward at the way power is distributed and maintained in the United States. to rectify past and current institutional inequities. We conclude this chapter by suggesting constructive ways to encourage the success and full participation of a broad range of diverse students in America's public schools.

REFERENCES

Adams, C.R., & Singh, K. (1998). Direct and indirect effects of school learning variables on the academic achievement of African American 10th graders. *Journal of Negro Education, 67*(1), 48–66.

Algozzine, B., Ysseldyke, J.E., & McGue, M. (1995). Differentiating low-achieving students: Thoughts on setting the record straight. *Learning Disabilities Research and Practice, 10* (3), 140–144.

Allen, J. (1999). *Actively seeking inclusion: Pupils with special needs in mainstream schools.* London, England: Falmer.

Allington, R.L., & McGill-Franzen, A. (1992). Unintended effects of educational reform in New York State. *Educational Policy, 6,* 396–413.

Apple, M.W. (1996). *Cultural politics and education.* New York: Teachers College Press.

Artiles, A.J., & Trent, S. (1994). Overrepresentation of minority students in special education: A continuing debate. *The Journal of Special Education, 27,* 410–437.

Asante, M.K. (1991). The Afrocentric idea in education. *Journal of Negro Education, 62,* 170–180.

Associated Press. (1999, May 15) Report documents gap in health-care for minorities. *The Herald-Times,* A3.

Ayers, W. (1990). Small Heroes: In and out of school with ten-year old city kids. *Cambridge Journal of Education, 20,* 205–212.

Banks, J.A. (1995). The historical reconstruction of knowledge about race: Implications for transformative teaching. *Educational Researcher, 24* (2), 15–25.

Banks, J.A. (1997). *Educating citizens in a multicultural society.* New York: Teachers College Press.

Barton, L. (1997). Inclusive education: Romantic, subversive or realistic? International *Journal of Inclusive Education, 1,* 231–242.

Bell, D.A. (1994). *Confronting authority: Reflections of an ardent protester.* Boston: Beacon Press.

Benson, P.L. (1991). *Private schools in the United States: A statistical profile, with comparisons to public schools.* Washington, DC: U.S. Department of Education.

Berliner, D.C., & Biddle, B.J. (1995). *The manufactured crisis: Myths, fraud, and the attack on America's public schools.* Reading, MA: Addison-Wesley.

Bingham, R.D., Haubrich, P.A., White, S.B., & Zipp, J.F. (1990). Dual standards among teachers: This school is good enough for other kids but not my child. *Urban Education, 25,* 274–288.

Bourdieu, P. (1984). *Distinction: A social critique of the judgment of taste.* Cambridge, MA: Harvard University Press.

Bourdieu, P., & Passeron, J.C. (1977). *Reproduction in education, society, and culture.* Beverly Hills, CA: Sage.

Bourgois, P. (1995). *In search of respect: Selling crack in El Barrio.* New York: Cambridge University Press.

Brandau, D.M., & Collins, J. (1994). Texts, social relations, and work-based skepticism about schooling: An ethnographic analysis. *Anthropology and Education Quarterly, 25* (2), 118–136.

Brantlinger, E.A. (1985a). Low-income parents' perceptions of favoritism in the schools. *Urban Education, 20,* 82–102.

Brantlinger, E.A. (1985b). Low-income parents' opinions about the social class composition of schools. *American Journal of Education, 93,* 389–408.

Brantlinger, E.A. (1985c). What low-income parents want from schools: A different view of aspirations. *Interchange, 16,* 14–28.

Brantlinger, E.A. (1987). Making decisions about special education placement: Do low-income families have the information they need? *Journal of Learning Disabilities, 20,* 95–101.

Brantlinger, E.A. (1991). Social class distinctions in adolescents' reports of problems and punishment in school. *Behavioral Disorders, 17,* 36–46.

Brantlinger, E.A. (1992). Unmentionable futures: Aspirations and expectations of low-income teenagers. *The School Counselor, 39,* 281–291.

Brantlinger, E.A. (1993). *The politics of social class in secondary school: Views of affluent and impoverished youth.* New York: Teachers College Press.

Brantlinger, E.A. (1994). High-income and low-income adolescents' views of special education. *Journal of Adolescent Research, 9,* 384–407.

Brantlinger, E.A. (1996). The influences of preservice teachers' beliefs on attitudes toward inclusion. *Teacher Education and Special Education, 19* (1), 17–33.

Brantlinger, E.A. (1997). Using ideology: Cases of nonrecognition of the politics of research and practice in special education. *Review of Educational Research, 67,* 425–459.

Brantlinger, E.A., & Guskin, S.L. (1987). Ethnocultural and social psychological effects on learning. In M.C. Wang, H.J. Walberg & M.C. Reynolds (Eds.), *The handbook of special education: Research and Practice.* Oxford, England: Pergamon.

Brantlinger, E.A., & Guskin, S.L. (1992, April). *Barriers to integrated schools and classrooms: Affluent parents' thinking about their own and other people's children.* Paper presented at the Annual American Association of Educational Research Meeting in San Francisco, CA.

Brantlinger, E.A., & Majd-Jabbari, M. (1998). The conflicted pedagogical and curricular perspectives of middle class mothers. *Journal of Curriculum Studies, 30* (4), 431–460.

Brantlinger, E.A., Majd-Jabbari, M., & Guskin, S.L. (1996). Self-interest and liberal educational discourse: How ideology works for middle class mothers. *American Educational Research Journal, 33,* 571–598.

Brown v. Board of Education, 347 U.S. 483, 493 (1954).

Brown, D.K. (1995). *Degrees of control: A sociology of educational expansion an occupational credentialism.* New York: Teachers College Press.

Britzman, D.P. (1997). The tangles of implication. *Qualitative Studies in Education, 10* (1), 31–37.

Burton, R.L. (1999). A study of disparities among school facilities in North Carolina: Effects of race and economic status. *Educational Policy, 13,* 280–295.

Carrier, J.G. (1986). *Learning disability: Social class and the construction of inequality in American education.* Westport, CT: Greenwood Press.

Carter, K. (1993). The place of story in the study of teaching and teacher education. *Educational Researcher, 22,* 5–12.

Christensen, C. (1996). Disabled, handicapped or disordered: 'What's in a name?' In C. Christensen & F. Rizvi (Eds.), *Disability and the dilemmas of education and justice* (pp. 63–78). Buckingham/Philadelphia, PA: Open University Press.

Cline, B.V., & Billingsley, B.S. (1991). Teachers' and supervisors' perceptions of secondary learning disabilities programs: A multi-state survey. *Learning Disabilities Research and Practice, 6,* 158–165.

Cochran-Smith, M. (1995). Uncertain allies: Understanding the boundaries of race and teaching. *Harvard Educational Review, 65,* 541–570.

Coles, G. (1987). *The learning mystique: A critical look at "learning disabilities."* New York: Pantheon Books.

Comer, J.P. (1991, April). *Education and the American future.* Presentation at the Indiana University School of Education Valuing Diversity Conference, Bloomington, IN.

Conforti, J.M. (1992). The legitimation of inequality in American Education. *The Urban Review, 24,* 227–238.

Conley, D. (1999). *Being black, living in the red: Race, wealth, and social policy in America.* Berkeley, CA: University of California Press.

Connell, R.W. (1993). *Schools and social justice.* Philadelphia, PA: Temple University Press.

Corbett, J. (1995). *Bad mouthing: The language of special needs.* London, England: Falmer.

Corson, D.J. (1992). Social justice and minority language policy. *Educational Theory, 42,* 181–200.

Cose, E. (1993). *The rage of a privileged class: Why are middle-class blacks angry? Why should America care?* New York: Harper Perennial Press.

Crawford, J. (1999). *Bilingual education: History, politics, theory and practice,* (4th ed.). Los Angeles, CA: Bilingual Education Services.

Cummins, J. (1989). *Empowering minority students.* Sacramento, CA: California Association of Bilingual Education.

Danforth, S. (1996). Autobiography as critical pedagogy: Locating myself in class-based oppression. *Teaching Education, 9* (1), 3–14.

deBettencourt, L.U., Zigmond, N., & Thornton, H. (1989). Follow-up of postsecondary-age rural learning disabled graduates and dropouts. *Exceptional Children, 56,* 40–49.

Delamont, S. (1989). *Knowledgeable women: Structuralism and the reproduction of elites.* London, England: Routledge.

Deloria, V. (1984). Land and natural resources. In L.W. Dunbar (Ed.). *What has happened to Blacks, Hispanics, American Indians, and other minorities in the eighties* (pp. 152–190). New York: Pantheon.

Delpit, L.D. (1992). Education in a multicultural society: Our future's greatest challenge. *Journal of Negro Education, 61,* 237–249.

Delpit, L.D. (1995). *Other people's children: Cultural conflict in the classroom.* New York: The New Press.

Deyhle, D., & Swisher, K. (1997). Research in American Indian and Alaska Native education: From assimilation to self-determination. In M.W. Apple (Ed.), *Review of Research in Education* (Vol. 22) (pp. 113–194). Washington DC: American Educational Research Association.

Dyson, M.E. (1993). *Reflecting black: African-American cultural criticism.* Minneapolis, MN: University of Minnesota Press.

Edelman, M. (1987). *Families in peril: An agenda for social change.* Cambridge, MA: Harvard University Press.

Eder, D. (1995). *School talk: Gender and adolescent culture.* New Brunswick, NJ: Rutgers University Press.

Elbaum, B.E., Schumm, J.S., & Vaughn, S. (1997). Urban middle-elementary students' perceptions of grouping formats for reading instruction. *The Elementary School Journal, 97,* 475–500.

Elias, M.J. (1989). Schools as a source of stress to children: An analysis of causal and ameliorative influences. *Journal of School Psychology, 27,* 393–407.

Emihovich, C. (1999). Compromised positions: The ethics and politics of designing research in the postmodern age. *Educational Policy, 13* (1), 37–46.

Finders, M.J. (1997). *Just girls: Hidden literacies and life in junior high school.* New York: Teachers College Press.

Fine, M. (1991). *Framing dropouts: Notes on the politics of an urban public high school.* Albany: State University of New York Press.

Fivush, R. (1991). The social construction of personal narratives. *Merrill-Palmer Quarterly, 37,* 59–82.

Ford, D.Y. (1992). The American achievement ideology and achievement differentials among preadolescent gifted and nongifted African American males and females. *Journal of Negro Education, 61,* 45–60.

Fordham, S., & Ogbu, J. (1986). Black students' school success: Coping with the "burden of 'acting' white" *The Urban Review, 18,* 176–206.

Foster, M. (1997). *Black teachers on teaching.* New York: The New Press.

Foster, M. (1999). Race, class, and gender in education research: Surveying the political terrain. *Educational Policy, 13* (1), 77–85.

Franklin, B.M. (1994). *From "backwardness" to "at-risk": Childhood learning difficulties and the contradictions of school reform.* Albany, NY: State University of New York Press.

Freire, P. (1973). *Education for critical consciousness.* New York: Seabury Press.

Fuchs, D., & Fuchs, L.S. (1994). Inclusive schools movement and the radicalization of special education reform. *Exceptional Children, 60,* 294–309.

Fuchs, E. (1973). How teachers learn to help children fail. In N. Keddie (Ed.), *The myth of cultural deprivation* (pp. 75–85). Harmondsworth, Middlesex, England: Penguin Education.

Futrell, M.H. (1999). Recruiting minority teachers. *Educational Leadership, 56* (8), 30–33.

Gamoran, A., & Berends, M. (1987). The effects of stratification in secondary schools: Synthesis of survey and ethnographic research. *Review of Educational Research, 57,* 415–435.

Garibaldi, A.M. (1992). Educating and motivating African American males to succeed. *Journal of Negro Education, 61,* 4–11.

Gartner, A., & Lipsky, D. (1987). Beyond special education: Toward a quality system for all students. *Harvard Educational Review, 57,* 367–395.

Gee, J.P. (1989). Literacy, discourse, and linguistics: Introduction. *Journal of Education, 171,* 5–17.

Gilbert, P. (1992). The story so far: Gender, literacy and social regulation. *Gender and Education, 4,* 185–200.

Gilborn, D. (1995). *Racism and anti-racism in real schools.* Buckingham/Philadelphia, PA: Open University Press.

Gilborn, D., & Gipps, C. (1996). *Recent research in the achievements of ethnic minority pupils.* London, England: Office for Standards in Education.

Giroux, H.A. (1989). *Schooling and the struggle for public life: Critical pedagogy in the modern age.* Minneapolis, MN: University of Minnesota Press.

Gollnick, D.M., & Chinn, P.C. (1990). *Multicultural education in a pluralistic society.* New York: Merrill.

Good, T.L., Slavings, R.L., Harel, K.H., & Emerson, H. (1987). Student passivity: A study of question asking in K-12 classrooms. *Sociology of Education, 60,* 181–199.

Goodlad, J. (1983). *A place called school.* New York: McGraw-Hill.

Gopaul-McNicol, S., Reid, G., & Wisdom, C. (1998). The psychoeducational assessment of Ebonics speakers: Issues and challenges. *Journal of Negro Education, 67* (1), 16–24.

Grant, C.A. (1990). Desegregation, racial attitudes and intergroup contact: A discussion of change. *Phi Delta Kappan, 72,* 25–32.

Greene, M. (1993). The passions of pluralism: Multiculturalism and the expanding community. *Educational Researcher, 22,* 13–18.

Gresham, F.M., & Forness, S.R. (1986). Full inclusion: An empirical perspective. *Behavioral Disorders, 21* (2), 145–159.

Gudmundsdottir, S. (1990). Curriculum stories. In C. Day, P. Denicolo, & M. Pope (Eds.), *Insights into teachers' thinking and practice* (pp. 107–118). London, England: Falmer Press.

Gutmann, A. (1996, October 11). Middle democracy. *The Chronicle of Higher Education*, p. b9.

Hakuta, K., & Snow, C. (1986). The role of research in policy decisions about bilingual education. In *Compendium of papers on the topic of bilingual education* (pp. 28–40) (Serial No. 99-R). Washington, DC: U.S. House of Representatives Committee on Education and Labor.

Haladyna, T.H., Nolan, S.B., & Haas, N.S. (1991). Raising standardized achievement test scores and the origins of test score pollution. *Educational Researcher, 20,* 2–7.

Harper, F.D., Braithwaite, K., & LaGrange, R.D. (1998). Ebonics and academic achievement: The role of the counselor. *Journal of Negro Education, 67* (1), 25–43.

Harris, M.D. (1992). Africentrism and curriculum: Concepts, issues, and prospects. *Journal of Negro Education, 61,* 300–316.

Harris, V.J. (1992). African-American conceptions of literacy: A historical perspective. *Theory Into Practice, 31,* 276–286.

Harry, B. (1992). *Cultural diversity, families, and the special education system: Communication and empowerment.* New York: Teachers College Press.

Harry, B. (1994). *The disproportionate representation of minority students in special education: Theories and recommendations.* Alexandria, VA: National Association of State Directors of Special Education.

Henry, A. (1995). Growing up black, female, and working class: A teacher's narrative. *Anthropology and Education Quarterly, 26,* 279–305.

Herrington, C.D., & Lazar, I. (1999). Evaluating integrated children's services: The politics of research on collaborative education and social service research. *Educational Policy, 13* (1), 47–58.

Hilliard, A.G., III. (1992a). The pitfalls and promises of special education practice. *Exceptional Children, 59,* 168–172.

Hilliard, A.G., III. (1992b). Behavioral style, culture, and teaching and learning. *Journal of Negro Education, 61,* 370–371.

Hooks, B. (1994). *Outlaw culture: Resisting representations.* New York: Routledge.

Horton, M. (with J. Kohl & H. Kohl) (1998). *The long haul: An autobiography.* New York: Teachers College Press.

Howe, K.R. (1996). Educational ethics, social justice and children with disabilities. *Disability and the dilemmas of education and justice.* Buckingham/ Philadelphia, PA: Open University Press.

Jencks, C. (1972). *Inequality: A reassessment of the effect of family and schooling in America.* New York: Harper & Row.

Jones, R. (1972). Labels and stigma in special education. *Exceptional Children, 38,* 553–564.

Jordan, J. (1988). Nobody mean more to me than you and the future life of Willie Jordan. *Harvard Educational Review, 58,* 363–374.

Kantor, H., & Lowe, R. (1995). Class, race, and the emergence of federal education policy: From the New Deal to the Great Society. *Educational Researcher, 24* (3), 4–11, 21.

Kauffman, J.M., & Hallahan, D.P. (1995). *The illusion of full inclusion: A comprehensive critique of a current special education bandwagon.* Austin, TX: Pro-Ed.

Keedy, J.L. (1992). Creative insubordination: Autonomy for school improvement by successful high school principals. *The High School Journal, 76,* 17–23.

King, S.H. (1993). The limited presence of African American teachers. *Review of Educational Research, 63,* 115–149.

Kirst, M.W., & McLaughlin, M. (1990). Rethinking children's policy: Implications for educational administration. *Policy Bulletin, 10,* 1–8.

Kornblum, W. (1984). Lumping the poor: What is the underclass? *Dissent, 31,* 295–302.

Kotlowitz, A. (1991). *There are no children here: The story of two boys growing up in the other America.* New York: Doubleday.

Kotlowitz, A. (1998). *The other side of the river: A story of two towns, a death, and America's dilemma.* New York: Doubleday.

Kozol, J. (1991). *Savage inequalities: Children in America's schools.* New York: Harper Perennial.

Kunjufu, J. (1986). *The conspiracy to destroy black boys* (Vol. 2). Chicago, IL: Afro-American publishing.

Labov, W. (1973). The logic of nonstandard English. In N. Keddie (Ed.), *The myth of cultural deprivation* (pp. 21–66). Harmondsworth, Middlesex, England: Penguin Education.

Ladson-Billings, G. (1992). Culturally relevant teaching: The key to making multicultural education work. In C.A. Grant (Ed.), *Research and* multicultural education: From the margins to the mainstream (pp. 106–121). Bristol, PA: Falmer.

Ladwig, J.G., & Gore, J.M. (1994). Extending power and specifying method within the discourse of activist research. In A. Gitlin (Ed.), *Power and method: Political activism and educational research* (pp. 227–238). New York: Routledge.

Lareau, A. (1989). *Home advantage: Social class and parental intervention in elementary education.* London, England: Falmer.

Latham, A.S., Gitomer, D., & Ziomek, R. (1999). What the tests tell us about new teachers. *Educational Leadership, 56* (8), 23–26.

Lather, P. (1986). Issues of validity in openly ideological research: Between a rock and a soft place. *Interchange, 17,* 63–84.

Lau v. Nichols, 414 U.S. 563, 566 (1973).

Lawrence-Lightfoot, S. (1994). *I've known rivers: Lives of loss and liberation.* New York: Penguin.

Lempers, J.D., & Clark-Lempers, D. (1990). Family economic stress, maternal and paternal support and adolescent distress. *Journal of Adolescence, 13,* 217–229.

Lipsky, D.K. & Gartner, A. (1996). Equity requires inclusion: The future for all students with disabilities. In C. Christensen & F. Rizvi, (Eds.), *Disability and the dilemmas of education and justice* (pp. 145–155). Buckingham/Philadelphia, PA: Open University Press.

Little, J.W. (1996). The emotional contours and career trajectories of (disappointed) reform enthusiasts. *Cambridge Journal of Education, 26,* 345–359.

Lomotey, K., & Brookins, C.C. (1988). Independent Black institutions: A cultural perspective. In D.T. Slaughter & D.J. Johnson (Eds.), *Visible now: Blacks in private schools* (pp. 163–183). New York: Greenwood Press.

Lucas, T., Henze, R., & Donato, R. (1990). Promoting the success of Latino language-minority students: An exploratory study of six high schools. *Harvard Educational Review, 60,* 315–340.

MacLeod, J. (1987). *Ain't no making it: Leveled aspirations in a low-income neighborhood.* Boulder, CO: Westview Press.

MacMillan, D.L., Semmel, M.I., & Gerber, M.M. (1994). The social context of Dunn: Then and now. *The Journal of Special Education, 27,* 466–480.

McCarthy, C. (1993). Beyond the poverty of theory in race relations: Nonsynchrony and social difference in education. In L. Weis & M. Fine (Eds.), *Beyond silenced voices: Class, race, and gender in United States schools* (pp. 325–346). Albany, NY: State University of New York Press.

McCaslin, M., & Good, T.L. (1996). *Listening in classrooms.* New York: Harper Collins.

McDermott, R., & Varenne, H. (1995). Culture as disability. *Anthropology & Education Quarterly, 26,* 324–348.

McGill-Franzen, S. & Allington, R.L. (1993). Flunk 'em or get them classified: The contamination of primary grade accountability data. *Educational Researcher, 22* (1), 19–22.

Mehan, H. (1992). Understanding inequality in schools: The contribution of interpretive studies. *Sociology of Education, 45,* 6–12.

Mehan, H., Hubbard, L., & Viallaneueva, I. (1994). Forming academic identities: Accommodation without assimilation among involuntary minorities. *Anthropology and Education Quarterly, 25,* 91–117.

Meier, D. (1993). Transforming schools into powerful communities. In R. Takanishi (Ed.), *Adolescence in the 1990s: Risk and opportunity* (pp. 199–202). New York: Teachers College Press.

Merton, D.E. (1994). The cultural context of aggression: The transition to junior high school. *Anthropology & Education Quarterly, 25* (1), 29–43.

Mitchell, D.E., Destino, T., Karam, R.T., & Colon-Muniz, A. (1998). The politics of bilingual education. *Educational Policy, 13* (1), 86–103.

Moran, M.R. (1984). Excellence at the cost of instructional equity? The potential impact of recommended reforms upon low achieving students. *Focus on Exceptional Children, 16,* 1–12.

Morrison, T. (1993). *Playing in the dark: Whiteness and literary imagination.* New York: Vintage.

Nader, L. (1996). Anthropological inquiry into boundaries, power, and knowledges. In L. Nader (Ed.), *Naked science: anthropological inquiry into boundaries, power, and knowledge* (pp. 1–25). New York: Routledge.

Nelson, J.I. (1995). *Post-industrial capitalism: Exploring economic inequality in America.* Thousand Oaks, CA: Sage.

Nicholls, J.R. (1989). *The competitive ethos and democratic education.* Cambridge, MA: Harvard University Press.

Oakes, J., & Guiton, G. (1995). Matchmaking: The dynamics of high school tracking decisions. *American Educational Research Journal, 32,* 3–33.

Oakes, J., & Lipton, M. (1992). Detracking schools: Early lessons from the field. *Phi Delta Kappan, 73,* 448–454.

Obiakor, F.E. (1992). Embracing new special education strategies for African-American students. *Exceptional Children, 59,* 104–106.

Obiakor, F.E. (1994). *The eight-step multicultural approach: Learning and teaching with a smile.* Dubuque, IA: Kendall/Hunt.

Ogbu, J.U. (1995). Understanding cultural diversity and learning. In J.A. Banks & C.A. Banks (Eds.), *Handbook of research on multicultural education* (pp. 582–593). New York: Macmillan.

Okundaye, J. (1999). Drug trafficking and addiction among low-income urban youths: An ecological perspective. *Journal of Children & Poverty, 5* (1), 21–42.

Olson, C.P. (1983). Inequality remade: The theory of correspondence and the context of French immersion in Northern Ontario. *Journal of Education, 165,* 75–98.

Onwuegbuzie, A.J. (1998). The underachievement of African American teachers in research methodology courses: Implications for the supply of African American school administrators. *Journal of Negro Education, 67* (1), 67.

Orfield, G. (1992). Money, equity, and college access. *Harvard Educational Review, 62,* 337–372.

Osborne, A.B. (1996). Practice into theory into practice: Culturally relevant pedagogy for students we have marginalized and normalized. *Anthropology and Education Quarterly, 27,* 285–314.

Oswald, D.P., Coutinho, M.J., Best, A.M., & Singh, N.N. (1999). Ethnic representation in special education: The influence of school-related economic and demographic variables. *The Journal of Special Education, 32,* 194–206.

Ovando, C.J. (1990). Politics and pedagogy: The case of bilingual education. *Harvard Educational Review, 60,* 341–356.

Ovando, C. (1999, April). *Bilingual education in the united states: Historical development and current is-*

sues. Presented at the American Education Research Association, Montreal, Canada.

Ovando, C.J., & Collier, V.P. (1998). *Bilingual and ESL classrooms; Teaching in multicultural contexts* (2nd ed.). Boston: McGraw Hill.

Page, R.N. (1991). *Lower-track classrooms: A curricular and cultural perspective.* New York: Teachers College Press.

Paley, V.G. (1990). *The boy who would be a helicopter: The uses of storytelling in the classroom.* Cambridge, MA: Harvard University Press.

Paley, V.G. (1999, May/June). K is for kindness. *Teacher Magazine,* 51–57.

Palonsky, S.B. (1987). Political socialization in elementary schools. *The Elementary School Journal, 87,* 493–505.

Parker, I., Gottlieb, J., Gottlieb, B.W., Davis, S., & Kunzweiller, C. (1989). Teacher behavior toward low achievers average achievers and mainstreamed minority group learning disabled students. *Learning Disabilities Research, 4,* 101–106.

Patton, J.M. (1998). The disproportionate representation of African Americans in Special Education: Looking behind the curtain for understanding and solutions. *The Journal of Special Education, 32* (1), 25–31.

Pelham, B.W., & Swann, W.B., Jr. (1989). From self-conceptions to self-worth: On the sources and structure of global self-esteem. *Journal of Personality and Social Psychology, 57,* 672–680.

Pinar, W.F., & Bowers, C.A. (1992). Politics of curriculum: Origins, Controversies, and significance of critical perspectives. In G. Grant (Ed.), *Review of research in education* (pp. 163–190). Washington, DC: American Educational Research Association.

Polakow, V. (1992). *Lives on the edge: Single mothers and their children in the other America.* Chicago, IL: University of Chicago Press.

Ray, C.A., & Mickelson, R.A. (1990). Corporate leaders, resistant youth, and school reform in Sunbelt City: The political economy of education. *Social Problems, 37,* 178–190.

Reyhner, J. (1992). American Indian Cultures and School Success. *Journal of American Indian Education, 32,* 30–39.

Richardson, J.G. (1994). Common, delinquent, and special: On the formalization of common schooling in the American states. *American Educational Research Journal, 31,* 695–723.

Robertson, P., Kushner, M.L., Starks, J., & Drescher, C. (1994). An update of participation rates of culturally and linguistically diverse students in special education: The need for a research and policy agenda. *The Bilingual Special Education Perspective, 41* (1), 1–9.

Robinson, J. (1994). White women researching/representing "Others": From anti-apartheid to postcolonialism. In A. Blunt & G. Rose (Eds.), *Writing women and space: colonial and postcolonial geographies* (pp. 197–226). New York: Guilford.

Roth, J. (1992). Of what help is he? A review of Foucault and education. *American Educational Research Journal, 29,* 683–694.

Ryan, W. (1971). *Blaming the victim.* New York: Vintage.

Sabornie, E.J., Marshall, K.J., & Ellis, E.S. (1990). Restructuring of mainstream sociometry with learning disabled and nonhandicapped students. *Exceptional Children, 56,* 314–323.

Sapon-Shevin, M. (1993). Gifted education and the protection of privilege: Breaking the silence, opening the discourse. In L. Weis & M. Fine (Eds.), *Beyond silenced voices: Class, race, and gender in United States schools* (pp. 25–44). Albany, NY: State University of New York Press.

Scheurich, J.J. (1993). Toward a white discourse on white racism. *Educational Researcher, 22* (8), 5–10.

Scheurich, J.J., & Young, M.D. (1997). Coloring epistemologies: Are our epistemologies racially biased? *Educational Researcher, 26* (4), 4–16.

Schoem, D. (1991). *Inside separate worlds: Life stories of young Blacks, Jews, and Latinos.* Ann Arbor, MI: University of Michigan Press.

Schumm, J.S., & Vaughn, S. (1995). Getting ready for inclusion: Is the stage set? *Learning Disabilities Research and Practice, 10,* 169–179.

Seginer, R. (1983). Parents' educational expectations and children's academic achievement: A literature review. *The Merrill-Palmer Quarterly, 29,* 1–23.

Sennett, R., & Cobb, J. (1972). *The hidden injuries of class.* New York: Vintage.

Sexton, P.C. (1961). *Education and income: Inequalities of opportunity in our public schools.* New York: Viking.

Shade, B.J. (1982). Afro-American cognitive style: A variable in school success. *Review of Educational Research, 52,* 243–248.

Shimahara, N.K. (1983). Polarized socialization in an urban high school. *Anthropology and Education, 14,* 109–130.

Shrum, W., Cheek, N.H., Jr., & Hunter, S.M. (1988). Friendship in school: Gender and racial homophily. *Sociology of Education, 61,* 227–239.

Shujaa, M.J. (1992). Afrocentric transformation and parental choice in African American independent schools. *Journal of Negro Education, 61,* 148–159.

Sieber, R.T. (1982). The politics of middle-class success in an inner-city public school. *Journal of Education, 164,* 30–47.

Skrtic, T.M. (1991). *Behind special education: A critical analysis of professional culture and school organization.* Denver, CO: Love.

Slee, R. (1996). Disability, class and poverty: School structures and policing identities. In C. Christensen & F. Rizvi (Eds.), *Disability and the dilemmas of social justice* (pp. 96–118). Buckingham/Philadelphia, PA: Open University Press.

Sleeter, C.E. (1986). Learning disabilities: The social construction of a special education category. *Exceptional Children, 53,* 46–54.

Sleeter, C.E. (1995). An analysis of the critiques of multicultural education. In J.A. Banks & C.A. McGee Banks (Eds.), *Handbook of research on multicultural education* (pp. 81–94). New York: Macmillan.

Smith, E.R., & Zarate, M.A. (1990). Exemplar and prototype use in social categorization. *Social Cognition, 8,* 243–262.

Spindler, G., & Spindler, L. (Eds.), (1994). *Pathways to cultural awareness: Cultural therapy with teachers and students.* Thousand Oaks, CA: Corwin.

Spivak, G.C. (1994). Bonding in difference. In A. Arteaga (Ed.), *An other tongue: Nation and ethnicity in the linguistic borderlands.* Durham, NC: Duke University Press.

Stainback, S., & Stainback, W. (1996). *Inclusion: A guide for educators.* Baltimore, MD: Paul H. Brookes.

Strahan, D. (1988). Life on the margins: How academically at-risk early adolescents view themselves and school. *Journal of Early Adolescence, 8,* 373–390.

Strahan, D. (1989). Disconnected and disruptive students: Who they are, why they behave as they do, and what we can do about it. *Middle School Journal*, 1–5.

Taylor, O.L. (1998). Ebonics and educational policy: Some issues for the next millennium. *Journal of Negro Education, 67* (1), 35–42.

Taylor, S.J. (1995). On rhetoric: A response to Fuchs and Fuchs. *Exceptional Children, 61,* 301–302.

Thorne, B. (1986). Girls and boys together; but mostly apart: Gender arrangements in elementary schools. In W.S. Hartup & Z. Rubin (Eds.), *Relationships and development*. Hillsdale, NJ: Lawrence Erlbaum.

Tinney, J.S. (1983). Interconnections. *Interracial Books for Children Bulletin, 14,* 4–6

Tobias, S. (1989). Tracked to fail. *Psychology Today, 23,* 54–60.

Tomasi, S.F., & Weinberg, S.L. (1999). Classifying children as LD: An analysis of current practice in an urban setting. *Learning Disabilities Quarterly, 22,* 31–42.

Tomlinson, S. (1982). *A sociology of special education*. Boston: Routledge & Kegan Paul.

Tomlinson, S. (1996). Conflicts and dilemmas for professionals in special education. *Disability and the dilemmas of education and justice* (pp. 175–186). Buckingham/Philadelphia, PA: Open University Press.

Tomlinson, S. (1999, June 15). *Race and special education*. Paper presented at the International Research Colloquium on Inclusive Education, University of Rochester, New York.

Troyna, B., & Vincent, C. (1996). "The ideology of expertism": The framing of special education and racial equality policies in the local state. In C. Christensen & F. Rizvi (Eds.), *Disability an the dilemmas of education and justice* (pp. 131–144). Buckingham/Philadelphia, PA: Open University Press.

U.S. Department of Education (1983). *A nation at risk*. Washington, DC: Author.

U.S. Department of Education (1991). *America 2000*. Washington, DC: Author.

Useem, E.L. (1992). Middle schools and math groups: Parents' involvement in children's placement. *Sociology of Education, 65,* 263–279.

Varenne, H., & McDermott, R. (1998). *Successful failure: The school America builds*. Boulder, CO: Westview.

Warner, G., Thrapp, R., & Walsh, S. (1973). Attitudes of children toward their special placement. *Exceptional Children, 39,* 37–38.

Weinstein, R.S., Madison, S.M., & Kuklinski, M.R. (1995). Raising expectations in schooling: Obstacles and opportunities for change. *American Educational Research Journal, 32,* 121–159.

Weis, L. (1990). *Working class without work: High school students in deindustrializing America*. New York: Routledge, Chapman & Hall.

Weis, L., & Fine, M. (1996). Narrating the 1980s and 1990s: Voices of poor and working-class white and African American men. *Anthropology & Education Quarterly, 27,* 493–516.

Weiss, C.H. (1995). The four "I's" of school reform: How interests, ideology, information, and institution affect teachers and principals. *Harvard Educational Review, 65,* 571–592.

Welch, O.M., & Hodges, C.R. (1998). *Standing outside on the inside: black adolescents and the construction of academic identity*. Albany, NY: State University of New York Press.

Wells, A.S., Hirshberg, D., Lipton, M., & Oakes, J. (1995). Bounding the case within its context: A constructivist approach to studying detracking reform. *Educational Researcher, 24,* 18–24.

Wells, A.S., & Serna, I. (1996). The politics of culture: Understanding local political resistance to detracking in racially mixed schools. *Harvard Educational Review, 66,* 93–118.

West, C. (1994). The new cultural politics of difference. In S. Seidman (Ed.), *The postmodern turn: New perspectives on social theory* (pp. 65–81). Cambridge, MA: Cambridge University Press.

Wildman, S.M. (1996). *Privilege revealed: How invisible preference undermines America*. New York: New York University Press.

Wilson, W.J. (1987). *The truly disadvantaged: The inner city, the underclass, and public policy*. Chicago, IL: University of Chicago Press.

Wolman, C., Bruininks, R., & Thurlow, M.L. (1989). Dropouts and dropout programs: Implications for special education. *Remedial Education and Special Education, 10,* 6–20.

Wright, E.O. (1994). *Interrogating inequality: Essays on class analysis, socialism, and Marxism*. London, England: Verso.

Wright, S.E. (1993). Blaming the victim, blaming society or blaming the discipline: Fixing responsibility for poverty and homelessness. *The Sociological Quarterly, 34,* 1–16.

Zane, N. (1994). When "discipline problems" recede: democracy and intimacy in urban charters. In M. Fine (Ed.), *Chartering urban school reform: Reflections on public high schools in the midst of change* (pp. 122–135). New York: Teachers College Press.

Zarate, M.A., & Smith, E.R. (1990). Person categorization and stereotyping. *Social Cognition, 8,* 161–185.

Zigmond, N., & Baker, J. (1990). Mainstream experiences for learning disabled students (Project MELD): Preliminary report. *Exceptional Children, 57,* 176–185.

Zisman, P., & Wilson, V. (1992). Table hopping in the cafeteria: An exploration of "racial" integration in early adolescent social groups. *Anthropology and Education, 23,* 199–220.

Chapter 3

TRENDS IN DISPROPORTIONATE REPRESENTATION: IMPLICATIONS FOR MULTICULTURAL EDUCATION

Donald P. Oswald and Martha J. Coutinho

The disproportionate representation of multicultural children in special education must be regarded as one of the most significant and longstanding issues educators have faced in the past 30 years (Dunn, 1968; Heller, Holtzman, & Messick, 1982; Kauffman, Hallahan, & Ford, 1998). Many estimates of the extent of disproportionality exist, and these vary considerably by disability condition and by ethnic category (Chinn & Hughes, 1987; Harry, 1992a, 1994; Reschly & Ward, 1991; Serwatka, Deering, & Grant, 1995; Trent & Artiles, 1995). There have also been many different interpretations of the significance of disproportionate representation. These reflect different perspectives about why disproportionate ethnic representation occurs, whether it is a problem, and, if so, how to respond.

School policies regarding multicultural education are influenced by beliefs about the extent and significance of disproportionate representation. This chapter presents information about the extent of disproportionate representation for Black, Hispanic, and American Indian students focusing on the disability conditions of mild mental retardation (MMR), serious emotional disturbance (SED), and learning disability (LD). In addition, the chapter documents how disproportionate representation has changed over time for the nation and three selected states. Trends are discussed from the perspective of legal and policy events that may be associated with changes in ethnic representation over time. The issues of what is disproportionate representation in special education and how to respond appropriately are discussed from the perspective of multicultural education policy. Emphasis is on the public goal to improve the educational experiences and outcomes of multicultural children.

LEGISLATION AND LITIGATION RELATED TO OVERREPRESENTATION

The Individuals with Disabilities Education Act (IDEA) of 1997 (P.L. 105-17; originally, the Education for All Handicapped Children Act, P.L. 94-142) sets forth provisions intended to ensure full, non-discriminatory assessment, identification, and placement of children with disabilities. The protection in evaluation procedures and the definitions of disability conditions in IDEA make it clear that those children whose educational difficulties are due to environmental disadvantage or differences in ethnic, linguistic or racial background are not to be identified as disabled. At the same time, P.L. 94-142 mandated the provision of a free, appropriate public education for all students with disabilities. Thus, P.L. 94-142 embodied public commitment to both entitlement (appropriate educational services for all children with disabilities) and equity (freedom from inappropriate identification).

During the 1980s, P.L. 94-142 was fully implemented across the nation. In the 1990 amendments to this law, IDEA (P.L. 101-476), was instituted. With IDEA, the U.S. Congress restated the national concerns about the (a) educational experience of multicultural children in special education; (b) apparent overrepresentation of multicultural learners in special education, particularly of Black children; and (c) inadequate quality of services provided to non-native-English speaking children. Congress amended IDEA in 1997 (P.L. 105-17) requiring states to collect ethnicity data for all students in special education with respect to identification, placement, and exit status and to implement procedures to reduce any apparent disproportionality. Over the past three decades, the United States Office for Civil Rights (OCR) has implemented its mandate to provide monitoring and oversight related to overrepresentation of multicultural children at the school district level.

Educational policymakers have been sometimes influenced by court cases regarding the overrepresentation of multicultural learners and assessment of non-native-English speaking students. The Equal Protection Clause of the 14th Amendment to the United States Constitution, Title VI of the Civil Rights Act of 1964, and Section 504 of the Rehabilitation Act of 1973 all prohibit discrimination against racial and ethnic minorities. Thus, the overrepresentation of ethnic and linguistic multicultural children in special education was cited frequently as evidence of discrimination and resulted in a number of court cases. Notable among these were the *Diana* (1970) and *Guadalupe* (1972) cases, in which guidelines were issued for assessing non-native-English speaking students. With respect to the overrepresentation of multicultural learners, the case of *Larry P. v. Riles* (1972, 1974, 1979) was one of the longest and most contentious court cases in educational law history. California schools were ordered to eliminate overrepresentation of Black students in programs for EMR children and, ultimately, were barred from using traditional IQ tests for any purpose with Black students. However, other cases involving disproportionate representation produced different judgments. In *Parents in Action on Special Education v. Joseph P. Hannon* (1980), *Marshall v. Georgia* (1984), and *S-1 v. Turlington* (1986) overrepresentation, per se, was not found to be sufficient evidence of discrimination. Emphasis was placed on achievement rather than ability and the relative benefits of special education. Nonetheless, the central complaint in these cases was of discrimination, and they achieved national prominence as they were litigated. These cases called public attention once more to the implications of U.S. anti-discrimination statutes (e.g., the 14th Amendment to the U.S. Constitution, Title VI of the Civil Rights Act of 1964, and Section 504 of the Rehabilitation Act of 1973) for the practice of special education.

The last 20 years have seen policy studies and public debate about the causes, nature, and significance of disproportionate representation. In 1982, the National Academy of Sciences issued a major report about the nature of overrepresentation of multicultural learners in special education which included a number of far-reaching recommendations (Heller et al., 1982). Analyses of the implications of court cases have appeared frequently in the professional literature, as have regional and state analyses of ethnic proportionality in special education. In 1997, Congress once again called on the National Academy of Sciences to conduct a comprehensive national study on the issue. Although most public policy has regarded the over or underrepresentation of ethnic minorities in special education as a problem, there is considerable lack of agreement about how to define disproportionate representation and what extent of disproportionality constitutes a significant problem (Harry, 1994). Percentage figures in a variety of forms have been used to describe disproportionality for a given system or as the basis of regional and national estimates (Coulter, 1996; Harry 1992a, 1994; Markowitz, 1996). Other researchers have used estimates based on a definition of disproportionate representation as an odds ratio (i.e., the extent to which membership in a given ethnic group affects the probability of being identified with a particular disability condition) (Oswald, Coutinho, & Best, 1999). The lack of a standard method for characterizing dispro-

portionality has plagued the field from the beginning and has yielded substantial confusion. Rarely can two or more studies be compared with integrity because of the lack of a common metric.

In addition to the issue of varying ways of characterizing disproportionate representation, a decision about the threshold at which disproportionate representation signifies a problem is not trivial. Some studies have relied on a simple rule of thumb regarding difference of percentages across ethnic groups to establish such a threshold (e.g., Coulter, 1996). Others have employed chi-square analyses of representation figures to define significant disproportionality (Horner, Maddux, & Green, 1986). In any case, both the definition and the threshold issues have contributed to widely varying conclusions and recommendations across studies. Based on the many legislative, regulatory, and judicial initiatives that address the issue of disproportionality, multicultural education approaches have also been implemented in efforts to eliminate bias during the referral and assessment process and to assure culturally responsive and competent instruction. Taken together, these policy and professional development activities could be expected to produce a declining rate of minority identification in special education, particularly for the category of students identified as MMR, and for students who are Black and Hispanic. Very little change would be expected for multicultural groups who were underidentified. However, there have been few investigations to determine whether disproportionate representation has actually diminished at some point after, and in response to, policy initiatives or litigation. Even more rare have been efforts to track changes over extended periods of time to provide a longitudinal perspective on the question of progress in addressing disproportionate representation.

TRENDS IN ETHNIC REPRESENTATION AND RELATED POLICY EVENTS

Description of Data Analyses

Using data collected by the U.S. Office for Civil Rights, trends in disproportionate representation were examined for the nation as a whole and for three states. Descriptive analyses were conducted on extant data on ethnicity and special education identification of students with LD, MMR, and SED between the years 1980 and 1994, the most recent data available from OCR to date. California, Pennsylvania, and New Mexico were selected for detailed study because of their extensive and readily available history of public policy and litigation related to special education. The sample for the analyses consisted of the districts participating in the 1980 through 1994 administrations of the U.S. Department of Education Office of Civil Rights (OCR) Elementary and Secondary Civil Rights Compliance Report survey. The data were collected on a biannual basis, generating eight data points over this 14-year period. The sample size ranged from a low of 3,128 districts in 1982 to a high of 5,058 districts in 1980. Districts were selected using a stratified random sampling methodology and were weighted to account for the sampling procedure and for non-respondent districts. Data from each district were summed, using the as-signed weights, to yield projections to the state and national levels.

Race/ethnicity data in the OCR survey are reported in five non-overlapping categories: American Indian, Asian/Pacific Islander, Black, Hispanic, and White. Considerable controversy has surrounded the use of these categories, and the U.S. Census Bureau has more recently adopted a different system for describing race and ethnicity (Pallas, Natriello, & McDill, 1989). Nonetheless, these category names are retained in this chapter as they appeared in the survey in the interest of accurately reflecting the data as they were gathered. As educators, we recognize problems associated with this system, namely, among others, that the category names may be offensive to some readers, that the term "Hispanic" is not a designation of a race, and that the group "Asian/Pacific Islander" is a heterogeneous group comprised of vastly different cultures. We do not seek to defend this flawed system of categorizing people, but we maintain that the introduction of alternative category names would be misleading and that a correction of the other weaknesses of the categories is impossible in an existing data set.

Definition of Disproportionate Representation

The issue of disproportionate representation has been described in a variety of ways over the past 30 years. In this chapter, the degree of disproportionate representation is defined as the extent to which membership in a given ethnic group affects the probability of being placed in a specific special education disability category. The degree of disproportionate representation is calculated as an odds ratio using the following formula:

$$\text{Odds Ratio} = \frac{\dfrac{\text{\# of students of X ethnicity in Y "handicapping" condition}}{\text{\# of students of X ethnicity in the student population}}}{\dfrac{\text{\# of white students in Y "handicapping" condition}}{\text{\# of white students in the student population}}}$$

All odds ratios reported here compare identification rates for a particular ethnic group with that obtained for students who are White. Other odds ratios are also possible (e.g., comparing each ethnic group with the sum of all other ethnic groups). However, this study calculated odds ratios as *comparisons to the identification rate of students who are White*, in order to provide a consistent benchmark, and because the common practice in policy and litigation has been to use comparisons to White identification rates. Using the above formula, an odds ratio of one may be interpreted as an absence of disproportionate representation for the target ethnic group; that is, target ethnicity students and White students are equally likely to be identified with a given disability condition. If the odds ratio is two, target students are twice as likely to be identified, while an odds ratio of .5 indicates that the target students are one-half as likely to be identified.

In the following section, data are first presented regarding changes in disproportionate representation over time for the nation as a whole. Odds ratio are described for each of three relatively high incidence disability conditions, MMR, LD, and SED. The White student odds ratio is excluded because it is, by definition, equal to one. Trends in ethnic representation for each disability condition are discussed from the point of view of policy and legal events and trends in overall identification rates for each disability condition. A similar strategy for characterizing changes in three exemplar states follows the presentation of national trends.

REPRESENTATION TRENDS FOR THE NATION AS A WHOLE

Ethnic Disproportionality Among Students Identified as Learning Disabled

As shown below in Table 3.1, there is no disproportionate representation among Black and Hispanic students with LD (odds ratio = 1 in 1994). While there are some minimal variations between 1980–1994, the odds ratios over the time period were essentially equal to one, indicating that Black and Hispanic students were identified as LD at about the same rate as White students, for the nation as a whole. On the other hand, American Indian students were consistently about 1.2 to 1.3 times as likely to be identified as learning disabled throughout the entire time period (odds ratio = 1.2 in 1994). The finding for American Indian students is of particular significance because, between 1980 and 1994, rates of identification for all groups as LD increased at a relatively even pace.

The LD analyses indicate that, despite all of the public attention to disproportionate representation and despite increasing ethnic diversity, there was little change in proportionality for minority ethnic groups between 1980–1994. The proportional representation of Black and Hispanic students and the overidentification of American Indian students as LD remained relatively stable. While public attention was focused largely on other ethnic groups (i.e., plaintiffs in the most prominent court cases were Black or Hispanic students), the overidentification of American Indian students persisted throughout the entire period. These findings reinforce the importance of dissemination of accurate estimates of proportionality, by ethnicity and disability condition, to scholars and policymakers who are designing and implementing multicultural education policies as a part of school reforms.

Ethnic Disproportionality Among Students Identified as
Seriously Emotionally Disturbed

Data analyses indicated that between 1980–1994, for the nation as a whole, Black students were disproportionately overidentified as SED, compared to White students (see Table 3.1). The data, however, revealed a modest declining trend in the extent of disproportionate representation. In 1980, Black students were about 1.7 times as likely as White students to be identified as SED, while in 1994 the odds ratio was about 1.5. Over the 14-year period, the low point of disproportionate representation for Black students occurred in 1990 at an odds ratio of about 1.3 and the high point came in 1986 at just over 1.8. The data for 1988–1994 raise a question about whether declining disproportionate representation has "bottomed out" and may be entering a stable phase or may even begin increasing again. Data analyses also indicated a trend toward increasing overrepresentation of American Indian students as SED, particularly since 1984. As shown above in Table 3.1, the extent of disproportionate representation for American Indian students in 1994 was about 1.2. On the other hand, in 1994 Hispanic students were substantially underrepresented as SED as compared to White students (odds ratio = 0.6). Hispanic students were identified at nearly the same rate as White students at the beginning of the period, but have shown a trend of decreasing likelihood of identification over time, compared to

White students. Although SED rates of identification increased for all ethnic groups between 1980–1994, since 1988, rates for Black and American Indian students increased at a higher rate than the rate for White students, resulting in increasing disproportionality.

From a public policy perspective, the substantial and persistent overidentification of Black students as SED between 1980–1994 is significant. The initiatives related to Black overrepresentation in special education do not appear to have impacted SED identification rates. It is, however, difficult to interpret the significance of Black overidentification as SED when the White identification rate is substantially below national estimates of prevalence (1–3 percent) (Institute of Medicine, 1989), and the Black rate falls only within the lower range (about 1 percent) of that estimate. Similarly, although American Indian students were overrepresented as SED in 1990 and 1994, the American Indian identification rate for SED is only about .8 percent. In addition, Hispanic students were underidentified as compared to White students throughout the time period with identification rates of only around .4 percent. To assure appropriate educational experiences and equity for all students, multicultural education approaches must adopt policies that consider proportionality and also assure all children who are disabled are identified.

Ethnic Disproportionality Among Students Identified as
Mild Mentally Retarded

As shown in Table 3.1, Black students have been consistently overrepresented as MMR (odds ratio = 2.2 in 1994). However, the analyses showed declining disproportionate representation for Black students

over the 14-year period. Odds ratios for Black students exceeded 3 up until 1986, dropped significantly to between 2.5 and 3.0 between 1986 and 1990, and then appeared to have leveled off at about 2.2 for the most

Table 3.1
1994 ODDS RATIOS FOR BLACK, HISPANIC, AND
AMERICAN INDIAN STUDENTS

	LD	SED	MMR
U.S.			
Black	1.0	1.5	2.2
Hispanic	1.0	0.6	0.5
American Indian	1.2	1.2	1.2
California			
Black	1.3	2.2	1.1
Hispanic	0.8	0.3	0.9
American Indian	1.0	1.1	1.8
Pennsylvania			
Black	1.0	1.1	0.6
Hispanic	1.2	0.8	1.3
American Indian	1.0	1.5	0.6
New Mexico			
Black	1.5	1.8	1.6
Hispanic	0.9	0.8	1.4
American Indian	0.9	1.1	0.9

recent OCR data. American Indian students were also over-represented as MMR, but the extent of disproportionality was smaller than for Black students and gradually declined over time to approximately 1.2 in 1994. For most of the time period under investigation, Hispanic students were underidentified as MMR. As shown in Table 3.1, in 1994, Hispanic students were only about one-half as likely as White students to be identified as MMR (odds ratio = .5). Hispanic MMR odds ratios showed a declining trend over the last six data points. Consistent with expectations related to the policy and legal events between 1980–1994, the data show declining overrepresentation of Black students as MMR. However, the odds of being identified as MMR in 1994 for a Black student were still about 2.3 times that for a White student. Perhaps because of the legal spotlight on programs for students with MMR, the overrepresentation of American Indian students also decreased to about 1.2 by 1994. The decline in disproportionality for Black and American Indian students is all

the more significant given that it occurred when ethnic diversity in general was increasing and MMR identification rates for Black, American Indian, and Hispanic students were decreasing. It is not clear whether the trend in identification rates for Black, American Indian or other ethnic/racial groups will change in the future as a result of the most recent change in the AAMR definition in 1992 which promulgated a more liberal upper level IQ cut-off of 75 (Gresham, MacMillan, & Siperstein, 1995). The trend toward underrepresentation of Hispanic students as MMR is also noteworthy and bears closer study. The extreme caution and extensive guidelines implemented to assure non-discriminatory evaluation and identification of Hispanic students may not assure full identification of all Hispanic students who are, in fact, MMR. Finally, overall rates for MMR identification, like those for SED, are substantially lower than the estimated rates of prevalence of 3% (Halfon & Newacheck, 1999). To design effective multicultural education policies and programs, general and special educators must evaluate the significance of the disproportionate overrepresentation of Black and American Indian students, the disproportionate underrepresentation of Hispanic, and the possible underidentification of White students.

TRENDS IN DISPROPORTIONATE REPRESENTATION FOR SELECTED STATES

While disproportionate representation of multicultural learners in special education has been acknowledged as a national issue, much of the public policy response to disproportionate representation over the past 30 years has been at the level of the state education agency. Thus, to understand how the nations' school systems have evolved with regard to the problem, one must ask whether this state-level attention has yielded observable results at the level of individual states. Three states (Pennsylvania, California, and New Mexico) were selected on the basis of a recognized history with regard to the issue of disproportionate representation and on availability of information regarding significant policy initiatives and litigation. Pennsylvania and New Mexico also served as case study sites for a policy study conducted by the National Association of State Directors of Special Education (Markowitz, 1996). For each state, we examined trends over time by ethnic groups for students identified as LD, SED and MMR and related these to significant policy events during that time period.

Disproportionate Representation for California

California has been at the forefront of action regarding disproportionate representation for at least the past three decades. Much of this action was related to *Larry P.* and the ensuing regulatory and legislative responses that focused on disproportionately high identification of Black students as MMR. In spite of this history, until in 1994, Black students continued to be disproportionately overrepresented as MMR (see Table 3.1). Between 1980 and 1990, Black students were about 2.5 times as likely as White students to be identified as MMR. In 1992, however, the odds ratio fell to approximately 1.6 and approached 1 in 1994, indicating that, in the most recent survey data available, disproportionate representation of California's Black students in the MMR category has disappeared. American Indian students, however, show a dissimilar trend. Disproportionate overrepresentation of American Indian students as MMR has tended to increase. The odds ratio in 1994 was about 1.8. The American Indian odds ratios have been rather unstable over the time period, probably due to the relatively low number of American Indian students, but a line-of-best-fit over the entire time period under investigation would suggest that disproportionate representation of American Indian students as MMR has generally increased since 1980. Proportionality with respect to Hispanic students and MMR has also shown some change during the 14-year time period. In 1994, the Hispanic identification rates as MMR was approximately the same as that of White students (odds ratio = .9). However, between 1980–1992, Hispanic students tended to be overrepresented as MMR (odds ratios ranging between 1.2 to 1.6). MMR data for California must be understood in a context of identification rates that have declined substantially over the study period. California MMR rates across the board are at a startlingly low level. Less than .25% of White, Black, Hispanic, and Asian Pacific/Islander students were identified as MMR in 1994 and less than .4% of American Indian students. MMR identification rates for all ethnic groups except American Indian have declined and the pattern is particularly striking for Black students.

It is important to acknowledge that California is a state with a significant and somewhat unique history in special education public policy. In the late 1970s and early 1980s, California educators began full implementation of P. L. 94-142 (later amended as P. L. 105-17, IDEA) at the same time that they responded to major California-based court decisions affecting the assessment of students who were Limited English Proficient (Diana, 1970) and those who were Black (Larry P., 1972, 1974, 1979). As noted earlier, in *Larry P.* the judge ordered the elimination of disproportionate representation of Blacks as mentally retarded and prohibited the use of IQ testing for any purpose with Black students. During this time, California also fully implemented the California Master Plan for Special Education. Provisions of this plan included conversion to a less categorical system of identification that allowed only four subcategories. Given these policy events, both the decline in MMR identification rates overall, as well as the observed elimination of disproportionate representation among Black students as MMR between 1980–1994, are not unexpected. Most importantly, Judge Peckham's order to eliminate disproportionality, the more stringent definition of MMR (using the IQ cutoff at 70 rather than 86), the elimination of IQ tests without clear alternatives for assessing potential, and the elimination of MMR as a separate category all would be likely to have

the effect of reducing the identification of all students, and Black students in particular, as MMR. In fact, Forness (1985) observed that children served as MMR in the mid-1980s demonstrated quite significant disabilities and were not very much different from those formerly identified as trainable mentally retarded (TMR). Macmillan and Balow (1991) and Macmillan, Hendrick, and Watkins (1988) were concerned whether an appropriate education would be provided to the formerly EMR students who were now expected to succeed, without special supports, in the general education classroom and curriculum.

The general decline in disproportionate representation of Hispanic students as MMR over the time period appears consistent with policy events. However, the recent trend toward more overrepresentation of American Indian students as MMR reflects an increase in American Indian identification rates, and it is difficult to interpret the increasing disproportionality within the context of the described policy events. The elimination of disproportionate representation of Black students in California as MMR differs from the national trend (declining, but still substantial, overrepresentation), perhaps indicating the very powerful impact of the Larry P. decision in that state. The pattern of MMR identification of American Indian students in California was similar to that of the nation; that is, American Indian students were overrepresented as MMR in both nation and California, with the exception of two points of underrepresentation in 1984 and 1988 in California. The trend in California toward proportionate representation of Hispanic students as MMR also differs from the national pattern of underrepresentation. In California, Hispanic students were overrepresented until the most recent data collection in 1994, whereas for the nation as a whole, they were generally underrepresented as MMR between 1980–1994.

The California picture with regard to LD, however, is very different (see Table 3.1). Black students were disproportionately over-represented as LD between 1980–1994; the odds ratio for Blacks increased to approximately 1.4 in 1986 and remained relatively steady thereafter. American Indian students' identification as LD has been somewhat unstable, but in 1994 American Indian students were about as likely as White students to be so identified. Hispanic students have been slightly underrepresented as LD throughout the time period. In 1994, the odds ratio for identification as LD for Hispanic students was about .8. The extent of disproportionality decreased between 1980 and 1986 (odds ratios approached 1). With respect to overall LD identification in California, rates for each ethnic group increased over the time period. LD identification rates have gone up most dramatically for Black students from about 3.6 percent in 1980 to nearly 8 percent in 1994. This marked increase is primarily responsible for the increasing disproportionate representation of Black students identified as LD.

Within the context of the public policy events in California, it is not surprising that the disproportionate representation of Blacks as LD *increased,* and that LD identification rates also *increased* for all racial/ethnic groups throughout the 14-year period, although the national odds ratio for Black students remained steady. The increase in identification rates occurred despite California policy initiatives to adopt a *severe* discrepancy concept in the definition of LD and the more stringent guidelines for making the discrepancy determination (Forness, 1985). Looking at the trends over time in identification and disproportionality for both students with MMR and LD who are Black, a strong case could be made that overrepresentation as MMR was, to some extent, replaced by disproportionate identification as LD. Some of the "formerly EMR" students may have been reclassified as

LD. This possibility reinforces the need to examine the factors that contribute to disproportionality before responding, in order to avoid endorsing multicultural education policies that ameliorate a symptom of the problem (e.g., disproportionate representation of Black students as MR) but do not address the larger issue of improving students' educational experiences. The significance of the slight, but consistent trend of underrepresentation of Hispanic students merits further investigation. As a result of Diana (1970) and the assessment provisions of IDEA, current efforts to fully implement non-discriminatory assessment measures among students who are Limited English Proficient (LEP) may need to be improved to ensure that all children who are LD in California are appropriately identified.

California odds ratio data for SED identification are evident in Table 3.1. Black students have been identified at a disproportionately higher rate throughout the 1980–1994 time period. This was particularly striking in 1980, when they were over three times as likely as White students to be identified as SED. This odds ratio declined sharply to around 1.8 in 1982 and then further declined steadily to about 1.4 in 1992. Black disproportionality increased abruptly again, however, in 1994, at which point they were about 2.2 times as likely to be identified as SED as their White counterparts. American Indian students were identified at about the same rate as White students in 1994, but were both underrepresented between 1980 and 1990 and overrepresented in 1992 at earlier points in time. In 1994, and consistently throughout the 14-year time period, Hispanic students as compared to White students have been underrepresented as SED in California. SED identification rates in general in California dropped sharply for all ethnic groups from 1980 to 1982, but have been steadily increasing again for Black, White, and American Indian students. Notwithstanding, no ethnic group has more than about .4 percent of its students identified as SED and Hispanic and Asian/Pacific Islander students are identified at a rate of less than .1 percent.

No doubt, policy events in California may have accounted for some of the trends in disproportionality for students identified as SED. The Larry P. decision would be expected to foster caution in all special education eligibility decisions for Black students and particularly for identification as SED, a category often regarded as especially stigmatizing. With respect to the extremely low rates of identification for all groups, Forness (1985) had already reported a precipitous decline between 1977 and 1982 in SED enrollment in California. He noted that changes in disability categories had the result of spreading students with emotional or behavior categories across more than one category. The process could account for the declining identification rates for the federally recognized category of SED. No policy event could be identified, however, that accounts for the sharp increase in overrepresentation of Black students in 1994, or the change from under to overrepresentation of American Indian students as SED in 1992 and, to a lesser extent, in 1994. Overall, the trends in SED identification for California are similar to those observed nationally (i.e., the disproportionate representation of Black students decreased slightly over the 14 year period, underrepresentation of Hispanic students was a consistent pattern, and there was overrepresentation of American Indian students as SED in 1992 and 1994).

Trends in Representation for Pennsylvania

While the state of Pennsylvania has a considerable history of litigation regarding individuals with disabilities (e.g., *PARC v. Commonwealth of Pennsylvania*, 1972), attention to the disproportionate representation of ethnic minorities in special education is relatively recent. In the early 1980s, the Office of School Equity in the Pennsylvania State Department of Education began to focus attention on disproportionate representation with particular emphasis on students who are LEP. Educators were concerned that some LEP students were inappropriately placed in special education programs when they actually needed English as Second Language services.

In 1990, statewide data on the racial/ethnic distribution of students in special education became available and the State Department of Education was mandated to notify all school districts that displayed significant disproportionate representation. Also in 1990, Pennsylvania began training Instructional Support Teams (ISTs) to assist teachers in the general education classroom in developing appropriate instructions and accommodations for students with disabilities in order to foster their success in the general education environment. As of the 1994–95 school year, all Pennsylvania school districts had implemented the IST program in at least one school. More recently, Pennsylvania is the site for a Comprehensive System for Personnel Development (CSPD) grant aimed at providing technical assistance and multicultural training to school personnel.

The early 1990s saw the filing of a desegregation case that involved students in special education. In Pennsylvania, *Human Relations Commission v. School District of Philadelphia* (1994), the court ordered the school district to "determine whether its special education programs are in compliance with all applicable laws and whether the criteria for placement and the racial enrollment in these programs discriminate against Black and Hispanic students" (p. 6). In the 1995 appeal of this case, the court found that the school district was in compliance with the order in that the evaluation of over and underrepresentation of Black and Hispanic students was to be completed by January 1996. This case, however, together with federal monitoring of disproportionate representation in Pennsylvania, has led to notification of procedural violations. In 1993, the Pennsylvania legislature (Act 16, Section 112) required the State Department of Education to review 1991–92 student data and to identify school districts that displayed gender or ethnic disproportionality. According to the State Department of Education, disproportionality occurs when a group's representation in special education services exceeds five percent (5%) of that group's representation in the total student population. Currently, all school districts that demonstrate disproportionate representation of racial/ethnic groups in special education are required to submit a Corrective Action Plan (CAP). The CAP must address strategies for improving the general education environment, appropriate prereferral, evaluation, placement, and reevaluation procedures, as well as personnel information.

Data analyses were conducted to relate ethnic proportionality in special education to policy initiatives. With respect to students with LD, the extent of disproportionality changed markedly for non-White students between 1980 and 1994. As shown in Table 3.1, in 1994, Black students were about 1.2 times as likely to be identified as LD. They were initially underidentified (1980 odds ratio = .9), then disproportionately over identified for the rest of the time period. Black students were nearly 1.7 times as likely as White students to be identified as LD in 1982, but this disproportionality had virtually disappeared by 1994. Disproportionality for Hispanic students has similarly declined since 1982, to just over 1.2 in 1994. American Indian students have been both over and under identified as LD between 1980 and 1994, the most recent figures showing virtual parity with White students. Ethnic specific changes

in LD identification rates in Pennsylvania reveal how this substantial reduction in disproportionality was achieved. Identification rates increased markedly between 1980 and 1986 for Black, Hispanic, and American Indian students. However, these groups tended to level off, while rates for White students continued to climb, producing a near convergence in 1994 for all ethnic groups.

In 1994, American Indian students were overrepresented as SED, whereas Black and Hispanic students were at parity and slightly underrepresented, respectively. Black and Hispanic students were generally overidentified until 1992, and the disproportionality reached a high of 3.8 for Black students and 2.2 for Hispanic students. Hispanic student rates declined to the point of underrepresentation in 1992 and 1994 with odds ratios of about .75. American Indian students have been under and overidentified during the period with the 1994 data showing them about 1.5 times as likely as White students to be identified as SED. Apparently, from 1980–1994, overall SED identification rates in Pennsylvania showed a steady increase for White students. Black SED identification rates were also increasing through 1990 but showed a sharp drop in 1992 to a rate approximately equal to that of White students. American Indian student rates were somewhat erratic but showed a sharp increase in 1992. American Indian students were identified as SED at a rate higher than any other racial/ethnic group in 1992 and 1994.

The extent of disproportionality in the identification of students with MMR was relatively erratic in Pennsylvania between 1980 and 1994. As shown in Table 3.1, Hispanic students were overrepresented as MMR in 1994. This occurred throughout the time period, although the extent varied markedly. Disproportionality exceeded 3.5 in 1988 but fell to below 1.5 in 1994. Disproportionate identification of American Indian students resulted in a zigzag pattern of substantial over and underrepresentation over the 14-year time period. In 1994, American Indian students were underrepresented as MMR (odds ratio = 0.7). In 1984 and 1988, American Indian students were substantially overrepresented (odds ratios of approximately 2.7), while in 1986, the most substantial underrepresentation was reported (odds ratio of approximately .35). In 1994, Black students were underrepresented as MMR as compared to White students, but the pattern over the preceding 14-year period was one of declining overrepresentation. With respect to MR identification rates in Pennsylvania, rates for the ethnic groups had fallen to the .7 percent to 1.5 percent range by 1994. However, rates were unstable over time, particularly for Hispanic and American Indian students.

Overall, the pattern of identification rates across disabilities in Pennsylvania suggests that in the early 1980s the attention to disproportionate representation of Black students in EMR classes may have resulted in shifting some of those students into the LD category. The result was a striking growth among minority students in LD and a marked increase in disproportionate representation among LD students in 1982. The substantial decline in MMR identification rates for minority students in 1994 did not yield a corresponding increase in either LD or SED categories. For Black and American Indian students, the state appears to have "overshot the mark," decreasing MMR identification rates for these two ethnic groups to slightly over half of the White rate. With the exception of American Indian students in SED, Pennsylvania appears to have nearly achieved (or in some cases, exceeded) its apparent objective of reducing minority EMR, SED, and LD identification rates to levels comparable to those seen in White students.

Trends in Representation for New Mexico

In New Mexico, explicit state-level attention to the problem of disproportionate representation in special education is somewhat more recent. During the early 1980s, some concern over disproportionality was generated following a university study that documented disproportionate representation in some disability classifications. In 1988, the New Mexico Department of Special Education began collecting race and gender data for all students receiving special education services. By 1990, efforts were made to determine the extent of disproportionality in New Mexico school districts. Districts with significant disproportionate representation were notified and asked to explain the data.

Subsequently, in the early 1990s, statewide task forces were set up to examine congruence between federal and state regulations regarding disproportionality and to identify areas in which technical assistance was needed. Since 1995, New Mexico has published a series of documents aimed at providing guidance and assistance for appropriate special education services, with some emphasis on bilingual students.

Data analyses of disproportionate representation of ethnic minority students in special education in New Mexico showed substantial change over the period of the study. With respect to students with LD, most striking were changes over time for Hispanic and American Indian students. Odds ratios for these two groups showed substantial overrepresentation in the early 1980s, followed by a steady decline to a rate equal to that for White students in 1994. On the other hand, throughout the time period Black students were over represented as LD (odds ratio = 1.5 in 1994). The trend for Black students with LD is not clear; odds ratios have been somewhat erratic over the study period, ranging from about 1.3 to around 2.3, but failing to display an unambiguous direction. The backdrop of LD identification rates in New Mexico is a significant increase over time for all ethnic groups. LD identification rates were quite low, but by 1994 about 7 percent of White, Hispanic and Black students and approximately 10 percent of Black students were identified as LD.

Hispanic, American Indian, and Black students were markedly overrepresented among students with MMR in 1980, with odds ratios of 2.5, 3, and over 4, respectively. However, as shown in Table 3.1, by 1994, these odds ratios were reduced to about 1.4, .9, and 1.6, respectively. In New Mexico, therefore, there was a striking decline in disproportionate representation over the study period. The larger trends, however, should not disguise the fact that Black and Hispanic students were still significantly overrepresented among students with MMR at the end of the study period, and the data collected since 1990 suggest that the decline in odds ratios may have leveled off. It is important to note that MMR identification rates in New Mexico showed a dramatic drop over the study period. The identification rate for White students in 1980 was about .5 percent; the next 14 years saw a steady decline to around .2 percent in 1994. Identification rates for Black, Hispanic, and American Indian students, however, started between 1.3 and 2.2 percent and dropped sharply to around .2 to .3 percent by 1994. Thus, the decline in odds ratios for these groups is explained by a dramatic reduction in the rate at which they were identified as MMR. This trend has reached the point that MMR identification in New Mexico is a relatively rare event.

Disproportionate representation in the identification of students with SED in New Mexico is quite different from other disabilities. Black students have been consistently overrepresented among students with SED and there was no indication of decline be-

tween 1980 and 1994. Odds ratios for Black students were 1.75 in 1994 and in 1990 exceeded 2. Hispanic students, on the other hand, were consistently underrepresented (odds ratio = .7 in 1994). American Indian students were even more strikingly underrepresented until 1994 when, as shown in Table 3.1, the odds ratio reached 1.2. In the two-year period from 1992 to 1994, the odds ratio for American Indian students identified as SED had jumped from about .5 to about 1.2. Additional data will apparently be required to determine if this represents an anomaly or the beginning of a trend toward increasing overrepresentation. With respect to overall rates, SED identification rates in New Mexico for all ethnic groups were very low at the beginning of the study period, ranging between about 0 percent and about .3 percent in 1980. SED identification rates for all ethnic groups showed a sudden increase in 1982 and a correction downward in 1984. Rates for Black, White, and Hispanic students then settled into a pattern of increasing identification through 1994. SED identification among American Indian students remained stable at about .5 percent from 1984 through 1992 then nearly tripled in 1994 to about 1.4, accounting for the marked discontinuity in the odds ratios.

New Mexico is somewhat unique in terms of its late entry into compliance with the Education of All Handicapped Children's Act (P. L. 94-142), and this historical fact may account for the instability of identification rates in the early portion of the study period. The striking decline in MMR identification in 1982, however, also corresponds to substantial increases in LD and SED identification, suggesting that some reclassification may have occurred. In any case, New Mexico has shown significant decreases in disproportionate representation for some ethnic groups and some disability categories. The disproportionate identification of Black students as SED, however, has been relatively persistent, even in the face of other changes.

IMPLICATIONS OF DISPROPORTIONALITY TRENDS ON MULTICULTURAL EDUCATION SPECIAL EDUCATION

Nationally, the proportional representation of Hispanic and Black students as LD in the most recent data available is an important finding. On the other hand, the overrepresentation of American Indian students as LD, MR and SED and of Black students as MR and SED persists. In addition, current trends in individual States are often different from the national picture. For example, Black students are overrepresented as LD in California and New Mexico; Hispanic students are overrepresented as MR in Pennsylvania and New Mexico, and American Indian students are underrepresented as MR in Pennsylvania and as MR and LD in New Mexico. These descriptive analyses of trends in the identification of minority students as disabled offer many implications and suggestions for future research, policies, and practices related to the education of minority students. These implications are discussed in the following sub-headings.

The Importance of Disaggregated, Technically Adequate Estimates of Proportionality

Trends differ by region, disability, ethnicity, and gender. The difference between the national picture and state profiles observed in these analyses is consistent with a recent study of urban areas with large Black and Hispanic populations (Robertson, Kushner, Starks, & Drescher, 1994). As Robertson et al. concluded, "It would appear that the geographic location in which a student resides may be a significant determinant of whether the student is identified as disabled," (p. 19). Patterns of representation also vary by ethnicity. The national underrepresentation of Hispanics as SED and MR contrasts sharply with the overrepresentation of Blacks and American Indians as SED and MR. In addition, recently completed analyses provide strong evidence that, within an ethnic group, rates of identification differ sometimes dramatically by gender (Oswald et al., 1999). When disability categories or ethnic categories are combined, relationships between the disproportionate representation and policy or legal events are much less clear or no-existent.

Future research and effective responses to disproportionate representation must be based on analyses at the level of the prospective intervention (e.g., the school or community level) and must be designed to separate proportionality estimates by ethnicity, disability, and gender. In addition, estimates must be technically defensible and accurate. Researchers and policymakers are warned against intemperate use of percentages, which can be confusing to interpret correctly. The definition and calculation of disproportionate representation may be obtained most unambiguously with an odds ratio (Coutinho & Oswald, 1998; Oswald, Coutinho, Best, & Singh, 1999).

The Need for Research that Explores Social and Demographic Factors at the Local Level

The contribution of social and demographic variables to the prediction of disproportionality suggests that these factors may be influencing children's susceptibility to educational disability (Oswald, Coutinho, & Best, 1999; Oswald et al., 1999). The uneven distribution of social and economic disadvantage across ethnic groups may serve as an important limiting factor in decreasing disproportionality (Halfon & Newacheck, 1999). Individual localities should examine the relationship between social and demographic factors and rates of identification (Coutinho & Oswald, in press).

The Need for Research Investigating the Referral, Assessment, and Eligibility Process

Are the same decisions made for African American students as compared to White students, for example, during the referral, evaluation, and eligibility process in special education? Evidence suggests that in some cases individual student behaviors and symptoms differ, but there is also significant concern and evidence that decisions about referral and identification are sometimes made differently for multicultural learners as compared to White students. For example, Obiakor (1999) examined teacher expectations as a critical factor during the referral and evaluation process:

> In today's general and special education programs, students who behave, look, speak, and learn differently are at risk of misidentification, misassessment, misclassification, misplacement, and misinstruction due to traditional school expectations. . . . When teachers fail to respond to intraindividual and interin-dividual differences, the process of identification, assessment, classification, placement, and instruction becomes loaded with inappropriate assumptions, prejudicial expectations, negative stereotypes, and illusory conclusions. Put another way, the traditional ways teachers gather and disseminate information about minority learners for decision making have problems addressing the inevitable concepts of intraindividual and interindividual differences. (p. 41)

A few years ago, Harry (1994) examined the historical context and problems associated with the special education referral and assessment process for Black students. She pointed out several ways in which teacher bias, cultural differences between the students and the teacher, issues of IQ test validity for minority students, or a failure to implement alternative and best practices during the prereferral process may inappropriately influence identification rates for minority students. Teachers' failure to assume a posture of cultural reciprocity in their interactions with students may result in disproportionate representation (Harry, Rueda, & Kalyanpur, 1999). Apparently, the current knowledge base offers a starting point for understanding how individual student differences, system characteristics, and the current system of referral and assessment may influence identification rates for minority students (Bahr, Fuchs, Stecker, & Fuchs, 1991; Gottlieb & Alter, 1994; Harry, 1992b; MacMillan, Gresham, Lopez, & Bocian, 1996). Carefully designed research is needed to understand how specific system characteristics (e.g., the procedures and bases for decisions during referral and evaluation for special education identification), and individual student characteristics produce patterns of over and underrepresentation at the local level (Coutinho & Oswald, 1998; Coutinho & Oswald, in press). Obiakor (1999) offered several recommendations for specific research that is needed. These include a focus on helping practitioners incorporate the principles of individualized instructional programming, using valid and reliable research instruments, and above all, "address[ing] issues that advance the society rather than the politics of those issues" (p.

48). Many scholars have also offered similar recommendations for changes in policies and practices (Bondy & Ross, 1998; Harry, 1994; Utley & Mortweet, 1999). These must also be considered and, where necessary, empirically investigated, as a part of efforts to incorporate effective multicultural education into general education school reforms.

The Need to Evaluate the Impact of State and Local Efforts to Respond to Disproportionate Representation

Many States have implemented long-term corrective plans or other interventions. Although the U.S. Office for Civil Rights monitors and provides enforcement of U.S. statutes barring discrimination against multicultural individuals in education, most agree this has neither proved an effective response to disproportionate representation nor has it contributed in a convincing way to efforts to improve the quality and outcomes of education for multicultural learners. In addition, numerous national and state policy initiatives have been undertaken or have been recommended (Harry & Anderson, 1994; Markowitz, 1996). Utley and Mortweet (1999) offered recommendations related to assessment, effective instruction, teaching models, and policy at the local, state and national levels. Coutinho and Oswald (in press) argued for sustained and articulate public advocacy aimed at both improving minority student outcomes and eliminating discriminatory practices. Rarely, however, have the results of recommended approaches and recommendations been evaluated empirically. Clear effects of policy, legislation or litigation are difficult to establish and must be studied systematically.

Responses to disproportionate representation require careful scrutiny, including examination of unintended consequences, before judgments can be made regarding the results. For example, "label switching" is recognized as a serious threat, but careful investigation of this phenomenon and its consequences for multicultural children is needed. The analyses reported in this chapter for California directly illustrate the need for evaluations of system responses to disproportionality. As reported above, between 1980 and 1994, in response to Larry P. decision and other factors, California virtually eliminated the overrepresentation of Black students in the MR category. On the other hand, by the end of the same time period, Black students were overrepresented in the LD category.

The Need to Empirically Investigate the Conceptual Frameworks and Efficacy of Cultural Competence Training

Recently, Voltz, Dooley, and Jeffries (1999) provided a comprehensive assessment of progress and current status related to special education teacher preparation for diversity. Issues related to professional standards, organizational structures, and the current knowledge base in special education were presented. Mapping where "we are" is a significant and necessary step, and recommendations to better prepare general and special educators are important. In addition, however, empirical research related to the impact of cultural competence training of educators on the educational experience and outcomes of multicultural learners is needed. As conceptually based, empirical understandings of, and responses to, disproportionality emerge, teacher preparation models must also be examined empirically with respect to impact and effectiveness.

The Need to Examine System Factors that Deny Children Appropriate Educational Experiences

Singular focus on achieving proportionality and making comparisons to White rates of identification can detract from needed attention and research related to the gap between estimated rates of prevalence and actual rates of identification (Coutinho & Oswald, in press; Oswald & Coutinho, 1995). Social and political pressures may have produced a system in which children in need of special education are denied access because of the stigma surrounding categories, the cost to local systems, or other related factors. Disproportionality figures are uninterpretable if some ethnic/gender groups are markedly underidentified. Further, many have expressed concern about the poor quality of instruction received by minority students prior to special education referral (Harry & Anderson, 1994) or that offered when students are returned to the regular education programs that have already failed them (MacMillan et al., 1988).

Empirical research is needed to (a) understand how to respond to social, political, and other factors that interfere with the full identification of children who have disabilities, and (b) clarify how social phenomena associated with the devaluation of special education postpone reforms that may be needed in both the breadth and quality of educational programs. Multicultural education policies and practices then can draw from the findings of this research to ensure full identification and appropriate educational experiences implemented as a part of broader school reform efforts. In sum, effective responses to disproportionate representation must also examine the extent to which both general and special education programs benefit multicultural learners, and recommend reforms that eliminate misidentification, support full identification, and provide quality educational experiences to all students with and without disabilities.

CONCLUSION

In spite all of the attention and resources devoted to the issue of disproportionate representation in special education over the past three decades, surprisingly little effort has been made to document the effects of judicial, legislative, and regulatory action. The reasons for this neglect range from questions about the integrity of existing data to a belief that present circumstances call for political activism rather than empirical analyses. However, while data problems cannot be denied and the need for advocacy is evident, the path forward to an improved educational outcome for all multicultural learners must be informed by an understanding of events in recent history. Examples of unintended consequences of governmental action abound

and the effects of policy initiatives must not be assumed. Thoughtful responses to the issues raised by the observed disproportionate representation of ethnic minorities in special education require careful study of those effects. Multicultural education policies and programs must focus not only on the extent and significance of overrepresentation in special education, but also on the full identification of all students who are eligible for special education, and on the educational experience those children are offered.

In sum, only when we have determined the impact of past actions on children's educational experiences can we make reasonable decisions about how to shape effective multicultural education polices and practices. This chapter is not a beginning, for others have sought to explore these data before; nor is it an end, for much work remains to be done, both in improving and understanding the data and also considering the impact of broader school reform policies. It does, however, represent another step along the way of how the issues have evolved, how the nation's schools have responded, and some of the issues that must be considered when developing multicultural education programs and policies needed to fulfill the public goal for better outcomes for all learners.

REFERENCES

Bahr, M.W., Fuchs, D., Stecker, P.M., & Fuchs, L.S. (1991). Are teachers' perceptions of difficult-to-teach students racially biased? *School Psychology Review, 20,* 599–608.

Bondy, E., & Ross, E.D. (1998). Confronting myths about teaching black children: A challenge for teacher educators. *Teacher Education and Special Education, 21,* 241–254.

Chinn, P.C., & Hughes, S. (1987). Representation of minority students in special education classes. *Remedial and Special Education, 8,* 41–46.

Coulter, W.A. (1996). *Alarming or disarming: The status of ethnic differences within exceptionalities.* Paper presented at the Annual Convention of the Council for Exceptional Children, Orlando, FL. (ERIC Document Reproduction Services No. ED 394 257).

Coutinho, M.J., & Oswald, D.P. (1998). Ethnicity and special education research: Identifying questions and methods. *Behavioral Disorders, 24,* 66–73.

Coutinho, M.J., & Oswald, D.P. (in press). Disproportionate representation in special education: A synthesis and recommendations. *Journal of Child and Family Studies.*

Diana v. State Board of Education, C. A. No. C-70-37 (N. D. Cal., July 1970) (consent decree).

Dunn, L.M. (1968). Special education for the mildly retarded: Is much of it justifiable? *Exceptional Children, 23,* 5–21.

Education for All Handicapped Children Act of 1975, P. L. 94-142, 89 Stat. 773.

Forness, S.R. (1985). Effects of public policy at the state level: California's impact on MR, LD, and ED categories. *Remedial and Special Education, 6,* 36–43.

Gottlieb, J., & Alter, M. (1994). *An analysis of referrals, placement, and progress of children with disabilities who attend New York City public schools.* (ERIC Document Reproduction Service No. ED 414 372).

Gresham, F.M., MacMillan, D.L., & Siperstein, G.N. (1995). Critical analysis of the 1992 AAMR definition: Implications for school psychology. *School Psychology Quarterly, 10,* 1–19.

Guadalupe Organization v. Tempe Elementary School District #3, No. 71-435 (D. Ariz., January 24, 1972) (consent decree).

Halfon, N., & Newacheck, P. (1999). Prevalence and impact of parent-reported disabling mental health conditions among U.S. children. *Journal of the American Academy of Child and Adolescent Psychiatry, 38,* 600–609.

Harry, B. (1992a). *Cultural diversity, families, and the special education system.* New York: Teachers College Press.

Harry, B. (1992b). Restructuring the participation of African American parents in special education. *Exceptional Children, 59,* 123–131.

Harry, B. (1994). *The disproportionate representation of minority students in special education: Theories and recommendations.* Project FORUM Final Report. Alexandria, VA: National Association of State Directors of Special Education.

Harry, B., & Anderson, M.G. (1994). The disproportionate placement of African American males in special education programs: A critique of the process. *Journal of Negro Education, 63,* 602–619.

Harry, B., Rueda, R., & Kalyanpur, M. (1999). Cultural reciprocity in sociocultural perspective: Adapting the normalization principle for family collaboration. *Exceptional Children, 66,* 123–136.

Heller, K.A., Holtzman, W.H., & Messick, S. (1982). *Placing children in special education: A Strategy for equity.* Washington, DC: National Academy Press.

Horner, C.M., Maddux, C.D., & Green, C. (1986). Minority students and special education: Is overrepresentation possible? *NASSP Bulletin, 70,* 89–93.

Individuals with Disabilities Education Act, 20 U.S.C. §§ 1400 et seq. (1997).

Institute of Medicine (1989). *Research on children with mental, behavioral, and developmental disorders.* Washington, DC: National Academy Press.

Kauffman, J.M., Hallahan, D.P., & Ford, D.Y. (1998). Introduction to the special section. *The Journal of Special Education, 32,* 3.

Larry P. v. Wilson Riles. 343 F.Supp. 1306 (N.D. Cal. 1972) (preliminary injunction). Aff'd 502 F. 2d 963 (9th cir. 1974); 495F. Supp. 926 (N.D. Cal. 1979) (decision on merits). Aff'd (9th cir. No. 80-427 Jan. 23, 1984). Order modifying judgment, C-71-2270 RFP, Sept. 25, 1986.

MacMillan, D.L., & Balow, I.H. (1991). Impact of Larry P. on educational programs and assessment practices in California. *Diagnostique, 17,* 57–69.

MacMillan, D.L., Gresham, F.M., Lopez, M.F., & Bocian, K.M. (1996). Comparison of students nominated for prereferral interventions by ethnicity and gender. *The Journal of Special Education, 30,* 133–151.

MacMillan, D.L., Hendrick, I.G., & Watkins, A.V. (1988). Impact of Diana, Larry P., and P.L. 94-142 on minority students. *Exceptional Children, 54,* 426–432.

Markowitz, J. (1996). *Strategies that address the disproportionate number of students from racial/ethnic minority groups receiving special education services: Case studies of selected states and school districts, final report.* (ERIC Document Reproduction Service No. ED 396 473).

Marshall et al. v. Georgia. U.S. District Court for the Southern District of Georgia, CV482-233, June 28, 1984; Aff'd (11th cir. No. 84-8771, Oct. 29, 1985). Note, the Court of Appeals decision was published as Georgia State Conference on Branches of NAACP v. State of Georgia, Oct. 30–Dec. 20, 1983.

Obiakor, F.E. (1999). Teacher expectations of minority exceptional learners: Impact on "accuracy" of self-concepts. *Exceptional Children, 66,* 39–53.

Oswald, D.P., & Coutinho, M.J. (1995). Identification and placement of students with serious emotional disturbance. Part I: Correlates of state child-count data. *Journal of Emotional and Behavioral Disorders, 3,* 224–229.

Oswald, D.P., Coutinho, M.J., & Best, A.M. (1999). *Describing and predicting national ethnic representation as mentally retarded, emotionally disturbed, and learning disabled.* Paper presented at the International Convention of the Council for Exceptional Children, Charlotte, NC.

Oswald, D.P., Coutinho, M.J., Best, A.M, & Singh, N.N. (1999). Ethnic representation in special education: The influence of school-related economic and demographic variables. *The Journal of Special Education, 32,* 194–206.

Pallas, A.M., Natriello, G., & McDill, E.L. (1989). The changing nature of the disadvantaged population: Current dimensions and future trends. *Educational Researcher, 18,* 16 22.

Pennsylvania Association for Retarded Citizens v. The Commonwealth of Pennsylvania. (1972). 343 F. Supp. 279.

PASE (Parents in Action on Special Education) v. Joseph P. Hannon. (1980). U.S. District Court, Northern district of Illinois, Easter Division, No. 74 (3586), July, 1980.

Pennsylvania Human Relations Commission v. School District of Philadelphia, No. 1056 C.D. 1973, Commonwealth Court of Pennsylvania. (1994). LEXIS-NEXIS Academic Universe Document.

Rehabilitation Act of 1973, P.L. 93-112, 87 Stat. 355.

Reschly, D.J., & Ward, S. (1991). Use of adaptive behavior measures and overrepresentation of black students in programs for students with mild mental retardation. *American Journal on Mental Retardation, 96,* 257–268.

Robertson, P., Kushner, M.I., Starks, J., & Drescher, C. (1994). An update of participation rates of culturally and linguistically diverse students in special education. *The Bilingual Special Education Perspective, 14,* 1–9.

S-1 v. Turlington. (1986). Preliminary Injunction, U.S. district Court, Southern District of Florida, Case No. 70-8020-Civ-CA WPB, June 15, 1979. Affirmed United States Court of Appeals, 5th Circuit, January 26, 1981, 635 F. 2d 342 (1981). Trial on Merits, May 19–June 4, 1986. Order on Motion to Dismiss, No. 79-8020-Div-Atkins, U.S. district Court, Southern District of Florida, October 9, 1986.

Serwatka, T.S., Deering, S., & Grant, P. (1995). Disproportionate representation of African Americans in emotionally handicapped classes. *Journal of Black Studies, 25,* 492–506.

Title VI of the Civil Rights Act of 1964, P.L. 88-352, 78 Stat. 241.

Trent, S.C., & Artiles, A.J. (1995). Serving culturally diverse students with emotional or behavioral disorders: Broadening current perspectives. In J.M. Kauffman, J.W. Lloyd, D.P. Hallahan, & T.A. Astuto (Eds.), *Issues in educational placement: Students with emotional and behavioral disorders* (pp. 215–245). Hillsdale, NJ: Erlbaum.

U.S. Department of Education, Office of Civil Rights (1994). *1992 Elementary and secondary school civil rights compliance report.* Washington, DC: Author.

Utley, C.A., & Mortweet, S.L. (1999). The challenge of diversity. In M.J. Coutinho & A.C. Repp (Eds.), *Inclusion: The integration of students with disabilities* (pp. 59–90). Belmont, CA: Wadsworth.

Voltz, D.L., Dooley, E., & Jefferies, P. (1999). Preparing special educators for cultural diversity: How far have we come? *Teacher Education and Special Education, 22,* 66–77.

Authors' Notes

Preparation of this chapter was supported in part by the Field-Initiated Studies Program of the National Institute on Educational Governance, Finance, Policymaking, and Management; Office of Educational Research and Improvement, U.S. Department of Education (R308F70020). The views expressed do not necessarily reflect those of the supporting agency.

Chapter 4

CULTURAL AND LINGUISTIC DIVERSITY AS A THEORETICAL FRAMEWORK FOR UNDERSTANDING MULTICULTURAL LEARNERS WITH MILD DISABILITIES

ROBERT RUEDA AND SIMON KIM

In this chapter, we examine research issues confronting the field of education in the context of renewed interest about cultural and linguistic diversity and in the context of rapidly developing educational reform. A central argument proposed in this chapter is that there is a common thread which links both the school reform movement as it impacts the instructional process, curriculum, and content, and the area of research. More specifically, both areas are closely tied to the theoretical paradigms and models upon which they are based. We argue that at least some of the current debate about various aspects of school reform as well as many of the controversies regarding research issues in special education are more properly seen as conflicts over paradigmatic and theoretically based beliefs and understandings rather than arguments about changes in specific practices, procedures, or structural/organizational arrangements. Moreover, we argue that it is not possible to examine the role of cultural and linguistic diversity in special education research (or practice) without closer examination of these paradigms and theoretical models which guide (consciously or unconsciously) research and practice contexts in which this diversity is increasingly found.

This chapter begins by briefly examining major theoretical perspectives which have guided special education research and practice. It also considers the role of cultural and linguistic diversity and sociocultural factors within these frameworks. It then examines more recent aspects of sociocultural theory as a contrast to earlier frameworks and discusses various research and practice issues from both a methodological as well as a theoretical perspective. Finally, we conclude by examining the implications for the future of special education as a field.

THEORETICAL PERSPECTIVES IN SPECIAL EDUCATION

Prior to discussing the above issues more in detail and the research implications entailed by our position, we call attention to various models of learning which have impacted the field of special education at various stages of its history. These have included at various times and in overlapping fashion a Medical model, a Psychological Process model, a Behavioral model, and a Cognitive Psychology model. Poplin (1988) presented a more critical, comparative description of each of these models). A complete review of the frameworks to be discussed is beyond the scope of this chapter, but Byrnes (1996) had a more complete discussion of the major frameworks.

Medical/Biological Model

The fundamental basis of the medical model is that the primary causal factor in mental retardation (and other special education conditions) is presumed or identifiable central nervous system or other organic damage. The major emphasis of this model, which was especially widespread in the late 1940s and 1950s, was on the criteria for diagnosis and educational instruction. The very early impact of this model on special education can likely be traced to the medical background of the very first "special educators" (Mercer, 1973). This influence was provided impetus with the development of the learning disability category and the widespread use of various presumed measures of psychomotor processes (Kavale & Forness, 1985). More recent manifestations of the influence of this framework are found in the current concern with Attention Deficit Hyperactivity Disorder (ADHD), sex differences in learning and intelligence, and other biological and neurological factors in learning.

Psychological Process Model

In the 1960s, a major influence in special education was the psychoeducational model which moved the emphasis of work in the field from strictly a medical orientation to a more educational focus. One result of this educational emphasis was the widespread practice of retaining psychomotor skills because of their presumed role as prerequisites to more complex academic tasks and developmental processes. These prerequisite skills included such factors as auditory, visual, and other sensory perceptions. The field drew upon the psychological emphasis on standardized measurement and assessment heavily and these psychological factors were frequently assessed.

Behavioral Model

The behavioral model was appropriated from behavioral psychology and resulted in an emphasis on teaching the academic, as well as social behaviors, necessary to succeed in the school setting. In essence, this model proposed that academic learning and social skills were simply a subtype of operant behavior that could be learned through precise and systematic training techniques. It relied on precise task analyses and criterion-referenced tests to determine specific areas where development was needed for an individual student. One result of this was the extended use of skill-based programs such as Distar and other specific skill-based approaches, used in an overall context of direct instruction given in the classroom to meet the specific needs of a student (see, for example, Kameenui, Jitendra, Asha, & Darch, 1995; McEachin, Smith, & Lovaas, 1993).

Cognitive Psychology Model

The emphasis on cognitive approaches resulted from the use of cognitive processes in problem-solving and learning by experts as opposed to novice learners. Therefore, this approach emphasizes careful specification and study of the cognitive processes involved in learning and related processes such as text comprehension. It has resulted in the development of a wide array of programs used for training in learning strategies and study skills that are necessary to perform academic tasks. The focus has been on the active processes involved in learning, the development of self-regulation, and on emulating the learning and problem-solving of expert learners (see, for example, Borkowski & Day, 1987; Graham & Harris, 1996). Inspection of the current literature on learning and intervention in special education suggests that at present the cognitive framework is the dominant model. Because of the fact that this work was rooted in experimental psychology, much of the research and the tasks used to study learning processes have been based in real world tasks. However, as researchers have begun to push the generalizability of this work to schools and everyday settings, some investigators and theoreticians (e.g., Belmont, 1989; Greeno, 1989) have begun to broaden the theory to begin to take into account the role of the learner's understanding of the task, the effects of task and contextual differences, and the role of affect and motivation. In reviewing a recent volume on cognitive psychology research, Lajoie (1991) stated:

> (Cognitive) researchers are going beyond the laboratory confines by looking at the use of strategic knowledge in the classroom and in our daily activities. Cognitive strategy research is undergoing a reality test, where the robustness of theory is being tested in the real world. Ecologically valid contexts make the impact of complex interactions on learning more apparent. (p. 30)

It should be recognized that the above overview is necessarily simplistic and by no means complete or exhaustive. Rather, it is only meant to illustrate the general theoretical influences on special education practice over time. In reality, each of the models has an extensive theoretical and empirical foundation which is also beyond the scope of this chapter. Moreover, as Poplin (1988) and others have noted, there is a great deal of overlap in the above time frames suggested, and these should be treated as approximations for illustrative purposes only.

EMERGING CRITIQUES OF THE PAST AND PRESENT KNOWLEDGE BASE

There is a long history of criticism in the special education literature regarding various policies and practices (Marozas & May, 1988). Recently, however, criticism has begun to include not so much a criticism of specific practices but rather the assumptions, knowledge base, and especially the paradigmatic foundations on which that knowledge and those assumptions are based (Danforth, 1997; Iano, 1992). It is likely that this critical analysis is being accelerated at least in part because of the interrelated factors of increasing diversity and continued underachievement on the part of diverse learners in comparison to their mainstream peers. It is also likely related to the push toward the integration of general and special education (Lipsky & Gartner, 1992) and the self-reflective impetus of the school reform and restructuring movement.

Unlike previous calls for change, however, special education is being forced to examine not only the effectiveness of its practices and organizational configuration, but as noted above, the knowledge base on which it is founded as well (Skrtic, 1988). Although alternative treatment models have long been an issue of contention in the special education literature (e.g., Arter & Jenkins, 1979), the issue has begun to be debated at a more fundamental level. An increasing amount of attention in the special education literature has been directed toward the issue of theoretical and paradigmatic differences. These differences reflect substantially more than simple disagreements about the relative benefits of alternative treatments. Several authors have begun to examine critically how these paradigmatic assumptions and belief systems drive the very essence of what is embedded in special education policy, practice, and organizational structure (Heshusius, 1982; Poplin, 1988; Poplin & Stone, 1992; Skrtic, 1988). As an example, Poplin argued that while special education practice and theory had been dominated at different periods by one or more individual models described above, they really represented various versions of a single paradigm which Poplin termed Reductionism. Building on this argument, others (Heshusius, 1984, 1989; Iano, 1992) have suggested that the roots of the prevailing paradigm were to be found in scientific or logical positivism and a Newtonian mechanistic view of the world and reality.

One of the primary arguments made by Poplin (1988) in describing the prevailing models of special education is that they all share a propensity to break ideas, concepts, and skills into parts in an attempt to understand and deal better with the whole (Capra, 1983; Heshusius, 1984, 1989). This positivist or Newtonian mechanistic paradigm, as described by Heshusius (1989), reflects a view that:

> . . . complexity is to be broken down into components; translated into practice, this leads to, for instance, task analysis and isolated skill training. The whole is understood by understanding the components as logically and sequentially arranged–assumptions that lead to mastery learning, programmed materials, and behavioral objectives. Thus, causality, prediction, certainty, and control become inherently possible . . . (p. 404)

For example, the behaviorist might break a complex task into a hierarchy of sequential skills, or a cognitive psychologist might divide "cognition" into discrete processes such as working memory, short term memory, long term storage, and executive functioning. The lively responses both in favor and against these articles suggest the depth and intensity of the controversy that it sparked in the field. In addition to these criticisms, Poplin and Stone (1992) observed that the practices derived from these models, as they are implemented in school settings, tend to be superimposed on each other rather than on one practice supplanting earlier practices derived from the models which preceded it. In many classrooms, it is possible to observe a mixture of practices that draw on several and perhaps incompatible theoretical bases (Rueda & Garcia, 1996).

While the above points are important considerations for the field, there are at least two other characteristics that are of utmost concern for diverse learners in schools. First, it is clear that cultural diversity and/or language differences do not occupy a central role in any of the preceding frameworks. While culture or language may occasionally find its way into a research study, cultural and language factors are not core constructs. As just noted, this is not to argue that one could not examine different cultural settings or different culturally based behaviors in any of these models. However, in each case, the models focus on "universals" in learning, thinking, and development. As an example, one of the basic principles of the behaviorist approach is that operant behavior is controlled by its consequences. This invariant behavioral principle is assumed not to vary across cultural settings and language groups. In a like fashion, within a cognitive framework, metacognitive awareness and learning strategies are assumed to be universally effective in higher order thinking and problem-solving. That is, the efficient learner plans, employs appropriate learning and problem-solving strategies, self-regulates his or her behavior under changing task conditions, and monitors the effectiveness of these efforts over time.

The intent here is not to claim that existing models are not extremely powerful or even that they are fundamentally incorrect. This position creates a significant paradox since each of the frameworks embodies significant literature which points to its own validity. While it is possible to argue the validity of the data or the validity of the methodology used to collect the data within each framework, it is more difficult to discount any of these frameworks entirely. In fact, each seems to explain a piece of the world satisfactorily. It is possible to suggest, however, that the scope of these frameworks is incomplete with respect to characterizing learning in a variety of diverse settings or in understanding differences in culturally based behavior. How to overcome this problem will be discussed in the next section. At this point, however, the point being suggested is that the relative lack of attention to cultural and linguistic factors (other than that generated by court disputes over testing and placement issues) is at least in part due to the nature of the theoretical models that have formed the foundation for special education practice and research.

While much of our own and others' critical analysis have focused primarily on issues of assessment and instruction, we propose to advance the discussion by considering the research implications of this controversy for the field in general as well as research on multicultural persons with mental retardation in particular. Prior to doing that, however, we briefly introduce an emerging alternative sociocultural framework that might be termed an alternative paradigm. Although its roots can be traced back perhaps as far back as Socrates, its influence in special education is rather recent. A central argument we advance is that this framework can expand the concerns of the field to include the treatment of language and cultural differences while at the same time acknowledging the contributions of past work.

SOCIOCULTURAL THEORY: AN ALTERNATIVE FRAMEWORK

In the recent past, an emergent sociocultural framework has become increasingly visible in the research and practice communities. Much of this perspective derives from

Vygotsky and his followers (Belmont, 1989; Bruner, 1984; Fischer & Bullock, 1984; Greenfield, 1984; Minick, 1987; Moll, 1990; Ochs, 1982; Rogoff, 1982; Rogoff & Lave, 1984; Tharp & Gallimore, 1988; Vygotsky, 1978; Wertsch, 1985a, 1985b). The common thread of this framework is that higher order functions develop out of social interaction. Especially important is the emphasis placed on everyday activity and its connection to learning and development. As Vygotsky (1978) emphasized, development cannot be understood solely by studying the individual, especially the individual in artificial contexts. Rather, Vygotsky and later "neoVygotskians" argue that it is necessary to also examine the external social world in which that individual life has developed. Through participation in social activities that have embedded cognitive and linguistic functions, children are drawn into the use of these higher order functions in ways that gradually nurture and "scaffold" them. Finally, cognitive and other aspects of development are seen as rooted in a particular cultural/historical context, with language being a key element in carrying on and transmitting that cultural and historical tradition.

One of the more unique features of sociocultural theory is that it views teaching and learning as social, not individual activities. This suggests that learning takes place in activities in which novices and experts collaborate to solve a common problem or produce a common product (Rogoff, 1991; Tharp & Gallimore, 1988). This model of assisted performance by a "more competent other" is more characteristic of the learning which is often found in out-of-school settings. Typically the role of "student" and "teacher" are not fixed in this view. An additional fundamental premise of sociocultural theory is that language is a critical tool that helps mediate interaction with the world. In this view, thinking takes place through the medium of language, and language helps frame problems in new and important ways. Language is viewed as a cultural tool that serves to mediate interactions with the world. Finally, based on the sociocultural theory, teaching and learning must be contextualized, or situated in meaningful activities connected to everyday life (Forman, Minick, & Stone, 1993). This means that the focus of teaching/learning activities and joint problem-solving should focus on authentic issues and problems encountered in the context of participants' daily practice, not externally imposed. In practice, this means that both the problems addressed as well as the teaching/learning processes in these contexts are certain to be "messier" than those typically encountered in more controlled or artificial situations.

Fortunately, the development of these significant advances in understanding the social and cultural foundations of cognitive development have been especially useful in examining the educational experiences of students from diverse cultural backgrounds and languages. A relatively large body of research drawing on this theory has focused on improving the academic success of students in these groups at-risk for failure. Some of these at-risk factors include poverty, limited English proficiency, or background knowledge and experiences that do not map easily onto school expectations. Rather than focusing on presumed student deficits, however, sociocultural theory has stimulated work focused on ways that schools can scaffold learning, build on student characteristics as resources, and mitigate risk factors (Tharp, 1997). This work has taken place in a variety of settings and with a variety of groups, such as Native Americans (Tharp, Dalton, & Yamauchi, 1994; Vogt, Jordan, & Tharp, 1992; Yamauchi, 1993); Korean Americans (Scarcella & Chin, 1993); Haitian Americans (Warren & Roseberry, 1995); Latinos (Goldenberg & Gallimore, 1991; Moll, Amanti, Neff, & Gonzalez, 1992); native Hawaiians (Tharp, 1982;

Tharp & Gallimore, 1988; Tharp et al., 1984); and low socioeconomic (SES) students in European and Latino communities (Azmitia, Cooper, Garcia, & Dunbar, 1996). For instance, the work by Moll and his associates with teachers in diverse classrooms has focused on assisting teachers to investigate the communities and homes of students they teach. The extensive and complex "funds of knowledge" that they uncover (that are significant educational resources even for the most impoverished and at-risk families) then become the basis for developing the curriculum in thematic units. This approach has been widely cited in the literature for its effectiveness in promoting optimal classroom learning contexts. Given the sociocultural nature of learning, these resources can be seen as a strong foundation for culturally effective or responsive instruction.

In sum, sociocultural theory views teaching and learning as a social activity, characterized by providing mediation or assisted performance in a responsive fashion. An important recent extension of sociocultural theory by Rogoff (1994, 1995) and Rogoff, Baker-Sennett, Lacasa, and Goldsmith (1995) is especially relevant in the present discussion. Rogoff (1994) proposed a view of learning and development as a dynamic process of transformation of participation in a given community. Based on this framework, research is supposed to answer questions such as, What are the activities in which people participate? Why and with whom and with what? How do the activity, its purpose, and peoples' roles in it transform? How do different activities relate to each other currently, historically, and prospectively? As Rogoff (1995) suggested, the participation in any sociocultural activity, such as reading and literacy, occurs on many planes or levels of interaction. In addition, a complete account of learning and development must take into account three levels. First, the *individual or personal plane* involves individual cognition,

emotion, behavior, values, and beliefs. In educational research, this might correspond with studies of individual student or teacher actions, psychological characteristics, or competence. Second, the *interpersonal or social plane* includes communication, role performances, dialogue, cooperation, conflict, assistance, and assessment. In educational research, this is often addressed in studies of teaching/learning interactions, such as a study of cooperative learning groups. And third, the *community or institutional plane* involves shared history, languages, rules, values, beliefs, and identities. This is sometimes addressed in studies of entire schools, districts, professions, neighborhoods, tribes, or cultures. This last plane of development, often overlooked in behavioral science, focuses on factors such as past and current power relationships among various groups under consideration, including (a) how these are embedded in social institutions; and (b) how these are perceived and experienced by individuals and their communities (see Figure 4.1). Sociocultural theory, in general, emphasizes that these three planes are inseparable: moreover, language is the primary force that defines and connects these planes. While one plane might be "foregrounded" in a particular study or analysis, and the other planes "backgrounded," a complete account of learning and development needs to consider all three. In practice, the smallest unit of analysis which contains all three planes simultaneously is the activity setting, or the "who, what, when, where, why, and how" of the routines which constitute everyday life in and out of school. Importantly, the unit of analysis (the object of study, observation, or assessment) is larger than the individual – rather it is the individual in interaction with others in a specific activity setting.

While the above description is inadequate in describing the scope and complexity of this emerging sociocultural framework, it should provide a good sense of contrast to

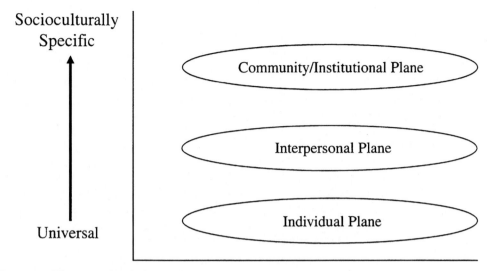

Figure 4.1. The interrelated planes of learning and development.

current and past models in the field. We argue that this framework represents a fundamentally different way of viewing teaching and learning and particularly of conducting research. In the remainder of the chapter, we discuss ways that this might impact research, especially with those persons from multicultural backgrounds.

Implications for Research in Multicultural Settings

As suggested, the models which have guided special education research and practice at various times during this century have two notable characteristics: they focus on universals in learning and development and fail to include language and cultural differences as core constructs, and they overwhelmingly focus on the individual's characteristics with little attention to the larger social context in which learning and development occur. This last feature has been overwhelmingly characteristic of the spectrum of special education assessment and instructional practices. In terms of research focus, it appears that a significant part of the field has focused on the individual plane of Rogoff's (1994, 1995) framework, and to a much less extent the interpersonal plane. Al-

most no work has focused on the last level, the community/institutional plane. One of the unfortunate aspects of this state of affairs is that arguably the individual plane of development is likely to be the most universal of the three planes, and the community/institutional plane to be the most "socioculturally specific" (see Figure 4.1). In a relatively homogenous context, inattention to the last plane of development may not necessarily be problematic because of the higher likelihood of shared understandings and experiences; in a highly diverse context, it can be highly significant. The cognitive problem-solving strategies necessary to solve a test item are universal, however a student's understanding of and personal meaning attached to the test-taking situation and the meaning of schooling in general is likely to be colored by his or her cultural-historical inheritance. Attention to the individual plane without consideration of the interaction of the other planes is reminiscent of the practice of developed nations providing technological advances to third world countries. Often a specific practice is introduced (birth control, for example) without attention to the larger sociocultural history and specific context. Important questions frequently not asked are, What is the historical significance of family size in this cultural context? What are the cultural beliefs and practices about childbirth and contraception? Inattention to these types of considerations has often led to the failure to adopt the "superior" innovation and condemnation of the "backwardness" of the group in question. Yet this same phenomenon is an important factor in the current intense efforts to reform and restructure schools. Introducing innovations and practices into a school setting without consideration of the existing cultural context is almost always problematic. In both cases, it is not that the innovations are not "superior" or desirable, nor is it the case that the intended recipients are deficient cognitively or otherwise. Rather, all learning and development take place in specific sociocultural contexts that reflect certain cultural and historical traditions. A complete account of learning and development requires considering the interactive effects of all three levels.

A Research Example

Currently, the first author of this chapter is engaged in a research project that is focusing on the issue of motivation in reading (known as reading engagement in the literature) among early elementary school students. The participants in the study are a small group of Latino students in an immigrant community in a central city school in a large urban school district. While most of the research in this area has examined reading engagement as an individual psychological characteristic of the child, in this study, particular attention has been paid to trying to examine variables at all three planes of development. Individual measures of reading engagement and other measures of learning and school achievement are being collected at the individual level, while observational data is being collected in classrooms and elsewhere to examine interpersonal factors. Finally, attention is being given to the larger community in which the school and the families exist (Rueda & MacGillivray, 1999).

Many of the students in this study are at high-risk for low achievement and failure by any criteria. At least one student has been placed in a special education program, and others are being assessed. They are from poverty-stricken homes, come from families where English is not spoken, live in overcrowded homes in presumed "dangerous" neighborhoods, and do not have access to the kinds of "cultural capital" that gives more advantaged children an head start in school. Not unexpectedly, on most school-based measures, they exhibit the profiles that one might expect given these risk factors. If one remains at the personal plane of analysis, it is easy to conclude that the children and/or their families are deficient along a variety of dimensions that need to be "fixed" before school success can be obtained.

In considering the other planes of analysis, however, the picture is not so straightforward. While there are many situations where students in the study are not engaged, there are times when they are. This appears to be related often to the types of academic tasks and activities that they are given. Specifically, in almost every classroom, students are often given low-level, programmed, inauthentic types of tasks to work on. It is not a simple matter of dismissing the teachers as incompetent. While the teachers in this school are extremely hardworking and dedicated, there are pressures from the larger sociocultural contexts which they must respond to. For example, in the state of California, the instruction of literacy is currently dominated by instructional approaches that emphasize phonics and basic skills. In addition, teachers must cope with the recent controversy and elimination of bilingual education as an accepted educational practice, a situation which has been particularly contentious at this school (the research setting). Finally, at this school (like countless others), there is a premium placed on "accountability" defined narrowly as performance on statewide standardized tests. In the single classroom where the teacher characteristically makes a concerted effort to provide students with authentic literacy activities and tries to connect their schoolwork with their outside experiences and lives, the level of engagement of students is noticeably different.

There are other factors related to the community/institutional plane which impact the nature of classroom interaction (and by extension, individual children's learning and performance). For example, there is notable hostility toward immigrants in general in California, a factor that was likely related to a recently passed ballot initiative to ban affirmative action and to actions of a nearby school district that passed a resolution to bill the Mexican government for the costs of educating immigrant students. There is constant fear among many of the families about immigration-related issues and the fear of deportation. There is reluctance on the part of families to keep a highly visible presence because of this. Further, economic problems in the central city garment industry where many of the parents work long hours in low-paying jobs are important as well. Transportation and health care are major issues for many of these families. While these factors constrain the ability of families in many ways, it is not the case that students never engage in litera-

cy activities outside of school or that families do not think schooling is important. In one family, for example, the mother avidly reads self-help books and even requires visitors to sit and read for a while when they first come to the house. Every family has high aspirations for its children with respect to future careers. Yet for many of these families being educated ("educado") is much broader than acquisition of academic skills, rather it implies being a "good" person. Moreover, because of their own impoverished school experiences and inability to speak English, almost none are able to help with homework or otherwise facilitate the lofty goals they have for their children.

While this study is still in progress, it nevertheless suggests that a straightforward analysis of individual cognitive and academic variables provides less than a complete picture of the issue of reading engagement and the larger issue of academic achievement for these students. It implies that a cultural-historical analysis of individuals and social contexts in which they operate are a necessary part of the research process especially (but not exclusively) where diverse populations are being studied. An important part of this view is that the meaning systems used by individuals are culturally and historically rooted, and embodied in such "tools" as language and linguistic categories and constructs used to make sense of the world (Vygotsky, 1978). Culture can be seen as an intersubjective meaning systems, then, which can be studied in the objective practices and institutions of society. As Iano (1992) stated:

> . . . The everyday activities, talks, and projects of people are carried out within larger and more enduring structures of society, such as social practices, conventions, norms, traditions, institutions, organizations, and agencies. People draw from these larger and more enduring structures for their everyday activities, but as they engage in their everyday activities people also contribute to sustaining, creating, and

recreating the larger and more enduring structures. (p. 325)

Apparently, not only are the meaning systems culturally determined, culture also plays a prominent role in the nature of the interpretations made by the observer. With respect to research, then, observations or basic data become available to scientists only through their particular theoretical conceptions and interpretations. This has been especially critical in the history of research on culturally and linguistically diverse children and families where "different" characteristics or behaviors (from the researcher's perspective) quickly come to be seen and labeled as deficits. The suggestion here is that in most cases the analysis is incomplete because of the overwhelming tendency to focus only at the individual plane of development. It is precisely this inattention to sociocultural factors (including cultural meaning systems and contextual factors) in investigating learning and development in general and assessing competence in particular (most often through standardized testing) which has tended to result in underestimations of the abilities of members of some linguistic, racial, or ethnic minority groups (Miller-Jones, 1989; Price-Williams & Gallimore, 1980). Conversely, increased attention to these factors provides a basis for understanding the often-noted variance in the competence of minority group children on apparently equivalent tasks in different settings (Gallimore, Tharp, & Rueda, 1989; Labov, 1972). It is this same respect for individual understandings and meaning systems that permits one to account for variances in behavior by context (Gallimore, Tharp, & Rueda, 1989). Moreover, it is precisely in this area that the special education knowledge is lacking. We argue that the absence of such a theoretical perspective in past research in the field has led to the minimal attention given to culture and language in that knowledge base.

Methodological Considerations

While data collection procedures and analytic procedures have advanced rapidly in the behavioral and social sciences, much of it has focused on the individual and to a lesser extend the interpersonal planes. The psychological foundations of the field have been especially useful in this respect. However, if one takes seriously the challenge to begin to consider all the planes of learning and development and their complex interactions, then clearly broader array of tools are needed and broader array of interpretations will result. What are particularly needed are methodological tools adequate to explore cultural-historical factors which impact current behavior, to examine emic (insider's) views of behavior and cognition, to look at behavior in everyday or natural settings, and to examine the development of culturally based meaning systems. Fortunately, disciplines such as anthropology, sociology and linguistics have provided an excellent source to draw on since these disciplines often deal with issues related to culture, language use, everyday behavior, and personal meaning systems in a more central fashion (Bogdan & Lutflyya, 1992; Stainback & Stainback, 1984, 1989; Taylor & Bogdan, 1984).

Although the first qualitative research involving persons with mental retardation appeared as early as the 1960s and 1970s (Edgerton, 1967; Edgerton & Bercovici, 1986), it is only more recently that the literature has begun to reflect this orientation in a more systematic fashion (Bercovici, 1983; Bogdan & Taylor, 1982; Bruininks, Meyers, Sigford, & Lakin, 1981; Edgerton, 1984; Ferguson, 1987; Mehan, Hertwick, & Miehls, 1986; Murray-Seegert, 1989; Zetlin & Hosseini, 1989). While research of this type has begun to focus on ethnic and linguistic minorities, it is still rare (Harry, 1992; Trueba, 1983).

It is important to note that the argument being made here is not that all past research in the field is unequivocally wrong and must be discarded. In contrast, each of the models described earlier has generated important information and knowledge. Rather, the argument being made here is that in an important sense they are incomplete because of the fact that they limit the scope of analysis to one or two planes of development only. Although traditional methodologies have provided powerful and complex models of learning, the goal of reforming teaching and learning in schools has only been partially realized at best. A gap in this research base is the investigation of social processes in learning and problem solving; of examining learning, thinking, and problem-solving in out of school contexts; of looking at behavior in natural contexts or on authentic and meaningful tasks; of understanding the culturally based meaning systems of students and their families and how these impact performance. It is the lack of attention to these factors, we propose, which is more directly related to the systematic underestimation of the competence of ethnic and linguistic minority students, more so than technical inadequacies and bias in the most commonly used assessment measures and procedures.

CONCLUSION

In the special education research focusing on ethnic and linguistic minority students, much attention with respect to cultural and linguistic diversity has been given to the issue of biased assessment and misplacement in stigmatizing settings (Artiles, Aguirre-Munoz, & Abedi, 1998; Artiles & Trent, 1994; Chinn & Hughes, 1987; Shannon & Hakuta, 1990). We argue that a research agenda based on the search for "less-biased" tests or procedures is essentially an incomplete question to be asking. Rather, it is the cultural meaning systems which students bring to school, as well as other related sociocultural and cultural-historical factors that interact with school or research-based tasks that should form the more pressing research agenda. We have argued that incomplete questions have been asked and investigated primarily due to the prevailing theoretical models and a paradigm which include only minimal attention to factors other than individual characteristics and that do not account for diversity in terms of culture, language, or other dimensions.

An alternative sociocultural framework discussed in this chapter is only beginning to find its way in the field (Keogh, Gallimore, & Weisner, 1997). Of importance to the special education research agenda, there are at least three specific research considerations which merit attention. The first is increased attention to behavior in a variety of settings and tasks (not just in school and not just on tests or experimental tasks). Experimental or standardized tasks such as test items are not de-contextualized, but rather represent a particular type of context, one which normally has little connection to everyday life and concerns. The same is often true of school in general. A central question is how to make use of each individual's everyday learning, problem-solving, and other cognitive activities in advancing school-based learning. Therefore, we need ways of talking about and studying contexts, as opposed to reducing them to formal artificial settings for study or worse, ignoring them. A second consideration is the unit of analysis. Thus far, it has almost exclusively been considered as the individual in isolation. However, sociocultural theory suggests it is the individual engaged in meaningful activity with more competent others. We need to look beyond the individual and to consider a unit such as "the individual in interaction with others in a particular sociocultural context." Finally, this framework indicates the need for an emic perspective–what is the understanding of the person in the setting we are observing in the course of everyday activity? As an example, Edgerton (1967), using ethnographic methods, was able to gain a unique perspective on the worldview of recently released institutionalized patients. We have almost none of this type of information on multicultural groups.

In sum, there is a pressing need for information on social and cultural-historical processes involved in learning in both formal and informal contexts. New research strategies need to be integrated with the powerful existing tools to provide a more complete picture of individuals and their communities. A major issue for the field will be to incorporate these challenges as it attempts to deal with the dual issues of increasing diversity and of calls for reform and restructuring. The type of framework adopted will provide the foundation for deciding what questions are important to ask; what methods are appropriate to use; and how to interpret and make sense of the results. Although traditional special education models are powerful, and have provided extensive and important empirical findings, they have limitations in the sense that they describe only a piece of the world. As the current restructuring movement gains momentum, and as special education is pushed to become less and less isolated, it can be expected that even more pressure will be exerted to scrutinize the knowledge base and theoretical assumptions of the field. As special education confronts research issues in the next decade and as these issues relate to multicultural persons, it seems that research tools and paradigmatically based beliefs and assumptions will need broadening beyond that which has been relied upon in the past.

REFERENCES

Arter, J.A., & Jenkins, J.R. (1979). Differential diagnostic-prescriptive teaching: A critical appraisal. *Review of Educational Research, 49,* 517–555.

Artiles, A.J., & Trent, S.C. (1994). Overrepresentation of minority students in special education: A continuing debate. *The Journal of Special Education, 27,* 410–437.

Artiles, A.J., Aguirrre-Munoz, Z., & Abedi, J. (1998). Predicting placement in learning disabilities programs: Do predictors vary by ethnic group? *Exceptional Children, 64,* 543–559.

Azmitia, M., Cooper, C.R., Garcia, E.E., & Dunbar, N. (1996). The ecology of family guidance in low-income Mexican-American and European-American families. *Social Development, 5,* 1–23.

Belmont, J.M. (1989). Cognitive strategies and strategic learning: The socio-instructional approach. *American Psychology, 44,* 142–148.

Bercovici, S. (1983). *Barriers to normalization.* Baltimore, MD: University Park Press.

Bogdan, R., & Lutfiyya, Z.M. (1992). Standing on its own: Qualitative research in special education. In W. Stainback & S. Stainback (Eds.), *Controversial issues confronting special education: Divergent perspectives* (pp. 243–252). Needham Heights, MA: Allyn and Bacon.

Bogdan, R., & Taylor, S. (1982). *Inside out.* Toronto, Ontario: University of Toronto Press.

Borkowski, J.G., & Day, J.D. (1987). *Cognition in special children: Comparative approaches to retardation, learning disabilities, and giftedness.* Norwood, NJ.: Ablex.

Bruininks, R., Meyers, C., Sigford, B., & Lakin, K. (Eds.). (1981). *Deinstitutionalization and community adjustment of mentally retarded people.* Washington, DC: The American Association on Mental Retardation.

Bruner, J.S. (1984). Vygotsky's zone of proximal development: The hidden agenda. In B. Rogoff & J.V. Wertsch (Eds.), *Children's learning in the zone of proximal development* (pp. 93–97). San Francisco, CA: Jossey-Bass.

Byrnes, J.P. (1996). *Cognitive development and learning in instructional contexts*. Needham Heights, MA: Allyn &Bacon..

Capra, F. (1983). *The turning point*. New York: Simon & Schuster.

Chinn, P.C., & Hughes, S. (1987). Representation of minority students in special education classes. *Remedial and Special Education, 8* (4), 41–46.

Danforth, S. (1997). On what basis hope: Modern progress and postmodern alternatives. *Mental Retardation, 35* (2), 93–106.

Edgerton, R. (1967). *The cloak of competence*. Berkeley, CA: University of California Press.

Edgerton, R. (1984). *Lives in process*. Washington, DC: American Association on Mental Deficiency.

Edgerton, R., & Bercovici, S.M. (1986). The cloak of competence–years later. *American Journal of Mental Deficiency, 80,* 485–490.

Ferguson, D. (1987). *Curriculum decision making for students with severe handicaps: Policy and practice*. New York: Teacher's College Press.

Fischer, K.W., & Bullock, D. (1984). Cognitive development in school-aged children: Conclusions and new directions. In W. A. Collins (Ed.), *Development during middle childhood: The years from six to twelve* (pp. 70–146). Washington, DC: National Academy Press.

Forman, E.A., Minick, N., & Stone, C.A. (1993). *Contexts for learning: Sociocultural dynamics in children's development*. New York: Oxford University Press.

Gallimore, R., Tharp, R. & Rueda, R. (1989). The social context of cognitive functioning in the lives of special education students. In D.A. Sugden (Ed.), *Cognitive approaches in Special Education* (pp. 51–82). London, Britain: Falmer Press.

Goldenberg, C., & Gallimore, R. (1991). Local knowledge, research knowledge, and educational change: A case study of first-grade Spanish reading improvement. *Educational Researcher, 20* (8), 2–14.

Graham, S., & Harris, K.R. (1996). Self-regulation and strategy instruction for students who find writing and learning challenging. In C.M. Levy & S. Ransdell (Eds.), *The science of writing: Theories, methods, individual differences and applications* (pp. 347–360). Mahwah, NJ: Lawrence Erlbaum.

Greenfield, P.M. (1984). A theory of the teacher in the learning activities of everyday life. In B. Rogoff & J. Lave (Eds.), *Everyday cognition: Its development in social contexts* (pp. 117–138). Cambridge, MA: Harvard University Press.

Greeno, J.G. (1989). A perspective on thinking. *American Psychologist, 44,* 134–141.

Harry, B. (1992). Making sense of disability: Low-income, Puerto Rican parents' theories of the problem. *Exceptional Children, 59* (1), 27–40.

Heshusius, L. (1982). At the heart of the advocacy dilemma: A mechanistic world view. *Exceptional Children, 49* (l), 6–11.

Heshusius, L. (1984). Why would they and I want to do it? A phenomenological-theoretical view of special education. *Learning Disability Quarterly, 7,* 363–368.

Heshusius, L. (1989). The Newtonian mechanistic paradigm, special education, and contours of alternatives: An overview. *Journal of Learning Disabilities, 22,* 403–415.

Iano, R.P. (1992). Role of interpretation in the human sciences with some applications to education. In W. Stainback & S. Stainback (Eds.), *Controversial issues confronting special education: Divergent perspectives* (pp. 323–333). Needham Heights, MA: Allyn & Bacon.

Kameenui, E.J., Jitendra, A.K., Asha, K., & Darch, C.B. (1995). Direct instruction reading as a contronym and eonomine. *Reading and Writing Quarterly: Overcoming Learning Difficulties, 11* (1), 3–17.

Kavale, K.A., & Forness, S.R. (1985). *The science of learning disabilities*. San Diego, CA: College Hill Press.

Keogh, B., Gallimore, R., & Weisner, T. (1997). A sociocultural perspective on learning and learning disabilities. *Learning Disabilities Research and Practice, 12,* 107–113.

Labov, W. (1972). *Language in the inner city: Studies in the Black English vernacular*. Philadelphia, PA: University of Pennsylvania Press.

Lajoie, S.P. (1991). Reality testing for cognitive strategy research. *Educational Researcher, 20* (3), 30–33.

Lipsky, D.K., & Gartner, A. (1992). Achieving full inclusion: Placing the student at the center of educational reform. In W. Stainback & S. Stainback (Eds.), *Controversial issues confronting special education: Divergent perspectives* (pp. 3–12). Needham Heights, MA: Allyn & Bacon.

Marozas, D.S., & May, D.C. (1988). *Issues and practices in special education.* New York: Longman.

McEachin, J.J., Smith, T., & Lovaas, T. (1993). Long-term outcome for children with autism who received early intensive behavioral treatment. *American Journal on Mental Retardation, 97,* 359–372.

Mehan, H., Hertwick, A., & Miehls, J.L. (1986). *Handicapping the handicapped: Decision making in students' educational careers.* Stanford, CA: Stanford University Press.

Mercer, J.R. (1973). *Labeling the mentally retarded.* Berkeley: University of California Press.

Miller-Jones, D. (1989). Culture and testing. *American Psychologist, 44* (2), 360–366.

Minick, N. (1987). Implications of Vygotsky's theories for dynamic assessment. In C.S. Lidz (Ed.), *Dynamic assessment: An interactional approach to evaluating learning potential* (pp. 116–140). New York: Gilford Press.

Moll, L.C. (1990). *Vygotsky and education: instructional implications and applications of sociohistorical psychology.* Cambridge, England: Cambridge University Press.

Moll, L.C., Amanti, C., Neff, D., & Gonzalez, N. (1992). Funds of knowledge for teaching: Using a qualitative approach to connect homes and classrooms. *Theory Into Practice, 16* (2), 132–141.

Murray-Seegert, C. (1989). *Nasty girls, thugs, thing and humans like us.* Baltimore, MD: Paul Brookes.

Ochs, E. (1982). Talking to children in western Samoa. *Language in Society, 11,* 77–104.

Poplin, M.S. (1988). The reductionistic fallacy in learning disabilities: Replicating the past by reducing the present. *Journal of Learning Disabilities, 27,* 389–400.

Poplin, M.S., & Stone, S. (1992). Paradigm shifts in instructional strategies: From reductionism to Holistic/Constructivism. In W. Stainback & S. Stainback (Eds.), *Controversial issues confronting special education: Divergent perspectives* (pp. 153–180). Needham Heights, MA: Allyn & Bacon.

Price-Williams, D., & Gallimore, R. (1980). The cultural perspective. In D. Price-Williams & R. Gallimore (Eds.), *Advances in Special Education* (Vol. 2, pp. 165–192). Greenwich, CT: JAI Press.

Rogoff, B. (1982). Integrating context and cognitive development. In M.E. & A.L. Brown (Eds.), *Advances in developmental psychology* (Vol. 2, pp.125–170). Hillsdale, NJ: Lawrence Erlbaum.

Rogoff, B. (1991). Social interaction as apprenticeship in thinking: Guidance and participation in spatial planning. In L.B. Resnick, J.M. Levine, & S. Teasley (Eds.), *Perspectives on socially shared cognition* (pp. 349–364). Washington, DC: American Psychological Association.

Rogoff, B. (1994). Developing understanding of the idea of communities of learners. *Mind, Culture, and Activity, 1,* 209–229.

Rogoff, B. (1995). Observing sociocultural activity on three planes: Participatory appropriation, guided participation, and apprenticeship. In J.V. Wertsch, P. Del Rio & A. Alvarez (Eds.), *Sociocultural studies of mind* (pp. 139–164). Cambridge, England: Cambridge University Press.

Rogoff, B., & Lave, J. (1984). *Everyday cognition: Its development in social contexts.* Cambridge, MA: Harvard University Press.

Rogoff, B., Baker-Sennett, J., Lacasa, P., & Goldsmith, D. (1995). Development through participation in sociocultural activity. In J. Goodnow, P. Miller, & F. Kessel (Eds.), *Cultural practices as contexts for development* (pp. 45–65). San Francisco, CA: Jossey-Bass.

Rueda, R., & Garcia, E. (1996). Teachers' perspectives on literacy assessment and instruction with language minority students: A comparative review. *The Elementary School Journal, 96,* 311–332.

Rueda, R., & MacGillivray, L. (1999). *Interest and engagement as a function of community and task in high-risk children.* Final Report. Ann Arbor, MI: University of Michigan: Center for the Improvement of Early Reading Achievement (CIERA).

Scarcella, R., & Chin, K. (1993). *Literacy practices in two Korean-American communities* (Research Report No. 8.). Washington, DC: Center for Applied Linguistics and the National Center for Research on Cultural Diversity and Second Language Learning.

Shannon, S.M., & Hakuta, K. (1990). Challenges for Limited English Proficient students and the schools. In M.C. Wang, M.C. Reynolds, & H.J. Walberg (Eds.), *Handbook of special education: Research and practice* (pp. 215–233). New York: Pergamon Press.

Skrtic, T.M. (1988). The crisis in special education knowledge. In E.L. Meyen & T.M. Skrtic (Eds.), *Exceptional children and youth: An introduction* (3rd ed.) (pp. 415–448). Denver, CO: Love.

Stainback, S., & Stainback, W. (1984). Broadening the research perspective in special education. *Exceptional Children, 80* (5), 400–408.

Stainback, W., & Stainback, S. (1989). Using qualitative data collection procedures to investigate supported education issues. *Journal of the Association for Persons with Severe Handicaps, 14,* 271–277.

Taylor, S., & Bogdan, R. (1984). *Introduction to qualitative research methods: The search for meaning* (2nd ed.). New York: Wiley.

Tharp, R.G. (1997). *From at-risk to excellence: Research, theory, and principles for practice.* Santa Cruz, CA: Center for Research on Education, Diversity, and Excellence.

Tharp, R.G. (1982). The effective instruction of comprehension: Results and description of the Kamehameha early education program. *Reading Research Quarterly, 17,* 503–527.

Tharp, R.G., & Gallimore, R. (1988). *Rousing minds to life: Teaching, learning and schooling in social context.* New York: Cambridge University Press.

Tharp, R.G., Dalton, S., & Yamauchi, L.A. (1994). Principles for culturally compatible Native American education. *Journal of Navajo Education, 11* (3), 21–27.

Tharp, R.G., Jordan, C., Speidel, G.E., Au, K.H., Klein, T.W., Calkins, R.P., Sloat, K.C.M., &

Gallimore, R. (1984). Product and process in applied developmental research: Education and the children of a minority. In M.E. Lamb, A.L. Brown, & B. Rogoff (Eds.), *Advances in developmental psychology* (Vol. 3, pp. 91–144). Hillsdale, NJ: Lawrence Erlbaum.

Trueba, H.T. (1983). Adjustment problems of Mexican and Mexican-American students: An anthropological study. *Learning Disability Quarterly, 6,* 395–415.

Vogt, L.A., Jordan, C., & Tharp, R.G. (1992). Explaining school failure, producing school success: Two cases. In E. Jacob & C. Jordan (Eds.), *Minority education: Anthropological perspectives* (pp. 43–66). Norwood, NJ: Ablex.

Vygotsky, L.S. (1978). *Mind in society: The development of higher psychological processes.* Cambridge, MA: Harvard University Press.

Warren, B., & Roseberry, A. (1995). Equity in the future tense: Redefining relationships among teachers, students and sciences in linguistic minority classrooms. In W. Secada, E. Fennema, & L. Adajian (Eds.), *New directions for equity in mathematics education* (pp. 290–326). New York: Cambridge University Press.

Wertsch, J.V. (1985a). *Culture, communication, and cognition: Vygotskian perspectives.* Cambridge, MA: Harvard University Press.

Wertsch, J.V. (1985b). *Vygotsky and the social formation of mind.* Cambridge, MA: Harvard University Press.

Yamauchi, L.A. (1993). *Visions of the ideal Zuni classroom: Multiple perspectives on Native American education.* Unpublished Doctoral Dissertation, University of Hawaii, Honolulu.

Zetlin, A.B., & Hosseini, A. (1989). Six post-school case studies of mildly learning handicapped young adults. *Exceptional Children, 55,* 405–411.

AUTHORS' NOTES

Partial support for the preparation of this work was provided to the first author under the Educational Research and Development Centers Program, PR/Award No. R305R-7004, the Center for the Improvement of Early Reading Achievement (CIERA) as administered by the Office of Educational Research and Improvement, U.S. Department of Education (USDOE). However, the comments do not necessarily represent the positions or policies of the U.S. Department of Education and endorsement by the Federal Government should be assumed.

Chapter 5

LEARNING PROBLEMS OR LEARNING DISABILITIES OF MULTICULTURAL LEARNERS: CONTEMPORARY PERSPECTIVES

CHERYL A. UTLEY AND FESTUS E. OBIAKOR

A myriad of legislative mandates to reform and restructure special education practices has been promulgated to benefit all students despite their racial, cultural, and socioeconomic backgrounds. For example, the 1964 Civil Rights Act, and the 1994 Goal 2000 Educate America Act have been well-meaning societal efforts to assist all students in maximizing their full potential. Ironically, these legislative efforts appear to have had little or no effect on the traditional Eurocentric educational system. For all practical purposes, this traditional system has resisted meaningful modifications to accommodate multicultural learners.

The institution of the 1997 Individuals with Disabilities Education Act (IDEA '97, P.L. 105-17) elucidated many fundamental concepts of special education. The public was reassured that multicultural students would receive (a) unbiased identification and nondiscriminatory assessment procedures, (b) placement in the least restrictive environment, (c) confidentiality of information, (d) parental consent, (e) procedural safeguards, and (f) individualized educational programming. The general consensus was that old mistakes would be remedied. Today, the old troublesome debates continue to rage and two critical questions seem to surface: What general and special education reform and restructuring programs will best meet the needs of multicultural learners who are at-risk of misidentification, misassessment, mislabeling, and misinstruction? Can real progress be made in special education without at least modifying the entrenched culture of traditional Eurocentric educational pedagogy?

The field of learning disabilities is one aspect of special education where issues of definition, identification, appropriate assessment, and instructional practices continue to be heavily debated. Over the past ten years, the category of learning disabilities (LD) has changed its definition and identification parameters to incorporate a significant number of students with low intelligence, underachievers, and students who are low achievers. Distinguishing the child with true learning disabilities from the underachiever and low achiever has become very challenging. In addition, leaders in the field have proposed that there are generalized characteristics which are representative of many individuals identified as having a mild intellectual, learning, or behavioral disability (Henley, Ramsey, & Algozzine, 1993; Kavale & Forness, 1998; MacMillan, Gresham, & Bocian, 1998; MacMillan & Reschly, 1997). More recently, Kavale and Forness described the school population of students with LD when they wrote:

> The LD category has thus become a catch-all classification with little substantive foundation. Research demonstrating a decline in IQ [intelligent quotient] scores and the increasing recognition of social/emotional deficits among students with LD reveals a fundamental change in the nature of LD caused by incorporating students who would previously have been designated mentally retarded (MR) or emotionally/behaviorally disordered (E/BD). Thus, LD covers not only students experiencing specific academic difficulties but also those who possess learning problems with an overlay of lowered intellectual ability or mild behavior problems. When combined with this perception that LD is a "better," less stigmatizing, and more acceptable classification, the desire for LD, rather than MR or E/BD, designation becomes irresistible and the political climate appears quite willing to accommodate this desire. (p. 250)

The current state of affairs reveals that multicultural learners are still confronted with multidimensional problems because schools are not structured to serve their interests and the interests of students from low-income backgrounds or students whose first language is not English (Sleeter & Hartney, 1992). In other words, multicultural students are at-risk in relation to disability status because schools are not well-prepared to deal with differences in learning behavior, culture, and language either separately or in combination. We believe that general and special educators must recognize the important role of cultural, linguistic, and environmental influences on children's learning problems. Therefore, they must acknowledge different approaches to understanding LD and incorporate this knowledge base in assessment and intervention efforts in teaching multicultural learners. In this chapter, we discuss (a) traditional conceptual frameworks used in identifying the etiology, causes, and types of learning disabilities; and (b) present problems associated with the use of traditional standardized, norm-referenced assessment procedures in classifying students with LD. Additionally, we differentiate between the concepts of learning problems and learning disabilities in multicultural learners by examining three contemporary paradigms: sociocultural, transactional, and ecobehavioral analysis. Also, we review critical issues in assessment and examine alternative assessment procedures for maximizing the capabilities of multicultural learners.

TRADITIONAL CONCEPTUAL MODELS FOR UNDERSTANDING LEARNING DISABILITIES

Within the field of special education, the category of LD is a relatively new field of exceptionality. Hardman, Drew, and Egan (1999) described the field of LD as controversial, confused, and polarized because it represents the largest single service delivery program for exceptional children in the United States. They agreed that "in the past, many children now identified as having specific LD would have been labeled as remedial readers, remedial learners, or emotionally disturbed or even mentally retarded, if they received any special attention or additional instructional support at all" (p. 173). The percentage of students with LD, ages six to 21, comprised 51 percent of all students identified in 1995–1996, and tend to be served primarily in general education and resource room classrooms (U.S. Department of Education, 1998). Many professionals agree that the controversial issues about this specific disability category are rooted in variations of the definition and identification procedures.

Overview of Definitions of LD

There are many definitions by professional organizations and state education agencies. However, P. L. 94-142, included in its legislation, the definition recommended by the National Advisory Committee on Handicapped Children (NACHC). In 1967, the NACHC developed the following definition of LD:

> *Specific learning disability* means a disorder in one or more of the basic psychological processes involved in understanding or in using language, spoken or written, which manifest itself in an imperfect ability to listen, think, speak, read, write, spell, or to do mathematical calculations. The term includes such conditions as perceptual handicaps, brain injury, minimal brain dysfunction, dyslexia, and developmental aphasia. The term does not include children who have learning problems which are primarily the result of visual, hearing or motor handicaps, of mental retardation, of emotional disturbance, or of environmental, cultural, or economic disadvantage. (National Joint Committee on Learning Disabilities, 1994, p. 4)

Over the years, this definition has been misinterpreted and has resulted in a number of issues and problems affecting the delivery of services to students, namely:

1. Persons with LD are a homogeneous group of individuals and require a standard approach to assessment and intervention.
2. This definition does not recognize the developmental nature of LD and that this disability may occur in early childhood and continue into adult life. The definition limits the applicability of this term to individuals 0–21 years of age.
3. The etiology of LD is not stated clearly in the definition. Disorders represented by the term LD should be viewed as intrinsic to the individual and that the basis of the disorder is presumed to be due to central nervous system dysfunction.
4. The wording of the "exclusion clause" in the definition lends itself to the misinterpretation that individuals with LD cannot be multihandicapped, gifted, or be from cultural and linguistic backgrounds.

In 1981, a revised definition of LD was developed by the National Joint Committee on Learning Disabilities (NJCLD) and adopted by the following NJCLD member organizations: American Speech-Language-Hearing Association, Council for Learning Disabilities, Division for Children with Communication Disorders, International Reading Association, Learning Disabilities Association, National Association of School Psychologists, and Orton Dyslexia Society. The revised definition recommended by NJCLD (1994) reads as follows:

> *Learning disabilities* is a general term that refers to a heterogeneous group of disorders manifested by significant difficulties in the acquisition and use of listening, speaking, reading, writing,

reasoning, or mathematical abilities. These disorders are intrinsic to the individual, presumed to be due to central nervous dysfunction, and may occur across the life span. Problems in self-regulatory behaviors, social perception, and social interaction may exist with learning disabilities but do not by themselves constitute a learning disability. Although learning disabilities may occur concomitantly with other handicapping conditions (for example, sensory impairments, mental retardation, serious emotional disturbance), or with extrinsic influences (such as cultural differences, insufficient or inappropriate instruction), they are not the result of those conditions or influences. (p. 65)

This revised definition of LD addressed a number of issues resulting from the earlier definition. These issues included (a) recognizing "LD"as a general term consisting of a heterogeneous group of disorders with difficulties in listening, speaking, reading, writing, reasoning, and mathematical abilities; (b) identifying different subgroups of individuals with LD; (c) using a multifaceted approach in the identification, assessment, instruction, remediation, and management in programs for persons with LD; (d) identifying problems in the ability of individuals with LD to self-regulate their behaviors and to engage in appropriate social interactions; (e) recognizing the developmental nature of LD continuing from early childhood throughout adult life; (f) understanding that the etiology of LD may be due to several reasons such as a central nervous system dysfunction, failure to learn because of inherently altered processes of acquiring and using information, poor instruction, and the interaction between the learner and his/her social and cultural environment; and (g) recognizing that LD may occur within the different disability categories as well as different cultural and linguistic groups.

There are popular scientific terminologies that explicate learning disabilities (e.g., agraphia and dysgraphia, alexia and dyslexia, acalculia and dyscalculia, and aphasia and dysphasia) (Hallahan, Kauffman, & Lloyd, 1999; Raymond, 2000). To a large measure, these terminologies represent the 3Rs (reading, writing, and arithmetic). According to Faas (1980), more than two decades ago, agraphia is the "inability to recall the kinesthetic patterns required to write words or express oneself in writing" (p. 399), and dysgraphia is the "partial inability to express ideas by means of writing or written symbols; usually associated with being dysfunctional" (p. 403). He defined alexia as the "loss of the ability to read written or printed language" (p. 399), and dyslexia as the "partial inability to read, or understand what one reads, silently or aloud; usually, but not always, associated with brain impairment" (p. 403). He explained acalculia as the "loss of the ability to manipulate arithmetic symbols and perform simple mathematical calculations" (p. 399), and dyscalculia as the "partial loss of the ability to calculate and to manipulate number symbols" (p. 403). Additionally, he defined aphasia as the "loss of the ability to comprehend spoken words in speech, words, or signs" and dysphasia as the "partial inability to comprehend the spoken word (receptive aphasia) and to speak (expressive aphasia), believed to be the result of injury, disease, and maldevelopment of the brain" (p. 403). These explanations make learning disability a perplexing disability, even though it is tied to academic instruction. While learning disability creates classification problems, general and special educators must be cognizant of certain "red flags." For example, students must be identified when they demonstrate (a) linguistic deficits, (b) academic deficits, (c) neuropsychological deficits, and (d) social behavior deficits (Blackhurst & Berdine, 1993). But then, general and special educators must be careful that they do not classify students without discovering their specific problems. This is especially important for multicultural learners with school problems.

Traditional Classification Systems for Identifying Causes of Learning Disabilities

Many conceptual frameworks or models have been used to identify the causes of learning disabilities: medical (i.e., neurological, genetic, and biochemical), cognitive-information processing, and achievement-behavioral (Cunningham, 1998; Smith, Price, & Marsh, 1986). From a medical perspective, neuropsychological models attempt to explain certain types of academic failure in terms of damage to specific brain functions. The category of major organic problems includes organic brain damage, brain injury, neurological disabilities, and central processing disorders. Research on the genetic transmission of reading disabilities has demonstrated that approximately 50 percent of all variability in the phonological processes that cause specific reading disabilities can be attributed to genetic factors (Olson, 1997; Torgensen, 1998; Wood, 1997). In addition, brain mapping research has demonstrated that a relationship exists between learning disabilities and subtle abnormalities in parts of the brain that process language (e.g., word-finding problems and identifying 40 segments or phonemes in spoken words) (Manis, 1996).

Biochemical imbalances have been identified as one of the causes of learning disabilities. This category, also referred to as "minor organic problems that are compounded by poor environments" includes maturational lags, vitamin deficiencies, allergic reactions, and sugar or food additives. Biochemical research related to learning disabilities has revealed that there is no scientific evidence linking the nature or extent of this factor on learning and behavior problems in children identified as LD. A cognitive-information processing model taps psychological processes that attempts to understand how individuals with learning disabilities acquire, retain, and interpret information received through the senses. General and special educators attempt to understand how thinking processes operate in order to complete such complex cognitive tasks as summarizing a chapter in a book, solving complex math problems, writing a mystery novel, and comparing and contrasting theories of learning. An achievement-behavioral model is based upon the assumption that academic failure in one or more of academic skill areas is due to inadequate learning environments. This category (without organic problems) includes poor teaching, poor curricula and focused on observable academic behaviors for the purposes of remediation of skill deficits (Berninger & Abbott, 1994; Greenwood, 1996).

Assessment Issues

Given the controversy surrounding the definition of learning disabilities, the question remains as to how to assess individuals with LD accurately. However, embedded within the definition are four major components related to the types of assessment used to document eligibility for services: an ability-achievement discrepancy clause, an emphasis on psychological processes, a central nervous system dysfunction etiology, and an exclusion clause differentiating the category of learning disability from other disability categories. Bender (1995) outlined the components of the LD definition in relation to the types of assessments suggested to document eligibility for services (see Table 5.1). The psychological processes component examines the types of ability deficits (i.e., intelligence, visual perception/motor, auditory perception, and language) that hinder learning. Earlier re-

Table 5.1
COMPONENTS OF THE LD DEFINITION AND ASSESSMENT INSTRUMENTS
USED FOR ELIGIBILITY FOR SPECIAL EDUCATION SERVICES

Components of the LD Definition	Assessment Instruments
Psychological Processing Problems	
IQ assessment	Wechsler Intelligence Scale for Children-III
Subtest scatter/verbal	Stanford Binet
Performance deficit/subtest grouping	Woodcock Johnson
	Kaufman Assessment Battery for Children
Visual perception/visual motor	Bender Visual Motor Gestalt Test
	Woodcock Johnson
	Visual Motor Integration
	Wechsler Intelligence Scale for Children-III
Auditory perception/language	Test of Language Development
	Woodcock Johnson
	Wechsler Intelligence Scale for Children-III
	Peabody Picture Vocabulary Test
Discrepancy	
Intraindividual differences	Wechsler Intelligence Scale for Children-III
	Woodcock Johnson
Ability-achievement discrepancy	Wechsler Intelligence Scale for Children-III
	Woodcock Johnson
	Peabody Individual Achievement Test-Revised
	Test of Written Language
	Kaufman Assessment Battery for Children
Exclusionary Clause	
Mental retardation	IQ tests
Behavioral disorders	Class observation
	Teacher ratings of behavior
	Teacher ratings of behavior
Mental disability	Physician's examination
Cultural/environmental/economic	Examination of school records
	History of speech improvements

Source: Bender, W. N. (1995). *Learning disabilities: Characteristics, identification, and teaching strategies* (3rd ed.). Needham Heights, MA: Allyn & Bacon.

search studies conducted by McKinney and Feagans (1981), Kaufman (1981), and Galagan (1985) showed that the assessment of basic psychological processes is not possible psychometrically due to the low reliability and validity of the majority of instruments. In addition, eligibility for special education services was not based on the assessment of psychological processes in children with LD. Rather, children were diagnosed primarily in terms of a discrepancy between measures of intelligence and measures of achievement in specific areas of learning. The discrepancy component is based on the observation that children with LD score below their age-mates in overall achievement and perform below expectations on their measured potential. A major discrepancy between the verbal IQ and performance IQ on an intelligence test has been used as an indicator of a potential learning disability. Two types of discrepancies (i.e., intraindividual and ability-achievement) and four major types of ability-achievement discrepancy formulas (e.g., standard score calculations, regression-score tables, discrepancies between grade placement and achievement, and discrepancies based upon achievement, intelligence, and grade placement) have been derived using ability-achievement discrepancy calculations to document deficits in the psychological processes and academic achievement.

Lyon (1996) remarked that "there is no universally accepted test, test battery or standard for identifying children with LD. While a discrepancy between intelligence quotient (IQ) and achievement has been widely accepted criteria for the identification of learning disabilities and still serves as the driving clinical force in the diagnosis of learning disabilities, there is considerable variation in how the discrepancy is derived and quantified" (p. 58–59).The operationalization of the exclusionary clause has been very difficult because assessment methods distinguishing characteristics describing the categories of MR, EBD, and medically based conditions have been vague with very little information available. In addition, the use of assessment methods for differentiating children from different cultural backgrounds, who have been raised in poor and low-socioeconomic (SES) environments, and students who are low achieving continues to be problematic. Criteria for assessing individuals with LD must be clear, observable, measurable, and agreed upon by professionals in the field. However, the federal definition of learning disabilities does not specify criteria or guidelines for distinguishing the disability category of learning disability from other disability categories nor does it stipulate that students with learning disabilities cannot demonstrate deficits related to other categories of disability.

CONTEMPORARY PERSPECTIVES ON LEARNING DISABILITIES

In this section, we review the concept of learning disabilities from three contemporary perspectives: sociocultural, transactional, and ecobehavioral analysis. The sociocultural perspective addresses issues of definition, classification, and student characteristics, and the interplay of these variables in relation to cultural and linguistic contextual factors. The transactional model is based upon the interaction of person and environmental factors and their effects on the learning outcomes of children. The ecobehavioral analysis approach examines classroom and instructional factors that are "temporarily and spatially removed from the behavior of individuals, including those in the broader social, professional, institutional, and cultural contexts" (Morris & Midgley, 1990, p. 11).

Sociocultural Perspective

The social construction of learning disabilities has been a topic of great debate by scholars (e.g., Kavale & Forness, 1998). As mentioned earlier, scholars espoused the philosophy that the field of learning disabilities originated from a medical model focused on the neurobiological and organic bases of learning problems, while other researchers asserted that learning disabilities is a construct of society and that its etiology and history directly correlate with the changing standards in education as a result of societal beliefs (Sleeter, 1986). Kavale and Forness noted that the process of identifying children as learning disabled is primarily a function of ideology that is "shaped by the social forces in the environment" (p. 254). In order to promote change in the system of classifying individuals with LD, researchers and educators need to understand how society, culture, and language influence education and the learning process.

Recently, Keogh, Gallimore, and Weisner (1997) suggested that researchers and educators examine a sociocultural perspective on learning disabilities in order to understand learning problems within multicultural groups. They further remarked that without a "sociocultural perspective it is impossible to separate the learning competencies and problems of individual children from the contexts in which they live and function" (p. 107). Garcia, Wilkinson, and Ortiz (1997) explained that "difficulties experienced by educators in distinguishing cultural or linguistic differences from disabilities can be partially explained by their unfamiliarity with cultural, linguistic, and other influences on student learning, attitudes, and behavior" (p. 631). Other researchers (e.g., Cole & Means, 1981; Gindis, 1995; Rogoff & Chavajay, 1995; Wertsch, 1991) have observed that sociocultural activities and how people think, remember, reason, and express their ideas influence the intellectual and social development of children. Also, in non-Western cultures, learning is affected by neurological and biological factors in addition to sociocultural contexts in which children live. As a result, the development of learning disabilities in children is inherently related to children's sociocultural experiences and biological and organic factors. Therefore, an examination of a sociocultural perspective has implications for defining the construct of learning disabilities and the assessment and intervention of multicultural learners.

In the U.S. society, literacy, education, and performance on standardized assessment tests are highly valued. If educational performance is used as an index of learning, then *one* critical component of defining learning disabilities is the normative performance of individuals in reading, mathematics, science, and other academic areas. However, in non-Western countries where intelligence test scores or performance on cognitive ability tests have little relevance to survival in society, educational competencies related to literacy are not emphasized and relevant to being productive members in society. In examining a sociocultural perspective, Keogh et al. (1997) questioned many assumptions about the concepts of ethnicity and culture in defining and classifying individuals with learning disabilities. These issues are focused on (a) using ethnicity as a marker variable for culture in the classification of persons as learning disabled; (b) defining cultural characteristics of multicultural groups with precision and accuracy; (c) identifying characteristics of subgroups and of individuals within specific ethnic and cultural groups; and (d) distinguishing ethnicity and culture by acknowledging variations in three different ways: among ethnically defined groups, within ethnically defined groups, and among individuals within ethnic and cultural groups. In differentiating aspects of culture and ethnicity, Longstreet (1978) and Byrd (1995) outlined five areas that must be taken into consideration: (a) intellectual modes (e.g., ethnic influence and emphasis on the development of intellectual abilities and approaches to learning); (b) verbal communication (e.g., categories describing oral language, verbal communications, and sociability); (c) nonverbal communication (e.g., gestures and body language, personal space, and touching); (d) orientation modes (e.g., body and spatial orientations, and attention modes); and (e) social value patterns.

As researchers and educators become aware of the influence of sociocultural factors on children's learning, they must conceptually and empirically validate the concepts of ethnicity and culture. Bos and Fletcher (1997) concurred with Keogh et al. (1997) and proposed adopting a sociocultural framework that includes student and contextual variables to reflect the dynamic interactions between learner and context.

Student variables include (a) sex, (b) age, (c) race and ethnicity, (d) socioeconomic status, (e) geographic region and locale, (f) grade level, (g) intelligence, (h) academic achievement, (i) time in special education placement, (j) level of special education placement, (k) primary and secondary language (proficiency), (l) cultural background, and (m) linguistic background. Contextual variables involve multiple layers of contexts within students' formal education programs. Three broad categories of contextual variables include community and family context (e.g., family and community cultures), district and school context (e.g., educational philosophy, size, location, curriculum, student achievement levels), and classroom context (e.g., size of class, students' and teachers' characteristics, curriculum, and culturally relevant pedagogy). In order to further understand multicultural learners, general and special educators must recognize, examine, incorporate, and document student variables within the broader sociocultural context. Earlier, Adler (1993) remarked that:

> Each year children from ghettos, barrios, and reservations enter our public schools with substantial handicaps in education readiness related to their culturally different heritages. These children bring with them unique experiences and differences in standards and values. They possess a culture of their own with different learning and living styles and different speech and language patterns. The manifestations both of speech and language patterns and of other cultural styles that differ significantly from those used by members of the dominant culture, however, are frequently rejected not only by their peers, but also, too frequently, by their instructors. (p. 15)

Massey (1996) further stated that the "study of language development cannot be separated from the study of the cultural dictates of the community that the language user is a part of. As important, the relation between primary language, the cultural experiences that shape the use of that language, and success with later societal demands (e.g., school) cannot be ignored" (p. 290).

Apparently, educational and research priorities must differentiate between students with learning disabilities, communication and language disorders, and developmental delay from multicultural learners who have normal language skills (Craig, 1996; Hallahan, Kauffman, & Lloyd, 1999; Hamayan & Damico, 1991; Ortiz, 1997; Seymour & Bland, 1991; Taylor, 1986). Smith (1998) noted that "many children who are multiculturally and linguistically diverse enter school with sociolinguistic conventions that are mismatched with the content and structure of the school curriculum, thereby causing confusion and misunderstanding" (p. 106). Unfortunately, the cultural mismatch between the school's expectations and students' cultural, linguistic, and socioeconomic backgrounds has resulted in serious problems in teacher attitudes, classification, assessment, and educational services provided to multicultural learners who speak African American English (AAE) (also referred to Black English and Ebonics) and Limited English Proficient (LEP) learners. For example, Seymour, Champion, and Jackson (1995, p. 98) reported that teacher attitudes about child AAE speakers were that (a) they equated a lack of school vocabulary with an overall lack of vocabulary; (b) they characterized children as not speaking in sentences or in complete thoughts and as strange grammatical constructions; (c) they complained that children's mispronounciations resulted from failure to use their tongue, teeth, and lips; and (d) they thought children did not know the correct English sounds. Earlier, Kretschmer (1991) argued that there has been an overlap between the classification of LEP students as "language-learning disabled," "language disordered," or "learning disabled." When language profiles show difficulties in conversational interaction and oral communication, LEP students are typically labelled "language disordered," while profiles of LEP students that show evidence of academic problems result in the classification of students as "learning disabled." Some of the problems manifested by students with language-learning disabilities, as identified by Roseberry-McKibbin (1995), include (a) problems in learning language at a normal rate; (b) a family history of learning difficulties; (c) maturational lag in development than siblings; (d) communication difficulties (e.g., poor sequencing skills, lack of organization, structure, and sequence in spoken and written language, poor conversational and social

interaction skills); (e) difficulties in using precise vocabulary words (e.g., noting and producing homophones and synonyms); (f) using concrete word meanings, deictic spatial terms, and syntax; and (g) using appropriate grammar, generating simple sentences.

Collier (1998) described several characteristics of multicultural learners who are suspected of having learning disabilities. Four areas characteristic of specific learning disabilities are under the categories of (a) achievement below ability, (b) receptive expressive language deficits, (c) behavior problems, and (d) problems associated with cognitive learning strategies. A detailed analysis of the sociocultural characteristics of African American, Asian/Pacific Islander, Hispanic, and American Indian students with LD and their instructional implications are described in Table 5.2 (see Table 5.2).

Transactional Perspective

The transactional model is based upon the reciprocal interplay of person and his/her environment and this encompasses a comprehensive perspective to understanding learning problems in children (Adelman & Taylor, 1993). Theoretically, a transactional model describes person and environmental factors as the "locus of cause" of learning problems on a continuum of 3 types of learning problems: Type I, Type II, and Type III (see Figure 5.1). As illustrated in Figure 5.1, Type I learning problems are caused by factors in the environment. These factors include (a) insufficient stimuli, (b) excessive stimuli, and (c) intrusive and hostile stimuli. Type II learning problems are caused by factors in the environment and person. These factors include (a) physiological insult, (b) genetic anomaly, (c) cognitive activity and affective states experienced by self as deviant, (d) physical characteristics shaping contact with the environment and/or experienced by

self as deviant, and (e) deviant actions of the individual. Type III learning problems are caused by factors in the person (e.g., learning disabilities). These factors include (a) severe to moderate personal vulnerabilities and environmental defects and differences, (b) minor personal vulnerabilities not accommodated by the situation, and (c) minor environmental defects and differences not accommodated by the individual (see Table 5.3). In studying the learning problems of children, Adelman and Taylor suggested that learning is a function of the transactions between the learner and classroom environment. They also acknowledged that:

A learner brings to a learning situation both capacities and attitudes that have been accumulated over time, and current states of being and behavior. These transact with each other and also with the learning environment. The learning environment consists of not only of instructional processes and content, but also the

Table 5.2

LEARNING DISABILITY CHARACTERISTICS OF MULTICULTURAL LEARNERS

African American

Characteristics of Exceptionality	Sociocultural Characteristics	Instructional Implications
• Achievement below ability	• Ability often misjudged because of test bias	• Students with learning disabilities may be misdiagnosed as mentally retarded
• Difficult perceiving and interpreting patterns in language environment (e.g., words, sounds, numbers hyperactive, attention deficit disorders	• Words not spoken with familiar intonation not paid attention to	• Students may appear to have auditory perceptual problems when there is simply a failure to recognize meaning without the cues of dialect
	• Interactive style	• Teacher may view student as hyperactive when he/she interacting normally with peers
	• Boredom can lead to distractibility	

Asian American

• Achievement below ability	• Value placed on high academic achievement, industriousness	• Student may try to compensate for disability by working extra hard, memorizing materials, etc., so as not to bring shame on family
• Difficulty perceiving and interpreting patterns in language environment (e.g., words, sounds, numbers)	• Failure to perceive unfamiliar sounds; or remember words out of context for non-English speaking children	• Teacher should use alternative assessment strategies
• Attention deficit disorders	• Culture values appearances of self-control, but expects emotion.	• Behavior may be a source of shame to parents and self
• Limited level of educational achievement	• Social class and self-esteem determined by level of education	• Teacher needs to assist student with culturally appropriate strategies
		• Teacher will need to assist student with self esteem and guide out of learned helplessness

Table 5.2 (continued)

LEARNING DISABILITY CHARACTERISTICS OF MULTICULTURAL LEARNERS

Hispanic American

Characteristics of Exceptionality	Sociocultural Characteristics	Instructional Implications
• Achievement below ability	• Impact of inadequate disrupted education	• Teacher needs to use appropriate alternative assessment
	• Differences in learning deficiencies	
• Difficulty perceiving and interpreting patterns in language environment (e.g., words, sounds, numbers)	• Disrupted early experiences result in both native language and English differences	• Teacher needs to assist student with a variety of appropriate cognitive learning strategies.
• Hyperactive, attention deficit disorders	• Many English words sound alike to Spanish speakers	• Teacher should assist student in using active-processing, analogy and other cognitive learning strategies related to language development

American Indian

• Achievement below ability	• Impact of inadequate instruction	• Teacher should facilitate cognitive learning strategies
	• Children are taught to observe first and not to act until they are sure of doing it correctly	
• Difficulty perceiving and interpreting patterns in language environment (e.g., words, sounds, number)	• Disrupted by experiences may lead to both native language and English deficiencies	• Teacher needs to learn to separate learning and behavior problems due to difference from disability
• Attention deficit disorders		• Teacher should assist student in using active-processing, analogy, and other cognitive learning strategies related to s selfmonitoring and learning to learn

Source: Adapted from Collier, C. (1998b). *Separating difference from disability: Assessing diverse learners.* Ferndale, WA: Cross-Cultural Developmental Education Services. Adapted from: Nazarro, N.N. (1981). Special problems of exceptional minority children. In J.N. Nazarro (Ed.), Culturally diverse exceptional children in school, Virginia: ERIC 1-12. Adapted from Utley, C.A. (1993). Culturally and linguistically diverse students with mild disabilities. In C.A. Grant (Ed.), *Educating for diversity: An anthology of multicultural voices* (pp. 301–324). Boston, MA: Allyn & Bacon.

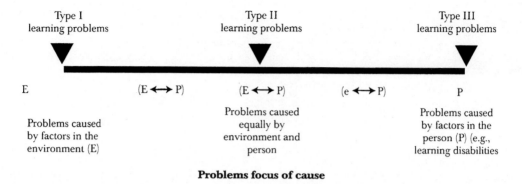

Figure 5.1. A Continuum of Learning Problems Reflecting a Transactional View of the Focus of Primary Instigating Factors.

physical and social context in which instruction takes place. Each part of the environment transact with the others. The outcome of all of these transactions may be positive learning or learning problems. Because the nature of the transactions can vary considerably, so can the outcomes. In general, the types of outcomes can be described as (a) deviant learning (i.e., capacities and attitudes change and expand, but not in desirable ways, (b) disrupted learning (i.e., interference with learning and possibly a decrease in capacities), (c) delayed and arrested learning (i.e., little change in capacities, and (d) enhanced learning (i.e., capacities and attitudes change and expand in desirable ways. (pp. 21–23)

In any school situation, multicultural learners bring characteristics (e.g., race/ethnicity, language, and culture, family, and economic status) to classrooms that differ significantly from monolingual, English-speaking Caucasian learners who have no apparent physical or cognitive disabilities. Gonzalez, Brusca-Vega, and Yawkey (1997) stated that "strong relationships exist between certain characteristics of these students and indicators of school failure, including those between poverty and low reading and math scores, racial and ethnic minority status and high drop-out rates, and disability and under-

or unemployment after graduation. Less attention, unfortunately, has been paid to analyzing relationships between characteristics of the learning environment itself and aspects of school failure. While culturally and linguistically diverse students may have personal characteristics that contribute to a lack of academic progress (e.g., a genuine disability or an unstable home life), they may also be at-risk because characteristics of the school setting are detrimental to the learning process" (pp. 5–6).

By examining transactions between person and environmental factors, researchers and educators become knowledgeable about the influence of sociocultural characteristics of multicultural learners (e.g., cultural values, beliefs, and customs) and how these factors interact within the classroom environment. The transactional model is focused on interactions of the student with the environment as an explanation of academic learning and social development. Environmental variables that influence the learning environment may be broadly categorized as (a) setting and context characteristics (e.g., organizational format, locale and geographic location, and climate), (b) characteristics of the participants (e.g., parent, student, demographics, individual differences

Table 5.3
FACTORS INSTIGATING LEARNING PROBLEMS

Environment (E) (Type I problems)	Person (P) (Type III problems)	Interactions and Transactions Between E and P* (Type II problems)
1. Insufficient stimuli (e.g., prolonged periods in impoverished environments; deprivation of learning opportunities at home or school such as lack of play and practice situations and poor instruction; inadequate diet)	1. Physiological insult (e.g., cerebral trauma, such as accident or stroke; endocrine dysfunctions and chemical imbalances; illness affecting brain or sensory functioning)	1. Severe to moderate personal vulnerabilities and environment defects and differences (e.g., person with extremely slow development in a highly demanding, understaffed classroom, all of which equally and simultaneously instigate the problem)
2. Excessive stimuli (e.g., overly demanding home or school experiences such as overwhelming pressure to active and contradictory expectations)	2. Genetic anomaly (e, g., genes that limit, slow down, or lead to any atypical development)	2. Minor personal vulnerabilities not accommodated by the situation (e.g., person with minimal CNS disorders resulting in auditory perceptual disability enroled in a reading program based on phonics; very active student assigned to classroom that does not tolerate this level of activity)
3. Intrusive and hostile stimuli (e.g., medical practices, especially at birth, leading to physiological impairment; conflict in home or fault child-rearing practices, such as long-standing abuse and rejection migratory family; language used in school is a second language; social prejudices related to race, sex, age, physical characteristics and behavior)	3. Cognitive activity and affective states experienced by self as deviant (e.g., lack of knowledge or skills such as basic cognitive strategies; lack of ability to cope effectively with emotions, such as low self-esteem)	3. Minor environmental defects and differences not accommodated by the individual (e.g., student is in the minority racially or culturally and is not participating in many school activities and class discussions because he or she thinks others may be unreceptive)
	4. Physical characteristics shaping contact with environment and/or experienced by self as deviant (e.g., visual, auditory, or motoric deficits; excessive or reduced sensitivity to stimuli; easily fatigued; factors such as race, sex, age, unusual appearance that produce stereotypical responses)	
	5. Deviant actions of the individual (e.g., performance problems, such as excessive errors in reading and speaking; high or low levels of activity)	

Source: Adelman, H.S., & Taylor, L. (1993). *Learning problems & learning disabilities: Moving forward.* Pacific Grove, CA: Brooks/Cole.

in current motivation and development, and criteria for judging person characteristics), and (c) task-process-outcome characteristics (e.g., quantitative and qualitative features of instruction, types of tasks, and procedural methods, materials, and techniques).

For multicultural learners, the environment consists of the society, community, school, and family and the interactions across these contexts dramatically affects children's abilities and disabilities. Thus, a classroom learning environment can work to habilitate or further debilitate a student's potential to learn (Ruiz, 1995). Garcia et al. (1995) remarked that, "although instruction occurs primarily in a classroom context, other factors beyond that context are important influences on decisions that teachers make during the instructional process. For example, at the societal level, the low performance of language minority students is embedded in the interactions between majority and "minority" groups, which influence educator role definition and the school climate. . . . The societal interaction also influences orientations of language minority students and their families toward education and schooling, thereby affecting the quality of home-school, parent-teacher, and student-teacher interactions" (pp. 444–445).

Ecobehavioral Analysis Model

General and special educators face unique challenges in teaching multicultural learners, some of which include (a) their lack of understanding of how to incorporate language effectively in the classroom, (b) difficulty in designing a classroom where teachers make instructional time challenging for students, (c) teachers' use of native language while teaching a second language, and (d) developing a classroom atmosphere of mutual understanding and accommodation. Over the past years, an emerging knowledge base has developed to address these classroom-based instructional challenges. Two instructional questions appear critical for a general or special educator. How do I design a classroom environment that will optimize learning and student performance in multicultural learners? What are the most crucial instructional variables that are likely to affect student outcomes?

Researchers at the Juniper Gardens Children's Project of the University of Kansas, have adopted an ecobehavioral analysis approach to (a) analyzing a broad range of environmental variables that are temporarily and spatially removed from the behavior of individuals, including those variables that are within environmental, social, and cultural contexts; and (b) evaluating the effectiveness of instruction and interventions in special education and bilingual education settings as a means of addressing classroom contextual factors that affect the student outcomes of multicultural children with and without disabilities. By examining classroom process variables (i.e., the assessment of teacher behavior, student behavior, and contextual variables), students' interactions with the environment (or ecological factors) can be studied to determine if instruction is optimizing or limiting the performance of multicultural learners. Thus, ecobehavioral analysis is a technology for evaluating instructional interventions in relation to program aspects (e.g., instructional environment components, teacher behaviors, and student behaviors) and identifying instructional variables that reliably influence academic and linguistic performance and the design of instructional technology based on this knowledge (Arreaga-Mayer, Carta, & Tapia, 1994).

In research studies with teachers, the concepts of "opportunity to respond" and "student engagement" were identified as important variables that facilitate academic achievement. Opportunity to respond refers to "the need to promote higher rates of academic behavior for all students for longer periods by ensuring that instruction occasioned active academic responding in the classroom" (Greenwood, Hart, Walker, & Risley, 1994, p. 214). More specifically, "opportunity to respond (also referred to as student engagement) can be defined as the interaction between (a) teacher formulated instruction . . . (the materials presented, prompts, questions asked, signals to respond), and (b) its success in establishing the academic responding desired or implied by materials, the subject matter goals of instruction" (Greenwood, Delquadri, & Hall, 1984, p. 64).

Observational instruments have been developed and validated through empirical research studies (Arreaga-Mayer, Tapia, & Carta, 1993; Carta, Greenwood, & Atwater, 1985; Carta, Greenwood, Schulte, Arreaga-Mayer, & Terry, 1987; Greenwood, Carta, Kamps, & Delquadri, 1997; Greenwood & Delquadri, 1988). Emerging from this database are descriptive studies conducted with (a) students with LD (Bulgren & Carta, 1993; Ysseldyke, Christenson, Thurlow, & Bakewell, 1989); (b) at-risk students in urban poverty environments (Greenwood, 1991), and bilingual students with developmental disabilities (Arreaga-Mayer, 1992; Arreaga-Mayer, Carta, & Tapia, 1994) documenting causal relations between achievement, academic responding, and instruction.

Supportive Data

In a review of literature, Bulgren and Carta (1992) examined the amount of academic engaged time students with LD spent in different instructional activities and classroom settings. These settings included general education and self-contained classrooms, consulting-teacher classrooms, and resource rooms. The results showed (a) differences in student engagement for students with LD compared to students without LD; and (b) that students with LD spent more time in individualized structures while students without LD spent more time in whole-group teaching structures. There were no differences in active engagement of students with and without LD in small group structures used across settings.

Over the years, a knowledge base has developed documenting why children living in urban poverty communities are academically delayed as early as kindergarten and first grade (Snow, Burns, & Griffin, 1998). To address questions regarding the causes and solutions to academic delay, learning disability, MR, and school failure in urban poverty classrooms, Greenwood, Carta, and Atwater (1991) remarked that "ecobehavioral analysis offers education a powerful, expanded process measure for the study of the delivery of teaching and its effects on students, including the causes of academic success and failure" (p. 63). Earlier studies of ecobehavioral assessments describing the ecological features of classroom practices in second, third, and fourth grade samples revealed important differences in practices and school achievement levels between at-risk students in low-SES schools compared to students schools in middle-high SES schools (Greenwood, Delquadri, Stanley, Terry, & Hall, 1986). Greenwood et al. (1991) summarized these results as follows:

First, high-SES students received significantly more time per day in subject matter instruction. Second, the ecological structure of instructional programs serving these students differed in terms of multiple qualitative and quantitative factors (e.g., materials used, grouping arrangements, and teachers' behaviors) compared to those received by low-SES students. Third, low-SES students, who were significantly less skilled on academic tests and measured IQ, were also significantly less engaged in academic behaviors ($M_{difference}$ = 11 minutes per day, range = 9–110 minutes of engagement per day) during their daily lessons than were high-SES, higher-skilled students. Fourth, the instructional arrangements employed by teachers of high-SES students covaried with higher levels of students' academic engagement. (p. 66)

These descriptive data provide important evidence that the ecological arrangements of classrooms and the delivery of instructional practices in classrooms can accelerate or decelerate academic responding and engagement and affect the overall rate of academic development, especially in children divergent in SES, achievement levels, and measured intelligence. As illustrated in Figure 5.2, when teachers implement instructional practices (i.e., ecological features of instruction) that promote low levels of academic responding and engagement, then, slower rates of academic growth on weekly test scores are observed. Conversely, when teachers implement instructional practices that promote high levels of academic responding and engagement, then, higher rates of academic growth on weekly test scores are observed (see Figure 5.2). Not along ago, Arreaga-Mayer (1992) conducted a study using *The Ecobehavioral System for the Contextual Recording of Interactional Bilingual Environments* (ESCRIBE) to describe in quantifiable terms assessment, methodological, and instructional variables related to the delivery of services for bilingual students at risk for developmental disabilities. Collectively, the results revealed that (a) the most frequently occurring activities were math (20%), reading (18%), and language arts (16%); (b) English was the most frequently used language of instruction (58%); and (c) the total "active engagement" of students in academic behaviors (44%) was slightly less than one-half of a typical school day.

NON-DISCRIMINATORY ASSESSMENT STANDARDS AND PROCEDURES

The underlying principle of non-discriminatory assessment, as stipulated in IDEA '97 is to provide an unbiased, multifaceted, multidisciplinary and professionally sound evaluation. To a large extent, this ensures that an evaluation process adheres to assessment standards and procedures. The evaluation team must follow specific IDEA standards related to cultural bias and the validation of tests. Turnbull and Turnbull (2000) outlined IDEA standards and procedures relating to the student, cultural bias, test validity, and administration, as follows:

1. Tests and other materials are provided and administered in the student's native language or other mode of communication unless it is not feasible to so [20 U.S.C. § 1414 (b)(3)(A)ii].

2. Tests and other materials that are selected and administered to children with limited English proficiency measure the extent to which the child has a disability and needs special education, rather than measuring the child's English language skills [34 C.F.R. 300.532(a)(2)].

3. The team must ensure that all standardized tests [20 U.S.C. § 1414 (b)(3)(B)] have been validated for the specific purpose for which they are used.

4. Tests and other materials are administered by trained and knowledgeable personnel; and are administered in accordance with any instruction from the test's producers. (p. 140)

Not long ago, Turnbull, Turnbull, Shank, and Leal (1999) noted that nondiscriminatory as-

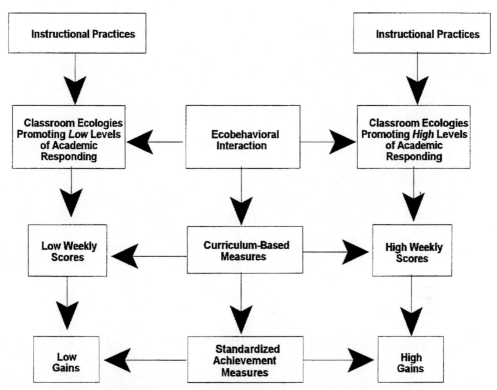

Figure 5.2. Hypothesized Relationships Between Instruction, Its Ecobehavioral Effects and Rate of Growth in Curriculum-Based and Standardized Measures of Academic Achievement.
Source: Greenwood, C.R., Carta, J.J., & Atwater, J. (1991). Ecobehavioral analysis in the classroom: Review and implications. *Journal of Behavioral Education 1* (1), 59–77.

sessment helps to (a) determine whether or not a student has a disability; (b) determine the nature of the disability and the special education and related services that he/she should receive; and (c) identify specific special education and related services in order to develop an appropriate, individualized educational plan (IEP) for a student with a disability. Within non-discriminatory assessment standards and procedures are (a) breadth of the assessment, (b) administration of the assessment procedures, (c) timing of the assessment, parental notice and consent, and (d) interpretation of the assessment information are included as components. Although the provisions of IDEA '97 are to guarantee an ap-

propriate education for students with disabilities, problems of misclassification, misidentification, and misassessment continue to exist when multicultural learners are evaluated using conventional, traditional psychometric testing procedures (Obiakor, 1994, 1999).

One major criticism regarding the use of standardized and norm-referenced assessments is that they may be culturally biased against poor, multicultural children as compared to majority children because of differences in culture, language, values, and experiential background, and therefore may not be appropriate tools with which to assess the intelligence of multicultural learners. The arguments against the use of standardized, norm-referenced assessments with multicultural learners have centered around claims of test bias from a variety of sources (Grossman, 1995; Karr & Schwenn, 1999; Midgette, 1995; Obiakor, 1994, 1999; Samuda, Feuerstein, Kaufman, Lewis, & Sternberg, 1998; Sandoval, Frisby, Gelsinger, Scheuneman, & Grenier, 1998). According to Midgette (1995), the potential sources of test bias may be summarized as follows:

1. Intelligence tests have a cultural bias. Standardized intelligence and aptitude tests have a strong White, Anglo-Saxon, and middle class bias.
2. National norms are inappropriate for minorities. National norms based primarily on White, middle class, and Anglo-Saxon samples are inappropriate for use with ethnically and racially different children.
3. Ethnically and racially different children are generally less privileged and sophisticated in test-taking skills. For example, African American children are handicapped in taking tests because of (a) deficiencies in motivation, test practice, and reading; (b) failure to appreciate the aspects of the test situation;

and (c) limited exposure to White, middle class, and Anglo-Saxon culture.
4. The fact that most examiners are White has the effect of depressing the scores of ethnically and racially different children. Rapport and communication problems exist between White examiners and ethnically and racially different children. These problems interfere with the children's ability to respond to the test items. (p. 12)

In conducting assessments with multicultural learners, psychologists must be knowledgeable about the weaknesses of traditional standardized, norm-referenced testing procedures. For assessments to be fair and non-discriminatory for multicultural learners and differentiate between multicultural learners with learning problems from learning disabilities, psychologists and practitioners must (a) be sensitive to their cultural and linguistic backgrounds; (b) provide assessment situations with suitable testing procedures; and (c) provide culturally appropriate descriptions and interpretations of the learners' skills. Recommendations for psychologists when testing multicultural learners are presented in Table 5. 4.

Alternative Assessment Procedures

One very important issue that must be resolved in the assessment of multicultural learners is the utility of standardized, norm-referenced assessments in developing effective, educational programs. Although norm-referenced assessments are used for purposes of classification and diagnosis, they are not prescriptive and do not (a) identify a child's *functional* needs (e.g., cognitive processing, and adaptive motivation); (b) recognize obstacles that may or may not interfere with their learning ability; and (c) develop instructional practices designed to minimize

the discrepancy between performance and learning potential. In addition, general and special educators need assessment procedures that allow them to document student progress as it related to curricular objectives and instructional methods and guide instructional decision making (Rivera & Smith, 1997). Therefore, it is imperative that school psychologists and practitioners employ alternative assessments (in addition to using multiple assessment methods) related to instruction for multicultural learners with learning problems and learning disabilities.

Table 5.4
RECOMMENDED ASSESSMENT PRACTICES

Awareness and Sensitivity

1. The assessor must learn as much as possible about the client's culture. This knowledge needs to include the values and beliefs of the culture.
2. The assessor must learn about the educational process in the client's culture. In particular, one needs to understand the methods of assessment the client has experienced.
3. One needs to become aware of any stereotypes that are personally held regarding the client and to take steps to minimize the impact of person biases when testing.
4. The tester must recognize that language issues significantly affect the accuracy of assessment. Using translators or client advocates may improve the fairness of the assessment process when working with limited-English-proficiency clients.
5. The assessor, either formally or informally, needs to assess the client's level of acculturation. The greater the acculturation, the greater the feasibility of comparing the client's score to the published norms of a test.
6. The assessor must be aware of professional and ethical considerations when working with a diverse client. These guidelines are discussed in the last chapter of this book.

Appropriate Assessment Situation and Procedures

1. Assessors must understand that single-score assessment is inappropriate and select only tests that provide a comprehensive picture of the client's abilities. Information should be sampled from a number of areas in order to demonstrate the client's potential keeping in mind that comprehensive assessment involves triangulation of testing, observation, and archival analysis in addition to a client's educational, social, and cultural history.
2. The examiner needs to use tests to power rather than speed, as many culturally diverse clients are not accustomed to highly speeded tests. This procedure assures their performance is based on their ability, rather than their inability to finish the test.
3. An assessor should use both verbally oriented or non-verbal tests. By using both formats, one can promote a more balanced and, therefore, fair assessment process.
4. Culturally diverse clients exhibit more anxiety during a test situation than mainstream clients, due to the unfamiliarity of the task. To lessen the impact of this anxiety, the assessor must take time, albeit longer than usual, to establish rapport and describe any assessment expectations to the client.
5. Determination of the client's language dominance must be done prior to testing. If the client's dominant language is not English, the tester must consider supplementing the assessment with non-verbal instruments. For this purpose, the Raven matrices or other culture-reduced tests are recommend.
6. If the client's dominant language is not English, the assessor needs to use a test translated or adapted into the client's language, in conjunction with a nonverbal instrument. It is incumbent upon the assessor to evaluate translated and adapted instruments.
7. The assessor needs to ensure that the examinee understands the test directions. This allows the tester to evaluate the viability of using a particular test.
8. An assessor should view non-verbal tests as culture-reduced, rather than culture-free, instruments. The structure of the items and strategies to obtain correct responses have a cultural component and therefore, remain culturally loaded.
9. The SOMPA provides useful adaptive behavior indicators and sociocultural information, but it is not to be used to make clinical or psychoeducational decisions on culturally diverse children because the validity of the ELP score is questionable.

Table 5.4. Continued

10. Testing-of-limits procedures must be implemented whenever feasible. These procedure needs to be used with individual tests of ability, as well as with group measures of aptitude. The client's ability to improve test performance when procedures are modified will help an assessor gain a clearer picture of a client's functioning.
11. Assessor must become skilled a test-train-test via mediation methods. Using a formal dynamic assessment procedure, such as the LPAD, helps the tester identify a client's learning style and ability to profit from tutorial guidance. This shift from product-oriented to process-oriented assessment allows the client to demonstrate learning potential within the context of his or her social and cultural background.

Culturally Appropriate Interpretations

1. The assessor cannot assume that the rules of test interpretation are applicable to the test results of a minority client in the same way they are applied to the test results of a middle-class, mainstream clients. Testers need to be flexible when judging cultural factors that are clearly affecting a client's test performance.
2. Acknowledge of the client's level of acculturation and the effect this level might have on the test result is required. If a lack of acculturation is suspected to have had a role in determining the client's performance, it is necessary to reassess the client when the level acculturation has increased.
3. The assessor needs to use comprehensive assessment data, testing-of-limits results, and other dynamic assessment intervention methods. A qualitative description is needed to outline the strengths and possible deficits of the client.
4. When interpreting scores, the tester must take into account that many traditional tests have not been normed adequately with various cultural groups. They need to be wary of the fact that some examinees are not well-represented by national test norms and make interpretations accordingly.
5. When making recommendations, the examiner must focus on describing strengths rather than weaknesses, potential rather than deficiencies.
6. Recommendations must link assessment to culturally appropriate interventions. These interventions need to focus on helping clients develop their potential.
7. One must never use a single test score to categorize and place a client into a program. A comprehensive approach must always be used.
8. Test results need to eliminate prejudice, racism, and inequities, rather than promote inadequate treatment of culturally diverse clients by providing accurate meaningful scores linked to appropriate intervention strategies.

Source: Lewis, J.E. (1998). Nontraditional uses of traditional aptitude tests. In R.J. Samuda, R. Feuerstein, A.S. Kaufman, J.E. Lewis, & R.J. Sternberg (Eds.), *Advances in cross-cultural assessment* (pp. 218–241). Thousand Oaks, CA: Sage.

Performance-Based Assessment

Performance-based assessment refers to "assessment relying on real-world tasks and often involving evaluation of performance through rubrics or benchmarks that identify characteristics of exemplary performance, acceptable performance, or unacceptable performance" (Rueda, 1977, p. 12). Performance assessment includes a variety of measures such as essays, portfolios, projects, and videotapes and is designed to assess higher order thinking, complex learning, authenticity, and active responses of students.

Under this broad category of assessment, general and special educators have become familiar with how to use portfolio assessment with other traditional methods of assessment and evaluation procedures. Rivera and Smith (1997) noted that portfolio assessment can be "used to examine student progress as it related to curricular objectives and instructional methods, to focus more on process than just on product, to measure more directly student academic achievement and classroom learning, and to assist teachers in evaluating the effectiveness of their instruction" (p. 183). The contents of the portfolio may consist of measures of (a) behavioral and adaptive functioning, (b) academic and literacy growth, (c) strategic learning and self regulation; and (d) cultural and language work samples (Karr & Schwenn, 1999; Swicegood, 1994). When portfolios are used with multicultural learners, the assessments should include completed products, learning problems of students (e.g., reading and math errors), and the problem-solving strategies used to analyze students' learning problems (e.g., auditory and visual aids). Portfolio samples of work may be acquired when different instructional strategies are implemented in the classroom. For example, when peer tutoring and cooperative arrangements are implemented, general and special educators would maintain anecdotal notes, work samples, and reports concerning the learning problems and academic progress of students. The portfolio assessment process should assist general and special educators to make adaptations, accommodations, and decisions about student performance. The frequent analysis and monitoring of student progress (e.g., fluency in oral reading) ensures that multicultural learners profit from instruction.

With regard to multicultural learners, portfolio assessment has several advantages (Rueda, 1997; Rueda & Garcia, 1997). Portfolio assessment can be used as (a) a support for primary language instruction; (b) a documentation for funds of knowledge; (c) a documentation of the nature of activities that students are involved in and the different learning conditions of instruction; (d) support

for documenting learning processes in children as they engage in meaningful activities and projects; and (e) documentation of student outcomes. In view of problems encountered by multicultural learners, general and special educators are responsible for using the psychological information obtained from standardized assessments to prepare individualized educational plan (IEPs). It is, therefore, important that they (a) address cultural and language characteristics of multicultural learners; (b) understand the influence of culture and environmental risk factors on learning; (c) become knowledgeable about how multicultural learners acquire strategies for learning; (d) understand patterns of thinking and learning that are reinforced by the family and community; and (e) pay attention to learning and communication styles of multicultural learners. In addition, general and special educators must have realistic expectations and use the "Teach-Reteach Modification Model" that encourages the continuous retesting and reteaching of concepts for multicultural students' learning mastery (Obiakor, 1994).

An important benefit of performance-based assessment is the link between portfolios and IEPs. Portfolios assist general and special educators in preparing and monitoring student academic progress in IEPs. In developing IEPs for multicultural learners, special considerations must be taken into account (Garcia & Malkin, 1993). The selection of IEP goals and objectives and instructional strategies must (a) accommodate the student's current instructional and cognitive levels of performance, (b) focus on the development of basic and higher cognitive skills; and (c) be responsive to cultural and linguistic variables. The instructional strategies described in IEPs must (a) take into consideration whether or not multicultural students with learning disabilities have had exposure to the curriculum; and (b) provide accommodations for learning, literacy, language development, and communication and motivational styles. Thus, performance-based assessment can be used as an alternative assessment procedure that can be used in conjunction with or as an alternative to standardized, norm-referenced assessment procedures.

CONCLUSION

In this chapter, we discussed (a) issues related to the definition and classification of individuals as LD, and (b) reviewed traditional conceptual frameworks used in identifying the etiology and causes of learning disabilities, and (c) presented problems associated with the use of traditional assessment procedures in classifying students with LD. In addition, we examined the concept of learning disabilities from three contemporary perspectives: sociocultural, transactional, and ecobehavioral analysis. Each contemporary paradigm has significant implications for assessing multicultural learners. The sociocultural perspective examines the distinct roles of culture and language and the interaction of these variables to differentiate learning problems and learning disabilities in multicultural learners. The transactional model emphasizes transactions between person and environmental risk factors along a continuum of describing Type I, Type II, and Type III learners The ecobehavioral analysis approach examines how the delivery of instruction affects the progress and rate of academic growth of multicultural learners.

We strongly believe general and special educators must continue to challenge themselves and implement non-discriminatory assessment procedures in order to ensure that multicultural learners are not misidentified, misassessed, misdiagnosed, miscategorized, misplaced, and misinstructed. We must be willing to collaboratively move beyond using traditional psychometric testing and shift our paradigm thinking focus on performance-based assessment models linked to instruction, learning mastery, student outcomes, and IEPs in order to maximize the learning potential of multicultural learners. The fields of general and special education can never be deemed reformed unless multicultural learners are properly assessed using alternative measurement models in relation to instruction in inclusive classroom settings.

REFERENCES

Adelman, H.S. & Taylor, L. (1993). *Learning problems & learning disabilities: Moving forward.* Pacific Grove, CA: Brooks/Cole.

Adler, S. (1993). *Multicultural communication skills in the classroom.* Needham Heights, MA: Allyn & Bacon.

Arreaga-Mayer, C. (1992). Ecobehavioral assessment of exceptional culturally and linguistically diverse students: Evaluating effective bilingual special education programs. *Proceeding of the Third National Research Symposium on Limited English Proficient Student Issues: Focus on middle and high school issues.* Washington, DC: Office of Bilingual Education and Minority Languages Affairs.

Arreaga-Mayer, C., Carta, J.J., & Tapia, Y. (1994). *Ecobehavioral assessment: A new methodology for evaluating instruction for exceptional culturally and linguistically diverse students.* (Monograph 1). Reston, VA: Council for Exceptional Children, Division of Diverse Exceptional Learner.

Bender, W.N. (1995). *Learning disabilities: Characteristics, identification, and teaching strategies* (2nd ed.). Needham Heights, MA: Allyn & Bacon.

Berninger, V.W., & Abbott, R.D. (1994). Redefining learning disabilities: Moving beyond aptitude-achievement discrepancies to failure to respond to validated treatment protocols. In G.R. Lyon (Ed.), *Frames of reference for the assessment of learning disabilities: New views on measurement issues* (pp. 163–184). Baltimore, MD: Brookes.

Blackhurst, A.E., & Berdine, W.H. (1993). *An introduction to special education* (3rd ed.). New York: Harper Collins.

Bos, C.S., & Fletcher, T.V. (1997). Sociocultural considerations in learning disabilities inclusion research: Knowledge gaps and future directions. *Learning Disabilities Research & Practice, 12*(2), 92–99.

Bulgren, J.A., & Carta, J.J. (1993). Examining the instructional contexts of students with learning disabilities. *Exceptional Children, 59*(3), 182–191.

Byrd, H.B. (1995). Curricular and pedagogical procedures for African American learners with academic and cognitive disabilities. In B.A. Ford, F.E. Obiakor, & J.M. Patton (Eds.), *Effective education of African American learners: New perspectives* (pp. 123–150). Austin, TX: Pro-Ed.

Carta, J.J., Greenwood, C.R., & Atwater, J. (1985). *Ecobehavioral system for the complex assessment of preschool environments: ESCAPE.* Kansas City, KS: Juniper Gardens Children's Project, Bureau of Child Research, University of Kansas.

Carta, J.J., Greenwood, C.R., Schulte, D., Arreaga-Mayer, C., & Terry, B. (1987). *Code for the Instructional Structure and Student Academic Response: Mainstream Version (MS-CISSAR).* Kansas City, KS: Juniper Gardens Children's Project, Bureau of Child Research, University of Kansas.

Civil Rights Act of 1964, P.L. 88-352, 78 Stat. 241.

Cole, M., & Means, B. (1981). *Comparative studies of how people think: An introduction.* Cambridge, MA: Harvard University Press.

Collier, C. (1988a). *Assessing minority students with learning and behavior problems.* Lindale, TX: Hamilton Publications.

Collier, C. (1998a). Developing instructional plans and curriculum for bilingual special education students. In L.M. Baca, & H.T. Cervantes (Eds.), *The bilingual special education interface* (3rd ed.) (pp. 28–35). Columbus, OH: Merrill.

Collier, C. (1998b). *Separating difference from disability: Assessing diverse learners.* Ferndale, WA: Cross-Cultural Developmental Education Services.

Craig, H.K. (1996). The challenges of conducting language research with African American children. In A.G. Kamhi, K.E. Pollack, & J.L. Harris (Eds.), *Communication development and disorders in African American children: Research, assessment, and intervention* (pp. 1–18). Baltimore, MD: Paul H. Brookes.

Cunningham, J.L. (1998). Learning disabilities. In J. Sandoval, C.L. Frisby, K.F. Geisinger, J.D. Scheueman, & J.R. Grenier (Eds.), *Test interpretation and diversity: Achieving equity in assessment* (pp. 317–347). Washington, DC: American Psychological Association.

Delquadri, J.C., Greenwood, C.R., Stretton, K., & Hall, R.V. (1983). The peer tutoring spelling game: A classroom procedure for increasing opportunity to respond and spelling performance. *Education and Treatment of Children, 6,* 225–239.

Faas, L.A. (1980). *Children with learning problems: A handbook for teachers.* Boston, MA: Houghton Mifflin.

Feuerstein, R., Falik, L.H., & Feuerstein, R. The learning potential assessment device: An alternative approach to the assessment of learning potential. In R.J. Samuda, R. Feuerstein, A.S. Kaufman, J.E. Lewis, & R.J. Sternberg (Eds.), *Advances in cross-cultural assessment* (pp. 100–161). Thousand Oaks, CA: SAGE.

Galagan, J.E. (1985). Psychoeducational testing: Turn out the lights, the party's over. *Exceptional Children, 52,* 244–265.

Garcia, S.B., & Dominguez, L. (1997). Cultural contexts that influence learning and academic performance. *Academic Difficulties, 6*(3), 621–655.

Garcia, S.B., & Malkin, D.H. (1993). Toward defining programs and services for culturally and linguistically diverse learners in special education. *Teaching Exceptional Children, 27*(1), 52–58.

Garcia, S.B., & Ortiz, A.A. (1988). *Preventing inappropriate referrals of language minority students to special education.* (New Focus, No. 5). Washington, DC: National Clearinghouse for Bilingual Education.

Garcia, S.B., Wilkinson, C.Y., & Ortiz, A.A. (1995). Enhancing achievement for language minority students: Classroom, school, and family contexts. *Education and Urban Society, 27,* 441–462.

Gindis, B. (1995). The social implication of disability: Vygotsky's paradigm for special education. *Educational Psychologist, 30*(2), 77–81.

Gonzalez, V., Brusca-Vega, R., & Yawkey, T. (1997). *Assessment and instruction of culturally and linguistically diverse students with or at-risk of learning problems: From research to practice.* Needham Heights, MA: Allyn & Bacon.

Gottlieb, J., & Weinberg, S. (1999). Comparison of students referred and not referred for special education. *The Elementary School Journal, 99*(3), 187–199.

Greenwood, C.R. (1991). A longitudinal analysis of time to learn, engagement, and academic achievement in urban versus suburban schools. *Exceptional Children, 57,* 521–535.

Greenwood, C.R. (1996). The case for performance-based instructional models. *School Psychology Quarterly, 11,* 283–296.

Greenwood, C.R., Carta, J.J., & Atwater, J.(1991). Ecobehavioral analysis in the classroom. *Journal of Behavioral Education, 1,* 59–77.

Greenwood, C.R., Carta, J.J., Kamps, D., & Delquadri, J.C. (1997). Ecobehavioral Assessment Systems Software *(EBASS Version 3.0): Practitioner's manual.* Kansas City, KS: Juniper Gardens Children's Project, University of Kansas.

Greenwood, C.R., & Delquadri, J.C. (1988). Code for instructional structure and student academic response: CISSAR: In M. Hersen & A.S. Bellack (Eds.), *Dictionary of behavioral assessment techniques* (pp. 120–122). New York: Pergamon.

Greenwood, C.R., Delquadri, J.C., & Hall, V.R. (1984). Opportunity to respond and student academic performance. In W. Heward, T. Heron, D. Hill, & J. Trap-Porter (Eds.), *Behavior analysis in education* (pp. 58–88). Columbus, OH: Merrill.

Greenwood, C.R., Delquadri, J.C., & Hall, V.R. (1989). Longitudinal effects of classwide peer tutoring. *Journal of Educational Psychology, 81,* 371–383.

Greenwood, C.R., Hart, B., Walker, D., & Risley, T. (1994). The opportunity to respond and academic performance revisited: A behavioral theory of developmental retardation and its prevention. In R. Gardner III, D.M. Sainato, J.O. Cooper, T.E. Heron, W.L. Heward, J. Eshleman, & T.A. Grossi (Eds.), *Behavior analysis in education: Focus on measurably superior instruction* (pp. 213–224). Pacific Grove, CA: Brooks/Cole.

Grossman, H. (1995). *Teaching in a diverse society.* Needham Heights, MA: Allyn & Bacon.

Hallahan, D.P., Kauffman, J.M., & Lloyd, J.W. (1999). *Introduction to learning disabilities.* Needham Heights, MA: Allyn & Bacon.

Hamayan, E.V., & Damico, J.S. (1991). *Limiting bias in the assessment of bilingual students.* Austin, TX: Pro-Ed.

Hardman, M.L., Drew, C.J., & Egan, M.W. (1999). *Human exceptionality: Society, school and family* (6th ed). Needham Heights, MA: Allyn & Bacon.

Henley, M., Ramsey, R.S., & Algozzine, R. (1993). *Characteristics of and strategies for teaching students with mild disabilities.* Needham Heights, MA: Allyn & Bacon.

Individual with Disabilities Education Act of 1990, P.L. 104-476, 104 Stat. 1103.

Individuals with Disabilities Education Act, 20 U.S.C. § 1400 et seq. 1997.

Karr, S., & Schwenn, J.O. (1999). Multimethod of assessment of multicultural learners. In F.E. Obiakor, J.O. Schwenn, & A.F. Rotatori (Eds.), *Multicultural education for learners with exceptionalities* (Vol. 12, pp. 105–120). Stamford, CT: JAI Press.

Kaufman, A.S. (1981). Assessment: The Wechsler scales and learning disabilities. *Journal of Learning Disabilities, 16,* 616–620.

Kavale, K. A., & Forness, S. R. (1998). The politics of learning disabilities. *Learning Disability Quarterly, 21*(4), 245–275.

Kea, C.D. & Utley, C.A. (1998). To teach me is to know me. *The Journal of Special Education, 32*(1), 44–47.

Keogh, B. K., Gallimore, R., & Weisner, T. (1997). A sociocultural perspective on learning and learning disabilities. *Learning Disabilities Research & Practice, 12*(2), 107–113.

Kretschmer, R.E. (1991). Exceptionality and the Limited English Proficient Student: Historical and practical contexts. In E.V. Hamayan & J.S. Damico (Eds.), *Limiting bias in the assessment of bilingual students* (pp. 1–38). Austin, TX: Pro-Ed.

Lewis, J.E.(1998). Nontraditional uses of traditional aptitude tests. In R.J. Samuda, R. Feuerstein, A.S. Kaufman, J.E. Lewis, & R.J. Sternberg (Eds.), *Advances in cross-cultural assessment* (pp. 218–239). Thousand Oaks, CA: Sage.

Longstreet. W. (1978). *Aspects of ethnicity.* New York: Teachers College Press.

Lyon, G.R. (1996). Learning disabilities. *The Future of Children: Special Education for Students with Disabilities, 6*(1), 54–76.

MacMillan, D.L., Gresham, F.M., & Bocian, K.M. (1998). Curing mental retardation and causing learning disabilities: Consequences of using various WISC-III IQ's to estimate aptitude of Hispanic students. *Journal of Psychoeducational Assessment, 19*(1), 36–54.

MacMillan, D.L., & Reschly, D.J. (1997). Issues of definition and classification. In W.E. MacLean, Jr. (Ed.), *Ellis' handbook of mental deficiency, psychological theory, and research* (3rd ed.) (pp. 47–74). Mahwah, NJ: Erlbaum.

Manis, F.R. (1996). Current trends in dyslexia research. In B.J. Cratty & R.L. Goldman (Eds.), *Learning disabilities: Contemporary viewpoints* (pp. 27–42). Amsterdam, The Netherlands: Harwood Academic.

Massey, A. (1996). Cultural influences on language: Implications for assessing African American children. In A.G. Kamhi, K.E. Pollack, & J.L. Harris (Eds.), *Communication development and disorders in African American children: Research, assessment, and intervention* (pp. 285–306). Baltimore, MD: Paul H. Brookes.

McKinney, J.D., & Feagans, L. (1981). The pattern of exceptionality across domains in learning disabled children. *Journal of Applied Developmental Psychology, 1,* 313–328.

Midgette, T.E. (1995). Assessment of African American exceptional learners: New strategies and perspectives. In B.A. Ford, F.E. Obiakor, & J.M. Patton (Eds.), *Effective education of African American exceptional learners: New perspectives* (pp.3–26). Austin, TX: Pro-Ed.

Moll, L.C. (1992). Bilingual classroom studies and community analysis: Some recent trends. *Educational Researcher, 21*(2), 20–24.

Morris, E.K., & Midgley, B.D. (1990). Some historical and conceptual foundations of ecobehavioral analysis. In S.R. Schroeder (Ed.), *Ecobehavioral analysis and developmental disabilities: The twenty-first century* (pp. 1–32). New York: Springer-Verlag.

National Joint Committee on Learning Disabilities (1994). *Collective perspectives on issues affecting learning disabilities: Position papers and statements.* Austin, TX: Author.

Obiakor, F.E. (1994). *The eight-step multicultural approach: Learning and teaching with a smile.* Dubuque, IA: Kendall/Hunt.

Obiakor, F.E. (1999). Teacher expectations of minority exceptional learners: Impact on "accuracy" of self-concepts. *Exceptional Children, 66,* 39–53.

Obiakor, F.E., Schwenn, J.O., & Rotatori, A.F. (1999). *Advances in special education: Multicultural education for learners with exceptionalities* (Vol. 12). Stamford, CT: JAI Press.

Obiakor, F.E., & Utley, C.A. (1997). Rethinking preservice preparation for teaches in the learning disabilities field: Workable multicultural strategies. *Learning Disabilities Research & Practice, 12,* 100–106.

Olson, R. (1997, May). *The genetics of LD: Twin studies.* Paper presented at the Conference of Progress and Promise in Research and Education for Individuals with Learning Disabilities, Washington, DC.

Ortiz, A.A. (1997). Learning disabilities occurring concomitantly with linguistic differences. *Journal of Learning Disabilities, 30*(3), 321–342.

Raymond, E.B. (2000). *Learners with mild disabilities: A characteristics approach.* Needham Heights, MA: Allyn & Bacon.

Rehabilitation Act of 1973, P. L. 93-112, 87 Stat. 355.

Rivera, D., & Smith, D. (1997). *Teaching students with learning and behavior problems* (3rd ed.). Needham Heights, MA: Allyn & Bacon.

Rogers-Warren, A. (1984). Ecobehavioral analysis. *Education and Treatment of Children, 7,* 283–303.

Rogoff, B., & Chavajay, P. (1995). What's become of research on the cultural bases of cognitive development? *American Psychologist, 50,* 859–877.

Roseberry-McKibbin, C. (1995). *Multicultural students with special language needs: Practical strategies for assessment and intervention.* Oceanside, CA: Academic Communication Associates.

Rueda, R. (1997). Changing the context of assessment: The move to portfolios and authentic assessment. In A.J. Artiles & G. Zamora-Duran (Eds.), *Reducing the disproportionate representation of culturally diverse students in special and gifted education* (pp. 7–26). Reston, VA: The Council for Exceptional Children.

Rueda, R., & Garcia, E. (1997). Do portfolios make a difference for diverse students? The influence of type of data on making instructional decisions. *Learning Disabilities Research & Practice, 12*(2), 114–122.

Ruiz, N.T. (1995). The social construction of ability and disability: I. Profile types of Latino children identified as language learning disabled. *Journal of Learning Disabilities, 28*(8), 476–490.

Samuda, R.J. (1998). *Psychological testing of American minorities: Issues and consequences* (2nd ed.). Thousand Oaks, CA: SAGE.

Samuda, R.J., Feuerstein, R., Kaufman, A.S., Lewis, J.E., & Sternberg, R.J. (1998). *Advances in cross-cultural assessment.* Thousand Oaks, CA: SAGE.

Sandoval, J., Frisby, C.L., Gelsinger, K.F., Scheuneman, J.D., & Grenier, J.R. (1998). *Test interpretation and diversity: Achieving equity in assessment.* Washington, DC: American Psychological Association.

Seymour, H.N., & Bland, L. (1991). A minority perspective in the diagnosing of child language disorders. *Clinics in Communication Disorders 1*(1), 39–50.

Seymour, H.N., Champion, T., & Jackson, J. (1995). The language of African American learners: Effective assessment and instructional programming for children with special needs. In B.A. Ford, F.E. Obiakor, & J.M. Patton (Eds.), *Effective education of African American exceptional learners: New perspectives* (pp. 89–121). Austin, TX: Pro-Ed.

Sleeter, C.E. (1986). Learning disabilities: The social construction of a special education category. *Exceptional Children, 53*(1), 46–54.

Sleeter, C.E., & Hartney, C. (1992). Involving special educators in challenging injustice in education. In C. Diaz (Ed.), *Multicultural education for the 21st century* (pp. 150–165). Washington, DC: National Education Association.

Smith, C.R. (1998). *Learning disabilities: The interaction of learner, task, and setting.* Needham Heights, MA: Allyn & Bacon.

Smith, E.C., Price, B.J., & Marsh, G.E. (1986). *Mildly handicapped children and adults.* St. Paul, MN: West.

Snow, C., Burns, M.S., & Griffin, P. (1998). *Preventing reading difficulties in young children.* Washington, DC: National Research Council.

Stanley, S.O. & Greenwood, C.R. (1981). *CISSAR: Code for Instructional Structure and Student Academic Response: Observer's Manual.* Kansas City, KS: Juniper Gardens Children's Project, Bureau of Child Research.

Swicegood, P. (1994). Portfolio-based assessment practices. *Interventions in School and Clinic, 30*(1), 6–15.

Taylor, O.L. (1986). *Nature of communication disorders in culturally and linguistically diverse populations.* Austin, TX: Pro-Ed.

Thurlow, M.L., Graden, J., Greener, J., & Ysseldyke, J.E. (1983). LD and non-LD students' opportunities to learn. *Learning Disability Quarterly, 6,* 172–183.

Tomasi, S., & Weinberg, S.L. (1999). Classifying children as LD: An analysis of current practice in an urban setting. *Learning Disability Quarterly, 22*(1), 31–42.

Torgensen, J.K. (1998). Learning disabilities: An historical and conceptual overview. In B.Y.L. Wong (Ed.), *Learning about learning disabilities* (pp. 3–34). San Diego, CA: Academic Press.

Turnbull, H.R., & Turnbull, A.P. (2000). *Free appropriate public education: The law and children with disabilities* (6th ed.). Denver, CO: Love.

Turnbull, H.R., Turnbull, A., Shank, M., & Leal, D. (1999). *Exceptional lives: Special education in today's schools* (2nd ed). Upper Saddle River, NJ: Merrill.

U.S. Department of Education (1994). *The Goals 2000: Educate America Act.* Washington, DC: Author.

U.S. Department of Education. (1998). *To assure the free appropriate public education of all children with disabilities. Twentieth annual report to Congress on the implementation of the Individuals with Disabilities Act.* Washington, DC: U.S. Government Printing Office.

Utley, C.A., Haywood, H.C., & Masters, J.C. (1992). Policy implications of psychological assessment of minority children. In H.C. Haywood & D. Tzuriel (Eds.), *Interactive assessment* (pp. 445–469). New York: Springer-Verlag.

Wertsch, J.V. (1991). *Voices of the mind: A sociocultural approach to mediated action.* Cambridge, MA: Harvard University Press.

Ysseldyke, J.E., Christenson, S.L., Thurlow, M.L., & Bakewell, D. (1987). *Instructional tasks used by mentally retarded, learning disabled, emotionally disturbed and nonhandicapped elementary students* (Research Report No. 2). Minneapolis, MN: Instructional Alternatives Project, University of Minnesota.

Ysseldyke, J.E., Thurlow, M.L., Mecklenburg, C., & Graden, J. (1984). Opportunity to learn for regular and special education students during reading instruction. *Remedial and Special Education, 5,* 29–37.

Chapter 6

SCHOOL REFORM AND MULTICULTURAL LEARNERS WITH EMOTIONAL AND BEHAVIORAL DISORDERS: ISSUES, CHALLENGES, AND SOLUTIONS

SUE ANN KLINE, RICHARD L. SIMPSON, DALE P. BLESZ, BRENDA SMITH MYLES, AND WILLIAM J. CARTER, JR.

The launching of Sputnik in October 1957 by the Russians was an important historical event that forced the U.S. government to initiate numerous reforms in educational programs (Obiakor, Algozzine, & Schwenn, 1995). While various reforms have been proposed to deal with the shortcomings and inequities that characterized U.S. schools in *A Nation at Risk* (National Commission on Excellence in Education, 1983), most have fallen short of their anticipated outcomes. These early reform movements consistently focused on general education students with little regard to students with disabilities, including those with emotional and behavioral difficulties (Shaw, Biklen, Conlon, Dunn, Kramer, & DeRoma-Wagner, 1990). Earlier, the National Council on Disability (1989) observed that for the most part school reform efforts have not been directed toward addressing the special challenges faced by students with disabilities. Indeed, Ysseldyke, Algozzine and Thurlow (1992) observed that "in a summary of the 'education reform decade,' there was not a single mention of students with disabilities or even special education" (p. 140).

Significant changes have occurred in the last two decades as current reform movements in general education do involve special education. These reforms in special education can be traced to both the school restructuring movement and to what came to be known as the regular education initiative. This initiative started in the late 1980s and was led by Madeline Will, who was the director of the Office of Special Education and Rehabilitation Services (OSERS) at that time. In a monograph entitled, *Educating Children with Learning Problems A Shared Responsibility,*

Will (1986) criticized the dual system of delivering services to students with special needs. Concerns over the separation and segregation of students in special classes was later incorporated into the conceptual framework of the "inclusion movement." The focus was to make sure that all students, including those from multicultural backgrounds do not get left out in the educational process. Educational reform reached a sociopolitical point with the issuance of Goals 2000 by President Bush (National Educational Goals Panel, 1991). In the most recent version (National Educational Goals Panel, 1995), there is an explicit commitment to have all children achieve certain standards and to increase graduation rates and performance on achievement tests. While the appropriateness of some of the goals for children with special needs, including those with severe disabilities, has been questioned (Guetzloe, 1996; Hallahan & Kauffman, 1994), the intent of the language is to hold relevant stakeholders accountable for higher standards for all students, including those in both general and special education. Revised conceptualizations in special education have grown out of numerous debates related to general education restructuring, special education programs or product outcomes, special education costs, and political effects on educational policies. However, despite the lively debates over these issues, little consideration has been given to such complicating factors as cultural and linguistic diversity on both students and special educational restructuring designs. The neglect of students with disabilities in school reform and restructuring initiatives has been particularly problematic for multicultural learners with EBD (Cartledge, 1999; Leone, McLaughlin, & Meisel, 1992). Increasingly, the impact of cultural, linguistic, and social factors is being recognized as significant in conceptualizing and fostering learning (Tharp, 1989). Unfortunately, within the field of special education, there has been little em-phasis placed on relevant instructional practices and pedagogical issues (Rueda & Forness, 1994).

The Individuals with Disabilities Education Act (IDEA, 1990), originally authorized in 1975 as the Education for All Handicapped Children Act, is designed "to assure that all children with disabilities have available to them. . . . a free appropriate public education which emphasizes special education and related services that are designed to meet their unique needs" (20 U.S.C § 1401(c), 1996). Nevertheless, almost 30 years of data have demonstrated that multicultural learners, especially males, are disproportionately and inappropriately placed in special education (Artiles & Trent, 1994; Coutinho & Oswald, 1998). It is our contention that school reform efforts will only be effective if they accommodate students of varying multicultural backgrounds. The literature supports the notion that multicultural learners are disproportionately placed in classes for students with serious emotional and behavioral disorders (Russo & Talbert-Johnson, 1997). Demographic studies also repeatedly show that multicultural students, particularly African American males, are disproportionately referred for behavior and learning problems compared to their majority counterparts (Wagner, 1995). For example, African Americans currently make up approximately 16% of the public school population (U.S. Department of Education, Office of Civil Rights, 1994); however, depending on the disability, African American students actually make up as much as 28–32%, almost double their representation, of the population of students in special education (Coutinho & Oswald; Lara, 1994; National Clearinghouse for Professions in Special Education, 1991).

In the present chapter, we discuss issues related to problems of (a) definition and eligibility, (b) tolerance and discipline, (c) assessment, (d) intervention, (e) family involvement, and (f) the impact of school reform initiatives on multicultural learners with emotional and behavioral disorders (EBD). We offer solutions and suggestions for facili-tating successful education of these children and youth in restructured and reformed schools.

SCHOOL-BASED ISSUES: CHALLENGES FACING MULTICULTURAL LEARNERS WITH EMOTIONAL AND BEHAVIORAL DISORDERS

Definition and Eligibility Issues

It is apparent that school reform and re-structuring initiatives must include in their amendments mechanisms for more objec-tively and fairly judging students, especially multicultural learners with alleged behav-ioral excesses and deficits. Forness and Knitzer (1992) proposed that students from any background should not be labeled as EBD for displaying traits reflective of their cultural upbringing. School reformers must address two primary policy issues related to assessment of children and youth with emo-tional and behavioral concerns: definition and eligibility criteria. Indeed, as noted by numerous scholars, a more consistent defini-tion of students who have behavioral con-cerns must be adopted so that interpretations of student behaviors are not prone to dis-criminatory biases (Ishii-Jordan, 1997). There is general agreement that the criteria and procedures used to identify students as EBD are problematic. Central to this prob-lem is the IDEA definition of "emotional dis-turbance" itself. This definition has been characterized as vague and confusing (For-ness, 1988; Wood, 1990). Because of this, there continues to exist a lack of consensus among educational professionals on the in-terpretation and operationalization of the de-finition, as well as the belief that this definition excludes students who need ser-vices. The notion of excluding students who are "socially maladjusted" from being identi-fied as emotionally disturbed is particularly problematic in this current definition. A new definition has been proposed by the Nation-al Special Education and Mental Health Coalition. In this definition "emotional or behavioral disorder" was suggested to re-place the federal term "seriously emotionally disturbed," and the description of "inappro-priate behaviors" was revised to reflect "re-sponses in school so different from appropriate age, cultural, or ethnic norms that they adversely affect educational perfor-mance." The Coalition proposal is at least one attempt to address the discriminating ef-fect that the category of EBD has had on multicultural learners (Ishii-Jordan, 1997). Nevertheless, controversy over the proposed terminology and definition continues to be a significant challenge.

As it appears, controversy still exists re-garding the terminology and definition of EBD, especially as they relate to multicultur-al learners. Cline (1990) suggested that "am-biguity in language" (p. 160) has resulted in a lack of consensus among the field. This am-biguity is further compounded by the policy problems that result in wide-ranging inter-pretations of eligibility. While the current fed-eral definition improves upon previous criteria in some ways, many scholars argue that the very clause intended to prevent over-representation of multicultural learners in special education may instead actually deny services to deserving pupils (McIntyre, 1993). As McIntyre (1993) pointed out, it was intended to prevent multicultural learners without labels from being labeled, it might instead be misused by those who may wish to exclude pupils in need of services. He identified four groups of students at risk for being denied services: children and youth from the urban socially maladjusted subculture; those with a homosexual orientation; historically oppressed minorities; and those from low income households. According to Ishii-Jordan (1997), when so much liberty is given in interpreting the types of behaviors that make a child eligible for services, opportunities for discrimination can occur for select groups of students. Thus, it is imperative that cultural differences be reflected in our eligibility criteria and that a clear definition of EBD be adopted by the field.

Characteristics of Multicultural Learners with EBD

Professional knowledge concerning the emotional and behavioral problems experienced by multicultural learners and the interactive effects of culture and behavior within the context of behavior disorders has been limited. Cartledge, Lee, and Feng (1995) remarked that cultural patterns impact social behaviors in the classroom. Special characteristics, traits, and attributes distinguish cultural groups from the mainstream culture and it is essential that educators have "some understanding of cultural distinctions as a prerequisite to planning and orchestrating a program that ensures the total integration of all children" (p. 329). General and special educators are therefore challenged to interpret the behaviors of learners from multicultural backgrounds accurately, to distinguish learning and behavioral differences from deficits, and to employ instructional strategies that will maximize the schooling experiences of these individuals.

Each specific cultural group has great diversity in its composition, definition, understanding, acceptance, and treatment of deviance. Therefore, general and special educators are also challenged to let go of their misconceptions about the concept of homogeneity within cultural groups and false assumptions about stereotyped images of different cultural groups; and make the effort to understand that there is great variation within cultural groups due to linguistic, environmental, and developmental factors. In addition, a lack of knowledge and understanding about different cultural groups and their characteristics may lead to misunderstandings and culture conflict. Without accurate knowledge and understanding of students' cultural and linguistic backgrounds, general and special educators will not be able to identify their learning and behavioral needs and provide them with appropriate educational services. Peterson and Ishii-Jordan (1994) remarked that "for a special educator concerned with student behavior, factors of cultural attitude towards deviancy, mental illness or health, appropriate behavior and treatment come into play. It is the specific culture, not the categorical makeup which defines the individual's attitudes toward education, deviance, treatment and other issues crucial to effective special education for behaviorally disordered students" (pp. 7–8). Table 6.1 presents the sociocultural characteristics and the behaviors of different cultural groups in the disability category of emotional disturbance (see Table 6.1).

Table 6. 1
EXCEPTIONALITY CONSIDERATIONS

Characteristics of Exceptionality	Sociocultural Characteristics	Instructional Implications
African American Exceptional Students		
Emotionally Disabled		
• Depressed, anxious, withdrawn, suicidal	• Conflict when forced into a role that contradicts values Normal side-effects of severe culture shock	• Teacher should develop awareness of cultural values and process of acculturation
• Delinquency	• Youths may rebel against system where they believe they have little hope for success	• Teachers and counselors will need to assist students to achieve success Requires special effort of community to combat abuse
• Substance	• Youth may become drug or alcohol dependent in environment where narcotics are commonly used as an escape	• Teachers need to become adept at early identification of at-risk behaviors
• Aggressive, acting out, challenging, militant	• Desire to assert racial identity	• Teachers needs to assist student to channel energy into constructive activities
Hispanic American Exceptional Students		
• Depressed, anxious, withdrawn, suicidal	• Conflicts when forced into a role that contradicts values	• Teacher should develop this communication resource
• Delinquency	• Youths may rebel against system when they believe they have little hope for success	• Teacher should facilitate coping strategies
• Substance	• Youths may turn to drugs or alcohol in situations where family roles and responsibility have broken down	• Requires special extended family and community effort to combat abuse
• Aggressive, acting out, challenging, militant	• Desire to assert cultural identity	• Teacher needs to assist students to channel energy into constructive activities

Table 6. 1 (continued)

Asian American Exceptional Students

Characteristics of Exceptionality	Sociocultural Characteristics	Instructional Implications
	Emotionally Disabled	
• Depressed, anxious, withdrawn, suicidal	• Acculturative stress may result in heightened anxiety, resistance to change, response fatigue, and other side effects.	• Teacher should facilitate student's acculturation in appropriate ways.
• Delinquency	• Youths may become angry at racial barriers then feel guilty for denying their own ethnicity.	• Teacher should facilitate reduction in racial barriers so youth will not desire to deny ethnicity.
• Substance	• One stage in the acculturation process can be when youths refuse to give unquestioning obedience to parental views.	• Teachers should work with parents and community. • Requires special understanding by educators of cultural practices and appropriate interventions
• Aggressive, acting out, challenging, militant	• Phobia may be resulting from not being able to satisfy achievement; demands of home and school. Japanese culture once reinforced this alternative as a way of ending a shameful situation. • Desire to assert ethnic identity power as part of positive self-image	• Teacher should learn as much as possible about student's cultures. • May be particularly shame producing for more traditional parents • Teachers should work with community.

American Indian Exceptional Students

• Depressed, anxious, withdrawn, suicidal	• Continued discrimination can lead to feelings of unworthiness and values conflicts.	• Teacher should use appropriate self concept strategies.
• Delinquency	• Discrimination and inability to succeed may lead to rebellion.	• Peer ridicule may be more effective deterrent than other punishments.
• Substance	• Acceptance of addictive patterns	• Requires special extended family and community effort.
• Aggressive, acting out, challenging, militant	• Desire to assert cultural identity and reaction to discrimination	• Teachers should assist student to direct concern to productive channels.

Source: Adapted from Collier, C. (1998). *Separating difference from disability: Assessing diverse learners.* Ferndale, WA: Cross-Cultural Developmental Education Services. Adapted from: Nazarro, N.N. (19981). Special problems of exceptional minority children. In J.N. Nazarro (Ed.), *Culturally diverse exceptional children in school,* Virginia: ERIC 1-12. Adapted from Utley, C.A. (1993). Culturally and linguistically diverse students with mild disabilities. In C.A. Grant (Ed.), *Educating for diversity: An anthology of multicultural voices* (pp. 301–324). Boston, MA: Allyn & Bacon.

Cultural Perspectives on Tolerance and Discipline

The overrepresentation of multicultural learners, specifically African American males and underrepresentation of Asian American students (Ishii-Jordan, 1997) in programs for students with disabilities (including those for students with EBD) can be explained to some degree by the cultural mismatch that commonly exists between professionals and students they serve (McIntyre, 1996). This cultural gap between students and general and special educators is significant. An example of this mismatch is the fact that although African Americans currently make up 16% of the public school population, only 8% of the public school teachers and approximately 4% of teacher educators in institutions of higher learning are African American (Coker, Menz, Johnson, & McAlees, 1996; King, 1993). Projections suggest that sooner or later multicultural learners will make up 46% of the public school population, yet fewer than 5% of the teachers will be from a multicultural heritage. Consequently, difficulties related to a cultural mismatch or a gap in communication between multicultural learners and educators will be heightened in the future. Cartledge and Talbert-Johnson (1998) noted that:

> We are all products of our environment, and those experiences greatly determine how we perceive the world and respond to environmental events. With a largely White female teaching force, cultural discontinuities enter in when the student population consists of racially/ethnically diverse youngsters who are disproportionately impoverished. When teachers and students are out of sync, they clash and confront each other, both consciously and unconsciously in matters concerning proxemics (use of interpersonal distance), paralanguage (behaviors accompanying speech such as voice tone and pitch and speech rate and length), and verbal behavior (gesture, facial expression, and eye gaze). Examples of these transactions are the ways status in the classroom is determined,

the degrading connotations attached to the use of other languages and dialects, and the ways we differentially affirm group membership and cultural identity. The resulting dissonance in communicative processes (e.g., perceptions, assumptions, gestures, and turn-taking procedures) contributes to the development of communication gaps and misunderstandings. (pp. 8–9)

Behavioral patterns and value orientations often vary by culture, as do actions considered to be aberrant (Light & Martin; 1985; McIntyre, 1996). McIntyre proposed that this commonly resulted in actions considered "normal" in some cultures as being misinterpreted as "abnormal" by teachers not from those groups. For example, in the Asian American culture, children do not express how they feel nor demonstrate negative emotions as reactions to environmental situations and interpersonal relationships. Within their own culture, this type of response to a situation is valued and is viewed as a demonstration of perseverance. However, within a different culture or setting, this type of response is viewed as docile and unhealthy. Ishii-Jordan (1997) remarked that "when a great disparity exists between a cultural/familial interpretation of a child's behavior and the school's interpretation of this behavior, there is also likely to be a disagreement on how the behavior is viewed and handled. Some of the differing concerns include (a) certain behavioral manifestations may not be deemed pathological or deviant among all cultural groups; (b) the stigma of the EBD label can be a negative mark in the cultural beliefs prominent among subgroups; (c) interventions used with students whose behaviors or emotional reactions are considered inappropriate to school personnel (i.e., those who make placement decisions) may not be consistent with the way the student's cultural group may handle the behavior" (pp. 30–31).

Knitzer, Steinberg, and Fleisch (1990) reported that EBD identification may depend more on local tolerance levels and resources, or on the student's race, class, or socioeconomic status, instead of on individual needs. That is, students are often diagnosed and identified for special education because they are "mad, bad, sad and can't add," and because their teachers are unable to tolerate them, rather than diagnosis and placement based on valid clinical assessments (Wagner, 1995). Grossman (1991) also reported that social and ethnic variables were significant considerations in assignment of students to ability groups. Although neither ethnicity nor social class were the sole criterion educators used to make ability group assignments, teachers often assigned minority and working class students to lower ability groups than was indicated by objective data, such as test scores. In addition, he stated that educators maintained more prejudicial behavioral expectations for minority students than for nonminority students and found that when teachers evaluate the severity or deviancy of students' behavior problems that they judge the exact same transgressions as more severe or deviant when they are committed by, for example, African American male students. Other related data indicated that compared to majority populations, (a) multicultural learners with disabilities are more likely to be suspended at a younger age; (b) given lengthier suspensions; (c) programmed into punishment facilities such as juvenile court rather than treatment; (d) given more pathological labels than warranted; and (e) are less likely to have appropriate family involvement in their treatment plans (Ewing, 1995; Forness, 1988). These statistics are alarming not only for African Americans but also for other multicultural groups. Other disturbing statistics include the fact that males are placed in programs for serious emotional and behavioral disorders significantly more often than females (U.S. Department of Education, Office of Civil Rights, 1994; U.S. Department of Education, 1998).

Controversy surrounds the policy issue concerning suspension and expulsion. This is a particularly important matter because students with EBD tend to be excluded from school more often than their higher achieving peers (Cartledge, 1999; Grossman, 1991). Under the reauthorization of the Individuals with Disabilities Act (IDEA '97), these issues were specifically addressed. The 1997 Amendments to the IDEA require educators to consider the effects of behavior on learning. Specifically, IDEA mandates that the relationship between behavior and learning must not only be considered, but must be acted upon. The Amendments have addressed this issue by requiring teams charged with developing Individualized Education Plans (IEPs) to conduct a functional behavioral assessment to implement behavior intervention plans that utilize positive behavioral interventions and supports to address behaviors which interfere with the learning of others (or require disciplinary action) (Center for Effective Collaboration and Practice, 1998). The disciplinary provisions outlined within IDEA indicated that (a) out-of-school suspensions that do not exceed 10 days in a school year do not require any alternative educational services; (b) any out-of-school suspensions that exceed 10 days in a school year requires services, including a meeting of the IEP team to determine if a functional behavioral assessment was done prior to the incident that resulted in an out-of-school suspension, review and modification of an existing behavior intervention plan, and determination of whether the conduct leading to the disciplinary action was a manifestation of the disability (manifestation determination); (c) out-of-school suspensions that exceed 10 days and create a pattern of suspension must be viewed as a change of placement; (d) students possessing a dangerous weapon, or using or selling drugs, may be placed in a 45-calendar day alternative educational placement, followed by a review within 10 school days of the functional behavioral assessment and behavioral support plan. Additionally a manifestation determination hearing is to be held. Furthermore long-term suspension and expulsion can be used with students with disabilities, but only if the Individualized Education Plan (IEP) team determines that the conduct was not a manifestation of the disability; and finally, and most importantly, especially for students with EBD; (e) the school district is still required to provide a free and appropriate public education and access to the general curriculum during the period of the suspension or expulsion.

The above changes in the statutory language serve to provide strong safeguards for students identified with EBD in maintaining their rights to a free and appropriate education. Concerns persist, however, that multicultural learners with EBD are particularly vulnerable to suspension and expulsion, a vulnerability which tends to increase their probability of dropping out of school and experiencing further problems in the community and throughout their adult life. McIntyre (1993) argued that administrators who wish to save money or retain their ability to suspend these students will argue that the behaviors of students from the aforementioned groups are traits that were developed and promoted by their culture and thus should not qualify these students for special education services. In these situations, denial of services and the use of restrictive disciplinary practices such as detention, suspension and expulsion will only serve to further alienate culturally, sexually and/or economically different youth.

Of all the students in schools, with and without disabilities, students placed in programs for EBD have the poorest outcomes in terms of academic underachievement, graduation rates, and encounters with the criminal justice system (Guetzloe, 1996). Not surprisingly, students with EBD tend to have chronic mental health problems in adult life. Unfortunately, there continues to be strong evidence that students with EBD receive few supportive or mental health services (Forness, 1988; Shalala, 1999). Lack of success in school translates into poor transition outcomes for students with EBD, with just over 25% being employed three to five years after leaving school (National Center for Education Statistics, 1992). Long-term, students with EBD tend to fare better, although approximately one-third of students with EBD remain unemployed or underemployed as older adults (Neel, Meadows, Levine, & Edgar, 1988).

One graphic example of the failure of the current system is the disproportionate number of incarcerated youth who are multicultural (Cartledge & Talbert-Johnson, 1997). As reported in the *Digest of Education Statistics* (U.S. Department of Education, National Center for Education Statistics, 1995), more than 40% of these students have criminal records within three years of leaving school. Findings from the National Longitudinal Transition Study (Wagner, Newman, D'Amico, Jay, Butler-Nalin, Marder, & Cox,1991) reported that 44% of students with EBD who drop out of school for two years had arrest records. Sizable numbers of these youths have emotional and/or behavioral problems that have not been properly assessed or treated. According to Cartledge, Kea, and Ida (1999), many problems could be alleviated if appropriate early intervention strategies were in place, or if there was more emphasis on prevention and providing a healthy environment for these children and adolescents before serious problems develop. More than a decade ago, Kazdin (1987) argued that one of the main reasons for the lack of long-term success in dealing with challenging behaviors include insufficient assessments of the factors maintaining those behaviors. Thus, accurate assessment and diagnosis are critical to the development of an appropriate treatment plan.

Assessment and
Intervention Issues

Issues of educational equity continue to focus on effective assessment and instruction (Rotatori & Obi, 1999). Researchers and practitioners have long argued that assessment of students with EBD is highly subjective (Wood, 1990). This issue becomes even more pronounced when multicultural learners are assessed for possible emotional and behavioral problems. According to Obiakor and Schwenn (1996), cultural and linguistic diversity can no longer be ignored in the assessment nor in the instruction of individuals with behavior problems. Earlier, Duran (1989), for example, questioned the reliability and validity of current evaluation methods for multicultural learners, citing (a) language differences or limited-English proficiency; (b) student lack of exposure to test item content; (c) lack of test-taking strategies; and (d) lack of sensitivity on the part of the examiner to individual social and cultural behaviors. Other researchers have reported that norm-referenced assessment instruments for identification of emotional and behavior disorders administered to multicultural populations (a) fail to account for environmental factors; (b) assume cross-setting generalizability; and (c) are irrelevant to classroom settings. The result of these inadequate testing procedures is that multicultural learners are both underrepresented and overrepresented in EBD programs (Galagan, 1985; Heward, 1999; Ysseldyke & Thurlow, 1984). Arguably, one of the most controversial issues surrounding the placement of multicultural learners in special education is "test bias." Despite language in the federal regulations on special education that requires that "testing and evaluation materials and procedures used for the purposes of evaluation and placement of children with disabilities must be selected and administered in a manner that is not

racially or culturally discriminatory" (34 C.F.R. § 300.500(b), 1996), the issue to date has not been satisfactorily resolved (Russo & Talbert-Johnson, 1997). There is a clear need for assessment practices that reduce cultural and language biases and improve the abilities of general and special educators to identify and intervene with students exhibiting challenging behaviors. Therefore, it is important to ensure that not only traditional assessment measures are used appropriately but that different forms of assessment are used. Appropriate use of these tools is needed to determine the kinds of instruction and services needed by each child and to identify individual strengths and areas of concern. According to the Council for Children with Behavioral Disorders (CCBD, 1989), the needs of multicultural learners with EBD would be best served through a functional assessment approach. This assessment should examine student performance under existing teaching conditions, alter instructional practices to improve student performance, and monitor student performance on a continuous basis in order to assess the effects of various strategies. This assessment should be conducted by a team of competent professionals, using multiple measures that are valid and reliable in order to render an ecologically and culturally sensitive judgment about a given student's needs in the context of his or her community and school (Park, Pullis, Reilly, & Townsend, 1994). Several questions to consider are (a) Is there agreement concerning the assessment process among the various professionals? (b) Did the professionals use family information about the child's functioning at home and in the community to aid in making a diagnosis? and (c) Does the family believe the assessment is accurate? If children from specific multicultural groups appear to be overrepresented in the program that has been recommended for a child, parents should carefully examine the procedures for determining the child's placement. If the parents believe that placement decisions are not culturally biased and cultural and linguistic factors are considered an integral part of the assessment process, then they will have increased confidence in the educational programs and interventions selected for their child. Despite best attempts to reduce cultural biases, a certain amount of ethnocentrism is inevitable. Peterson and Ishii-Jordan (1994) suggested that this may be true because people deal with the "affective" in cultural issues and not purely with objective cognition. As they pointed out, people's repertoire of experiences influence how they see and understand foreign concepts and behaviors. If assessors would rely more on large numbers of direct observations and functional assessments in natural settings, they would be better able to observe the behaviors of non-referred peers in order to determine if problem identification is the result of quantifiable behavioral differences or the result of intolerance of cultural diversity (Rosenberg, Wilson, Maheady, & Sindelar, 1997). With a reliance on functional assessments for students with EBD, special education placements would be reserved for those students whose behaviors would be viewed as deviant by most (if not all) cultures. One of the primary purposes of a functional assessment is to improve instruction and subsequently to enhance students' academic and behavioral performance (Maheady, Algozzine, & Ysseldyke, 1984). To accomplish this, it is necessary to assess students within the context of their respective instructional environments. Functional behavioral assessment may reveal factors or conditions within the learning environment, itself, that may be precipitating problem behavior. Researchers have suggested that a va-

riety of factors can serve as precursors to problematic behavior. These factors, for example, can range from the physical arrangement of the classroom or student seating assignment to the difficulty level of an academic assignment.

When developing a behavior intervention plan, IDEA dictates that the IEP team should explore the need for strategies and support systems to address any behavior that may impede learning. Support systems necessary to help students use appropriate behavior may include a variety of school personnel, family members, peers and other adults in and around the school and community. The Center for Effective Collaboration and Practice (1998) suggested that regardless of the specific approach, the more closely the behavior plan reflects the results of the functional behavioral assessment, the more likely it is to succeed. It further indicated that options for positive behavioral interventions may include (a) replacing problem behaviors with appropriate behaviors that serve the same (or similar) function as the inappropriate one; (b) increasing reinforcement for existing appropriate behaviors; (c) making changes to the environment that eliminate the possibility of engaging in an appropriate behavior; and (d) providing the supports necessary for the child or youth to use appropriate behaviors. It is further recommended that systems of care be developed that are family-centered and include such practices as those that (a) involve the family in assessment, decision making, planning and service delivery at all levels, including family, agency, and system levels; (b) develop services not just for the child, but also for the entire family; (c) use the family's priorities for services and goals to guide service provision; (d) respect the family's choice as to their level of involvement and participation with child and family services agencies; and (e) embrace a strengths-based focus (Grant & Sleeter, 1998).

MULTICULTURAL FAMILY INVOLVEMENT ISSUES:
REDUCING RISK FACTORS

Family configurations have continued to change in recent years. A growing number of children and youth live in single parent homes, in blended families, and in poverty. Factors associated with these circumstances, include divorce, teen pregnancy and homelessness, severely impact children's capacity to successfully function in school (Fish, 1991; Fradd & Weismantel, 1989; Hetherington & Cox, 1985; Simpson, 1996). In addition, these significant social and family factors not only affect parents' and families' abilities to respond to the needs of children and youth with emotional and behavioral problems, but also their ability to effectively consume available services. Accordingly, school reform programs should include methods of strengthening entire families, rather than exclusively focusing on children with EBD, independent of their families. Without such efforts, general and special educators may find that many multicultural families, such as those who live in poverty, are forced to choose the daily challenge of sheer survival over the needs of a child with an emotional or behavioral problem.

Parental involvement in mental health, treatment and educational programs for students with EBD tends to be generally limited. Concerns and issues of parents and families of multicultural learners with emotional and behavioral problems (e.g., housing and employment) may further exacerbate these engagement difficulties. Moreover, according to Forness (1988) and others (Rotatori & Obi, 1999), parents of multicultural learners with EBD are often not well-informed about their rights, nor is there a strong parent advocacy and/or self-help movement. In this regard, the National Special Education and Mental Health Coalition has voiced concern about the paucity of parent advocacy groups for stu-

dents with EBD. This body of advocates indicated that parents are often overwhelmed by the necessity of coping both with the needs of a child with an emotional disturbance and with the complex bureaucratic service systems. As evidence of this problem, Rosenberg, Reppucci, and Linney (1983) reported that a program designed to provide parent education and support to 130 low-income families whose children were at risk for developmental delay, abuse, or emotional disturbance served only about 25 families. They further speculated that immediate problems were too overwhelming to allow parents to attend to more long-term needs.

Information regarding these predictors of later academic, social and behavioral difficulties could be used for screening and early identification of at-risk individuals. While research has documented the potential impact of certain risk factors, it should be noted with caution that any one risk factor by itself is unlikely to lead to negative outcomes. Rather, it is the accumulation of multiple risks for any one individual such as the ones listed below that increases the probability of enduring problems (English, 1998) (see Table 6.2). As illustrated in Table 6.2, these environmental risk factors include (a) child characteristics, (b) caregiver characteristics, (c) the parent/child relationship, (d) severity of child and physical abuse and neglect, (e) chronicity of child and physical abuse and neglect, (f) perpetrator access, and (g) social and economic factors. It is essential that general and special educators become alert to these risk factors and provide environments that enhance the ability of students with EBD to cope with the multiple risks in their lives. At the present time, early identification and treatment is the approach that has the clearest record of effectiveness (Lane & Burchard, 1983; Nelson

Table 6.2
MAIN CATEGORIES IN RISK-ASSESSMENT MODEL

Child Characteristics
- Age of child
- Physical/mental/social disability or developmental delay
- Behavioral problems
- Self-protection, ability to resist abuse
- Fear of caregiver or home environment

Caregiver Characteristics
- Victimization of other children
- Mental, physical, or emotional impairment
- Substance abuse, past or current
- History of abuse or neglect as a child
- Poor parenting skills or knowledge, inappropriate expectations
- Inability to nurture child
- Failure to recognize problem or accept responsibility
- Unwillingness or inability to protect child
- Uncooperative with child protective services (CPS) agency

Parent/Child Relationship
- Inappropriate response to child's behavior
- Poor attachment and bonding
- Child has inappropriate family role

Severity of Child Abuse/Neglect
- Dangerous acts that create risk of injury
- Extent of physical injury or harm
- Extent of emotional harm
- Inadequate medical care, routine and in case of injury or illness
- Failure to provide for basic needs
- Inadequate supervision for child's age
- Sexual contact

Chronicity of Child Abuse/Neglect
- Chronic or repeated maltreatment

Perpetrator Access
- Has unsupervised access to child (in case of abuse)
- Has sole responsibility for care of child (in case of neglect)

Social and Economic Factors
- Stress on caregiver
- Unemployed caregiver
- Lack of social support for caregiver
- Lack of economic resources

Source: Adapted from Department of Social and Health Services (1987). *Washington Risk Assessment Matrix.* Olympia, WA: Author.

& Pearson, 1998). Intervention and treatment programs must include not only school-based programs but also home and community-based programs. Stumphauser (1986) described the services and programs that constitutes community-based treatment: community programs and prevention, including such programs as behavioral family contracting; social skills training for youths; school-based learning strategies and school survival skill training; and job finding and job skills training, and group treatment homes. These services and programs could be accessed in a least-to-most intrusive and restrictive hierarchy according to individual needs of the child or youth. Educational systems and community agencies must establish collaborative and ongoing working relationships in order to address all of the important ecological and behavioral variables that impact the lives of multicultural learners. In addition, educational systems and agencies must encourage culturally competent exchanges and collaborations among families, professionals, students, and communities.

School reformers will obviously find solutions to social and family problems difficult to implement. We believe these solutions must extend well beyond traditional school boundaries. General and special educators must be motivated to work cooperatively with ancillary school personnel and community professionals to provide equitable services for multicultural children and their families (see Chapter 11). Systemic and creative approaches are needed to comprehensively address the needs of multicultural families of children and youth with EBD.

IMPLICATIONS FOR SCHOOL REFORM IN MULTICULTURAL AND SPECIAL EDUCATION

As general and special educators consider cultural and linguistic factors, the emotional and behavioral problems of students with EBD must be dealt with in relation to issues such as economic conditions, family living conditions, family values, beliefs, and traditions, and community services. That is, school personnel should not attempt to respond to emotional and behavioral problems of students without awareness and sensitivity to cultural, environmental, family, and community factors. Policy makers have voiced that solutions to these problems will require family stability, support systems for single-parent homes, decreased teenage pregnancy, and meaningful job opportunities to lure people from welfare to work. Many solutions to the problems of students with EBD, including multicultural learners with EBD, will require that educational reform and restructuring initiatives occur in combination with appropriate societal changes. Thus, while school reform initiatives will not be able to address all problems of multicultural learners with EBD, there are a number of consid-erations that are within their range of authority; and still others that should be undertaken in collaboration with community, state, and national leaders. As a consequence, school reforms should seek to identify empirically based best practices methodology which can be cooperatively implemented by educators, related services personnel, mental health professionals, parents and others involved in serving multicultural learners with EBD in public schools and other least restrictive settings. As a result, we offer the following school reform considerations which we believe are essential in accommodating multicultural learners with EBD in schools of the future (a) strengthening home, school and community capacity and partnerships; (b) restructuring teacher education programs by preparing teachers to become culturally competent and responsive; (c) recruiting and retaining multicultural general and special educators; (d) promoting appropriate functional assessments; and (e) creating learning environments that value and address diversity.

Strengthen Home, School, and Community Capacity and Partnerships

Multicultural learners with EBD are a heterogeneous group of young people with a variety of strengths and needs. While much is known about the family, school and community factors that place young people at risk for developing emotional disturbance, there is gap between what is known and what is done. Promoting systems change resulting in the development of coherent services built around the individual needs of children and youth at-risk of developing serious emotional disturbance is essential. Nevertheless, schools cannot, nor should they, attempt to integrate school and community services alone. School personnel, parents, and community leaders must, however, advocate for the development of interagency programming to provide a comprehensive system of care for multicultural learners with EBD. Models for interagency programming abound, including the Ventura Model for Mental Health Services, the Bluegrass Impact Model, and the Alaska Youth Initiative, as well as, Wraparound Milwaukee and Project Wraparound (Nelson & Pearson, 1992). A common thread throughout these model programs is that they provide for systems change, are needs based, and are family-centered.

In addition, it is imperative that a "set of congruent behaviors, attitudes, and policies that come together in a system, agency, or among professionals enables that system, agency, or those professionals to work effectively in cross-cultural situations" (King, Sims, & Osher, 2000, p. 3). The system must become culturally competent by incorporating the following elements in their structures, policies, and services (a) value diversity, (b) have the capacity for cultural self-assessment, (c) be conscious of the "dynamics" inherent when cultures interact, (d) institutionalize cultural knowledge, and (e) develop adaptations within human service agencies to reflect an understanding of diversity between and within cultures (Cross, Bazron, Dennis, & Issacs, 1989).

Restructuring Teacher Education Programs

It is important for training programs to produce culturally competent professionals and organizational systems. Teacher training institutions must assume a larger share of the burden for imparting cultural information to current and future teachers (Rotatori & Obi, 1999; Utley, Delquadri, Obiakor, & Mims, 2000). The overrepresentation of multicultural learners in special education programs is probably not a result of conscious prejudice but rather due to a variety of factors, including ethnocentricity on the part of teachers (McIntyre, 1993). Grossman (1990) suggested that the vast majority of general and special educators are unaware of cultural differences in their behavior and how influential their behaviors are on students.

General and special educators need to develop an understanding of how cultural and linguistic factors affect the way one behaves, and conversely, how these factors influence how one perceives and judges the behaviors of those that are different from oneself. That is, in order to minimize the cultural discontinuities evidenced in culturally based learning and behavioral styles of multicultural learners, general and special educators must become skilled in adapting and modifying traditional assessment and intervention procedures that are congruent with the student's cultural traits.

Current and future teachers will need information regarding cultural characteristics, differing values and customs, instructional modifications, and culturally sensitive behavior management practices. Teacher education programs need to assist teachers in methodology and best practices for improved student learning and outcomes. This match of teaching and learning styles will enhance positive learning opportunities and results for both general and special educators and multicultural learners in their classrooms. As Rotatori and Obi (1999) pointed out, it is important to diversify instruction so that general and special educators can ensure that they reach *all* children. For example, a more inductive presentation on cooperative learning activities might be used with multicultural, low socioeconomic status (SES), and socially maladjusted students, given that this strategy tends to be associated with generally positive outcomes (Johnson & Johnson, 1990; McIntyre, 1993).

Recruiting and Retaining Multicultural General and Special Educators

The increasing diversity of students and decreasing diversity of teachers highlight the urgent need to increase the number of multicultural teachers in school systems. According to Ransom, Maurer, McLean, Simmons, and Duvall (2000), the teaching shortage in urban schools has grown even worse over the last three years. These authors suggested that as teachers retire and children of the baby-boomers enroll, urban schools are scrambling to find teachers. Given the shortages across the nation, general and special educators must make a concerted effort to attract more and more highly qualified teachers. Several urban districts have been successful in their attempts to counter teacher shortages by pioneering the use of special recruitment efforts such as (a) offering induction and support programs to keep talented new teachers in the classroom; (b) offering alternative certification routes to bring professionals with backgrounds in shortage subject areas into the classroom; (c) offering on-the-spot contracts to hire teachers without the waiting on red tape that in the past often resulted in teachers not taking jobs in urban schools; (d) recruiting at historically Black colleges (HBCUs) and other minority institutions (OMI's) to address teacher shortages; and (e) offering financial incentives for teaching in high-need subject areas (Ransom et al., 2000).

Enhanced recruitment of educational professionals from diverse cultural backgrounds could ultimately lead to the countering of lowered teacher expectations and the overrepresentation of multicultural learners in programs for EBD (McIntyre, 1996). School districts must be sensitive to educational practices and hiring procedures to ensure that educational procedures address the unique needs of multicultural learners with disabilities by having available a diverse faculty and staff.

Promoting Appropriate Functional Assessments

It seems clear that fundamental changes will have to take place in schools to address the needs of diverse populations of students. Assessment practices need to move beyond the traditional standardized testing to methods that take into account the complex interactions among a number of variables inherent in each student, including race, ethnicity, religion, nationality, gender, sexual orientation, membership in different cultures, and disability label (Singh, Ellis, Oswald, Wechsler, & Curtis, 1997).

Professionals who work with multicultural learners with EBD suggest that assessment be radically changed to include a functional perspective. It is not enough to merely alter the currently used norm-referenced assessment model, but rather it is mandatory that general and special educators dramatically alter the assumptions which underlie evaluations of students. School reform initiatives must embrace assessment practices that are culturally appropriate, ethical and functional. The overall goal of these types of assessment is to assist teachers in guiding maximally efficient and effective instruction. Thus, general and special educators must promote practices that ensure that assessment is integral to the identification, design, and delivery of services for multicultural learners with EBD.

Creating Learning Environments that Value and Address Diversity

The culture of the school must change to provide learning environments that are responsive to a wide range of students' needs in urban settings. Schools should embrace the diversity of the student body, respecting and appreciating the rich ethnic and cultural differences in a safe environment conducive to students' learning styles and needs (Russo & Talbert-Johnson, 1997; Tam & Gardner, 1997). Embracing diversity means highlighting the value of all students, including those who represent different learning styles, behavior profiles, physical abilities, languages, and cultural backgrounds. Research into the characteristics of effective teachers of multicultural learners indicates that such teachers (a) have high expectations for their students and believe that all students are capable of academic success; (b) communicate clearly, pace lessons appropriately, involve students in decisions, monitor students' progress, and provide frequent feedback; (c) use culturally relevant teaching approaches that integrate the students' native language and dialect, culture, and community into classroom activities to make input more relevant and comprehensible to build trust and self-esteem, and to promote cultural diversity and pluralism; and (d) use curricula and teaching strategies that promote coherence, relevance, progression, and continuity (Grant & Gomez, 1995).

Additionally, cultural sensitivity includes practicing respect for culturally different behaviors. Instead of viewing a behavior as right or wrong, it should be best judged by how well it is suited to the demands of a given educational environment (Rotatori & Obi, 1999; Singh, 1995). McIntyre (1994) suggested that in order to better deal with behavior changes, general and special educators need to develop an awareness of how cultural background affects the way people behave. Other researchers such as Light and Martin (1985) noted that "an understanding of cultural expectations and roles can contribute to the development of behavior management techniques specifically designed to eliminate value differences between a child's family, the school system, and the larger society" (p. 42).

Specific pedagogical strategies within a multicultural curriculum are critical to the success of creating positive learning environments. A critical variable linked to effective instruction is the use of pedagogical strategies such as active student responding and student-centered instructional practices (e.g., language experience approaches) which have been found to improve academic instruction of students from various populations (Gardner, Heward, & Grossi, 1994). In addition, Tam and Gardner (1997) proposed that "the curriculum of a school should reflect the diversity of the school's population and should include a core body of knowledge that takes into account the students" various cultural backgrounds? (p. 3). Guiding principles for the infusion of multicultural content into the curriculum have been identified by Hilliard, Payton-Stewart, and Williams (1990). These principles include (a) helping students to understand the history of their own culture; (b) providing assistance to teachers in how to use curriculum materials; (c) acquiring curriculum materials such as books, videos, and films; (d) encouraging community members to participate in the infusion of curriculum materials; and (e) providing staff training to promote curricular change. As a result, general and special educators must encourage culturally competent collaborations that will foster equitable outcomes for all students and result in the identification and provision of services that are responsive to issues of race, culture, gender, as well as social and economic status.

CONCLUSION

We acknowledge that implementing effective and efficient programs for multicultural learners with EBD is not an easy chore. Yet, we consider this task to be so integral to the school reform movement that it can neither be delayed nor assumed to be a matter that has little relevance for the majority of educators. It is firmly our contention that revitalization and reform are needed at all levels of general and special education to meet the complex needs of multicultural learners with EBD and their families. Accordingly, educators, parents, and community and business leaders must aggressively strive to develop and implement programs and support systems for those students who experience emotional and behavioral difficulties. Tremendous gains have been made in serving multicultural learners with EBD. At the same time, much remains to be accomplished toward implementing more effective programs. Providing a quality education for multicultural learners with EBD is a complex task that not only requires sensitivity to cultural and linguistic differences, but also requires an understanding of early intervention, family involvement, transdisciplinary teaming, functional assessment, and positive behavioral supports.

REFERENCES

Artiles, A.J., & Trent, S.C., (1994). Overrepresentation of minority students in special education: A continuing debate. *The Journal of Special Education, 27,* 410–437.

Cartledge, G. (1999). African American males and serious emotional disturbance: Some personal perspectives. *Behavioral Disorders, 25* (1), 76–79

Cartledge, G., Kea, C.D., & Ida, D.J. (2000). Anticipating differences-celebrating strengths: Providing culturally competent services for children and youth with serious emotional disturbance. *Teaching Exceptional Children, 32* (3) 30–37.

Cartledge, G.W., & Milburn, J.F. (1995). *Teaching social skills to children and youth: Innovative approaches* (3rd ed.). Needham Heights, MA: Allyn & Bacon.

Cartledge, G., & Talbert-Johnson, C. (1997). School violence and cultural sensitivity. In A.P. Goldstein & J.C. Conoley (Eds.), *School violence intervention: A practical handbook* (pp. 391–425). New York: Guilford Press.

Cartledge, G., & Talbert-Johnson, C. (1998). *African American males and serious emotional disturbance (SED): Genetic disposition versus social bias*. Paper presented at the American Education Research Association, San Diego, CA.

Center for Effective Collaboration and Practice (1998). *Addressing student problem behavior: An IEP Team's introduction to functional behavioral assessment and behavior intervention plans*. Washington, DC: Chesapeake Institute. On line at, http://www.airdc.org/cecp/resources/problem behavior.html.

Cline, D.H. (1990). A legal analysis of policy initiative to exclude handicapped/disruptive students from special education. *Behavioral Disorders, 15,* 159–173.

Coker, C.C., Menz, F.E., Johnson, L.A., & McAlees, D.C. (1996). *School outcomes and community benefits for minority youth with serious emotional disturbances: A synthesis of the research literature. [OSEP Research in Education of Individuals with Disabilities Program]*. Washington, DC: U.S. Department of Education, Office of Special Education Programs. (CFDA No. 84.023E).

Council for Children with Behavioral Disorders (CCBD) (1989). *A new proposed definition and terminology to replace serious emotional disturbance in the Education of the Handicapped Act*. Reston, VA: Author.

Coutinho, M.J., & Oswald, D.P. (1998). Ethnicity and special education research: Identifying questions and methods. *Behavioral Disorders, 24,* 66–73.

Cross, T., Bazron, B., Dennis, K., & Issacs, M. (1989). *Towards a culturally competent system of care* (Vol. 1). Washington, DC: Georgetown University Development Center, CASSP Technical Assistance Center.

Division of Child and Family Services, Children's Administration, Department of Social and Health Services (1987). *Washington risk assessment matrix*. Olympia, WA: Author.

Duran, R.P. (1989). Assessment and instruction of at-risk Hispanic students. *Exceptional Children, 56,* 154–158.

English, D.J. (1998). The extent and consequences of child maltreatment: Protecting children from abuse and neglect. *The Future of Children, 8* (1), 39–53.

Ewing, N.J. (1995). Restructured teacher education for inclusiveness: A dream deferred for African American children. In B.A. Ford, F.E. Obiakor, & J.M. Patton (Eds.), *Effective education of African*

American exceptional learners: New perspectives (pp. 189–207). Austin, TX: Pro-Ed.

Fish, M.C. (1991). Exceptional children in nontraditional families. In M.J. Fine (Ed.), *Collaboration with parents of exceptional children*. Brandon, VT: Clinical Psychology Publishing.

Forness, S.R. (1988). Planning for the needs of children with serious emotional disturbance. The national special education and mental coalition. *Behavior Disorders, 13* (2), 127–139.

Forness, S.R., & Knitzer, J. (1992). A new proposed definition and terminology to replace "serious emotional disturbance" in *Education of the Handicapped Act*. Alexandria, VA: National Mental Health and Special Education Coalition, c/o National Mental Health Association.

Fradd, S.H., & Weismantel, M.J. (Eds.) (1989). *Meeting the needs of culturally and linguistically different students: A handbook for educators*. Austin, TX: Pro-Ed.

Galagan, J.E. (1985). Psychoeducational testing: Turn out the lights, the party's over. *Exceptional Children, 52,* 288–299.

Gardner, R., & Heward, W.O., & Grossi, T.A. (1994). Effects of response cards on student participation and academic achievement: A systematic, replication with inner-city students during whole class science instruction. *Journal of Applied Behavior Analysis, 27,* 63–71.

Grant, C.A., & Gomez, M.L. (1995). *Making schooling multicultural: Campus and classroom*. Englewood Cliffs, NJ: Prentice Hall.

Grant, C.A., & Sleeter, C.E. (1998). *Turning on learning: Five approaches for multicultural teaching plans for races, class, gender, and disability* (2nd ed.). Upper Saddle River, NJ: Merrill/Prentice Hall.

Grossman, H. (1990). *Trouble-free teaching; Solutions to behavior problems in the classroom*. Mountainview, CA: Mayfield.

Grossman, H. (1991). Special education in a diverse society: Improving services for minority and working-class student. *Preventing School Failure, 36,* 19–27.

Guetzloe, E. (1996). Facts pertaining to children and youth with emotional/behavioral disorders. *Council for Children with Behavioral Disorders Newsletter, 10,* 34.

Hallahan, D.P., & Kauffman, J.M. (1994). Toward a culture of disability in the aftermath of Deno and Dunn. *The Journal of Special Education, 27,* 496–508.

Hetherington, E.M., & Cox, M. (1985). Long term effects of divorce and remarriage on the adjustment of children. *Journal of the American Academy of Child Psychiatry, 24,* 518–530.

Heward, W.L. (1994). Three "low tech" strategies for increasing the frequency of active student response during group instruction. In R. Gardner, D.M. Sainato, J.O. Cooper, T.E. Heron, W.L. Heward, J. Eshleman, & T.A. Grossi (Eds.), *Behavior analysis in education: Focus on measurably superior instruction* (pp. 283–316). Pacific Grove, CA: Brooks/Cole.

Heward, W.L. (1999). *Exceptional children: An introduction to special education* (6th ed.). Englewood Cliffs, NJ: Merrill/Prentice Hall.

Hilliard, A.G., Payton-Stewart, L., & Williams, L. (1990). *Infusion of African and African American content in the school curriculum.* Morristown, NJ: Aaron Press.

Individuals with Disabilities Act (IDEA), 20 U.S.C.§§ 1401 *et seq.* (1996).

Ishii-Jordan, S.R. (1997). When behaviors differences are not disorders. In A.J. Artiles & G. Zamora-Duran (Eds.), *Reducing disproportionate representation of culturally diverse students in special and gifted education* (pp. 27–46). Reston, VA: Council for Exceptional Children.

Johnson, D., & Johnson, R. (1990). Cooperative small-group learning. *NASSP Curriculum Report, 14* (1), 1–4.

Kazdin, A.E. (1987). Treatment of antisocial behavior in children: Current status and future directions. *Psychological Bulletin, 102,* 187–203.

King, S.H. (1993). *The limited presence of African American teachers. Review of Educational Research, 63,* 115–149.

King, M.A., Sims, A., & Osher, D. (2000). *How is cultural competence integrated in education?* On line at, http://www.air-dc.org/cecp/cultural/Q_integrated. html.

Knitzer, J., Steinberg, Z., & Fleisch, B. (1990). *At the schoolhouse door: An examination of programs and policies for children with behavior and emotional problems.* New York: Bank Street College of Education.

Lane, T.W., & Burchard, J.D. (1983). Failure to modify delinquent behavior: A constructive analysis. In E.B. Foa & P.M.G. Emmelkamp (Eds.), *Failures in behavior therapy* (pp. 355–377). New York: John Wiley & Sons.

Lara, J. (1994). *State data collection and monitoring procedures regarding overrepresentation of minority students in special education.* Washington, DC: Special Education Program (ED/OSERS). (ERIC Document Reproduction Service No. 369247).

Leone, P.E., McLaughlin, M.J., & Meisel, S.M. (1992). School reform and adolescents with behavior disorders. *Focus on Exceptional Children, 25,* 1–15.

Light, H., & Martin, R. (1985). Guidance of America Indian children. *Journal of American Indian Education, 25,* 42–46.

Maheady, L., Algozzine, B., & Ysseldyke, J.E. (1984). Minority overrepresentation in special education: A functional assessment perspective. *Special Services in the Schools, 1,* 5–19.

McIntyre, T. (1993). Reflections on the new definition for emotional or behavioral disorders: Who still falls through the cracks and why? *Behavior Disorders, 18* (2), 148–160.

McIntyre, T. (1994). Teaching urban behavior disordered youth. In R.L. Peterson & S. Ishii-Jordan (Eds.), *Multicultural issues in the education of students with behavioral disorders* (pp. 33–50). Cambridge, MA: Brookline Books.

McIntyre, T. (1996). Guidelines for providing appropriate services to culturally diverse students with emotional and/or behavioral disorders. *Behavioral Disorders, 21* (2), 137–144.

National Center for Education Statistics (1992). *Announcement: New report focuses on dropout rates in the United States.* Washington, DC: Author.

National Clearinghouse for Professions in Special Education (1991). *The severe shortage of minority personnel.* Washington, DC: U.S. Department of Education, National Center for Education Statistics.

National Commission on Excellence in Education (1983). *A Nation at Risk: The Imperative for Educational Reform.* Washington, DC: U.S. Department of Education.

National Council on Disability (1989). *The education of students with disabilities: Where do we stand?* Washington, DC: Author.

National Educational Goals Panel. (1991). *Where are we?* Washington, DC: Author.

National Educational Goals Panel. (1995). *Improving education through family-school-community partnerships.* Washington, DC: Author.

Neel, R., Meadows, N., Levine, P., & Edgar, E. (1988). What happens after special education: A statewide follow-up study of secondary students who have behavioral disorders. *Behavioral Disorders, 13,* 209–216.

Nelson, C.M., & Pearson, C.A. (1992). *Integrating services for children and youth with emotional and behavioral disorders*. Reston, VA: The Council for Exceptional Children.

Nelson, C.M., & Pearson, C.A. (1998). Juvenile delinquency in the context of culture and community. In R.L. Peterson & S. Ishii-Jordan (Eds.), *Multicultural issues in the education of students with behavioral disorders* (pp. 40–62). Cambridge, MA: Brookline Books.

Obiakor, F.E., Algozzine, B., & Schwenn, J. (1995). Where are we in educating African-American students with problem behaviors? *The Western Journal of Black Studies, 19* (3), 203–210.

Obiakor, F.E., & Schwenn, J. (1996). Assessment of culturally diverse students with behavior disorders. In A. F. Rotatori, S. Burkhardt, & J. O. Schwenn (Eds.), *Advances in special education* (Vol. 10, pp. 37–57). Greenwich, CT: JAI Press.

Park, E.K., Pullis, M., Reilly, T.F., & Townsend, B.L. (1994). Cultural biases in the identification of students with behavioral disorders. In R.L. Peterson & S. Ishii-Jordan (Eds.), *Multicultural issues in the education of students with behavioral disorders* (pp. 40–62). Cambridge, MA: Brookline Books.

Peterson, R.L., & Ishii-Jordan, S. (1994) *Multicultural issues in the education of students with behavioral disorders*. Cambridge, MA: Brookline Books.

Ransom, S., Maurer, M., McLean, D., Simmons, A., & Duvall, H. (2000). *The urban teacher shortage*. Washington, DC: Recruiting New Teachers, Inc.

Rosenberg, M.S., Reppucci, N.D., & Linney, J.A. (1983). Issues in the implementation of human service programs: Examples from a parent training project for high-risk families. *Analysis and Intervention in Developmental Disabilities, 3,* 215–225.

Rosenberg, M.S., Wilson, R., Maheady, L, & Sindelar, P.T. (1997). *Educating students with behavior disorders* (2nd ed.). Needham Heights, MA: Allyn & Bacon.

Rotatori, A., & Obi, S. (1999). Directions for the future: Empowering the culturally diverse exceptional learners. In F.E. Obiakor, J. Schwenn, and A.F. Rotatori (Eds.), *Advances in special education* (Vol. 12, pp. 233–242). Stamford, CT: JAI Press.

Rueda, R.S., & Forness, S. (1994). Childhood depression: Ethnic and cultural issues in special education. In R.L. Peterson & S. Ishii-Jordan (Eds.), *Multicultural issues in the education of students with behavioral disorders* (pp. 40–62). Cambridge, MA: Brookline Books.

Russo, C.J., & Talbert-Johnson, C., (1997). The overrepresentation of African American children in special education: The resegregation of educational programming? *Education and Urban Society, 29,* 136–148.

Shalala, D.E. (1999). *Mental health: A report of the surgeon general.* Online at, http://www.surgeon-general.gov/library/mentalhealth/home.html.

Shaw, S., Biklen, D., Conlon, S., Dunn, J., Kramer, J., & DeRoma-Wagner, V. (1990). Special education and school reform. In L.M. Bullock & R.L. Simpson (Eds.), *Critical issues in special education: Implications for personnel preparation.* Denton, TX: University of North Texas.

Simpson, R.L. (1996). *Conferencing parents of exceptional children.* Austin, TX: Pro-Ed.

Singh, N.N. (1995). In search of unity: Some thought on family-professional relationships in service delivery systems. *Journal of Child and Family Studies, 4,* 3–18.

Singh, N.N., Ellis, C.R., Oswald, D.P., Wechsler, H.A. & Curtis, W.J. (1997). Value and address diversity. *Journal of Emotional and Behavioral Disorders, 5,* 24–35.

Stumphauser, J.S. (1986). *Helping delinquents change: A treatment manual of social learning approaches.* New York: Hayworth Press.

Tam, B.K.Y., & Gardner, T. (1997). Developing a multicultural and student-centered educational environment for students with serious emotional disturbances. *Multiple Voices, 2* (1), 1–11.

Tharp, R.J. (1989). Psychocultural variables and constants: Effects on teaching and learning in schools. *American Psychologist, 44,* 349–359.

U.S. Department of Education (1994). *The national agenda for achieving better results for children and youth with disabilities.* Washington, DC: Office of Special Education Programs.

U.S. Department of Education (1998). *Twentieth annual report to congress on the implementation of* the *Individuals with Disabilities Education Act.* Washington, DC: Author

U.S. Department of Education, National Center for Education Statistics. (1995) *Digest of education statistics.* Washington, DC: Office of Educational Research and Improvement.

U.S. Department of Education, Office of Civil Rights (OCR). (1994). *1992 Elementary and secondary school civil rights survey: National summaries.* Washington, DC: DBS Corporation.

Utley, C.A., Delquadri, J.C., Obiakor, F.E., & Mims, V. (2000). General and special educators' perceptions of teaching strategies for multicultural students. *Teacher Education and Special Education, 23* (1), 34–50.

Wagner, M.M. (1995). Outcomes for youths with serious emotional disturbance in secondary school and early adulthood: Critical issues for children and youths. *The Future of Children, 5* (2), 90–139.

Wagner, M., Newman, L., D'Amico, R., Jay, E.D., Butler-Nalin, P., Marder, C., & Cox, R. (1991).

Youth with disabilities: How are they doing? The first comprehensive report from the National Longitudinal Transition Study of Special Education Students. Menlo Park, CA: Stanford Research International. (ERIC Document Reproduction Service No. ED 342 204).

Will, M.C. (1986). Educating children with learning problems: A shared responsibility. *Exceptional Children, 55* (5), 411–415.

Wood, F.H. (1990). Issues in the education of behaviorally disordered students. In M.C. Wang, M.C. Reynolds, & H.J. Walberg (Eds.), *Special education research and practice: Synthesis of findings* (pp. 101–118). New York: Pergamon.

Ysseldyke, J.E., Algozzine, B., & Thurlow, M.L. (1992). *Critical issues in special education.* Boston, MA: Houghton Mifflin.

Ysseldyke, J.E., & Thurlow, M.L. (1984). Assessment practices in special education: Adequacy and appropriateness. *Educational Psychologist, 9,* 123–136.

Chapter 7

RESPONDING TO THE LEARNING NEEDS OF MULTICULTURAL LEARNERS WITH GIFTS AND TALENTS

VERA I. DANIELS

Many efforts have been made to address the inequities in the educational structure that prejudice outcomes of students from diverse ethnic, cultural, linguistic, and socioeconomic backgrounds. Educational reform efforts of the 1970s, 1980s, and 1990s; judicial judgments rendered in court cases such as *Brown v. Topeka Board of Education* (1954), *Mills v. Board of Education of the District of Columbia* (1972), *Pennsylvania Association of Retarded Children (PARC) v. Commonwealth of Pennsylvania* (1972), *Lau v. Nichols* (1973), *Diana v. California Board of Education* (1970); and federal legislative mandates such as Public Law 94-142 (The Education for All Handicapped Children Act of 1975) and its subsequent Amendments, P.L. 101-476 (The Individuals with Disabilities Education Act of 1990) and P.L. 105-17 (The Individuals with Disabilities Education Act Amendments of 1997) represent a small, yet significant sample of these efforts.

For decades, multicultural learners have been overrepresented in special education programs. In 1968, Lloyd M. Dunn called the attention of special educators to this problem. His classic article, *Special Education for the Mildly Retarded–Is Much of it Justifiable?* brought widespread attention to issues involving the efficacy of special class placements and the disproportionate representation of minority students, particularly African Americans, in classes for the mildly mentally retarded. It is unfortunate that more than three decades years later, general and special educators are still struggling with issues of disproportionate representation of multicultural learners in gifted and special class placements. While the causes of overrepresentation and underrepresentation are not fully understood, it has been suggested that poverty rather than race/ethnicity, school bias in the use of assessments, limited English proficiency, residence in inner cities, age, gender, and maturation may account for some of the problem (U.S. Department of Education, 1998). Incongruent learning and teaching styles, a lack of understanding of diverse cultures, teacher expectations, and insensitivity to cultural differences may also influence placement decisions and disproportionality patterns of multicultural learners.

In this chapter, I present one defined perspective for affecting change in the disproportionality, achievement, and placement outcomes of multicultural learners, especially those whose gifts and talents cannot be exposed through traditional educational programming. I begin with a discussion on the problems and issues in identifying multicultural learners with gifts and talents. One solution to these problems is to examine learning and cognitive style (i.e., field-independence and field-dependence) research and to highlight the results of learning/cognitive style research studies conducted with various cultural groups residing in the United States. This chapter concludes with a discussion of the effects of teaching styles on student diversity and learning and how these variables influence student referrals and placement outcomes in special education.

PROBLEMS AND ISSUES IN IDENTIFYING MULTICULTURAL LEARNERS WITH GIFTS AND TALENTS

Creating equitable conditions in school settings for multicultural learners has been a centuries-old struggle in the United States (Davidman & Davidman, 1994). This struggle still continues in this new millennium. Problems of educational equality for multicultural learners are widely focused in the literature. They range from controversies about the skills of teachers in creating educational equity in the classroom to achievement outcomes of the various groups of diverse learners. Yet, in spite of the pervasive literature on the impact of culture on learning (Banks, 1977, 1994a, 1994b); research findings on effective practices for at-risk learners (Carbo & Hodges; Johnson, 1998; Sileo & Prater, 1998); mounting research evidence on teaching/ learning styles (Carbo & Hodges, 1988; Dunn & Dunn, 1992; Saracho, 1990; Saracho & Spodek, 1981); and research findings on culturally sensitive instructional practices for diverse learners (Burke, Hagan, & Grossen, 1998; Dunn, 1995; Franklin, 1992; Sileo & Prater, 1998), educational inequities still prevail in U.S. educational system. These inequities have not only perpetuated the continual overrepresentation of students from multicultural backgrounds in special education programs, but also the continual underrepresentation of this same population in programs for students with gifts and talents.

Between 1980 and 1990, the representation of multicultural learners in special education programs increased by 13.2 percent for African Americans, 53 percent for Hispanic Americans, and 107.8 percent for Asian/Pacific Islanders, while the rate of increase for White Americans surged by only 6 percent (U.S. Department of Education, 1998). Although the rate of increase for African Americans seems somewhat small, it has great significance. African Americans represent 16 percent of elementary and secondary enrollments and 21 percent of total enrollments in special education (U.S. Department of Education). Further, it has been noted that the underrepresentation of multicultural learners (particularly, African Americans, Hispanic Americans, and American Indians) in gifted programs may be as much as 30 to 70 percent with an average of about 50 percent (Ford & Thomas, 1997). Addressing this problem of disproportionality in placement patterns of multicultural learners in gifted and special education placements can be a highly complex task because it is so difficult to isolate the specific variables that are inherent in the education system that influence disproportionality. It is equally difficult to isolate those variables that account for the disproportionate representation of males (particularly, African Americans) in special education. Research indicate that males, rather than females, account for more than two-thirds of all students served in special education programs (U.S. Department of Education). The question is, Why is this kind of representation not visible for African American males in programs for students with gifts and talents?

It is widely known that norm-referenced assessments can and do play a major role in influencing educators' decisions about placement outcomes for multicultural learners. Although such assessments have generated widespread debate regarding the efficacy of their use in assessing the cognitive abilities (i.e., intellectual and academic) of multicultural learners, they are still being used extensively in current educational systems; and their use still remains problematic despite attempts to eliminate or minimize cultural biases that are inherent in their use. While there is a clear need to discuss assessment practices related to multicultural learners, there is an equally important need to discuss instructional variables that influence learning, particularly in lieu of demographic projections related to the racial and ethnic composition of students and teachers in schools. By the year 2001, it is projected that "one-third of America's students will be culturally and linguistically diverse, while 95% of the teachers will be white" (Education Commission of the States 1990, cited in Hill, Carjuzaa, Aramburo, & Baca, 1993, p. 259). These de-

mographic projections of increasing discontinuity between the racial and ethnic composition of students and teachers has a number of implications for multicultural learners—the most salient being student-environment compatibility as related to instructional match (or mismatch) between teachers' teaching styles and students' learning styles and achievement outcomes.

How to respond to the learning and instructional needs of multicultural learners with gifts and talents continues to be a major area of great concern and relentless debates. Shade, Kelley, and Oberg (1997) noted the influence of cultural, social, and historical backgrounds of children and the impact these variables have on how multicultural learners perceive school and the educational process. As they stated:

> Culture represents a collective consciousness or a group state of mind. If people in a group share situations and problems, share the same geographical space, belong to the same tribe or clan, are of the same ethnicity or religion, or participate in the same social system or institution, they develop a common way of speaking, acting, thinking, and believing. As the behavior is institutionalized through intergenerational transmission, it becomes culture. Not only does culture provide behavioral and cognitive guidelines for functioning, it provides a sense of belonging and a special bond or unity that every human being needs. (pp. 18–19)

Thus, the cultural orientation of multicultural groups is a way of appraising and interpreting interactions with events, people, or ideas encountered in daily living, and this frame of reference has a substantial influence on multicultural learners and their approach to the learning process. As multicultural learners enter the classroom, they come in with developed rules, guidelines, and patterns that represent frames of reference for normal ways of acting, feeling, and ways of perceiving, judging, and organizing information in their daily lives. Their unique culturally determined information processing strategies are reflected in their behavioral expectations and social interaction patterns, communication style, linguistic style and vernacular, and learning styles (Shade & New, 1993).

Because the cultural orientation and learning styles of multicultural learners differ significantly from school standards and requirements, their academic and social behaviors may be viewed as incompatible with demands of the school. McIntyre (1996) wrote:

Upon entering school, students attempt to gather and process incoming information via strategies that have been rewarded previously in similar situations. If their culturally determined processing procedures are incompatible with the required cognitive style of the task, dysfunction (e.g., cognitive and emotional conflict, poor academic performance, and low self-esteem) can result. Unfortunately, the instructional methods typically used in educational settings are often incompatible with the cognitive styles and experiences of culturally and linguistically different students. (p. 355)

OVERVIEW OF LEARNING AND COGNITIVE STYLE RESEARCH

Learning styles characterize a person's way of thinking, perceiving, remembering, and understanding as well as judging and problem solving once the individual stores, transforms, and processes information (Cohen, 1969; Ramirez, 1989; Saracho, 1989; Saracho & Spodek, 1981). In educational settings, learning styles represent the characteristic way in which individuals learn, react, and respond to the various circumstances, situations, and events within their instructional (learning) environment (Saracho, 1989). As many as 13 different learning style theories (Goldstein & Blackman, 1978; Guilford, 1980) and 14 learning styles (e.g., impulsivity/reflectivity, convergent vs. divergent thinkers) have been proposed in the psychological and educational literature (Nieto, 2000; Shade, 1997; Vernon, 1972), all of which focus on a wide range of learning processes.

Dunn and Dunn (1992) identified five major domains through which individuals learn–(a) environmental (e.g., classroom noise levels, lighting, and temperatures); (b) emotional (e.g., persistence, motivation, responsibility, and need for structure); (c) sociological (e.g., students' ability to learn from or with others); (d) physiological (e.g., best

time of day for learning); and (e) psychological (e.g., preferences for learning new information). Age, gender, achievement level, poverty, socioeconomic status, and culture also contribute to the development of learning preferences, as do the teaching styles of family members and the types of learning behaviors that they encourage (Ramirez, 1989). But how students learn is dependent upon their individual learning (cognitive) style preferences (Dunn, 1995).

More than two decades ago, Gregorc (1979) described learning styles as "consisting of distinctive behaviors which serve as indicators of how a person learns from and adapts to his (her) environment" (p. 234). Learning styles are the ways in which a person "concentrates on, processes, internalizes, and remembers new and difficult academic information or skills" (Shaughnessy, 1998, p. 141). Regardless of how learning styles are defined, the educational implications are that "when students have a strong preference for the manner in which new material is presented, it may be difficult or impossible to learn when educators fail to present material in their preferred way" (Wakefield, 1993, p. 402). The greatest concern, however, is that teachers "are not equipped to identify, interpret, and respond to the variant styles of multicultural populations" (Durodoyle & Hildreth, 1995, p. 7).

Learning Style and Cross-Cultural Research

Culture has been recognized as a significant factor affecting the development of learning styles in children and adolescents (Hainer, Fagan, Bratt, Baker, & Arnold, 1990). Empirical studies on learning style (also referred to as cognitive style) have been conducted to understand life-styles, the process of adaptation, and cultural patterns for different ethnocultural groups. In earlier cross-cultural research, Berry (1976), Witkin (1978), and Witkin and Berry (1975) examined cognitive/learning style preferences of societies with different lifestyles. These researchers found that communities which relied upon their entrepreneurial ability to obtain food through hunting and migratory activities developed ecological, social, and familial interaction patterns which fostered field-independence as a coping strategy to facilitate adaptation. By contrast, societies whose life-style was more sedentary, agricultural, and cooperative developed behavioral, social, and familial patterns which fostered a field-dependence within their community. These researchers concluded that cognitive/learning styles were developed in response to the life-styles and cultural patterns of certain communities.

Research on learning style has been extended to examine the influence of culture and socialization patterns (e.g., family beliefs, religious practices, child-rearing practices, and values) on the cognitive/learning styles in multicultural groups in different geographical regions in the United States (e.g., Castaneda, 1984; Ramirez & Castaneda, 1974). For example, in their classical work, Ramirez and Castaneda (1974) found that children from traditional Mexican-American families which emphasized (a) the role of a supernatural force in explaining the meaning of life, (b) loyalty to the family and community, and (c) cooperative interpersonal relationships were more field-dependent than children reared in modern Mexican-American families which emphasized the role of science in explaining the origins of life, developed an individualistic identity, and fostered competitive interpersonal relationships. As it appears, cross-cultural research studies of field-independence and field-dependence have been conducted in non-Western and Western countries that differ in ecological adaptations, values and beliefs, socialization, and child-rearing practices (Irvine & York, 1995). Based upon this research, results have suggested that the development of field-independence and field-dependence in children are influenced by (a) life-styles and interactions of individuals within different ecological environments; and (b) traditional (e.g., strong family ties and personal relationships in the community) and non-traditional (e.g., competitiveness and individualism in the family and community) values, beliefs, and life-styles.

Field-Independent vs. Field-Dependent Learners

Learning styles and behaviors (academic and affective) characteristic of field-independent and field dependent learners have been discussed extensively in the literature (Latham, 1997; Shade, 1994,1997). Descriptions of perceptual, intellectual, and personality characteristics identified with learning and cognitive styles of field-independent and field-dependent individuals have been identified by (Saracho & Spodek, 1981) (see Table 7.1).

Field-Independent Learners

Field-independent learners have preferences for learning materials that focus on general principles rather than social content (Saracho, 1990; Saracho & Spodek, 1981). They are better able to reorganize, restructure, and process information, and can easily learn material that is devoid of structure and organization (Nieto, 2000; Saracho). Additionally, they exhibit greater competence in using their cognitive skills and abilities in learning situations to comprehend information (Saracho, 1988, 1993; Saracho & Spodek, 1981). They are more analytic rather than global in their thinking and tend to prefer and perform well in abstract subject areas such as math and science (Ramirez, 1989; Saracho & Spodek). Field-independent learners are task-oriented learners who favor instruction that is direct and impersonal (Ramirez; Saracho; Saracho & Spodek). Socially, these learners are less interactive with their classmates, and they like to work independently on academic tasks (Ramirez). Field-independent learners tend to exhibit greater cognitive competence than field-dependent learners (Saracho, 1988) and are generally not affected (distracted) by environmental stimuli when working on learning tasks (Ramirez). These learners enjoy discovery or trial-and error-learning experiences and like to try new tasks without teachers' help or guidance (Ramirez). In ad-

dition, field-independent learners also like to compete with their classmates and gain individual recognition for their accomplishments (Ramirez).

Field-Dependent Learners

Field-dependent learners are sensitive to the feelings and opinions of others (Ramirez, 1989). They seek guidance from teachers and are highly motivated by working relationships with teachers. These learners also seek rewards from teachers to strengthen their relationships with teachers, function best when the curriculum content is relevant to their personal interests and experiences, and perform better when learning objectives are carefully explained (or modeled) before engaging in an activity or lesson (Ramirez). Field-dependent learners are global, holistic learners. They have preferences for learning materials with social content and depend on teachers to define their learning goals (Saracho, 1988, 1990; Saracho & Spodek, 1981). Field-dependent learners perform well in group-oriented and cooperative learning arrangements (Franklin, 1992) which allow them to interact with others to achieve a common goal (Ramirez), and they tend to prefer group and exploratory types of experiences in the classroom (Saracho & Spodek). In addition, field dependent learners tend to learn better when teacher expectations are made clear and when school rules and learning outcomes are clear and explicit (Banks, 1994a) and when demonstrations and modeling are used during instruction (Ramirez). These learners also learn better when materials are organized and structured, have explicit instructions in problem solving techniques, and have clearly defined performance outcomes (Saracho, 1993).

Table 7.1

CHARACTERISTICS OF FIELD-INDEPENDENT AND FIELD-DEPENDENT LEARNERS

Characteristics of Field-Independent Individuals	Characteristics of Field-Dependent Individuals
• Perceive objects as separate from the field	• Rely on surrounding perceptual field
• Can abstract an item from the surrounding field and solve problems that are presented and reorganized in different contexts	• Experience their environment in a relatively global fashion by conforming to the effects of the prevailing field or context
• Experience an independence from authority which leads them to depend on their own standards and values	• Depend on authority
• Are oriented towards active striving	• Search for facial cues in those around them as a source of information
• Appear to be cold and distant	• Are strongly interested in people
• Are socially detached but have analytic skills	• Get closer to the person with whom they are interacting
• Prefer occupations that allow them to work by themselves	• Have a sensitivity to others which helps them to acquire social skills
	• Prefer occupations which require involvement with others

Source: Saracho, O. N., & Spodek, B. (1981). Teachers' cognitive styles: Educational implications. *The Educational Forum, 45*(2), 153-159.

Learning Style Dispositions of Multicultural Learners

Historically, students from multicultural backgrounds have been maligned with educational systems that thwart educational equity. This is due primarily to the fact that schools are extremely analytic (field-dependent) in their instructional approaches (Cohen, 1969), and they tend to ignore the field-dependent cognitive styles engendered by most multicultural learners (Durodoyle & Hildreth, 1995). Such prejudices have resulted in the negative mislabeling of some students, (particularly, African Americans) as being incompetent, lazy, or unwilling to learn (Durodoyle & Hildreth); misdiagnosis of cognitive (intellectual) abilities of multicultural learners; the overrepresentation of multicultural learners in special education programs; and the underrepresentation of multicultural learners in programs for students with gifts and talents.

African American Learners

The research literature has identified African American learners as field-dependent (field-sensitive) as compared to Anglo-Saxon students (Franklin, 1992; Durodoyle & Hildreth, 1995; Shade, 1994, 1997; Shade & New, 1993). They tend to be "relational, visual, mobile/kinesthetic, concrete/global tactile learners" (Ford & Webb, 1994, p. 363) who "relate best to teachers who are flexible, supportive, accepting, creative, tolerant of individual differences, and determined to ensure that learning occurs" (Banks, 1977, p. 24). With regard to instruction, African

American learners prefer group rather than individual learning experiences, cooperative rather than competitive learning situations (Byrd, 1995; Ford & Webb, 1994; Hale-Benson, 1986), and settings with subdued rather than bright light (Byrd, 1995).

Hispanic American Learners

In the research literature, Hispanic American learners have been identified as field-dependent learners as compared to Anglo-Saxon students (Ramirez & Castaneda, 1974; Saracho, 1997). They learn best in cooperative learning arrangements and in environments that are noise-free or with few distractions (Baruth & Manning, 1992). Hispanic American learners often seek close relationships with their teachers, and are more comfortable in learning broad concepts rather than component facts and specifics (Guild, 1994).

Asian American/Pacific Islander Learners

Asian American/Pacific Islander learners have been identified as field-dependent learners (Timm & Chiang, 1997). They too work best in a well-structured, quiet, learning environment in which specific goals have been established (Baruth & Manning, 1992). Asian American/Pacific Islander learners mostly learn by observation, memorization, patterned practice, and rote rather than discovery learning (Sileo & Prater, 1998). These

learners often seek teacher approval and make decisions (personal/academic) based on what the teacher thinks is best (Baruth & Manning; Yao, 1985). In the classroom, Asian American/Pacific Islander learners seldom express their opinions, ideas, or abilities voluntarily (Baruth & Manning). Some Asian American/Pacific Islander learners(those of Japanese and Korean decent) prefer formal relationships with teachers and prefer to work individually for teacher recognition (Sileo & Prater).

American Indian Learners

American Indian learners, most of whom are field-independent in their learning styles, are reflective thinkers (Guild, 1994; Kaulback, 1997). These students are soft spoken, cooperative, and patient. American Indian students have acute skills in visual discrimination and in the use of imagery (Guild) and they tend to process information in a global/analytic manner (Baruth & Manning, 1992). American Indian learners prefer to learn using visual/perceptual/spatial information and the use of mental images to enhance their memorization, recall, and understanding of words and concepts (Baruth & Manning; Utley, 1983). With regard to instruction, teachers should establish a context for the presentation of new information, provide quite times for students to engage in reflective thinking, and incorporate the use of various types of visual stimuli in their teaching methods (Guild).

LEARNING STYLES: IMPLICATIONS FOR MULTICULTURAL LEARNERS WITH GIFTS AND TALENTS

The implications of learning styles on multicultural learners have been discussed extensively throughout the literature (Banks, 1994a, 1994b; Carbo & Hodges, 1988; Dunn, 1995; Dunn & Dunn, 1992; Franklin, 1992; Grant & Sleeter, 1998; Saracho, 1990; Shade, Kelly, & Oberg, 1997; Sileo & Prater, 1998). In short, the literature suggests that teachers who use culturally responsive teaching styles, positively influence the learning outcomes of their students. Yet, the teaching methods and instructional practices that are currently used in schools are in stark contrast to learning styles of most multicultural learners with gifts and talents. Bridging cultural barriers in teaching/learning styles can be particularly challenging. Teachers must become sensitive to cultural differences and develop skills in recognizing the gifts and talents of students across the spectrum of culture, class, and color. Failure to use culturally responsive teaching styles further perpetuate the educational injustices that already exist in schools. Although researchers are still grappling with issues on how cultural learning styles interact with instructional approaches, it is clear that current instructional practices that prevail in the educational system necessitate major changes.

How do general and special educators respond to instructional needs of multicultural learners in gifted education programs? Based on what is known about learning characteristics and learning styles (preferences) of multicultural learners, one can assert that instructional practices for at-risk, disadvantaged, and atypical learners are also effective for multicultural learners. One can further surmise that a student's educational placement (special class or gifted) does not diminish the effectiveness of these instructional practices. Carbo and Hodges (1988) identified and expounded upon several instructional practices derived from learning-styles-based instruction that were found to be effective for at-risk learners. These practices include such strategies such as identifying and matching students' learning styles; the sharing of learning styles information with students; reduced emphasis on skill work that require strong analytic thinking; the initial teaching of new concepts from a global rather than analytic perspective to help students develop relevant context and meaning for the concepts to be learned; quiet work environments; and the use of a variety of instructional methods and cooperative learning arrangements. Johnson

(1998) identified and summarized instructional principles for at-risk learners. These principles emphasized the maintenance of high expectations for all students; the use of praise and encouragement; the use of teaching and learning strategies that facilitate student learning; the use of a wide range of stimuli (environmental and emotional) to accommodate students' learning styles to maximize learning; a focus on skills, concepts, and activities that have relevance and meaning to students; the use of examples and demonstrations during the instructional process to enhance students' learning and performance; active engagement of students in the learning process; cooperative learning methods; the use of questioning methods to stimulate students thinking and learning; and the celebration of cultural diversity in the classroom through multicultural education.

A few years ago, Franklin (1992) delineated culturally sensitive instructional practices for African American learners with disabilities. Interestingly, these same techniques could help maximize the learning potential of intellectual students with gifts and talents. She noted that strategies that (a) incorporated various formats of instructional presentation; (b) embodied culturally sensitive teacher-student interactions (e.g., the occasional use of dialect in conversations with students); (c) included instructional activities that are meaningful and realistic to the cultural environment; and (d) included cooperative learning arrangements such as peer-tutoring, peer/cross-age grouping were more effective in fostering learning and helping relationships between learners. In short, the delivery of appropriate and equitable educational services to students from multicultural backgrounds is not an easy simplistic process. The problem is that the current system of education is heavily influenced by Anglo American perspectives in which most teachers (who are also Anglo Americans) are not prepared to create and maintain learning environments to meet the need of students from diverse, racial, ethnic, cultural, linguistic, and socioeconomic backgrounds. Although identical styles matching (learning-based-styles instruction) is the most effective and preferred means of educational delivery (general, inclusion, special, and gifted education) for students from culturally divergent backgrounds, general and special educators must also "concentrate on teaching students about their learning style strengths, how to teach themselves and each other, and how to bypass their teachers' styles when they are mismatched with their learning styles" (Dunn, 1995, p. 30).

TEACHING STYLES: IMPACT ON LEARNING OUTCOMES OF MULTICULTURAL LEARNERS WITH GIFTS AND TALENTS

Teaching styles may be described as a pervasive way of approaching learners through the use of carefully selective methods of teaching (Henson & Borthwick, 1984). They may also be viewed as the instructional approaches and strategies that teachers use to affect learning. Discussions on teaching styles are also rooted in research on cognitive style. According to Saracho (1990), studies on teaching styles reflect a wide range of outcomes with regard to the issue of educational desirability for matching cognitive styles of teachers and students. These studies have generally focused on two dimensions—those that propose a match with teacher and student personality types (Smith & Renzulli, 1984), that is identical matching styles (Saracho); and those that focus on various teaching strategies and their appropriateness for diverse learners, (Smith & Renzulli), that is, performance matching styles (Saracho). Although both of these approaches to matching have yielded mixed results, it is generally believed that congruence or matching of similar personality types between teachers and students results in greater achievement outcomes, especially for students who are culturally different from the dominant culture.

Personality Traits and Teaching Styles

The personality traits and teaching styles of field-independent teachers are distinctly different from field-dependent teachers. Field-independent teachers are analytic or differentiated; field-dependent teachers are global or undifferentiated (Saracho, 1989). The differences in teaching approaches of field-independent and field-dependent teachers can be summarized in the following discussions.

Field-Independent Teachers

Field-independent teachers tend to be task-oriented, impersonal, and socially detached from their students (Saracho, 1993; Saracho & Spodek, 1981). These teachers interact mostly with their students as a whole class (Saracho, 1988, 1990). Field-independent teachers prefer to use the lecture approach to teaching (Hunt & Marshall, 1994) and teaching situations that are impersonal. These teachers have limited teacher-student interactions with their students, and their teaching is oriented more toward abstract cognitive elements (Saracho, 1988). In addition, field-independent teachers use questioning methods that are analytic in nature to promote, encourage, and enhance student learning; and they organize and direct students' learning, and encourage independent (individual) student achievement and competition among students (Gollnick & Chinn, 1991, 1994; Hunt & Marshall, 1994; Saracho, 1988). Last, field-independent teachers tend to extend more classroom freedom to students in their classes (Saracho).

Field-Dependent Teachers

Field-dependent (field-sensitive) teachers are interpersonally oriented (Gollnick & Chinn, 1991, 1994; Hunt & Marshall, 1994), compassionate, and understanding of student needs. They prefer to use personal conversational techniques with their students (Gollnick & Chinn), and interpersonal teaching methods (such as discussion and discovery approaches) that permit, encourage, and foster interpersonal interactions among students (Hunt & Marshall; Saracho, 1988, 1990). Field-dependent teachers interact frequently with their students in small groups as well as individually and they involve students more in establishing their own goals, structuring their learning activities, and guiding their learning. These teachers also infuse the questioning method during their instruction to assess students' learning, and they use instructional practices that incorporate the use of concrete instructional elements (Sara-

cho). Field-dependent teachers also exercise more control of students' learning in their classroom with regard to instruction, class activities, classroom management, evaluation, and supervision.

It is important to note that the implications of teaching styles on multicultural learners are boundless. Apparently, field-independent and field-dependent teachers differ in their academic and social interactions with students, their conceptual levels of instructional activity, the kinds of feedback they provide to their students, the methods of assessment that they use to evaluate students' learning, and the methods they use to encourage and promote learning. Thus, when teachers' teaching styles are incongruent or remarkably different from the learning styles of their students, it makes learning difficult for both the teacher and the student (Hunt & Marshall, 1994). Such a mismatch between teaching/learning styles can evoke a number of potentially devastating outcomes for multicultural learners, especially those with gifts and talents. These outcomes may include underachievement, low academic performance, substantially higher rates of referral to special education, lower referral rates for gifted education, and low teacher expectations. It may also cause students to have inaccurate self-knowledge, self-esteem and self-ideal (Obiakor, 1999).

NEW VISION FOR MULTICULTURAL LEARNERS WITH GIFTS AND TALENTS

Teaching students in ways that compliment their learning styles can enhance students' learning; improve their overall academic performance; accentuate their gifts and talents which may otherwise be unrecognizable; and reduce underachievement, low academic performance, and the disproportionate representation patterns of multicultural learners in gifted and special education programs. While

there are limits to how much educational equality can be legislated (Heward & Cavanaugh, 1993), teachers can provide equitable education to students with diverse backgrounds, abilities, and experiences by embracing and respecting cultural differences, obtaining knowledge about learning styles, and by endorsing the ideology of educational matching (teaching and learning) in their instructional styles. In short, effective teachers of multicultural learners guard against "overteaching" by their own preferred learning styles (Friedman & Alley, 1984). These teachers also excel in five domains—content knowledge, teaching for student learning, creating a classroom community for student learning, teacher professionalism, and the incorporation of culturally responsive pedagogy in their teaching methods (Garcia, 1994). When properly done, the potential of multicultural learners with gifts and talents will be eventually maximized.

Many scholars and educators (Ford & Webb, 1994; Kranz, 1994; Patton, 1992) have discussed the limitations of traditional assessment instruments in predicting the abilities of students from diverse cultural backgrounds. While such instruments may provide a basis for addressing students' needs with regard to enrichment, often these tests fail to identify underachievers who have gifts and talents (Ford & Webb; Kranz) and they tend to place diverse learners at greater risk for referral to special education. Researchers have also noted a number of interesting findings with regard to identification practices. First, students from multicultural populations are more likely to be identified by their teachers as having learning difficulties (mental retardation, learning disabilities, and emotional disturbance). Second, teachers' rates of referral to special education are significantly higher for multicultural learners than for their White Anglo American counterparts. Third,

most referrals of students from multicultural backgrounds often end in special education placements, which ultimately leads to the overrepresentation of multicultural learners in special education. Moreover, researchers have found that students from multicultural backgrounds are gravely underrepresented in gifted education programs.

Recognizing gifts and talents of students across the spectrum of ethnic and cultural groups must be an imperative for educators. Gifts and talents are multidimensional and multimodal (Ford & Webb, 1994) and they tend to be found across all cultural, racial, ethnic, and socioeconomic groups (Hilliard, 1992; Kranz, 1994). As Ford and Webb explained, "Tapping the talents and potential of all children requires a broadened vision of giftedness which reflects the understanding that talent and creativity may vary markedly depending upon students' cultural, ethnic, economic, and linguistic backgrounds" (1994, p. 371). It is crucial that general and special educators understand factors that place multicultural learners at greater risk for misclassification, misidentification, or inappropriate placements, higher referrals for special education, and lower referrals for gifted education. These factors include teachers' methods of instruction (teaching style), inflexibility in teaching style, pace of learning, curriculum content, low achievement expectations, insensitivity to individual differences, and lack of knowledge, understanding, and responsiveness to cultural differences.

CONCLUSION

The disproportionate representation of students from multicultural backgrounds in gifted and special education programs is a complex and persistent problem. Although many legal and legislative efforts have been made to ameliorate this problem, these ef-

forts have not fully deterred discriminatory educational practices in the assessment, education, and placement of multicultural learners (Obiakor, 1992). The use of culturally sensitive instructional practices is essential to effective teaching, so is the recognition of social-environmental (social-cultural) variables that may have negative consequences for children from diverse racial and ethnic backgrounds. It is unfortunate that our public schools are dominated by field-independent and discovery-oriented instructional approaches and methods which are in stark conflict with the ways in which most diverse students learn (Ramirez, 1989). Providing individualized, meaningful, relevant, and developmentally appropriate curricular and learning experiences reflective of instructional practices that are sensitive to the unique needs, cognitive abilities, learning styles, and cultural and linguistic experiences of diverse learners is central to best practices and equitable educational opportunities for multicultural learners.

REFERENCES

Banks, J.A. (1977). *Multiethnic education: Practices and promises.* Bloomington, IN: Phi Delta Kappa Educational Foundation.

Banks, J.A. (1994a). *An introduction to multicultural education.* Needham Heights, MA: Allyn and Bacon.

Banks, J.A. (1994b). *Multiethnic education: Theory and practice* (3rd ed.). Needham Heights, MA: Allyn and Bacon.

Baruth, L.G., & Manning, M.L. (1992). *Multicultural education of children and adolescents.* Needham Heights, MA: Allyn and Bacon.

Berry, J. (1976). *Human ecology and cognitive style: Comparative studies in cultural and psychological adaptation.* New York: John Wiley & Sons.

Burke, M.D., Hagan, S.L., & Grossen, B. (1998). What curricular designs and strategies accommodate diverse learners? *Teaching Exceptional Children, 3*(1), 34–38.

Byrd, H.B. (1995). Curricular and pedagogical procedures for African American learners with academic and cognitive disabilities. In B.A. Ford, F.E. Obiakor, & J.M. Patton (Eds.), *Effective education of African American exceptional learners: New perspectives* (pp. 123–150). Austin, TX: PRO-ED.

Carbo, M., & Hodges, H. (1988). Learning styles strategies can help students at risk. *Teaching Exceptional Children, 20*(4), 55–58.

Castaneda, A. (1984). Traditionalism, modernism, and ethnicity. In J.L. Martinez & R.H . Mendoza (Eds.), *Chicano psychology* (pp. 35–40). San Diego, CA: Academic Press.

Cohen, R.A. (1969). Conceptual styles, culture conflict and nonverbal tests of intelligence. *American Anthropologist, 71,* 826–828.

Davidman, L., & Davidman, P.T. (1994). *Teaching with a multicultural perspective: A practical guide.* White Plains, NY: Longman.

Dunn, R. (1995). *Strategies for educating diverse learners.* Bloomington, IN: Phi Delta Kappa Educational Foundation.

Dunn, R., & Dunn, K. (1992). *Teaching elementary students through their individual learning styles.* Needham Heights, MA: Allyn & Bacon.

Durodoyle, B., & Hildreth, B. (1995). Learning styles and the African-American student. *Education, 116*(2), 241–247.

Ford, D.Y., & Thomas, A. (1997). *Underachievement among gifted minority students: Problems and promises* (ERIC Digest No. E544). Reston, VA: The Council for Exceptional Children.

Ford, D.Y., & Webb, K.S. (1994). Desegregation of gifted educational programs: The impact of Brown on underachieving children of color. *Journal of Negro Education, 63*(3), 358–375.

Franklin, M.E. (1992). Culturally sensitive instructional practices for African-American learners with disabilities. *Exceptional Children, 59*(2), 115–122.

Friedman, P., & Alley, R. (1984). Learning/teaching styles: Applying the principles. *Theory Into Practice, 23*(1), 76–81.

Garcia, E. (1994). *Understanding and meeting the challenge of student cultural diversity.* Boston, MA: Houghton Mifflin.

Goldstein, K.M., & Blackman, S. (1978). *Five approaches and relevant research.* New York: John Wiley & Sons.

Gollnick, D.M., & Chinn, P.C. (1991). *Multicultural education for exceptional children* (ERIC Digest

No. E498). Reston, VA: The Council for Exceptional Children.

Gollnick, D.M., & Chinn, P.C. (1994). *Multicultural education in a pluralistic society* (4th ed.). New York: Macmillan.

Grant, C.A., & Sleeter, C.E. (1998). *Turning on learning: Five approaches for multicultural teaching plans for race, class, gender, and disability* (2nd ed.). Columbus, OH: Merrill.

Gregorc, A.F. (1979). Learning/teaching styles: Potent forces behind them. *Educational Leadership, 36*(4), 234–236.

Guild, P. (1994). The culture/learning style connection. *Educational Leadership, 51*(8), 16–21.

Guildford, J.P. (1980). Cognitive styles: What are they? *Educational and Psychological Measurement, 40,* 715–735.

Hainer, E.V., Fagan, B., Bratt, T., Baker, L., & Arnold, N. (1990). *Integrating learning styles and skills in ESL classrooms.* Washington, DC: National Clearinghouse for Bilingual Education.

Hale-Benson, J. (1986). *Black children: Their roots, culture, and learning styles.* Baltimore, MD: John Hopkins University Press.

Henson, K.T., & Borthwick, P. (1984). Matching styles: A historical look. *Theory Into Practice, 23*(1), 3–9.

Heward, W.L., & Cavanaugh, R.A. (1993). Educational equality for students with disabilities. In J.A. Banks & C.A. McGhee Banks (Eds.), *Multicultural education: Issues and perspectives* (2nd ed., pp. 239–261). Needham Heights, MA: Allyn & Bacon.

Hill, R., Carjuzaa, J., Aramburo, D., & Baca, L. (1993). Culturally and linguistically diverse teachers in special education: Repairing or redesigning the leaky pipeline. *Teacher Education and Special Education, 16*(3), 258–269.

Hilliard, A.G. (1992). The pitfalls and promises of special education practice. *Exceptional Children, 59*(2), 168–172.

Hunt, N., & Marshall, K. (1994). *Exceptional children and youth: An introduction to special education.* Boston, MA: Houghton Mifflin.

Irvine, J.J., & York, D.E. (1995). Learning styles and culturally diverse students: A literature review. In J.A. Banks & C.A. McGhee Banks (Eds.), *Handbook of research on multicultural education* (pp. 484–497). New York: Macmillan.

Johnson, G.M. (1998). Principles of instruction for at-risk learners. *Preventing School Failure, 42*(4), 167–174.

Kaulback, B. (1997). Styles of learning among Native-American children: A review of research. In B.J. Shade (Ed.), *Culture, style, and the educative process: Making schools work for racially diverse students* (2nd ed., pp. 92–104). Springfield, IL: Charles C Thomas.

Kranz, B. (1994). *Identifying talents among multicultural children.* Bloomington, IN: Phi Delta Kappa Educational Foundation.

Latham, A.S. (1997). Responding to cultural learning styles. *Educational Leadership, 54*(7), 88–89.

McIntyre, T. (1996). Does the way we teach create behavior disorders in culturally different students? *Education and Treatment of Children, 19*(3), 354–370.

Nieto, S. (2000). *Affirming diversity: The sociopolitical context of multicultural education* (3rd ed.). White Plains, NY: Longman.

Obiakor, F.E. (1992). Self-concept of African-American students: An operational model for special education. *Exceptional Children, 59*(2), 160–167.

Patton, J.M. (1992). Assessment and identification of African American learners with gifts and talents. *Exceptional Children, 59*(2), 150–159.

Ramirez, M. (1989). A bicognitive-multicultural model for a pluralistic education. *Early Child Development and Care, 51,* 129–136.

Ramirez, M., & Castaneda, A. (1974). *Cultural democracy, bicognitive development and education.* New York: Academic Press.

Saracho, O.N. (1988). Cognitive styles: Implications for the preparation of early childhood teachers. *Early Child Development and Care, 38,* 1–11.

Saracho, O.N. (1989). Cognitive style: Individual differences. *Early Child Development and Care, 53,* 75–81.

Saracho, O.N. (1990). The match and mismatch of teachers and students' cognitive styles. *Early Childhood Development and Care, 54,* 99–109.

Saracho, O.N. (1993). Sociocultural perspectives in the cognitive styles of young students and teachers. *Early Child Development and Care, 84,* 1–17.

Saracho, O.N. (1997). Cultural differences in the cognitive style of Mexican-American students. In B.J. Shade (Ed.), *Culture, style, and the educa-*

tive process: Making schools work for racially diverse students (2nd ed., pp. 118–125). Springfield, IL: Charles C Thomas.

Saracho, O.N., & Spodek, B. (1981). Teachers' cognitive styles: Educational implications. *The Educational Forum, 45*(2), 153–159.

Shade, B.J. (1994). Understanding the African American learner. In E.R. Hollins, J.E. King, & W.C. Hayman (Eds.), *Teaching diverse populations: Formulating a knowledge base* (pp. 175–190). Albany, NY: SUNY Press.

Shade, B.J. (1997). *Culture, style, and the educative process: Making schools work for racially diverse students* (2nd ed.). Springfield, IL: Charles C Thomas.

Shade, B.J., Kelley, C., & Oberg, M. (1997). *Creating culturally responsive classrooms*. Washington, DC: The American Psychological Association.

Shade, B.J., & New, C. (1993). Cultural influences on learning: Teaching implications. In J.A. Banks & C.A. McGhee Banks (Eds.), *Multicultural education: Issues and perspectives* (pp. 317–331). Needham Heights, MA: Allyn & Bacon.

Shaughnessy, M.F. (1998). An interview with Rita Dunn about learning styles. *The Clearing House, 71*(3), 141–145.

Sileo, T.W., & Prater, M.A. (1998). Creating classroom environments that address the linguistic and cultural backgrounds of students with disabilities: An Asian Pacific American perspective. *Remedial and Special Education, 19*(6), 323–337.

Smith, L.H., & Renzulli, J.S. (1984). Learning style preferences: A practical approach for classroom teachers. *Theory Into Practice, 23*(1), 44–50.

Timm, J., & Chiang, B. (1997). Among culture and cognitive style. In B.J. Shade (Ed.), *Culture, style, and the educative process: Making schools work for racially diverse students* (2nd ed., pp. 105–117). Springfield, IL: Charles C Thomas.

U.S. Department of Education. (1998). *Twentieth annual report to congress on the implementation of the individuals with disabilities education act.* Washington, DC: Author.

Utley, C.A. (1983). *A cross-cultural investigation of field-independence/field-dependence as a psychological variable in Menominee Native American and EuroAmerican grade school students.* Unpublished doctoral dissertation, University of Wisconsin-Madison.

Vernon, P. (1972). The distinctiveness of field-independence. *Journal of Personality, 40,* 366–391.

Wakefield, A.P. (1993), Learning styles and learning dispositions in public schools: Some implications of preference. *Education, 113*(3), 402–406.

Witkin, H.A. (1978). *Cognitive styles in personal and cultural adaptation.* Hartford, CT: Hartford Clark Press.

Witkin, H.A., & Berry, J. (1976). Psychological differentiation in cross-cultural perspective. *Journal of Cross-Cultural Psychology, 6,* 65–87.

Yao, E.L.(1985). Adjustment needs of Asian immigrant children. *Elementary School Guidance and Counseling, 19,* 222–227.

Chapter 8

MULTICULTURALISM AND DISABILITY IN A RESULTS-BASED EDUCATIONAL SYSTEM: HAZARDS AND HOPES FOR TODAY'S SCHOOLS

MARTHA L. THURLOW, J. RUTH NELSON, ELLEN TEELUCKSINGH, AND INGRID L. DRAPER

The issue of bias in assessment has been present since the introduction of the intelligence test. According to Kamin (1975), "Since its introduction to America, the intelligence test has been used more or less consciously as an instrument of oppression against the underprivileged–the poor, the foreign born, and racial minorities" (p. 1). There has been considerable research conducted in this area, especially on the development of assessment tools and devices that are not biased toward members of certain groups. However, there continues to be ongoing concern among educators about finding an appropriate and unbiased measure to administer to individuals from varying backgrounds (Ysseldyke, Algozzine, & Thurlow, 2000).

To understand specific issues related to bias in assessment and its impact on multicultural students with disabilities, the issue of bias must be first examined more broadly. One major concern related to bias in assess-ment involves the disproportionate represen-tation of multicultural students in special ed-ucation (Reschly, 1997). More general concerns in this area were uncovered in testimony given before the congressional committee on the Protection in Evaluation Procedures Provisions of PL 94-142. Ys-seldyke, Algozzine, and Thurlow (2000) noted that bias in the entire assessment process includes the inappropriate and indiscriminate use of tests, bias in the assessment of children with disabilities, bias in the identification of children who might be incorrectly labeled as having a disability, bias throughout the decision making process, and bias following assessment.

Historically, bias-in-assessment issues have emerged for assessments used for eligibility or certification determinations. However, state and district assessments now are becoming the kind of assessments that students more frequently encounter as they progress through school. And, in the past five years, these types of large-scale assessments have taken on importance as states and districts stress accountability for the results of education. As the nation moves toward increased emphasis on educational accountability, it is important to step back and examine the relationship between multicultural concerns and these large-scale assessments. As it appears, educational outcomes are the subject of much controversy. The nation's concern about the results of education—its outcomes—has come about through the realization that simply providing youngsters with an education does not ensure that they will leave school with skills needed to be good workers and contributing members of society. Concerns about outcomes of education are reflected in many national reform initiatives, including the development of a common set of national educational **goals,** repeated calls to raise educational **standards,** and increased emphasis on **assessment.** These reform initiatives are reflected in both general and special education laws. For example, Title I now is to be evaluated by progress toward standards, measured through state assessments, and the 1997 reauthorization of the Individuals with Disabilities Education Act (IDEA 97, PL 105-17) requires that states report on test-based outcomes of students with disabilities. All of these reform efforts have contributed to a push toward focusing on the *results* of education, rather than on the process of education.

There is an incredible push in education for schools, teachers and students to be held accountable for the results of instruction (American Federation of Teachers, 1998; Education Commission of the States, 1998a, 1998b; Erickson, Ysseldyke, Thurlow, & Elliott, 1998; Rouse, Shriner, & Danielson, 1999). Although the emphasis on results-based education seems new, it really is ingrained in educational theory. Foundational theorists have equated education to a system with inputs and resources, processes, and results (see Oakes, 1986; Shavelson, McDon-

nell, & Oakes, 1989; Shavelson, McDonnell, Oakes, & Carey, 1987). Inputs to an educational system refer to teachers and students who have certain characteristics (e.g., qualifications and socioeconomic status) and resources of the school district such as federal and state funds. The process of education is a description of what happens in the classroom on a daily basis (e.g., the number of minutes spent in instruction and the curricula being used). Together, inputs and the process of education produce results for students, teachers, and schools (e.g., student performance, dropout rates, and graduation rates). Based on these results, different stakeholders may experience direct and indirect consequences (e.g., graduation, monetary rewards for exemplary schools, and intervention assistance teams). General and special educators have encountered this accountability for any or all of the above components of an educational system, but the emphasis today is clearly on the results of education.

Some would argue that accountability initiatives have contributed to practices and procedures that are incompatible with the increasing multiculturalism and student diversity evident in schools today. Of particular concern are those students who are from different cultural and ethnic backgrounds and who also have disabilities. Jesse Jackson (cited in Tennyson & Leung, 1993), Executive Director of Rainbow Coalition, referred to the lack of attention to these individuals in a report from the National Council on Disability when he noted that "people with disabilities have always been excluded from the bounty of our nation's resources. Minorities with disabilities, in particular, have been the most disenfranchised of the disenfranchised. It is time that we bring them into the fold as full, first-class participants in our society" (p. 1).

In this chapter, we explore the hopes and hazards of a results-based educational system in relation to student diversity in today's schools. First, an overview of the move from access to results and the IDEA '97 requirements is provided, including information on school and student accountability and how multiculturalism fits within this system. Then, the critical educational outcomes being identified by various groups and in various locations are explored. This is followed by an examination of assessment issues that accompany a results-based educational system. We conclude the chapter with a discussion of some possible hazards of a results-based educational system, along with our hopes for a results-based accountability system that truly includes all students. Innovative ways to meet the challenges of student diversity (including both multiculturalism and disability) in today's schools are explored.

MOVEMENT FROM ACCESS TO RESULTS

With the reauthorization of IDEA in 1997, the accountability movement has stepped forward to include the performance of students with disabilities. In the past, the emphasis of education reform for students with disabilities focused on the inputs, resources, and processes of special education (e.g., number of students served and educational placements). However, IDEA '97 officially added a results-based focus to a focus on access for the education of students with disabilities. Thus, special education has moved to a system with accountability for both services and student learning. As a consequence, state education agencies (SEAs) must report, with the same frequency as for non-disabled students, the number of students participating in regular and alternate assessments. Furthermore, performance data for students with disabilities must now be disaggregated in the reporting of results for students. States must document results for students with disabilities in the context of their developing educational accountability systems. The requirement to report aggregate and disaggregate results for students with disabilities reflects the belief that educators and the public need to know how well these groups of students are profiting from their educational experiences.

Although IDEA '97 is intended to illuminate the educational progress of students with disabilities, there continues to be a gap in the knowledge about students with disabilities who come from multicultural backgrounds. IDEA '97 requires that states report on the numbers of students with disabilities served by minority status, but it does not specify that *results* for students with disabilities should be disaggregated by minority status Aggregated results provide only a general picture of how all students with disabilities are performing. Pertinent information about the performance of subgroups of these students may not be revealed without looking at their results separately. Furthermore, if scholars and educators do not clearly understand how multicultural learners or any other group of students with disabilities is performing in statewide assessments, how can educational reform initiatives accurately reflect any improvements intended to benefit these students? With IDEA '97 came the presumption that if accountability systems are built with high standards and schools and students are held accountable, the performance of schools and students will improve. Challenging standards should guide the choices of assessments, curriculum, and instructional practices that enable students to meet the standards. Professional development that equips teachers with the skills and knowledge to enact these practices, and accountability based on assessments, are intended to help motivate teachers to change (David & Shields, 1999).

Educational Accountability Systems

Educational accountability systems are the vehicles that embody results-based education. Accountability is the systematic collection, analysis, and use of information to hold schools, educators, and others responsible for the performance of students and the education system (Education Commission of the States, 1998a, 1998b). How do states and educators evaluate and communicate the outcomes of all students? To accomplish this goal, most States are in the process of designing inclusive accountability systems and public reports of student performance to ensure the attainment of higher educational standards for all students. A few states have already designed their accountability systems to ensure those inside and outside the educational arena that students, including students with disabilities, are moving toward desired goals (Westat, 1993).

By definition, a complete school accountability system includes (1) information about the organization's performance (e.g., dropout rates and test scores); (2) standards for judging the quality or degree of success of organizational performance; (3) significant consequences to the organization (i.e., rewards, such as bonuses to teachers in school, and sanctions, such as firing staff), and (4) an agent or constituency that receives information on organizational performance, judges the extent to which standards have been met, and distributes rewards and sanctions (Newmann, King, & Rigdon, 1997). Nationally, there are 40 states that distribute consequences for schools or staff (Education Commission of the States, 1998a, 1998b). There is no doubt that educational accountability systems are the sine quo non of student accountability. Student accountability means that students are held accountable for their educational performance and consequences are attached to their performance. Half of the states (N=25) have a test with high stakes consequences for students (e.g., graduation requirement) (Education Commission of the States). Twenty states have a graduation test that must be passed in order for a student to graduate from high school (Guy, Shin, Lee, & Thurlow, 1999). The majority of states (N=41) have alternative types of exit documents including certificates of attendance, achievement, or completion, and/or an IEP diploma (Guy et al.).

CRITICAL EDUCATIONAL OUTCOMES FOR TODAY'S STUDENTS

Educational outcomes continue to be defined at a variety of levels. With continued emphasis on educational reform at the national level, six national educational goals were originally identified at the summit of the nation's Governors and the President in the Fall of 1989. When Goals 2000: Educate America Act was passed in 1994 (Public Law 103-224), these six goals were expanded to encompass eight goals. It is also worthwhile to look at the outcomes and standards defined by State Departments of Education as an indicator of what are considered critical educational outcomes. Finally, outcomes defined by the National Center on Educational Outcomes to encompass the needs of students with disabilities provide another view of what are considered to be critical educational outcomes. The delineation of outcomes can be evaluated to determine the commonalities and differences in outcomes that are being defined and their relevance to students from diverse cultural backgrounds with disabilities.

National Education Goals

The eight national education goals established in 1994 were to direct the nation's reform efforts through the year 2000. As society begins the new millennium and looks ahead to the future, national education goals will continue to be relevant to the nation's educational reform efforts. The eight goals are:

- All children in America will start school ready to learn.
- The high school graduation rate will increase to at least 90 percent.
- All students will leave grades 4, 8, and 12 having demonstrated competency over challenging subject matter including English, mathematics, science, foreign languages, civics and government, economics, arts, history, and geography, and every school in America will ensure that all students will use their minds well, so they may be prepared for responsible citizenship, further learning, and productive employment in our Nation's modern economy.
- The Nation's teaching force will have access to programs for the continued improvement of their professional skills and the opportunity to acquire the knowledge and skills needed to instruct and prepare all American students for the next century [now the new millennium].
- United States students will be first in the world in mathematics and science achievement.
- Every adult American will be literate and will possess the knowledge and skills necessary to compete in a global economy and ex-

ercise the rights and responsibilities of citizenship.
- Every school in the United States will be free of drugs, violence, and the unauthorized presence of firearms and alcohol and will offer a disciplined environment conducive to learning.
- Every school will promote partnerships that will increase parental involvement and participation in promoting the social, emotional, and academic growth of children. (National Education Goals Panel, 1998)

The above goals have been criticized to some extent by their primary focus on academics. Yet, as the National Education Goals Panel members noted, the goals were not written to define all that is important in education. Rather, they represent some very important outcomes that the nation needs to be measuring to monitor its progress in its educational reform efforts. Still, the goals have spurred a range of other activities (e.g., standards setting and assessment development) that are focused on academics. Although significant progress toward these goals may not seem apparent, there has been some encouraging news in the past few years that are worth noting. The nation has made progress toward Goal 1: Ready to Learn, Goal 3: Student Achievement and Citizenship, and Goal 5: Mathematics and Science (National Education Goals Panel, 1998). It is also important to note that individual states are continuing to make significant progress toward meeting the goals (National Education Goals Panel, 1998).

Outcomes Defined by States

States have developed and continue to develop a range of goals, standards, expectations, outcomes, and objectives in the wake of the national education goals. All but one state now have established content standards

that define what students should know and be able to do. Performance standards also have been developed by individual states (N=21) to better gauge how well students must perform in school (American Federation of Teachers, 1998). Currently, states have not yet defined Opportunity to Learn (OTL) standards. Such standards would address what must be provided so that students can meet content and performance standards.

Outcomes Identified by the National Center on Educational Outcomes

The National Center on Educational Outcomes (NCEO) engaged in a comprehensive effort in 1990 to identify outcomes that reflect a broad range of perspectives and that are appropriate for *all* students, including students with disabilities. The identification of outcomes involved a wide array of people, including policymakers, parents, teachers, administrators, school board members, legislators, and others in an intensive consensus-building approach. In addition to Academic and Functional Literacy, the outcome domains identified by NCEO were Presence and Participation, Accommodation and Family Involvement, Physical Health, Social and Emotional Adjustment, Responsibility and Independence, Contribution and Citizenship, and Satisfaction.

Later, the National Association of State Directors of Special Education (NASDSE) developed a conceptual model for a "balanced system of accountability" that includes system standards, inputs and processes, and student learning outcomes (Ahearn & Crocker, 1995). Then, NCEO revised its outcomes into a framework for educational accountability (shown in Figure 8.1) that can be used to implement parts of the NASDSE model (Ysseldyke, Krentz, Elliott, Thurlow, Erickson, & Moore, 1998). Educational outcomes and indicators are specified for six developmental levels (ages three and six, grades four, eight, and twelve, and post-school). The key outcome domains of education results for systems and individuals that have been identified again and again by the NCEO consensus meeting participants are:

- Academic and Functional Literacy
- Physical Health
- Responsibility and Independence
- Citizenship
- Personal and Social Well-being
- Satisfaction

The key domains that have been identified for Educational Processes are:

- Participation
- Family Involvement
- Accommodation

See Table 8.1 for further description of educational results and processes (Ysseldyke et al., 1998).

Commonalities and Differences in Outcomes

Outcomes that have been identified within national, State, and local systems are fairly consistent with each other, for the most part. Nevertheless, the emphasis tends to be given to the outcomes that are considered academic in nature. One of the reasons for this, undoubtedly, is because the academic outcomes are easier to objectify and measure. In the first attempts by the National Education Goals Panel (1991) to identify measures for monitoring progress on Goal 3, it was concluded that the National Assessment of Educational Progress (NAEP) would be used to measure the academic area, but that there were no measures currently available to measure other aspects of the goal (e.g., using

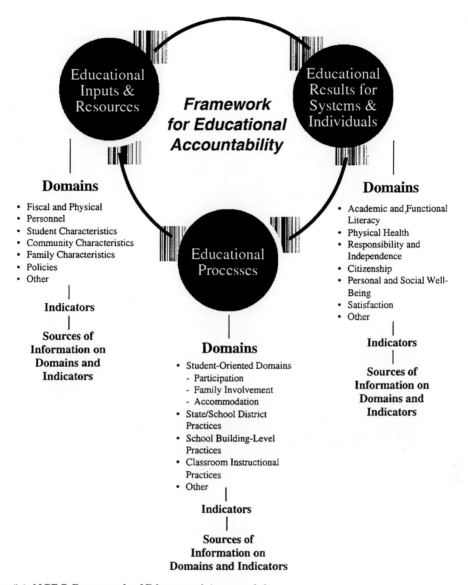

Figure 8.1. NCEO Framework of Educational Accountability

one's mind well, responsible citizenship, further learning, and productive employment). The National Council on Educational Standards and Testing (NCEST) then was formed to investigate the possibility of developing standards for content and performance (e.g., what students should know and be able to do). The results of this effort, summarized in a report entitled *Raising Standards for American Education* (National Council on Educational Standards and Testing, 1992), further promoted the importance of academic goals within the educational system. Only after much discussion was attention turned back to

Table 8.1
GRADE 8 NAEP MATH, READING, AND CIVIC RESULTS
Grade 8 NAEP Results (% At or above Basic Level)

Group	Math, 1996	Reading, 1998	Writing, 1998	Civics, 1998
All	61%	74%	84%	70%
White	73%	73%	90%	80%
Black	27%	36%	72%	50%
Hispanic	37%	40%	69%	45%
Asian/Pacific Islander	58%	69%	90%	71%
American Indian	50%	47%	73%	49%

Note: Data in table were pulled from documents of the National Center for Education Statistics (Donahue, Voekl, Campbell, & Mazzeo, 1999; Greenwald, Persky, Campbell, & Mazzeo, 1999; Lutkas, Weiss, Campbell, Mazzeo, & Lazer, 1999; Shaughnessy, Nelson, & Norris, 1998).

the other aspects of Goal 3. State goals have generally identified nonacademic goals as well as academic ones. Yet, most states have not incorporated these non-academic goals into their measurement systems. Thus, state assessment systems remain almost totally focused on the academic areas of reading, math, science, and social studies (National Center on Educational Outcomes, 1993; Ysseldyke, Thurlow, Langenfeld, Nelson, Teelucksingh, & Seyfarth, 1998). The issue of whether state-defined educational outcomes might pose a problem for the multicultural student with a disability has been exemplified by the vocal outcries of a group called the Committee for Excellence in Education. In the early 1990s, this group focused its criticisms on the Outcomes-Based Education (OSE) approach, specifically on the inappropriateness of some of the outcomes, such as the quest for an understanding of the value of cultural diversity originally identified by the State of Pennsylvania. But, this belief that cultural diversity is an inappropriate topic for education is just one side of the coin. On the other side is the issue of whether some identified goals are appropriate from a multicultural perspective. For example, the emphasis on inquiry of scientific standards may be difficult for some English language learners who have different oral language traditions (Lee & Fradd, 1998).

ASSESSING OF OUTCOMES OF MULTICULTURAL LEARNERS

Assessment has been and continues to be a major source of questions, both in general and special education as related to the multicultural perspective. Generally, the key assessment issue continues to be bias in assessment. What this means is that a test, just by the nature of the way it was written or normed, may be biased in its measurement of student performance. Volumes have been written about this issue (e.g., Berry & Lopez, 1977; Goldman & Hewitt, 1976; Jensen, 1976, 1979; Newland, 1973; Nuttall, Romero, & Kalesnik, 1992; Utley, Haywood, & Masters, 1992; Vasquez, 1972; Ysseldyke, Algozzine, & Thurlow, 2000), but it remains a key issue nevertheless. Several professional organizations have developed policy statements addressing the possibility of bias in mental tests (e.g., American Education Research Association, American Psychological Association, National Council on Measurement in Education). Basically, the issue is whether an assessment can produce a fair, valid, and reliable measure of a student's performance when there are differences among students in culture, language, values, and experiential background, all of which may lead to an inappropriate appraisal of a student's abilities.

Bias in National Assessments

Although there are no clear performance results reported for multicultural students who are receiving special education services, there are results reported for various ethnicity groups and "all" students as a whole on the National Assessment of Educational Progress in 1996 and 1998. The most recent data (see Table 8.1) highlight a performance trend for multicultural students and the performance gap that is evident. There appears to be a performance gap between White students and students from other ethnic groups (excluding the Asian/Pacific Islander subgroup).

In the latest Condition of Education Report (Wirt et al., 1998), a longitudinal look at Black student performance on the NAEP was examined. In 1971, there was a large gap in the reading performance between White and Black students; however, by 1996, these gaps had considerably narrowed (Wirt et al.). Similarly, when the first NAEP math assessment was given in 1973, a significant difference existed between Black students and their White counterparts. Again, this gap has narrowed over time (Wirt et al.). A similar trend in positive reductions has occurred in science between 1973 and 1996. Although the gap of achievement appears to have narrowed be-

tween Black and White students, Black students still lag behind White students in *all* four subject areas of reading, math, science, and writing (see Wirt et al.). Researchers and education coalitions (e.g., National Association of State Boards of Education) have suggested a number of explanations for these gaps in testing performance:

- Cultural biases in test construction and content
- Differences in learning styles among racial and ethnic groups
- Environmental variables, such as higher poverty rates and lower educational levels among families in minority groups
- Lack of [some] minority students' proficiency in standard English
- Less access by minority students to rich curricula and other educational resources.(Claycomb, Kysilko, & Roach, 1997)

While scholars and educators might hypothesize that the performance of multicultural learners with disabilities from different multicultural groups would mirror that of multicultural learners without disabilities, it is difficult to draw any general conclusions for multicultural learners with disabilities because the data simply are not there. More research is then needed in this area.

Bias in State Assessments

In the 1970s, many states started using minimal competency tests (MCTs). Often, they were used to determine eligibility for graduation or for a type of exit document. Some of the states using MCTs had specific policies about the participation and/or consequences for students with disabilities. Many states dealt with students with disabilities by waiving the requirement (Vitello, 1988). Nearly a decade ago, the "acceptable" accommodations for students with disabilities to participate in MCTs included exclusion of children from the MCT program, substitution of IEP goal attainment, establishment of differential standards, awarding of differential diplomas for students not taking or passing the MCT, modification of test administrations, and use of *different* MCTs.

Today, tests similar to the MCTs are still being used, with an emphasis on reaching either minimal or high standards. High school graduation exams are not on the decrease; rather, a few more states have added these mandatory exams (which are similar in intent and design to minimal competency tests) to a student's educational requirements (Guy, Shin, Lee, & Thurlow, 1999). The same issues arise and the same potential for bias toward students with disabilities and students from different multicultural backgrounds abound in the implementation of high school graduation exams.

Bias in Performance Assessments

In the past decade, assessment issues have been complicated by the introduction of new forms of assessment. In reaction to dissatisfaction with the meaningfulness of objective, multiple choice, fill-in-the-bubble assessments, districts, states, and national data collection programs have jumped on board the train pushing toward more authentic forms of assessment. Based on past research, many assessments are viewed as biased against students from different cultural backgrounds. The argument has been made that results-based assessments that are more authentic in nature may provide the opportunity to respond in other than traditionally accepted ways. It has also been argued that the standards movement's emphasis on authentic learning tasks may benefit students with diverse cultural experiences because learning tasks can be paired to their cultural frames of reference and their personal experiences, and thus, build upon their prior knowledge (Lachat, 1999). In a presentation at a conference on performance assessment, Baker (1992) noted that an assessment that required the student to diagram historical events promoted better performance in a student with learning disabilities than did a traditional multiple choice test of the same information. On the other hand, in the 1992 National Assessment of Educational Progress, the gap between the performance of White and Black students was much greater on open-ended math items than multiple choice and short-answer questions (Office of Educational Research & Improvement, 1993; Rothman, 1993). And, in a study of portfolio ratings (LaMahieu, 1999), it was found that White high achievers scored higher on portfolios than on the full body of their work while the portfolios of low-achieving predominantly minority group students were rated lower than the full body of work from which the portfolios had been selected. It is unclear whether this performance was related to poor decision-making by the student about what to include in the portfolio, whether bias occurred when teachers were evaluating students' work, or a combination of factors. However, due to the cost of administrating and grading performance-based assessments, many States are moving back to using traditional multiple-choice exams that may also address their particular state standards (CCSSO, 1998).

Bias in Alternative Assessment Systems

Very little is known about the technical adequacy of alternative assessment systems for students with disabilities from multicultural backgrounds. In those cases where technical adequacy has been examined, the results have been less favorable. This has led some to argue that a different set of criteria is needed for performance assessments (e.g., Linn, Baker, & Dunbar, 1991). Performance assessments, alternative assessments, and portfolio assessments will continue to command the attention of scholars and educators for many years to come.

HAZARDS OF RESULTS-BASED EDUCATION SYSTEMS

There are three salient "hazards" associated with a results-based accountability system for students from multiculturally diverse backgrounds, particularly when they also have a disability. These hazards are:

- Diversity is downplayed
- Outcomes are narrow
- Accountability produces exclusion

One of the hazards of results-based accountability approaches may be that they tend to promote the same outcomes for all students. In the "inclusivity" of its approach, it may be ignoring important differential outcomes that are needed for different students, particularly those students who are different in some ways from the outset.

Another hazard, one that in fact has been realized to some extent, is that the outcomes may be defined in a very narrow way. Thus, academic outcomes become the primary focus of interest, and as a result, the primary focus of instruction. This is a dangerous possibility when assessments are directed only toward the documentation of how students are doing academically. Current outcomes that have been documented for multicultural children with special needs include the overrepresentation in classes for children with disabilities (Artiles & Trent, 1994) and underrepresentation in gifted and talented classes (Patton, 1992). In comparison with dominant culture peers, multicultural learners receive remedial instruction, are tracked in low-ability classes (Oakes, 1994) and are retained in grade more often (Meisels & Law, 1993). Multicultural learners with disabilities

also drop out of school at higher rates (Rumberger, 1994). In 1996, only 6 percent of all undergraduates reported having a disability (Horn, Berktold, & Bobbitt, 1999). Of those 1995–1996 undergraduates who reported a disability, the total percentage with a disability by race/ethnicity was:

White	6.2%
Black	3.4%
Hispanic	4.1%
Asian/Pacific Islander	1.9%
American Indian/Alaskan Native	13.4%

(Horn et al., 1996)

These figures show that students with disabilities who enroll in an undergraduate institution are more likely to be White. The multicultural groups appear to be underrepresented (excluding the American Indian/ Alaskan Native subgroup). These outcomes are the few statistics available on multicultural students with disabilities. More information is needed on these narrow outcomes for these students, as well as results that are occurring for these students in broader contexts (e.g., employment and other postsecondary educational opportunities).

Another hazard for which there are some evidence is that results-based accountability may produce exclusion of students. In examination of both State and national assessment programs, McGrew, Thurlow, Shriner, and Spiegel (1992) and McGrew, Thurlow, and Spiegel (1993) found significant evidence of the exclusion of students with disabilities from assessments. The exclusion rates in State NAEP assessments ranged from 33% to

87%, and in State assessment systems from 0% to 100%. In national data collection programs, depending on the kind, exclusion rates approached 50% of students in the assessment sample. For example, the percent of 8th grade IEP students assessed in the 1992 and 1994 Math Exam of the NAEP was 44% and 38% (Olson & Goldstein, 1996). Thus, 56% and 62% of students with disabilities were excluded from the Math NAEP assessment. However, there was an increase in the percent of students on an IEP taking the math assessment from 1992 to 1994 (9% to 13%). These results were not disaggregated by ethnicity and IEP status, and researchers are not able to know how many ethnically diverse students receiving special education services were excluded from this national assessment. Along a similar vein, Lam and Gordon (1992) found that students whose first language was other than English, also were excluded from assessment systems at the State level. Exclusion becomes a significant issue because when it occurs researchers do not get full and accurate information about the status of education or students within it. In times of educational reform, it is critical that this information be available and used.

HOPES OF RESULTS-BASED EDUCATION SYSTEMS

There are three salient "hopes" associated with a results-based accountability system for students with multicultural diverse backgrounds, particularly when they also have a disability. These hopes are:

- Diversity drives outcomes
- Broad outcomes open opportunities for all students
- Accountability produces inclusive educational systems for all students

The hope that diversity drives outcomes really reflects the view that outcomes must be appropriate for a diverse range of students, and that a narrow focus is inappropriate. It also reflects the belief that there must be some recognition of the individual in the outcomes accountability system. More broadly, current theoretical paradigms that undergird current research on multicultural students with disabilities must also change. For example, scholars need to examine the context of their research by including the perspectives of investigators *and* of ethnic minority students (Artiles, 1998). Related to this mission is the hope that broad outcomes will be identified and that these will open opportunities for all students. It is important to know how students are performing on measures like this so educators can plan for needed changes in instruction and/or school personnel. Scholars and educators must have a picture of what the results of education are for all students in order to know what to do to change the picture (if deemed necessary).

Darling-Hammond (1992) summarized the gist of these hopes in one of her standards of practice for learner-centered schools. She wrote:

> School goals and expectations should be expressed in terms of desired social, personal, and academic learning outcomes and should be evaluated using assessment strategies that are appropriate and authentic measure of the goals being pursued. Assessment tools should provide instructionally useful indicators of individual student growth and performance. These measures, including samples of student work and project, observations of student performance, evaluation of student learning characteristics, and exhibitions or examinations should be culturally and developmentally sensitive and should permit students to demonstrate their capacities using diverse modes of expression and performance. (p. 24)

Likewise, following a one-year study of multiculturalism in education, the National Association of State Boards of Education (1992) included two recommendations related to assessments:

RECOMMENDATION #3

States should develop more sophisticated systems for gathering and analyzing data that affect learning. State school data should be compiled according to race, ethnicity, socioeconomic status, and gender to provide continuous information on state diversity and to determine a state's success in educating students from diverse backgrounds. (p. 12)

RECOMMENDATION #9

State boards of education should promote and adopt student assessments that are grounded in cultural diversity. Culturally biased assessments should be identified and eliminated. (p. 26)

MEETING TWENTY-FIRST CENTURY CHALLENGES TO CHANGE THROUGH OUTCOMES

The challenge of promoting educational reform that serves the needs of all students is greater today than ever before as general and special educators see increasing numbers of students from multicultural backgrounds and students who are likely to need special education services entering schools (Hodgkinson, 1996). A focus on outcomes has been seen as critical to educational reform by many (e.g., Finn, 1990; Oakes, 1986; Shavelson, McDonnell, & Oakes, 1989), not because it allows educators to ignore the needs of the educational process, but because an outcomes focus helps to identify where there are problems so that educators can then look at what kinds of changes might have an impact on those problems. Critical parts of the process of promoting educational change for students of diverse cultural and disability background will include at least the following three steps:

- Identifying outcomes for all students.
- Assessing outcomes through accommodated assessments.
- Identifying the outcomes deserving attention and moving toward system renewal directed at those outcomes.

Identifying Outcomes for All Students

The critical questions of what are the important outcomes for all students must continually be reexamined. Nearly every group that has developed lists of outcomes has used some kind of consensus process and has reached some level of agreement on the important outcomes of education. Not *all* groups doing this have kept all students in mind as they did so. It has been particularly true that students with disabilities and students from different cultural backgrounds have been forgotten when the goals of education have been discussed. This is a serious omission in the educational world of today. And, in the educational world of tomorrow, it will be a travesty. When outcomes of importance are identified, individuals who have disabilities and those individuals from varied ethnic and cultural backgrounds must be at the table.

Making Accommodations in Assessments of Outcomes

Literature reviews reveal that the assessment of outcomes is an area of concern whenever scholars and educators talk about students from the non-Caucasian, non-college-bound group. For others, there are serious questions of technical adequacy, bias, and usefulness. In both national and state assessment systems, considerable exclusion is seen of those students from whom it is most important that information is received (McGrew, Thurlow, & Spiegal, 1993; Ysseldyke et al., 1998). Accommodations and adaptations that are allowed in assessments are inconsistent and confusing (Thurlow, Ysseldyke, & Silverstein, 1993). There is a long way to go before general and special educators can say with confidence that they are able to assess with much accuracy outcomes of education for all students.

Moving to System Renewal

Perhaps the most difficult step, and the one about which educators know the least, is how to move to system renewal when they have the evidence that they need to do so. As Singham (1998) confirmed, "The educational achievement gap is not an artifact . . . we have to start looking at the problem in new and deep ways, and we must avoid the temptations to seek simplistic one-shot solutions if we are going to make any real headway" (p. 15).

Earlier, some reformers (e.g., Cook, 1992; Skrtic, 1987) have suggested that true renewal of an educational system can only happen following the build-up of unreconcilable differences that lead to a paradigm shift, when a radical transformation occurs. Others (e.g., Sarason, 1990) argued that while change cannot start from within, it must recognize the need to alter existing attitudes and power relationships. When these significant changes happen, then the major players are impelled to significant change. Some change advocates have argued that "change is a journey and not a blueprint" (Fullan, 1991, p. 126). In this view, change is a slow steady process that is influenced by itself. It is a journey the path of which is changed only as a function of the immediately preceding path. It is clear at this point that the nation will not be able to focus on outcomes alone. It will need to pay attention to outcome information in connection with information on the equitable delivery of education to students. The collection of data on school delivery or student opportunity to learn is sure to gain increased attention.

CONCLUSION

With the enactment of IDEA 97, all students with disabilities now must participate in state and district assessments, or in alternate assessments developed for them. Furthermore, the number of students with disabilities participating in these assessments is to be publicly reported, as is their performance. Participation in these assessments is important, for they are designed to measure the standards that have been defined by each state as those that students must meet. The designation of standards and measures of them is further supported by Title I legislation, which also requires that the performance of students with disabilities be disaggregated from the performance of other students (as well as aggregated with their performance), so that educators and service providers can be sure that these students are reaching standards too. The standards that currently are being measured by states and districts primarily are academic in nature. Many scholars and educators have questioned the validity, reliability, and utility of these standards, especially since they focus solely on academics and ignore cultural values of many of those tested.

Because of the importance of state and district assessments in today's results-based educational system, it is imperative to recognize the challenges and benefits when multiculturalism and disability are combined. This emphasis will probably be tempered in the future by adding other important outcomes, such as work-related skills (e.g., timelines and

ability to work with others). Within this context, it remains critical for educators, test developers, and policymakers to remain aware of the distinct possibility for bias in assessing the academic skills of students with disabilities from multicultural backgrounds. Despite the potential hazards of results-based education systems, there are some potential benefits for all students, including those students with disabilities from multicultural backgrounds. Only with information on how these students are doing, information like that obtained on other students, will we know that our education system is or is not working. This information appears necessary as we begin to adjust and improve the educational opportunities provided to these students, so that they achieve all of the important educational outcomes.

REFERENCES

Ahearn, E.M., & Crocker, M. (1995, February). *Summary report of accountability focus groups.* Alexandria, VA: National Association of State Directors of Special Education.

American Federation of Teachers (November, 1998). *Making standards matter 1998.* Washington, DC: Author.

Artiles, A.J. (1998). The dilemma of difference: Enriching the disproportionality discourse with theory and context. *The Journal of Special Education, 32* (1), 32–36.

Artiles, A.J., & Trent, S.C. (1994). Overrepresentation of minority students in special education: A continuing debate. *The Journal of Special Education, 27,* 410–437.

Baker, E. (1992). *Performance assessment: High hopes, high standards.* Paper presented at the CAREI Conference Performance-Based Assessment: A National Perspective, Minneapolis, MN.

Berry, G.L., & Lopez, C.A. (1977). Testing programs and the Spanish-speaking child: Assessment guidelines for school counselors. *School Counselor, 24,* 261–269.

Claycomb, C., Kysilko, D., & Roach, V. (1997, February). *Issues and trends in statewide assess-*

ments. Alexandria, VA: National Association of State Boards of Education.

Cook, W.J. (1992). *The urgency of change: The metamorphosis of America's schools* (rev. ed.). Montgomery, AL: Cambridge Management Group.

Darling-Hammond, L. (1992). *Standards of practice for learner-centered schools.* New York: National Center for Restructuring Education, Schools, and Teaching (NCREST).

David, J.L., & Shields, P.L. (1999). Standards are not magic. *Education Week, 18* (31), 40–42.

Donahue, P., Voelkl, K., Campbell, J., & Mazzeo, J. (1999). *NAEP 1998 reading report card for the nation and the states, NCES 1999-459.* Washington, DC: U.S. Department of Education, Office of Educational Research and Improvement & National Center for Education Statistics.

Education Commission of the States (1998a, January). *Accountability–State and community responsibility.* Denver, CO: Author.

Education Commission of the States (1998b, March). *Designing and implementing standards-based accountability systems.* Denver, CO: Author.

Erickson, R., Ysseldyke, J., Thurlow, M., & Elliott, J. (November/December, 1998). Inclusive assessments and accountability systems: Tools of the trade in educational reform. *Teaching Exceptional Children, 31* (2), 4–9.

Finn, C.E. (1990). The biggest reform of all. *Phi Delta Kappan, 21,* 584–592.

Fullan, M. (1993). Innovation, reform, and restructuring strategies. In G. Cawelti (Ed.), *Challenges and achievements of American education (1993 Yearbook of the Association for Supervision and Curriculum Development)* (pp. 116–133). Alexandria, VA: ASCD.

Goldman, R.D., & Hewitt, B.N. (1976). Predicting the success of black, Chicano, Oriental and white college students. *Journal of Educational Measurement, 13,* 107–117.

Greenwald, E., Persky, H., Campbell, J., & Mazzeo, J. (1999). *NAEP 1998 writing report card for the nation and the states, NCES 1999-462.* Washington, DC: U.S. Department of Education, Office of Educational Research and Improvement, & National Center for Education Statistics.

Guy, B., Shin, H., Lee, S.Y., & Thurlow, M. (1999). *State graduation requirements for students with and without disabilities (Technical Report 24).* Minneapolis, MN: University of Minnesota, National Center on Educational Outcomes.

Hodgkinson, H.L. (January, 1996). *Bringing tomorrow into focus: Demographic insights into the future.* Washington, DC: Center for Demographic Policy, Institute for Educational Leadership.

Horn, L., Berktold, J., & Bobbitt, L. (1999, June). *Students with disabilities in postsecondary education: A profile of preparation, participation, and outcomes.* Washington, DC: National Center for Education Statistics.

Jensen, A.R. (1976). Test bias and construct validity. *Phi Delta Kappan, 58,* 340–346.

Jensen, A.R. (1979). *Bias in mental testing.* New York: Free Press.

Kamin, L.J. (1975). Social and legal consequences of IQ tests as classification instruments: Some warnings from our past. *Journal of School Psychology, 13,* 317–323.

Lachat, M.A. (1999). *Standards, equity, and cultural diversity.* Providence, RI: Northeast and Islands Regional Educational Laboratory, Brown University.

Lam, T.C.M., & Gordon, W.I. (1992). State policies for standardized achievement testing of limited English proficient students. *Educational Measurement: Issues and Practice, 11* (4), 18–20.

Lee, O., & Fradd, S.H. (1998). Science for all , including students from non-English-language backgrounds. *Educational Researcher, 27* (4), 12–21.

LeMahieu, P. (September 15, 1999). Personal communication.

Linn, R.L., Baker, E.L., & Dunbar, S.B. (1991). Complex, performance-based assessment: Expectations and validation criteria. *Educational Researcher, 20* (8), 15–21.

Lutkas, A., Weiss, A., Campbell, J., Mazzeo, J., & Lazer, S. (1999). *NAEP 1998 civics report card for the nation, NCES 2000-457.* Washington, DC: U.S. Department of Education, Office of Educational Research & Improvement, & National Center for Education Statistics.

McGrew, K.S., Thurlow, M.L., Shriner, J.G., & Spiegel, A.N. (1992). *Inclusion of students with disabilities in national and state data collection programs (Technical Report 2).* Minneapolis, MN: University of Minnesota, National Center on Educational Outcomes.

McGrew, K.S., Thurlow, M.L., & Spiegel, A.N. (1993). An investigation of the exclusion of students with disabilities in national data collection programs. *Educational Evaluation and Policy Analysis, 15* (3), 339–352.

Meisels, S.J., & Law, F. (1993). Failure in grade: Do retained students catch up? *Journal of Educational Research, 87* (2), 69–77.

National Association of State Boards of Education. (1992). *The American tapestry: Educating a nation.* Alexandria, VA: Author.

National Council on Disability. (1993). *Meeting the unique needs of minorities with disabilities (A report to the President and the Congress).* Washington, DC: Author.

National Council on Educational Standards and Testing. (1992). *Raising standards for American education.* Washington, DC: National Education Goals Panel.

National Education Goals Panel. (1991, March). *Measuring progress toward the national education goals: Potential indicators and measurement strategies* (Discussion Document). Washington, DC: Author.

National Education Goals Panel. (1998). *Data volume for the national education goals report.* Washington, DC: Author.

Newland, T.E. (1973). Assumptions underlying psychological testing. *Journal of School Psychology, 11,* 316–322.

Newmann, F.M., King, B., & Rigdon, M. (1997). Accountability and school performance: Implications for restructuring schools. *Harvard Educational Review, 67* (1), 41–74.

Nuttall, E.V., Romero, I., & Kalesnik, J. (1992). *Assessing and screening preschoolers.* Needham Heights, MA: Allyn & Bacon.

Oakes, J. (1986). *Educational indicators: A guide for policymakers.* Santa Monica, CA: Rand Center for Policy Research in Education.

Oakes, J. (1994). Tracking, inequality, and the rhetoric of reform: Why schools don't change. In J. Kretovics & E.J. Nussel (Eds.), *Transforming urban education* (pp. 146–164). Needham Heights, MA: Allyn & Bacon.

Office of Educational Research and Improvement. (1993). *Data compendium for the NAEP 1992 mathematics assessment of the nation and the states.* Washington, DC: Author.

Olson, J.F., & Goldstein, A.A. (1996, July). *Increasing the inclusion of students with disabilities and limited English proficient students in NAEP.* Washington, DC: National Center for Education Statistics (NCES).

Patton, J.M. (1992). Assessment and identification of African American learners with gifts and talents. *Exceptional Children, 59* (2), 150–159.

Poplin, M. (1993). *A practical theory of teaching and learning: The view from inside the new transformative classroom: Contributions of constructivism.* Paper presented at the TED/DOE Conference in Tampa, FL.

Roeber, B., Bond, L., & Connealy, S. (1998). *Annual survey of state student assessment programs: Fall 1997* (Vols. I & II). Washington, DC: Council of Chief State School Officers.

Rothman, R. (1993, June 23). Wide racial gap found on open-ended math items. *Education Week, 12* (39), 18.

Rouse, M., Shriner, J., & Danielson, L. (1999). National assessment and special education in the United States and England and Wales: Towards a common system for all? In M. McLaughlin & M. Rouse (Eds.), *Special education and school reform in the United States and Britain* (pp. 1–34). Needham Heights, MA: Allyn & Bacon.

Rumberger, R.W. (1994). High school dropouts: A review of issues and evidence. In J. Kretovics & E. J. Nussel (Eds.), *Transforming urban education* (pp. 187–210). Needham Heights, MA: Allyn & Bacon.

Sable, J. (1998). The educational progress of black students. In J. Wirt, T. Snyder, J. Sable, S. Choy, Y. Bae, J. Stennett, A. Gruner, & M. Perie (Eds.), *The condition of education 1998* (pp. 2–10). Washington, DC: U.S. Department of Education, National Center for Education Statistics.

Sarason, S. (1990). *The predictable failure of educational reform.* San Francisco, CA: Jossey Bass.

Shaughnessy, C., Nelson, J., & Norris, N. (1998). *NAEP 1996 mathematics cross-state data compendium for the grade 4 and grade 8 assessment, NCES 1998-481.* Washington, DC: U.S. Department of Education, Office of Educational Research & Improvement, & National Center for Education Statistics.

Shavelson, R., McDonnell, L., & Oakes, J. (1989). *Indicators for monitoring mathematics and science education.* Santa Monica, CA: RAND Corporation.

Shavelson, R., McDonnell, L., Oakes, J. & Carey, N. (1987, August). *Indicator systems for monitoring mathematics and science education.* Santa Monica, CA: Rand Corporation. (ERIC Document Reproduction No. ED 294 738).

Singham, M. (1998, September). The canary in the mine: The achievement gap between black and white students. *Phi Delta Kappan, 80,* 8–15.

Skrtic, T.M. (1987). *An organizational analysis of special education reform.* (ERIC Document Reproduction Service No. ED 291 177).

Tennyson, J.W., & Leung, P. (1993). *Meeting the unique needs of minorities with disabilities: A report to the President and the Congress.* Washington, DC: National Council on Disability.

Thurlow, M.L., Ysseldyke, J.E., & Silverstein, B. (1993). *Testing accommodations for students with disabilities: A review of the literature* (Synthesis Report 4). Minneapolis, MN: University of Minnesota, National Center on Educational Outcomes.

Utley, C.A., Haywood, H.C., & Masters, J. (1992). Policy implications of psychological assessments of minority children. In H. C. Haywood

& D. Tzuriel (Eds.), *Interactive assessment* (pp. 445–469). New York: Springer-Verlag.

Vasquez, J. (1972). Measurement of intelligence and language differences. *Aztlan, 3,* 155–163.

Vitello, S.J. (1988). Handicapped students and competency testing. *Remedial and Special Education, 9* (5), 22–28.

Westat, Inc. (May, 1993). *Outcomes-based accountability: Policy issues and options for students with disabilities.* Rockville, MD: Author.

Wirt, J., Snyder, T., Sable, J., Choy, S., Bae, Y., Stennett, J., Gruner, A., & Perie, M., (Eds.). (1998). *The condition of education 1998.* Washington, DC: U.S. Department of Education, National Center for Education Statistics.

Ysseldyke, J., Algozzine, B., & Thurlow, M. (2000). *Critical issues in special education.* Boston, MA: Houghton Mifflin.

Ysseldyke, J., Krentz, J., Elliott, J., Thurlow, M., Erickson, R., & Moore, M. (1998). *National Center on Educational Outcomes Framework for educational accountability.* Minneapolis, MN: University of Minnesota, National Center on Educational Outcomes.

Ysseldyke, J., Thurlow, M., Langenfeld, K., Nelson, R., Teelucksingh, E., & Seyfarth, A. (1998). *Educational results for students with disabilities: What do the data tell us? (Technical Report 23).* Minneapolis, MN: University of Minnesota, National Center on Educational Outcomes.

Chapter 9

COLLABORATIVE CONSULTATION BETWEEN GENERAL AND SPECIAL EDUCATORS IN MULTICULTURAL CLASSROOMS: IMPLICATIONS FOR SCHOOL REFORM

ANN NEVIN, KATHLEEN C. HARRIS, AND VIVIAN C. CORREA

It is apparent that day-to-day operations of the public school have changed since the advent of P.L. 94-142 (1975) and its subsequent reauthorization as the Individuals with Disabilities Education Act Amendments of 1990. Also apparent is the fact that school reform processes must be sensitive to the needs of multicultural populations primarily because of the increasing numbers of learners who come from ethnically diverse cultures and who are developing proficiency in more than one language. The movement towards cultural pluralism has stimulated added responsibilities that ensure respect and equal participation from multicultural groups. What, then, can be learned from the school reform research and practice to address the needs of an increasingly diverse population of students, including students with disabilities who are multicultural? Does this knowledge base lead to recommendations for

exemplary practices in establishing effective communications with sustained and meaningful interactions with communities who are multicultural? What can be done to make school reform more inclusive for those who are different? Is ethnic representation on school reform committees used to change the school culture itself? What does it mean to go beyond acceptance of minority and cultural differences to supporting pluralistic outcomes? What advice might be derived from the literature to help general and special educators become better collaborators who contribute to school reform efforts?

This chapter responds to the initial questions indicated above. Our premise is that school reform involves changing the way business is conducted in schools. For this to occur, general and special educators have to organize their work relationships in ways that ensure appropriate education for students with disabilities. From our perspective, these ways include educational consultation (Heron & Harris, in press), teaming (Morsink, Thomas, & Correa, 1992), and collaborative consultation (Idol, Nevin, & Paolucci-Whitcomb, in press).

OPERATIONAL DEFINITIONS OF RELEVANT CONSTRUCTS

To properly discuss the impact of collaborative consultation, relevant definitions must be operationalized.

Multiculturalism

Multiculturalism refers to differences between groups of people related to class, ethnic heritage, language dominance, religious practices, race, and national origin (Banks, 1999; Gollnick & Chinn, 1994; Obiakor, 1999). Depending on the perspective taken, as well as the communication and interaction patterns employed, these differences can be treated as assets or deficits and can be exacerbated or ameliorated.

Educational Reform

Fullan (1993) distinguished between innovation (discrete changes such as a new curriculum or technology, flexible scheduling or team teaching) and reform or restructuring which refer to "fundamental, potentially sweeping changes" (p. 116) at the systemic level regarding assessment, staff development, teacher preparation, and certification. In addressing school reform from the perspective of multicultural learners, Cummins (1986, 1989) focused upon changing the relationships between educators and students and between school and communities. He described four components of the school context that must change so as to embrace diversity: cultural/linguistic incorporation, community participation, pedagogy, and assessment. In addition, he contended that the culture and language of students and community should be *added to* the school context; the community should *collaborate* with the school in the identification of the curriculum and the teaching/learning process; instruction should not be transmission-oriented but rather *reciprocal interaction-oriented;* finally, assessment should be used to empower students, *advocating for their success* not disabling them and legitimizing disabilities.

Collaborative Consultation

In order to implement school reform, a process to change the day-to-day way of doing business must be generated. A key ingredient to success has been identified by personnel in schools that have successfully restructured to meet the needs of all students–collaborative teams and the collaborative consultation decision-making process that they employ to conduct their daily operations (Thousand & Villa, 1990, 1992; Villa & Thousand, 1995, in press; Villa, Thousand, Stainback, & Stainback, 1992). Collaborative decision-making results in many of the desired outcomes of school reform such as shared ownership of problem definitions and solutions (Duke, Showers, & Imber, 1980), an exchange of skills (Thousand, Fox, Reid, Godek, Williams, & Fox, 1986; Villa & Thousand, 1995), the use of higher level thinking processes and the generation of more novel solutions (Thousand, Nevin, & Fox, 1987), attendance and participation at meetings and persistence in working on difficult tasks (Johnson & Johnson, 1989).

Collaborative consultation is defined by Idol, Nevin, and Paolucci-Whitcomb (in press) as an interactive process that enables groups of people with diverse expertise to generate creative solutions to mutually defined problems. The outcome is enhanced and altered from original solutions that group members would produce independently. Collaborative consultation can be characterized by the following basic elements (Nevin, Thousand, Paolucci-Whitcomb, & Villa, 1990; Raffaniello, 1981). Group members agree to view all members, including students, as possessing unique and needed expertise; they engage in frequent face-to-face interactions; they distribute leadership responsibilities and hold each other accountable for agreed-upon commitments; they understand the importance of reciprocity and emphasize task or relationship actions based on such variables as the extent to which other members support or have the skill to promote the group goal; they agree to consciously practice and increase their social interaction and/or task achievement skills through the process of consensus building.

These elements of collaborative consultation are particularly important when general and special educators from diverse cultures collaborate on school-based teams. For example, an exploratory collaboration between bilingual and special educators from two cultures (Anglo and Hispanic) in a southwestern metropolitan school district showed creative multicultural communication patterns (Harris, 1995; Harris & Nevin, 1993). Team members constructed respectful communication processes and reflective and authentic evaluation processes related to the team's impact on teachers who accessed the team's expertise. Elements of collaborative consultation were also found to be present for successful collaboration with parents as partners across different cultures (Jordan, Reyes-Blanes, Peel, Peel, & Lane, 1998; Sileo, Sileo, & Prater, 1996).

COLLABORATIVE CONSULTATION GUIDELINES IN GENERAL AND SPECIAL EDUCATION

Over 20 years ago, Goodenough (1976) argued that since role expectations differ with different social situations, each set of expectations constitutes a different culture to be learned. Therefore, advice from the consultation literature should be taken in light of the need for general and special educators to be multicultural. Three pertinent guidelines include (a) understanding models of consultation; (b) establishing and maintaining teams; and (c) developing and using effective consultant competencies for a multicultural society.

Understanding Models of Consultation

Models of consultation are useful as they help match goals of consultation with a process for conducting consultation. There are many models of consultation. Gallessich

(1982) referred to six broad consultation models: behavioral, clinical, education and training, mental health, organizational, and program. Babcock and Pryzwansky (1983) differentiated among collaborative, expert, mental health, and medical models. Gutkin and Curtis (1999) and Shields, Heron, Rubenstein, and Katz (1995) discussed the ecobehavioral model. However, there is widespread consensus that the behavioral, mental health, and organization-systems, and collaborative consultation models are the four major models used in schools (Curtis & Meyers, 1988; Idol et al., in press; Kratochwill, Elliott, & Rotto, 1990; Kratochwill, Sheridan, & Van Someren, 1988; West & Idol, 1987; Zins & Ponti, 1990a, 1990b).

Although organization and systems consultation models were originally conceptualized separately, current thinking views the models as conjoint due to their focus on change at the group or organizational level (see Gutkin & Curtis, 1999). Because of the focus on group process and change, the organizational-systems consultation model is the most relevant to establishing and maintaining effective school reform committees. This model focuses on modifying policies, procedures, group structure, and role responsibilities as the method for improving program effectiveness. Gutkin and Curtis (1999) discussed four crucial elements of success: mutual adaptation (referring to the ability of school personnel to configure innovations to make them fit within the particular ecology of the existing system), the "involvement of all primary stakeholders in all aspects of the change process" (p. 623), the support of change efforts by key administrators, and "a coherent system of collaborative problem solving" (p. 623). In a related vein, Zins and Illback (1995) stressed that:

Strategic change programs must reflect the complexity of the organizations that they are trying to change. Adequate effort must be devoted to gathering diagnostic data, to assessing organizational readiness, and to following up on the implementation process . . . many educational reforms fail because they are unidimensional and do not take into account the interactive elements of organizational structure, process, and behavior. . . . Furthermore, lasting, significant change takes time . . . Attempts to rush the process may be met with resistance and failure. (p. 239)

Knowledge of how each subsystem operates (Schmuck & Runkel, 1995) can help general and special educators work together more effectively. Four organizational structures that may potentially influence the behavior of participants as well as the outcome of the collaborative work have been highlighted: the authority structure, the decision-making structure, the reward structure, and the communication structure. This knowledge can help committee members and co-teaching team members to be sensitive to the individuals they represent and to guide the process of effective group interactions in light of the interactive elements of the organizational structure. The seven goals of this model of consultation, according to Schmuck and Runkel (1995), include clarifying communication, establishing collective goals, uncovering conflicts and interdependence, improving group procedures, solving problems, making decisions, and assessing changes. Schmuck and Runkel (1995) cautioned that any time a major curriculum, instructional, and/or management technique is broadly adopted within the school system, the "culture" of the school district is likely to change. Knowing this can help members of collaborative teams maintain trust, keep lines of communication open, and share decision-making (Sugai & Tindal, 1993).

Establishing and Maintaining Teams

The literature on teaming provides direction for ways to facilitate group interaction. Regardless of the nature of the team (e.g., teaching team and reform committee), the research on team development summarized by Ellis and Fisher (1994) indicated that teams develop as they strive to address their tasks. Regardless of the approaches used to describe team development, there are some commonalities. All teams go through at least three stages. The first stage is the orientation stage when team members adjust their individualities to group membership and accustom themselves to the task. All teams go through a conflict stage as a middle stage where differences of opinion on task achievement and group process can occur. The final stage is a completion stage when group members achieve a consensus and validate decisions made in the previous stages.

Factors that Facilitate the Team Process

To have an effective collaborative teaching team or school reform committee, general and special educators can improve the way they function as a team, sometimes using a consultant to help the team develop. There are at least four aspects that characterize effective teams (Friend & Cook, 1996). First, team goals need to be clear and group members should remain focused on the task. For reform committees, it is essential that the team goals reflect all constituents, supporting the "salad bowl" metaphor of nurturing and valuing diverse cultures. Second, the committee members' professional and personal needs are met through the team's interactions. This requires knowledge as well as recognition of each member's professional role as well as the type of interpersonal interaction and communication needed to promote effective functioning as a team member. Third, members need to understand the reciprocal relationship between their behavior and the team's output. Team members are interdependent upon one another. If all team members do not work well together, the team may not produce the desired results. Fourth, the group works within an organized system of leadership and participation, recognizing shared responsibility in a decentralized process. There is no "boss" of the team. All members of an effective team share responsibilities and goals, and are actively involved in the work of the team.

Factors that Inhibit Team Process

Just as the literature has identified characteristics of effective teams, there are also factors that inhibit the team process. More than a decade ago, Moore, Fifield, Spira, and Scarlato (1989) indicated that one of the main reasons for team failure is that members lack the skill to work together (i.e., arranging meetings, using a problem-solving process, or following up with recommendations). Another constraining factor is the inability to access the knowledge of multidisciplinary team members. If team members have mutual respect and knowledge of their own and each others' philosophies and roles, this factor can be minimized. However, knowledge is not sufficient.

Developing and Using Effective Consultant Competencies for a Multicultural Society

To work effectively in a multicultural society, general and special educators who work on co-teaching teams or other school reform committees can develop cross-cultural competence as well as consultation and collaboration skills. It is essential that team members understand their own culture and perspective, are aware of the roles and perspectives of others on the team, and use culturally effective interpersonal, communication and problem-solving skills (Harris, 1991, 1995, 1996).

Understanding one's perspective is a necessary prerequisite to any collaborative activity. To engage in team work, it is necessary for collaborators to understand their own attitudes, values, needs, beliefs, skills, knowledge, and limitations (Kurpius, 1978; West, Idol & Cannon, 1989). This understanding is necessary to establish a climate for the collaborative work that will foster growth and change (Heron & Harris, in press). According to Gibbs (1980), collaborators have an ethical responsibility to be aware of their own culture, values, and beliefs as well as to understand how these differ from others. Recognizing one's culture and how it influences his/her behavior is the first step. It is then necessary for team members to assess how their perspective differs from those with whom they will be working (Heron & Harris, in press). Team members can learn about other cultures through reading, interaction, and involvement. However, as pointed out by Lynch and Hanson (1998), assuming that the culture-specific information one learns from books or a study of the language applies to all members of the cultural group is not appropriate. It can be stereotyping to overgeneralize, and this can reduce one's understanding of individuals on the team. It is

better to learn about the culture by getting to know individuals as people rather than as a member of a group. Each collaborator must determine the degree of congruence between his or her beliefs and values and the beliefs and values of family members and others (Heron & Harris, in press). Team members must have the interpersonal and communication skills to access that knowledge. Harris (1991) urged team members to ask themselves questions such as "What are our beliefs regarding the abilities of various cultural groups, and what are the basis of those beliefs?"

Many scholars and educators have written extensively on specific interpersonal and communication skills necessary for successful consultation (Conoley & Conoley, 1982; De-Boer, 1986; Idol, Nevin, Paolucci-Whitcomb, in press; Rosenfield, 1987; Speece & Mandell, 1980; Tombari & Bergan, 1978). Some necessary interpersonal and communication skills identified by West, Idol, and Cannon (1989) include caring, respect, empathy, openness, enthusiasm, willingness to learn from others, risk-taking, flexibility, resiliency, ability to manage conflict and time, good listening, ability to interview effectively, and ability to problem-solve. Harris (1996) added other interpersonal and communication skills necessary for professionals who work in multicultural settings. These skills include respect for individuals from other cultures, identifying the needed multicultural knowledge base, working effectively with an interpreter or translator, acknowledging cultural differences in communication and relationship building, and ensuring that problem identification does not conflict with cultural beliefs. Accommodating for diversity in interpersonal interactions is addressed in the next section.

ACCOMMODATING FOR DIVERSITY IN
INTERPERSONAL INTERACTIONS

To accommodate for diversity in interpersonal interactions in multicultural classrooms, general and special educators must be aware of their interpersonal communication skills. These skills emphasize (a) understanding verbal and non-verbal communication patterns; (b) an awareness of the attitudes of members from multicultural groups in situations where they are required to disclose personal information about their beliefs and feelings; and (c) respecting silence as a form of communication.

Interpersonal Communication

Although much has been written on effective interpersonal communication skills necessary for collaboration and teaming, less is known about the complexities involved in communicating with individuals from multicultural backgrounds. Interpersonal communication between people from non-dominant cultures and professionals from dominant cultures can show up as challenges when general and special educators work together. As schools become more multicultural, school personnel must face challenges of communicating with students, parents, family members, and liaisons from the community. It is necessary for general and special educators to understand unique and idiosyncratic patterns of communication among individuals from multicultural backgrounds. To be effective communicators, general and special educators must find ways of bridging the cultural or linguistic communication gaps. Removing ethnic communication barriers involves understanding common communication patterns of individuals from multicultural communities and accommodating for diversity in interpersonal interactions. It is also important to note that in some cases, the non-dominant cultural norm can serve as a strength, not a barrier, to the effectiveness of the multicultural team. For example, Nieto (1996) noted cultural groups such as African Americans, Hawaiians, and Hispanics value cooperative strategies in learning and completing tasks. For professionals and parents who work together, collaboration is actually culturally compatible with these groups and should serve as an effective teaming method.

The interpersonal communication patterns of persons from multicultural backgrounds have been described in the special education, social work, and mental health literature (Lynch & Hanson, 1998; Kuambe, Nishida, & Hepworth, 1985; Ponterotto, Casa, Suzuki, & Alexander, 1995; Samovar & Porter, 1985; Sue & Sue, 1990; Wittmer, 1992). An important caution is to remember that the individual and not the cultural group is the focus (Wittmer, 1992). Overgeneralization of ethnic communication patterns to all members of an ethnic group is stereotyping and not productive in establishing effective communication patterns.

Verbal Communication

Individuals from multicultural backgrounds may have patterns of verbal communication that are different from those of Anglo Americans. Verbal communication can be challenging for team members when some members (e.g., parents and community representatives) are speakers of other languages. To accommodate for language differences, teams may use interpreters during meetings. Educational reform teams should be sensitive, however, to issues of preparing interpreters to serve as translators (Fradd & Weistmantel, 1989). In addition, the reciprocal issue of preparing listeners to interact with the speaker rather than the translator must also be addressed.

Not all challenges in verbal communication are related to non-English speaking team members. The verbal patterns of some groups who are fluent in English can be a cause for concern. For example, the "call and response" patterns of communication among African American individuals can be confusing to professionals from the (dominant) Anglo culture (Tharp, 1989). This pattern is associated with the communication patterns seen in church sermons where preachers exclaim a statement and the congregation responds with hand-clapping, amens, and head-nodding. In the case of school collaboration, an African American teacher speaking with an Anglo principal may think the principal is not listening if the response is not overt. The principal, on the other hand, is showing polite respect by not interrupting the African American teacher's discourse. For instance, researchers in Hawaii have found that a speech style called "talk-story" is a familiar linguistic event for some Hawaiian communities and should be accommodated within team meetings (Nieto, 1996). Some Asian and Middle Eastern groups speak in circles (i.e., they loop around a subject to avoid direct confrontation of a problem (Fukuyama & Inoue-Cox, 1992). Anglo Americans who want to be direct and honest in their communication style, may feel confused or frustrated with the amount of time it takes to decide upon or resolve an issue without direct confrontation. Often, confrontational issues may not surface until several meetings have occurred.

Individuals with accents or dialects are often misunderstood in the communication process. Team members who are not tuned attentively may disregard the speaker with an accent or dialect different from their own. Individuals are sometimes made to feel ignorant or unaware of what is being said. It takes a lot of practice to listen to intonations and to understand the accent or dialect (Fukuyama & Inoue-Cox, 1992). The effectiveness of a school reform committee with members from multiple cultures will be greater if people are comfortable asking each other to repeat themselves or clarify the points that are being communicated. Evidently, verbal communication is important in establishing rapport and enhancing interactions with multicultural families and professionals. However, reliance on culture-bound means of communication (i.e., language) is not sufficient. An in-depth exploration of the culture of the individual is necessary to understand others (Alexander & Sussman, 1995) including several aspects of non-verbal communication.

Non-verbal Communication

As with other aspects of communication, non-verbal communication among multicultural groups can be challenging to participants on educational reform teams. Several aspects of non-verbal communication are important to explore: eye contact, facial expressions, space and touch, and body language and gestures. For example, people from Native American cultures may prefer a simple head nod or gentle clasping of the hand when greeting others and feel uncomfortable with the common vigorous handshake and direct eye contact that Anglo Americans use in greeting others. The avoidance of direct eye contact has been documented for Asian/Pacific Islanders (Fukuyama & Inoue-Cox, 1992). Teachers from the dominant culture often reprimand children from these cultures for not looking at them when they are speaking, a behavior that is considered disrespectful in the cultures of the children's homes. In addition, the use of certain gestures such as touching a child's head may be offensive to family members from other cultures.

Eye Contact and Facial Expressions

Direct eye contact and expressions of emotion through smiling or laughter may confuse or offend others from the non-dominant culture. Professionals engaged in collaboration and teaming should be aware that eye contact might be interpreted as disrespectful with some Hispanic and African Americans, or shameful for some Asians (Lynch & Hanson, 1995). Similarly, some non-dominant groups may use smiling and laughing to cover emotions such as embarrassment or confusion, and may refrain from using emotional expressions until they are more comfortable and trusting of team members.

Personal Space and Touch

Hall (1966) described cultures as contact or non-contact-oriented in regard to personal space and touch during communication. Communication in contact cultures involves physical closeness, occasional touching, and frequent gestures while in non-contact cultures, interactions occur at a distance which precludes physical contact (Herring, 1990). For example, some Asian/Pacific cultures are non-contact-oriented. It is important to provide space at a meeting which avoids being overly intrusive in touch and space. On the other hand, a Middle Eastern, African American or Hispanic American parent who is more contact-oriented may perceive Anglo American general and special educators as being cold and withdrawn when they are communicating at a further distance. Similarly, greetings such as handshakes may be incompatible with Chinese or other Asians, but in some African American communities, there can be elaborate handshakes but limited to within group greetings (Lynch & Hanson, 1995). Professionals can best evaluate the appropriate levels of contact by observing how individuals from the multicultural backgrounds interact among themselves.

Personal Disclosure

The amount of personal (self) disclosure varies among cultural groups. Some Anglo Americans tend to be more self-disclosing while people from other groups such as Hispanic Americans or Asian/Pacific Islanders are more reserved (Atkinson & Lowe, 1995; Pickens, 1982). Unfortunately, if Anglo American professionals in general and special education are not aware of these differences, minority individuals will often be offended and embarrassed by the questions being asked of them. People from nondisclosive cultures can be embarrassed and even offended by questions which require personal disclosure (e.g., personal or financial needs or feelings). Parents from minority cultures can be placed in this uncomfortable disclosure situation when Anglo professionals ask questions related to feelings about their child with disabilities, personal problems, or the family's financial needs (Lynch & Hanson, 1995; Kuambe, Nishida, & Hepworth, 1985).

Silence

Silence in conversation for Anglo Americans may lead to feelings of discomfort; yet for others from diverse cultures, silence is a way of thinking and attending to the listener (Tantranon-Saur, 1989). Some cultures focus more on non-verbal messages (Wittmer, 1992). Anglo Americans who are wordy and dominate conversations may have less effective interactions with professionals from those cultures who respect silence and pauses. People from such cultures may not speak at team meetings because they do not want to interrupt the speaker. However, if they are to share in collaborative processes they may need to learn to graciously interrupt their Anglo American collaborators.

IMPLICATIONS OF COLLABORATIVE CONSULTATION IN SCHOOL REFORM

Today, school personnel involved in collaborative co-teaching teams and school reform committees must demonstrate skills in facilitative communication. Wittmer (1992) described facilitative communicators as attentive listeners accepting and respectful of diversity and aware of their own assumptions, cultural values, and biases. Apparently, collaborative consultation has social implications in school reform. The focus must be on increasing the spirit of intercultural communication within a multicultural society. To foster this spirit, the following collaborative activities are imperative:

1. School personnel and members of school reform committees should practice self-analyses of their beliefs and biases related to cultural diversity. Self-examination of one's own interpersonal communication style is helpful.
2. School personnel and members of school reform committees should learn about different cultures. Several strategies for learning about culture-specific aspects of interpersonal communication include consulting with members of the culture, reading textbooks on culturally specific information (Lynch & Hanson, 1995), and consulting guidebooks for cultural etiquette (e.g., Dresser, 1996). Valuable information can be gained through interacting with members from diverse cultural groups. When school personnel are unable to ascertain the families' cultural beliefs, a cultural mediator may be helpful. Individuals from the community (e.g., paraprofessionals, clergy, and neighbors) who are willing to share information about values, beliefs, and communication styles of their people can serve as cultural mediators for school personnel (Correa, 1991; Thomas, Correa, & Morsink, 1995). Cultural mediators can assist as language interpreters and can educate the team on idiosyncratic variations of their beliefs and interpersonal communication styles.
3. To better understand the interpersonal communication styles of individual team members, particularly those from culturally and linguistically diverse backgrounds, school personnel should observe team members in diverse settings. Many of the subtle aspects of communication such as space and touch can be observed in both school and community settings. For example, parents may be more comfortable in-

teracting with educators in their homes or community environments. Educators can observe the family's style of communication and learn how to better interact with family members. Furthermore, other team members such as general educators, school psychologists, occupational therapists, physical therapists, and administrators can be observed in school environments that are more familiar and comfortable for them. Facilitative communicators develop a better understanding of differences and similarities in interpersonal communication when they can study and analyze interactions of others in multiple settings. Collaboration can be enhanced when team members share their perspectives and observations with one another towards achieving the mutually agreed-upon goal of increased communication.

4. School personnel can become more effective collaborators if they understand that individuals may have different views about the purposes of education. For example, many Hispanic families believe their children are "bien educados" (well-educated socially) if they respect adults, speak only when spoken to, and are polite (Lynch & Hanson, 1995; Ortiz, 1993). Thus, school personnel from the dominant culture who place a high value on academic achievement may need to adjust expectations to include social competence and respect for authority which are valued by other cultures.

5. Issues should be identified and resolved based on the interdependent relationship of all representatives on the school reform committee or co-teaching teams.

6. Members of co-teaching teams and school reform committees should use effective problem-solving and facilitation techniques such as arranging meetings, running meetings, and following up with recommendations.

CONCLUSION

In this chapter, we have addressed the impact of collaborative consultation in general and special education. We believe schooling in America has served the dual role of transmitting the majority culture and supporting the development of individuals from minority cultures. Assimilation of those from diverse cultures has been understood to be the major outcome and has been overseen by those from the dominant culture. Traditionally, people from the dominant culture have served on the governing boards and the school reform committees (e.g., administrators, teachers, parents, students, and business and community leaders who themselves are members of the dominant culture). Individuals from multicultural cultures have approached changing the ways that schools operate primarily in a reactive mode (i.e., when enough people in the community become upset, or when their children are in trouble, come *en masse* to school board meetings, to protest policies or practices).

From our perspective, instead of assimilating diverse cultures by suppressing and devaluing their language and customs (i.e., the melting pot metaphor), schools are now expected to nurture and value diverse cultures (i.e., the salad bowl metaphor). Under these circumstances, general and special educators as well as governing boards and school reform committees are now expected to *reflect* the faces of the community itself. The challenge is to actively include those people who previously have been discouraged from participating, those who have no history or practice of participating (and therefore no skills to do so), and those who have sought assertively or aggressively to participate. Collaborative teaching teams, school reform committees, and governing boards committed to including members from diverse cultures as representatives on the committees may need to guard against doing business as usual rather than doing new business. That is, the representatives can become assimilated into the school culture rather than changing the culture of the school itself.

In summary, ensuring diversity of membership is not enough but must be combined with different ways of involving underrepresented people, families, and businesses from diverse cultures. Not only must the members of the minority culture learn how to negotiate the system, the interpersonal interactions of all team members must change. All must become sensitive to and more effective with diverse interpersonal and communication styles. Increasing the intercultural competence of members from minority and dominant cultures may be a beneficial outcome of acquiring and practicing facilitative communication skills. In the end, general and special educators who take the trouble to improve their multicultural competencies can do much to enhance school reform efforts in the education of all our children.

REFERENCES

Alexander, C.M., & Sussman, L. (1995). Creative approaches to multicultural counseling. In J. Ponterotto, J.M. Casa, L.A. Suzuki, & C.M. Alexander (Eds.), *Handbook of multicultural counseling* (pp. 375–386). Thousand Oaks, CA: Sage.

Atkinson, D., & Lowe, S. (1995). The role of ethnicity, cultural knowledge, and conventional techniques in counseling and psychotherapy. In J. Ponterotto, J.M. Casa, L.A. Suzuki, & C.M. Alexander (Eds.), *Handbook of multicultural counseling* (pp. 387–414). Thousand Oaks, CA: Sage.

Babcock, N.L., & Pryzwansky, W.B. (1983). Models of consultation: Preferences of educational professionals at five stages of service. *Journal of School Psychology, 21,* 359–366.

Banks, J.A. (1999). *An introduction to multicultural education* (2nd ed.). Needham Heights, MA: Allyn & Bacon.

Banks, J.A., & Banks, C.A. McGhee (1997). *Multicultural education: Issues and perspectives.* Needham Heights, MA: Allyn & Bacon.

Conoley, J.C., & Conoley, C.W. (1982). *School consultation: A guide to practice and training.* New York: Pergamon.

Correa, V.I. (1991). Involving culturally diverse families in the educational process. In S.H. Fradd, & J. Weismantel (Eds.), *Meeting the needs of culturally and linguistically different students: A handbook for educators* (pp. 130–144). Boston, MA: College-Hill.

Cummins, J. (1986). Empowering minority students: A framework for intervention. *Harvard Educational Review, 56,* 18–36.

Cummins, J. (1989). A theoretical framework for bilingual special education. *Exceptional Children, 56,* 111–119.

Curtis, M.J., & Meyers, J. (1988). Consultation: A foundation for alternative services in schools. In J.L. Graden, J.E. Zins, & M.J. Curtis (Eds.), *Alternative educational delivery systems: Enhancing instructional options for all students* (pp. 35–48). Washington, DC: The National Association of School Psychologists.

DeBoer, A. (1986). *The art of consulting.* Chicago, IL: Arcturus Books.

Dresser, N. (1996). *Multicultural manners: New rules of etiquette for a changing society.* New York: John Wiley & Sons.

Duke, D., Showers, B., & Imber, M. (1980). Teachers and shared decision-making: The costs and benefits of involvement. *Educational Administration Quarterly, 16,* 93–106.

Ellis, D.G., & Fisher, B.A. (1994). *Small group decision making: Communication and the group process* (4th ed.). New York: McGraw Hill.

Fradd, S., & Weismantel, J. (1989). *Meeting the needs of culturally and linguistically different students: A handbook for educators.* Boston, MA: College-Hill.

Friend, M., & Cook, L. (1996). *Interactions: Collaboration skills for school professionals* (2nd ed.). New York: Longman.

Fukuyama, M.A., & Inoue-Cox, C. (1992). Cultural perspectives in communicating with Asian/Pacific Islanders. In J. Wittmer (Ed.), *Valuing diversity and similarity: Bridging the gap through interpersonal skills* (pp. 93–111). Minneapolis, MN: Educational Media Corporation.

Fullan, M. (1993). Innovation, reform, and restructuring strategies. In S. Cawell (Ed.), *Challenges and achievements in American education* (pp. 116–133). Alexandria, VA: Association for Supervision and Curriculum Development.

Gallessich, J. (1982). *The profession and practice of consultation.* San Francisco, CA: Jossey-Bass.

Gibbs, J. (1980). The interpersonal orientation in mental health consultation: Toward a model of ethnic variations in consultation. *Journal of Community Psychology, 8,* 195–207.

Gollnick, D.M., & Chinn, P.C. (1994). *Multicultural education in a pluralistic society* (4th ed.). Columbus, OH: Merrill.

Goodenough, W.H. (1976). Multiculturalism as the normal human experience. *Anthropology and Education Quarterly, 7,* 4–7.

Gutkin, R.B., & Curtis, M.L. (1999). School-based consultation theory and techniques. In C.R. Reynolds & T.B. Gutkin (Eds.), *The handbook of school psychology* (3rd ed.) (pp. 598–637). New York: John Wiley & Sons.

Hall, E.T. (1966). *The hidden dimension.* New York: Doubleday.

Harris, K.C. (1991). An expanded view on consultation competencies for educators serving culturally and linguistically diverse exceptional students. *Teacher Education and Special Education, 14,* 25–29.

Harris, K.C. (1995). School-based bilingual special education teacher assistance teams. *Remedial and Special Education, 16,* 337–343.

Harris, K.C. (1996). Collaboration within a multicultural society: Issues for consideration. *Remedial and Special Education, 17,* 355–362, 376.

Harris, K.C., & Nevin, A. (1993). Exploring collaboration between bilingual and special educators. *The Consulting Edge, 5,* 1, 3, 5.

Heron, T., & Harris, K. (in press). *The educational consultant* (4th ed.). Austin, TX: Pro-Ed.

Herring, R.D. (1990). Nonverbal communication: A necessary component of cross-cultural counseling. *Journal of Multicultural Counseling and Development, 18,* 172–179.

Idol, L., Nevin, A., & Paolucci-Whitcomb, P. (in press). *Collaborative consultation* (3rd ed.). Austin, TX: Pro-Ed.

Individuals with Disabilities Education Act Amendments of 1990 (IDEA). P. L. 105-17. 20 U.S.C. §§ 1400 et seq.

Johnson, D., & Johnson, R. (1989). *Cooperation and competition: Theory and research.* Edina, MN: Interaction.

Jordan, L., Reyes-Blanes, M.E., Peel, B.B., Peel, H.A., & Lane, H.B. (1998). Developing teacher-parent partnerships across cultures: Effective parent conferences. *Intervention in School and Clinic, 33,* 141–147.

Kratochwill, T.R., Elliott, S.N., & Rotto, P. (1990). Best practices in behavioral consultation. In A. Thomas & J. Grimes (Eds.), *Best practices in school psychology II* (pp. 147–169). Washington, DC: The National Association of School Psychologists.

Kratochwill, T.R., Sheridan, S.M., & VanSomeren, K.R. (1988). Research in behavioral consultation: Current status and future directions. In J.F. West (Ed.), *School consultation: Interdisciplinary perspectives on theory, research, training, and practice* (pp. 77–102), Austin, TX: Research and Training Project on School Consultation, The University of Texas.

Kuambe, K.T., Nishida, C., & Hepworth, K.H. (1985). *Bridging ethnocultural diversity in social work and health.* Honolulu, HI: University of Hawaii, School of Social Work.

Kurpius, D. (1978). consultation theory and process: An integrated model. *Personnel and Guidance Journal, 56,* 335–338.

Lynch, E., & Hanson, M. (1995). *A guide for working with children and their families: Developing cross-cultural competence* (2nd ed.). Baltimore, MD: Paul H. Brookes.

Lynch, E., & Hanson, M. (1998). *Developing cross-cultural competence* (2nd ed.). Baltimore, MD: Paul H. Brookes.

Moore, K.J., Fifield, M.B., Spira, D.A., & Scarlato, M. (1989). Child study team decision making in special education: Improving the process. *Remedial and Special Education, 10,* 50–58.

Morsink, C., Thomas, C., & Correa, V. (1992). *Interactive teaming: Consultation and collaboration in special programs.* New York: Macmillan.

Nevin, A., Thousand, J., Paolucci-Whitcomb, P., & Villa, R. (1990). Collaborative consultation: Empowering public school personnel to provide heterogeneous schooling for all–or, Who rang that bell? *Journal of Educational and Psychological Consultation, 1,* 41–67.

Nieto, S. (1996). *Affirming diversity: The sociopolitical context of multicultural education* (2nd ed.). White Plains, NJ: Longman.

Obiakor, F.E. (1999). Multicultural education: Powerful tool for educating learners with exceptionalities. In F.E. Obiakor, J.O. Schwenn, & A.F. Rotatori (Eds.), *Advances in special education: Multicultural education for learners with exceptionalities Vol. 12* (pp. 1–14). Stamford, CT: JAI Press.

Ortiz, A.A. (1993). Cultural factors in educating students with emotional disturbance and behavior disorders. In J. Kauffman (Ed.), *Characteristics of emotional and behavioral disorders of children and youth* (5th ed.) (pp. 282–284). New York: Macmillan.

Pickens, J.C. (1982). *Without bias: A guidebook for non-discriminatory communication* (2nd ed.). New York: Wiley.

Ponterotto, J., Casa, J.M., Suzuki, L.A., & Alexander, C.M. (1995). *Handbook of multicultural counseling.* Thousand Oaks, CA: Sage.

P.L. 94-142, The Education of All Handicapped Children Act of 1975. (23 August 1977). 20 U.S.C. §§ 1401 et seq: *Federal Register, 42* (163), 42474–42518.

P.L. 101-476: Individuals with Disabilities Education Act. (1990). Title 20, U.S.C. §§ 1400 et seq: *U. S. Statutes at Large, 104,* 1103–1151.

Raffaniello, E.M. (1981). Competent consultation: The collaborative approach. In M.J. Curtis & J.E. Zins (Eds.), *The theory and practice of school consultation* (pp. 44–54). Springfield, IL: Charles C Thomas.

Rosenfield, S. (1987). *Instructional consultation.* Hillsdale, NJ: Lawrence Erlbaum.

Samovar, L., & Porter, R. (1985). *Intercultural communication: A reader.* Belmont, CA: Wadsworth.

Schmuck, R.A., & Runkel, P.J. (1995). *The handbook of organization development in schools* (3rd ed.). Palo Alto, CA: Mayfield.

Shields, J.M., Heron, T.E., Rubenstein, C.L., & Katz, E.R. (1995). The ecotriadic model of educational consultation for students with cancer. *Education and Treatment of Children, 18,* 184–200.

Sileo, T.W., Sileo, A.P., & Prater, M.A. (1996). Parent and professional partnerships in special education: Multicultural considerations. *Intervention in School and Clinic, 11,* 145–153.

Speece, D.L., & Mandell, C.J. (1980). Interpersonal communication between resource and regular teachers. *Teacher Education and Special Education, 3,* 55–60.

Sue, D.W., & Sue, D. (1990). *Counseling the culturally different: Theory and practice.* New York: Wiley.

Sugai, G.M., & Tindal, G.A. (1993). *Effective school consultation: An interactive approach.* Pacific Grove, CA: Brooks/Cole.

Tantranon-Saur, A. (1989). What's behind the "Asian mask?" *Our Asian Inheritance, 6,* 67–70.

Tharp, R.G. (1989). Psychocultural variables and constants: Effects on teaching and learning in schools. *American Psychologist, 44,* 349–359.

Thomas, C., Correa, V., & Morsink, C. (1995). *Interactive teaming: Consultation and collaboration in special programs* (2nd ed.). Columbus, OH: Merrill.

Thousand, J., Fox, T., Reid, R., Godek, J., Williams, W., & Fox, W. (1986). *The Homecoming Project: Educating students who present intensive educational challenges within regular classroom environments* (Monograph No. 7-1). Burlington, VT: University of Vermont Center for Developmental Disabilities.

Thousand, J., Nevin, A., & Fox, W. (1987). Inservice training to support education of learners with severe handicaps in their local schools. *Teacher Education and Special Education, 10* (1), 4–14.

Thousand, J., & Villa, R. (1990). Sharing expertise and responsibilities through teaching teams. In

W. Stainback & S. Stainback (Eds.), *Support networks for inclusive schooling: Interdependent integrated education* (pp. 151–166). Baltimore, MD: Paul H. Brookes.

Thousand, J., & Villa, R. (1992). Collaborative teams: A powerful tool in school restructuring. In R. Villa, J. Thousand, W. Stainback, & S. Stainback (Eds.), *Restructuring for heterogeneity: An administrative handbook for creating effective schools for everyone* (pp. 73–108). Baltimore, MD: Paul H. Brookes.

Tombari, M., & Bergan, J. (1978). Consultant cues and teacher verbalizations, judgments, and expectancies concerning children's adjustment problems. *Journal of School Psychology, 16,* 212–219.

Villa, R., & Thousand, J. (1995). *Creating inclusive schools.* Alexandria, VA: Association for Supervision and Curriculum Development.

Villa, R., & Thousand, J. (Eds.). (in press). *Restructuring for caring and effective education* (2nd ed.). Baltimore, MD: Paul H. Brookes.

Villa, R., Thousand, J., Stainback, W., & Stainback, S. (1992). *Restructuring for caring and effective education: An administrative guide to creating heterogeneous schools.* Baltimore, MD: Paul H. Brookes.

West, J.F., & Idol, L. (1987). School consultation (Part I): An interdisciplinary perspective on theory, models, and research. *Journal of Learning Disabilities, 20,* 388–408.

West, J.F., Idol, L., & Cannon, G. (1989). *Collaboration in the schools: An inservice and preservice curriculum for teachers, support staff, and administrators.* Austin, TX: Pro-Ed.

Wittmer, J. (1992). *Valuing diversity and similarity: Bridging the gap through interpersonal skills.* Minneapolis: MN: Educational Media Corporation.

Zins, J.E., & Illback, R.J. (1995). Consulting to facilitate planned organizational change in schools. *Journal of Educational and Psychological Consultation, 6,* 237–245.

Zins, J.E., & Ponti, C.R. (1990a). Best practices in school-based consultation. In A. Thomas & J. Grimes (Ed.), *Best practices in school psychology II* (pp. 673–693). Washington, DC: The National Association of School Psychologists.

Zins, J.E., & Ponti, C.R. (1990b). Strategies to facilitate the implementation, organization, and operation of system-wide consultation programs. *Journal of Educational and Psychological Consultation, 1,* 205–218.

Chapter 10

CULTURALLY RESPONSIVE TEACHER PREPARATION PROGRAMMING FOR THE TWENTY-FIRST CENTURY

FESTUS E. OBIAKOR AND CHERYL A. UTLEY

For millions of racial and language minority children, children who live in resource-poor urban and rural areas, and children who come from cultures considered non-mainstream, the future rests in the hands of policymakers, community leaders, and educators they will never meet. These children's future depends on the conditions of the schools, on whether these schools are culturally responsive to the students they serve. Most important, these children's future depends on the quality of teaching that occurs in their classrooms. (Futrell & Witty, 1997, p. 212)

Educational reform in teacher preparation programs is influenced by state and federal policies (e.g., 1997 IDEA Amendments) and national professional standards established by organizations such as the Council for Exceptional Children (CEC), the National Council for Accreditation of Teacher Education (NCATE), the National Board for Professional Teaching Standards (NBPTS), and the Interstate New Teacher Assessment and Support Consortium (INTASC). The accreditation of special education teacher preparation programs, to a large extent, depends upon the national standards, knowledge, and skills taught in the content and structure of their programs. Therefore, the responsibility of schools, colleges, and departments of education is to ensure that knowledge and information applicable to culturally-based learning and behavioral styles, teaching styles, culturally responsive educational practices, and family and community values are incorporated into teacher preparation programs.

A national dilemma, however, is that school reform in the teaching profession shows that teachers' degrees, qualifications, and licensing or certification status in affluent communities are impressive and increasingly improving, while teachers in the urban cities are underprepared and provided little knowledge about teaching and learning upon entering classrooms to teach at-risk and multicultural learners with disabilities. During the 1980s, commission reports, such as *A Nation at Risk* and *An Imperiled Generation: Saving Urban Schools,* and research-based books (e.g., Goodlad's 1984 *A Place Called School* and Kozol's 1991 *Savage Inequalities*) focused the nation's attention on the failure of U.S. schools to improve the status of education for multicultural children from low-socioeconomic (SES) backgrounds. These reports and books singled out teacher preparation programs, noting the degree to which these programs (a) perpetuated theories that support the assumption that poor education is caused primarily by cultural, family, or biological circumstances, and (b) supported retrogressive school practices (e.g., tracking) and program options (e.g., Chapter 1, remedial education, and special education) that have maintained separate and unequal education opportunities for at-risk and multicultural learners.

Undergraduate and graduate students in teacher preparation programs generally have little knowledge or experience about different ethnic groups in the United States and too often they hold negative attitudes about cultural groups other than their own (Ford, Obiakor, & Patton, 1995). Most general and special education programs have frames of reference based on dominant Eurocentric values without a systemic focus on characteristics of different cultural groups in terms of their unique strengths, characteristics, and contributions to society (Artiles & Aguirre-Munoz, 1995; Bynoe, 1998; Hilliard, 1995). The failure to enforce policies and the minimal attempts to upgrade educational standards and teacher knowledge in school districts where resources are scarce must be addressed by all members of the education community if United States schools are to change these troubling trends and overcome the challenges that urban schools face. For

teacher preparation programs to address the academic and social needs of multicultural learners with disabilities, graduating students must develop an in-depth understanding of the influence of culture and language on students' academic performance in order for them to distinguish between learning problems that reflect characteristics of second language learners or cultural differences versus those that are the result of a disability (Algozzine & Obiakor, 1995; Ford, Obiakor & Patton; Kea & Utley, 1998; Obiakor & Utley, 1997; Utley, 1995; Utley & Mortweet, 1999). Yet, in a survey of doctoral programs at 46 universities that were members of Higher Education Consortium in Special Education (HECSE), Bos, Roberts, Rieth, and Derer (1995) reported that there are only a few programs including multicultural/bilingual education programs as an area of focus (18%) or as a minor (5%). In another study of Office of Special Education Programs (OSEP) funded leadership training projects from 1990–1993, Smith and Salzberg (1994) reported that only 10% of the projects focused on multicultural issues. More recently, OSEP (1999) reported on the number of minority or underrepresented students that have been enrolled in doctoral leadership training programs.

In the OSEP's *Annual Performance Report* for the year 1995, the number of Caucasian (.76), African-American (.10), Hispanic (.07), American Indian (.01), Asian-American/Pacific Islander (.02), and students with disabilities (.03) was reported. Strikingly evident in reviewing survey results of doctoral-level programs in Institutions of Higher Education (IHEs) is that general and special educators have not been aggressive in meeting the challenge of developing special education programs infused with multicultural/bilingual education course work (Sindelar & Schloss, 1987). These data suggest that the situation has not changed since the 1980s and that teacher educators have not been retrained to respond to the unique needs of students who come from diverse races, cultures, and languages (Algozzine & Obiakor, 1995; Cartledge, Gardner, & Tillman, 1995; Ewing, 1995; Ladson-Billings, 1990; Obiakor, 1993, 1994; Obiakor, Algozzine, & Ford, 1994; Trent, 1995). This chapter presents the need to rethink traditional teacher preparation programs for general and special educators who teach multicultural learners with disabilities. We briefly review demographic and national trends in the supply-and-demand of multicultural general and special educators. We examine the knowledge base and outcomes of "culturally responsible" teacher preparation programs and CEC's professional standards of practice in special education and propose models of infusion to bridge the existing gap in the preparation of general and special educators in multicultural education competencies.

CULTURAL DIVERSITY IN SPECIAL EDUCATION PERSONNEL: A MISSING LINK

While cultural diversity in the student population has increased, the diversity of the teaching or professional force has decreased (American Association of Colleges for Teacher Education [AACTE], 1994; Ewing, 1995). According to AACTE, the number of minorities enrolled in teacher preparation programs is small when compared to the number of minority group children in public schools. It noted that "approximately 85 percent of teacher education students are White, 7 percent are Black/African-American, and 4 percent are Hispanic, 1 percent are International/non-Resident, 0.5 percent are Native American/American Indian, and Pacific Islander and Alaskan Native represent less than 1 percent of enrollments" (p. 5). In undergraduate special education programs, the percentage of enrollment for White students is 87.8, for Black/African-American students is 6.6, for Hispanic students is 3.1, for Asian/Pacific Islander students is .5, and for American Indian students is .5 (AACTE). Thus, the problem of educating teachers for diversity, in most instances, continues to be one of preparing White, monolingual, and mostly female teacher education students. Despite the language and cultural diversity in schools, the majority of general and special educators continue to be Euro-American, monolingual speakers of English.

National trends in the composition of the teaching workforce in special education reflect similar trends in general education (Wald, 1996). In supply-and-demand research in special education, Cook and Boe (1995) reported that the supply of special education teaching professionals representing diverse populations was 14%, whereas the percentage of students in special education programs representing multicultural populations was about 32%. The National Center for Education Statistics (1995) reported that 13.5% of the U.S. teaching work force was composed of multicultural personnel, whereas 31.4% of all students represented multicultural populations. The underlying issues associated with the supply and demand of culturally and linguistically diverse teaching professionals include (a) individuals representing multicultural populations do not consider teaching as a career because of the lure of alternative careers; (b) variables such as poverty, standardized tests, certification exams, continue to have a disparate effect on the number of multicultural students who are enrolling in postsecondary educational programs; (c) barriers of alienation and discrimination in institutions of higher education (IHE), (d) additional educational requirements necessary for certification, and (e) increased attrition/retention rates of multicultural teachers in urban, inner-city areas are greater than in suburban cities. Collectively, these findings indicate a negative impact on the number of special educators who are qualified to teach multicultural learners with mild disabilities.

Minority Faculty in Institutions of Higher Education

The severity of the supply-and-demand problem associated with professionals representing different cultural groups in doctoral programs in institutions of higher education (IHEs) must not be overlooked. In earlier research conducted by Smith and Tyler (1994), 48 IHEs were surveyed with doctoral-level comprehensive special education programs to determine the number of doctoral students from minority groups. Five of these IHE programs had enrollments ranging from 13 to 29 students, but the majority (27) reported fewer than 4 students, including three major university programs that had no minority doctoral students. More recently, in studying the supply and demand of special education faculty, Tyler and Smith (1999) surveyed 90 college/university programs and identified 374 doctoral graduates for participation in this study. Results indicated that the majority of doctoral graduates in special education programs were of European American descent. The total percentage of African American, Hispanic/Latino, Native-American, Middle Eastern, and Asian/Pacific Islander doctoral-level graduates ranged from 0.7 to 8.9. Thus, based collectively on trends in the shortages of culturally and linguistically diverse general and special educators and minority graduate doctoral students in teacher preparation programs, there is a critical need to rethink traditional teacher preparation programs and develop a culturally responsive teacher preparation programs.

TRADITIONAL UNIVERSITY-BASED TEACHER PREPARATION PROGRAMS

Colleges of Education have been designed to prepare prospective elementary and secondary teachers to serve students with disabilities in inclusive classroom settings. Teacher educators acknowledge that their programs must include both a knowledge base and a set of instructional skills focused on the actual delivery of instruction. Reitz and Kerr (1991) noted that the "knowledge base component of teacher preparation curricular is reflected in the didactic course offerings and generally includes emphasis in such areas as teaching theory, instructional methodology, child development, education-al research, and specific subject content (e.g., reading, math, and science). The skill development component of the curriculum is reflected in the practicum and student teaching experiences, where students are expected to put into practice the knowledge they have gained through their course work" (p. 362). Knowledge and skill-based competencies have been described by Welch and Sheridan (1993), Reynolds (1991), and OSEP (1997) and reflect the following core domains: ethical and legal principles, curriculum teaching, basic literacy skills, educational theories and systems, effective instruction, pupil and class management and behavioral principles, professional consultation and communication, teacher-parent relationships, student-student relationships, characteristics of students with disabilities, referral, individualized teaching, professional values, diagnosing problems, teaching and managing atypical learners, setting academic and behavior performance standards, teaching for self-regulation and strategic behavior, technology, and motivating students.

One major criticism of university-based teacher preparation programs is that teacher trainees spend the majority of their course work learning about educational principles and how students learn, but spend little time actually engaged in the process of teaching children with disabilities in restrictive and inclusive classroom settings (Burstein & Sears, 1998; Goodlad, 1991; Lenz & Deshler, 1990). There is an overwhelming emphasis on developing a knowledge base in teacher trainees, but very little time teaching the skills that will enable them to effectively apply that knowledge in different classroom settings. For university-based teacher preparation programs to be effective, teacher educators must recognize that change is needed where there is a shared commitment between university-based faculty and school district personnel in developing a critical knowledge base, skills, and field-based experiences for teacher trainees in a variety of public school settings. A central consideration in the university-based teacher preparation program is the composition of the student population to be served by its program graduates. Because of changing demographics of students served in the public schools, graduating teachers are responsible for the learning of a diverse group of children with respect to cultural and linguistic background, socioeconomic status, ability, and disability. The question is "How prepared are America's teacher preparation programs to meet the challenges presented by the changing demographics of the population?"

Presumptuous statements or myths about multiculturalism have traditionally permeated teacher preparation programs and continue to create problems for administrators, faculty, staff, and students of Colleges of Education in the United States. Obiakor (1993) provided a few examples:

1. Minority students must understand that this is America, a land of competition.
2. We cannot find qualified minority students for academic scholarships.
3. We cannot find qualified minority faculty for recruitment.
4. It is a preferential treatment to adopt policies to recruit and retain minority faculty, staff, and students.
5. Multicultural curriculum is expensive.
6. Multicultural curriculum is not necessary because there are a few minority students.
7. Multicultural curriculum is not necessary because racism does not exist anymore.
8. Affirmative action regulations are unfair to the majority in the university.
9. Changes to reflect multiethnicity in teacher education programs should be gradual.
10. Advocates of multiculturalism want to lower the quality of education.

As a consequence, colleges of education must remedy existing educational disparities by adopting a "culture of inclusiveness" policy that would be infused in every facet of society (Wisniewski, 1995). A multicultural/bilingual general and special education curricula would correct the miseducation of students, provide them with the total life experience, and advocate inclusion rather than exclusion in manpower. Traditional programs must revamp their philosophy, mission, and purpose to be more culturally responsive to teachers and students. Thus, essential components in the preparation of program graduates must be knowledge, skills, and field experiences in the discipline of multicultural/bilingual education to ensure that teachers are trained to be instructionally flexible and culturally competent (Obiakor & Utley, 1997).

CULTURALLY RESPONSIBLE PEDAGOGY IN GENERAL TEACHER PREPARATION PROGRAMS

Factors such as urban education, poverty, race, or membership in a particular culture group demand new forms of teacher preparation and practice. It is increasingly apparent that teacher educators can no longer support their traditional programs that emphasize the learners' age, the content to be taught, and disability. Also, apparent is the fact that they can no longer ignore and reject including variables such as urban poverty or cultural diversity in their preparation programs. The challenge today is on including those elements of curricula that touch on all facets of society. The infusion of multicultural knowledge and skills into the curricula is centered upon debates focused on what content best serves the vision of a society where diverse groups can retain their cultural heritages while simultaneously engaging in true cooperation to achieve universal ideals of equity and access for all. Teacher preparation programs must generate course work that address divergent aspects of ethnicity and culture of the peoples of America and the world. Grant (1997) noted that challenges of infusing a culturally responsible pedagogy into teacher preparation programs have generated consistent debates on how to reconfigure existing programs. Discussions have focused on whether teacher educators should create a new paradigm that is multicultural-social reconstructionist and/or infuse ethnic studies content and field experience in a multicultural site. In this chapter, we recommend a "culturally responsible pedagogy paradigm" for preparing teachers to work with multicultural learners with and without disabilities. As Garcia and Dominguez (1997) pointed out:

> For classrooms in which culturally and linguistically diverse students are served to reach its full developmental potential, instruction should be provided in ways that promote the acquisition of increasingly complex knowledge and skills in a social climate that fosters collaboration and positive interactions between participants. Such classrooms are inclusive in their emphasis on high outcomes for all students, including culturally and linguistically diverse students. Important features of such a setting include high expectations, exposure to academically rich curricula, materials, approaches that are culturally and linguistically responsive and appropriate, use of instructional technologies that enhance learning, and emphasis on student-regulated, active learning, rather than passive, teacher-directed transmission. In addition to using effective methods and materials, teachers possess cross-cultural communication understanding and skills that promote positive communication with their culturally and linguistically diverse students, who in turn, have opportunities to develop their own cross-cultural effectiveness. (p. 647)

Smith (1998), in defining a culturally responsible pedagogy for teacher education, stated that the mission of a "teacher preparation program is to prepare teachers to be respectfully sensitive to the cultures of their students, to learn about and know the cultures of their students, and to use understandings about how culture influences learning in their day-to-day planning for teaching students" (p. 20). She further noted that a moral and ethical imperative for schools, colleges, and departments of education is to "enable teachers to respond to the educational needs of their diverse student population by planning and developing culturally rich curricula and by using instructional methodologies that are based upon knowledge about how culture influences cognitive learning styles. Ideally, to have a culturally responsible teacher education program, a school, college, or department of education would have a mission statement that recognizes that multicultural teacher education is teacher education and would provide a series of multiculturally rich experiences consisting of formal course work and interactive classroom and field experiences that accomplish its mission" (p. 20). The goals of a culturally responsible teacher education program, as delineated by Smith, directly teaches facts about several cultural groups for the local rural and metropolitan communities of program graduates, presents the knowledge bases of theory and research studies about cultural groups, and provides opportunities for teachers to learn processes and methodologies for the study of other cultural groups. Grant (1997) confirmed that the knowledge base must come out of a "fund of knowledge from different disciplines that have been shaped by different multicultural perspectives and experiences acquired from working with race, class, and gender issues and culturally diverse groups of people" (p. 17). As can be seen in Table 10.1, eleven essential knowledge bases have been identified for infusion into the teacher education curriculum.

The outcomes associated with a culturally responsible pedagogy include research-based knowledge and practices related to student learning in both content and methodology. Thus, a culturally responsible teacher education program involves:

1. Teachers who think and act multiculturally rather than monoculturally.
2. Teachers who develop curricula that are multicultural rather than monocultural in content.
3. Teachers who use methods that are congruent with the students' cultural learning styles and who reflect about the relevance of knowledge bases in a variety of cultural contexts.
4. Teachers who understand that becoming a multicultural educator is a developmental process.

5. Teachers who understand and respect their own cultural heritage and develop the knowledge, skills, and attitudes to become functional within other ethnic cultures as well as the mainstream culture.
6. Teachers who understand that multicultural education will enable them to believe in their intrinsic worth, to transcend monoculturalism, and to become multicultural.
7. Teachers who are willing to learn about customs, belief systems, communication, and linguistic styles, mores, and behavior patterns of different cultural groups. They are willing to internalize a methodology for adapting to and learning about many other cultures from which their pupils may come.
8. Teachers who are willing to develop a curriculum that includes elements of different cultural groups.
9. Teachers who identify dominant culturally influenced cognitive styles and how to recognize the individual student variances from the dominant cognitive styles of that student's culture.
10. Teachers who view multicultural students as capable, motivated, and resilient.
11. Teachers who are change agents who work to fight injustice, social inequality, and inequities.

Field-based experiences are critical sources of teacher knowledge in teacher preparation programs. The classroom is the place where teachers have opportunities to integrate their conceptual knowledge base and skills to form an experiential knowledge base. The critical experiences associated with field-based experiences, as outlined by Grant (1997), include:

- Field experiences guided by theoretical and pedagogical research.
- Field experiences with a cooperating teacher and supervisor who have a thorough knowledge of multicultural education.

Table 10.1
KNOWLEDGE BASES FOR DIVERSITY IN TEACHER EDUCATION

1.0 Foundations of Multicultural Education
   1.1 Definitions of multicultural education
   1.2 Key terms that constitute the concepts and language of multicultural education such as diversity, cultural pluralism, assimilation, culture, acculturation, xenophobia, ethnocentrism, Eurocentrism, racism, classism, prejudice, discrimination, antiracism, antibias, inclusion, and exclusion
   1.3 Principles and philosophical tenets of multicultural education (i.e., differences are not deficits; culture influences the way students learn)
   1.4 Models of multicultural curriculum infusion
   1.5 Models of personal stages of development from ethnocentrism to multiculturalism and globalism
   1.6 Literature of theory and research that undergirds multicultural education as a discipline

2.0 Sociocultural Contexts of Human Growth and Psychological Development in Marginalized Ethnic and Racial Cultures
   2.1 Ethnic patterns of social, physical, and cognitive development
   2.2 Patterns and stages of ethnic identity including self-concept and self-image development
   2.3 Influences of culturally determined and unique patterns of family organization, child-rearing practices, and other processes of socialization and development
   2.4 Cultural influences on motivation
   2.5 Resilience among non-mainstream ethnic and racial cultures
   2.6 Critical theory perspectives regarding conventional norms and definitions of "developmentally appropriate practice"

3.0 Cultural and Cognitive Learning Style Theory and Research
   3.1 Descriptive profiles of cultural learning styles for African American, Hispanic American, Native American, Asian American, and other cultural groups
   3.2 Theory and research base that undergirds the cultural learning-style profiles for each group
   3.3 The skills to use cultural learning-style profiles wisely

4.0 Language, Communication and Interactional Styles of Marginalized Cultures
   4.1 The theory and research on language acquisition, particularly of native speakers of languages other than English and English dialects
   4.2 Cultural communication and interaction styles (verbal and nonverbal)
   4.3 Principles and strategies of teaching English as a second language to speakers of culturally unique English dialects and speakers of first languages other than English

5.0 Essential Elements of Cultures
   5.1 A schema for learning about any culture
      • Patterns of knowledge and ways of knowing
      • Patterns and relevance of values, belief systems, worldviews, cratoms, traditions, mores, and spirituality
      • An ancient through modern history of a culture's people (heroines and heroes), artifacts, music, dance, science, technology, mathematics, philosophy, architecture, government)
      • Unique ways different voices of a culture express relationships to other cultures, particularly the dominant culture
      • Patterns of unique skills and behaviors
      • Patterns of perception and cognition (cognitive styles)
      • Languages and communication styles including verbal and nonverbal nuances
   5.2 Study of each of the above essential elements in the context of specific or regional cultures (i.e., African American, Mexican American, Navajo, Korean American)

Table 10.1 (continued)

6.0 Principles of Culturally Responsive Teaching and Culturally Responsive Curriculum Development

   6.1 Principles of culturally responsive curriculum development
- Definitions: culturally responsive pedagogy, cultural synchronization, and cultural incongruity.
- Major premises

   6.2 Principles of culturally responsive curriculum development

7.0 Effective Strategies for Teaching Minority Students

   7.1 Effective teaching research
   7.2 Effective schools research
   7.3 Cooperative learning research
   7.4 Craft wisdom research
   7.5 Resilient child research
   7.6 Parental involvement research

8.0 Foundations of Racism

   8.1 History of prejudice, discrimination, and racism in the United States
   8.2 Theory and research on how racist attitudes, stereotypes, and prejudices are learned and integrated into self image, personality structure, and ethnic identity
   8.3 Effects of racism on members of the dominant white culture and members of minority cultures
   8.4 The literature of theory and research on changing negative racial attitudes and negative attitudes toward diversity
   8.5 Scales and instruments that purport to measure racism and attitudes toward diversity
   8.6 A study of anti-bias, anti-racist curricula

9.0 Effects of Policy and Practice on Culture, Race, Class, Gender, and Other Categories of Diversity

   9.1 Effects of ability grouping and curriculum tracking
   9.2 Effects of segregated schools by race and class
   9.3 Effects of school choice, privatization and vouchers
   9.4 Effects of inequitable school funding
   9.5 Effects of discipline policy and practice on minority students
   9.6 Effects of teacher expectations and teacher-student interactions
   9.7 Effects of standardized testing

10.0 Culturally Responsive Diagnosis, Measurement, and Assessment

   10.1 Theory and research on skewed diagnosis
   10.2 The validity literature on specific intelligence tests, achievement tests, and aptitude tests, K-higher education
   10.3 The literature that questions the use of tests to allocate educational opportunity in a democratic society
   10.4 The literature on alternative and authentic assessment

11.0 Sociocultural Influences on Subject-Specific Learning

   11.1 Theory and research on the influence of cultural belief systems, values, and expectations that influence non-White ethnic children's learning and achievement in specific subject areas (i.e., mathematics, science, standard English, reading, art)
   11.2 Theory and research on linguistic factors of non-native speaking and dialect speaking groups on mastery of skills in specific subjects

Source: Smith, G.P. (1998). Adapted from *Common sense about uncommon knowledge: The knowledge bases for diversity.* Washington, DC: American Association of Colleges for Teacher Education.

- Field experiences that are continuous and discussed in seminars.
- Prospective teachers of color who have broad-based experiences in schools and communities different from their own background.
- Prospective teachers of color who have opportunities to conduct action research.

CULTURALLY RESPONSIBLE PEDAGOGY IN SPECIAL EDUCATION TEACHER PREPARATION PROGRAMS

The document titled, *Building Partnerships: Preparing Special Education Teachers for the 21st Century* (OSEP, 1997) recommended that general and special educators should be trained in a common core of knowledge and skills prior to their moving on to specialty areas in elementary, middle, secondary, and special education. The core domains consist of (a) foundations in education, (b) cultural and learning diversity, (c) home-school partnerships, (d) foundations for learning, (e) assessment, (f) curriculum and instruction, (g) collaboration and teaming, (h) student and classroom management, and (i) technology. Recently, CEC has outlined a Common Core of Knowledge and Skills needed by special educators in the area of cultural and linguistic competence supported by a validation process. As illustrated in Table 10.2 , eight broad categories were divided into knowledge and skill components: (a) philosophical, historical, and legal foundations of special education, (b) characteristics of learners, (c) assessment, diagnosis, and evaluation, (d) instructional content and practice, (e) planning and managing the teaching and learning environment, (f) managing student behavior and social interaction skills, (g) communication and collaborative partnerships, and (h) professionalism and ethical practices (see Table 10.2). While CEC has made progress in identifying standards and competencies for professional practice in cultural and linguistic diversity, conceptual and structural frameworks for preparing general and special educators to become culturally competent in teacher preparation programs has not been developed (Voltz, Dooley, & Jefferies, 1999). If a major priority of teacher preparation programs is to serve the student population in urban, poverty, and multicultural classrooms, then teacher preparation programs must provide a knowledge base in courses and develop skills in field experiences related to this population in a variety of ways including (a) graduate programs (e.g., bilingual and special education) and (b) the infusion of course content throughout a course of study. Both of these approaches have merit, however, current trends suggest that the infusion of course content is the most contemporary method in preparing prospective general and special educators.

Models of Infusion

In a review of literature, four different infusion paradigms have been implemented in teacher preparation programs. The first model by Rodriguez (1982) examined the degree of exposure to multicultural issues into one's teaching. He recommended that special educators examine levels of multicultural understanding through which teacher trainees must move to gain competence in the (a) awareness-consciousness level, (b) knowl-

Table 10.2

COUNCIL FOR EXCEPTIONAL CHILDREN (CEC) COMMON CORE OF KNOWLEDGE AND SKILLS IN MULTICULTURAL EDUCATION AND SPECIAL EDUCATION

CEC Common Core of Knowledge and Skills

I. Philosophical, Historical, and Legal Foundations of Special Education
Knowledge:

1. Knowledge of how diverse populations cope with the legacy of former and continuing racism in their lives.
2. Knowledge of accurate characteristics of one's own culture and specific ways one's culture is like and differs from other cultures.
3. Knowledge of ways specific cultures are negatively stereotyped.
4. Knowledge of the impact of the dominant culture on shaping schools and the individuals who study and work in them.
5. Knowledge of the dichotomy in values and customs that often exists between the home and the schools.
6. Knowledge of the dynamics that may exist between, or among, two or more different cultural groups.
7. Knowledge of the one's own identity and how that identity has developed.
8. Knowledge of literature concerning the history of America and the world which is inclusive of the point of view and reveals the contributions of culturally diverse groups to the government of science, mathematics, and government in the world.

II. Characteristics of Learners
Knowledge:

9. Accurate knowledge of characteristics of the cultures of the students in the school and in the neighborhood.
10. Knowledge of the effects of cultural differences on child growth and development.

III. Assessment, Diagnosis, and Evaluation
Skills:

11. Skill in the development and administration of nonbiased, informal assessment procedures.

IV. Instructional Content and Practice
Knowledge:

12. Knowledge of strategies for preparing students to live harmoniously and productively in a multiclass, multiethnic, multicultural, multinational world.
13. Knowledge of ways of helping students who live in monocultural areas understand and appreciate diversity.

Skills:

14. Skill in adapting teaching styles to the learning styles of students.
15. Skills in designing curriculum and making appropriate educational decisions for implementing a multicultural, intercultural educational program.

V. Planning and Managing the Teaching and Learning Environment
Knowledge:

16. Knowledge of differing learning styles of culturally diverse students and how to adapt teaching style to learning styles.
17. Knowledge of ways of creating learning environments that allow students to retain and be proud of their own cultural heritage.

Skills:

18. Skill in inspiring and stimulating dialogue regarding differences.
19. Skill in using group dynamics in the classroom that empowers students and provides opportunities for developing student leadership abilities.
20. Skill in establishing equitable learning environments for all students, regardless of the diversity of the student's background.

Table 10.2 (continued)

21. Skill in teaching students from diverse groups in ways that enhance their abilities.
22. Skill in the positive use of whatever abilities the child brings with him/her to the school.
23. Skill in allowing students to retain their cultural identity while reaching for high levels of academic and personal development.

VI. Managing Student Behaviors and Social Interaction Skills
Skills:
24. Skills in using group dynamics effectively when working toward inclusion of diverse groups into an effective, efficient working group.
25. Skills useful for eliminating racism in schools.
26. Skill in mediating controversial, intercultural issues among students in ways that enhance (or do not demean, even I inadvertently) any culture, group, or person.
27. Skill in organizing, developing, and sustaining learning environments that support positive interracial expression.

VII. Communication and Collaborative Partnership
Skills:
28. Skill in effective communication with families of students from diverse backgrounds.
29. Skill in utilizing knowledge of culturally diverse families in making authentic connections with family members.
30. Skill in translating knowledge of one's own identity into attitudes, skills, and abilities that enable one to relate positively to persons from other ethnic groups.
31. Skills which will enable one to develop constructive intercultural, interpersonal relationships with parents of student from diverse groups.
32. Skill in communicating with students whose primary language is not English to the extent that students can achieve the subject matter of the classroom.

VIII. Professional and Ethical Practices
Knowledge:
33. Knowledge of alternative and more appropriate ways of perceiving and evaluating people and events than those often used by the macroculture.
34. Knowledge of differences in ways of behaving and communicating among cultures that may lend themselves to misinterpretation and misunderstanding.
35. Knowledge of one's own ethnocentrism and the impact of that ethnocentrism on others, especially students and parents from diverse populations.

VIII. Professional and Ethical Practices
Knowledge:
36. Knowledge that "different" is not necessarily "deviant."
37. Knowledge of one's own cultural biases and differences that affect one's teaching to the detriment of the students.
38. Knowledge that the values of one's own cultural group may not be appropriate for a different cultural group.
39. Knowledge of the "blind spots" in one's own culture and how those blind spots impact upon relations with other cultural groups.
40. Knowledge of the goals of multicultural education and the validity of those goals.

Skills:
41. Skills in researching, comparing, contrasting, and positively evaluating cultures.
42. Skills in advocating for students from diverse backgrounds
43. Skill in demonstrating sensitivity to other cultures.
44. Skill in demonstrating non-judgmental attitudes toward others.
45. Skill in demonstrating for other cultures.
46. Skill in intercultural competence.
47. Skill in allowing students from other cultures to challenge assumptions about their cultures.

edge-content level, and (c) skill-implementation level. In the second infusion model developed by Burstein, Cabello, and Hamann (1993), components consisted of (a) program goals and competencies to serve multicultural students throughout the special education program; (b) faculty development; (c) curriculum development/implementation; and (d) program evaluation. Additional goals assist educators in examining their beliefs about the influence of culture on students' academic and social behaviors, develop teachers' knowledge about multicultural learners, and develop teachers' skills to adapt instruction to the needs of their students. The third infusion model is focused on multicultural change in postsecondary courses and is a framework applicable to single courses, the larger university curriculum, K-12 schools, higher education, and business (Kitano, 1997). As illustrated in Figure 10.1, the instructor's goals are based upon principles of learning and multicultural education and the nature of the course. Once the goals of the course are determined, levels of course change and elements will be modified in the syllabus. For example, at the exclusive level of course change, the instructor maintains traditional mainstream experiences and perspectives of the discipline. Course material is presented in a didactic manner and the acquisition of knowledge is through subjective or objective written examinations. Instructor-student interactions use a question and answer format (without discussion) with little participation by the students. In an inclusive level of change, both traditional and multiple perspectives that reflect the cultural characteristics and experiences of students are presented. Content integration ranges from the inclusion of new viewpoints to analyzing reasons for historical exclusion. The student engages in active learning by the instructor using a variety of learning activities and encouraging student participation when learning course content. A transformed course involves the reconceptualizing of knowledge and ways of thinking. The instructor and student have a shared responsibility in the learning process and student experiences are an integral part of the course. Non-traditional assessments and evaluation methods (e.g., projects and self-evaluation) are incorporated into the course.

The fourth infusion model, as proposed by Gay (1997), presents a structural outline of how to infuse the components of multicultural education into the curricula of teacher education. She advocates a dual approach for infusing multicultural education into curricula. The first approach has multicultural education principles and concepts woven throughout all of the core or foundation courses such as human development, and principles of curriculum development, and educational philosophy. The second approach is a specialized program of study that is subject-specific across the elementary, middle, and high school grade levels. For multicultural education to be effective, the structural framework of teacher education must incorporate both strategies of infusion. A dual-dimensional infusion strategy that identifies conventional program features, multicultural education as a specialization, and as embedded in all other aspects of teacher education is presented in Table 10.3 (see Table 10.3).

Under each program of study, admission requirements, foundational courses and experiences, and subject-specific methods and materials are clearly defined to reflect similarities and differences in approaches. For example, for students who specialize in multicultural education, the admission degree requirements would consist of an interdisciplinary social/sciences/humanities major or concentration in ethnic and cultural pluralism. The program of study would examine issues related to ethnic groups such as cultural characteristics, historical experiences, and contributions from multiple perspec-

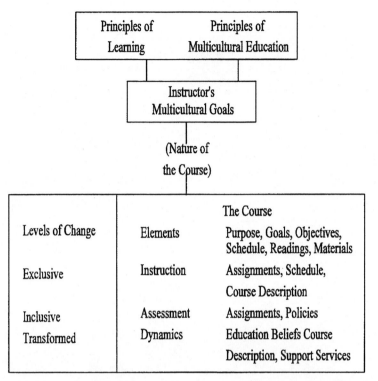

Figure 10.1. A model for multicultural course and syllabus change. Source: Kitano, M.K. (1997). A rationale and framework for course change. In A.I. Morey & M.K. Kitano (Eds.), *Multicultural course transformation in higher education: A broader truth.* Needham Heights, MA: Allyn & Bacon.

tives (i.e., foundational courses and experiences with content related to cultural characteristics that affect learning, philosophies of education, legal and policy regulations, and the multicultural curriculum). In teaching multicultural education, course work would be focused on instructional strategies, resources, materials, and the curriculum and student teaching would involve field-based experiences, practicum, and student teaching in multiethnic and multiracial schools and classrooms.

By contrast, in the embedded infusion approach, admission degree requirements would consist of some courses on ethnic and cultural diversity and experiences with multicultural learners in ethnic community set-tings. Foundational courses and experiences would incorporate culturally pluralistic perspectives, experiences, contexts, and examples to illustrate general education principles. With regard to field experiences, prospective teachers would be required to spend hours observing teachers and students in multiethnic and multiracial school settings. In teaching ethnic and cultural diversity in subject matter content, the program of study would consist of creating multicultural learning climates, addressing multicultural issues in the school, and student teaching in ethnically pluralistic schools and classrooms.

As a consequence, teacher educators, must be concerned about how future general and special educators will learn the knowledge

Table 10.3

A DUAL APPROACH TO MULTICULTURAL INFUSION IN TEACHER EDUCATION

Multicultural Specialization	Conventional Program Features	Embedded Multicultural Infusion
1. Admission Requirements • Interdisciplinary social science/humanities degree or major with emphasis in ethnic and cultural pluralism • Experience with children in ethnic communities	1. Admission Requirements • Degree or major in Introductory and Foundational Courses	1. Admissions Requirements • Some courses on ethnic and cultural diversity • Experience with culturally diverse children in ethnic community settings
2. Introduction to Multicultural Education • Scholarship, paradigms, historical perspectives • Cultural characteristics that affect learning opportunities, styles, outcomes for diverse ethnic groups • Culturally diverse philosophies of education • Culturally pluralistic characteristics of society and implications for education • Legal and policy regulations on equity and diversity Issues • Managing multicultural curriculum, instruction, and classroom	2. Introduction to teaching • Human growth, and development; learning theories; developmental paradigms; diagnosis and assessment • Philosophy of education • School and society • Teachers' legal rights subject content area • Experience with children and responsibilities • Classroom management and discipline • Conventional Program Features	2. Introduction to Teaching in Ethnically and Culturally Pluralistic Contexts • Culturally responsive teaching • Ethnic and cultural variations in developmental paradigms; sociocultural theories of development; ethnic learning styles; culturally appropriate diagnosis and assessment • Relationship between culture, ethnicity, and education • Cultural contextuality of education; pluralizing school culture • Law, policies, provisions that obstruct of facilitate multiculturalism • Culturally relevant discipline and management principles and techniques • Embedded multicultural infusio

Table 10.3 (continued)

Multicultural Specialization	Conventional Program Features	Embedded Multicultural Infusion
3. Teaching Multicultural Education Multicultural instructional strategies Selecting multicultural resources and materials • Designing multicultural curriculum • Multicultural climates for learning • Teaching multicultural education in the content areas	3. Subject-Specific Content, Methods, and Materials	3. Ethnic and Cultural Diversity in Subject Matter Content, Structure, and Process • Creating multicultural learning climates
4. Field-Based Observations, Experiences, Practicum, and Student Teaching in Multiethnic or Cross-Ethnic Schools and/or Classrooms	4. Field-Based Experiences • Observations • Practicum • Student Teaching	4. Observations and Practicum in Multiethnic Schools/Classrooms • Focus on multicultural issues in school culture and climate • Student teaching placements and task assignments in ethnically pluralistic schools and classrooms
5. Exit Criteria: Demonstrated Competency in Multiculturally Appropriate Teaching	5. Exit Competency According to Established Criteria and Supervisory Reviews	5. Successful Completion of Student Teaching Contingent upon Acceptable Performance on Multicultural Criteria Embedded in Regular Performance Appraisal Criteria and Procedures

Source: Gay G. (1997). Multicultural infusion in teacher education. In A.I. Morey & M.K. Kitano (Eds.), *Multicultural course transformation in higher education: A broader truth*. Needham Heights, MA. Allyn & Bacon.

and skills to teach multicultural learners with disabilities. Voltz and Dooley (1999) and Voltz, Dooley, and Jeffries (1999) posed some critical questions for teacher educators: How confident are special education teacher educators of their knowledge base in preparing teachers of diversity? What preparation to deliver culturally responsible instruction have they received? What gaps, if any, exist in their knowledge base and skills? What ways have been found most effective in retooling teacher educators in this area? Answers to these specific questions will enable teacher preparation programs in multicultural/bilingual and special education to map out a course of study that ensures that personnel are appropriately and adequately trained and retrained to meet professional standards of practice. Special education teacher educators must (a) bridge the gap between the knowledge base for a culturally responsible pedagogy and the standards knowledge and skills needed by special educators in the area of cultural and linguistic diversity, and (b) engage in a scholarly dialogue and discussion of how to address issues of diversity among departmental faculty members, students, curriculum, and instruction.

CONCLUSION

Given the nature of diversity and the dramatic demographic changes within America's classrooms, we are aware that general and special educators will be challenged to provide quality instruction to all children. However, we cannot accept a "deficit orientation" as a fundamental principle upon which we base the implementation of individualized, appropriate educational program for children with disabilities. We concur with Maheady (1997) that "individual differences in abilities, background experiences, and educational history, for example, interact in fairly complex ways (some predictable, others not so predictable) with specific facets of the learning environment (i.e., grouping arrangements, curricular content, instructional pacing, and specific pedagogical practices) to produce a wide array of educational outcomes" (p. 324). General and special educators must be trained to identify alterable factors (e.g., student engagement levels and use of teacher behaviors that decelerate student outcomes) that promote student learning and enhance responsiveness to instruction. Hence, general and special educators must learn through culturally responsive teacher preparation programs to apply pedagogical practices that accommodate students' needs and maximize the academic progress of all children, especially those who come from multicultural backgrounds. This has been the thrust of this chapter.

The "rat race" for educational reforms and initiatives is not the answer. The answer is within the realistic intent of teacher preparation programs to practice what they preach and attack inequities through practical implementation of change policies. Challenges that face the public schools today reflect challenges that face teacher preparation programs. These challenges will continue as long as these programs are not urged to respond to the needs of all members of society. In a majority of colleges of education, traditional strategies have failed to infuse cultural and linguistic principles of teaching into preservice and inservice training programs. Teacher education programs in special education have consistently prepared student teachers in terms of normative frames of reference based on Eurocentric values that minimize the success of persons from diverse cultural and linguistic backgrounds. This kind of archaic thinking has far-reaching implications for preparing undergraduate and graduate students in special education. It is a blatant deception to indicate that general and special educators are prepared for the "real world" when their programs of study fail to infuse multicultural principles and concepts as related to disability. We believe reforms must occur. For us to reap the rewards of reform programs, general and special educators, teacher educators, researchers, and practitioners must work collaboratively to translate research into practice. Our vision is that special education teacher preparation programs in this new millennium will reflect a change of attitudes, the modification of curricular content and instructional practices, and a transformation of concepts and principles that acknowledge the dynamic interaction of urban poverty conditions and cultural and linguistic diversity in the lives and communities of children with disabilities.

REFERENCES

Algozzine, B., & Obiakor, F.E. (1995). African American quandaries in school programs. *Scholar and Education, 17* (2), 75–87.

American Association of Colleges for Teacher Education (1994). *Teacher education pipeline III: Schools, colleges, and departments of education enrollments by race, ethnicity, and gender.* Washington, DC: Author.

Artiles, A.J., & Aguirre-Munoz, Z. (1995). Rethinking classroom management for students with emotional and behavior problems: The need for a contextualized research program for teaching. In F.E. Obiakor & B. Algozzine (Eds.), *Managing problem behaviors: Perspectives for general and special educators* (pp. 293–317). Dubuque, IA: Kendall/Hunt.

Bos, C., Roberts, R., Reith, H., & Derer, K. (1995). Doctoral preparation in special education: Current status and trends. *Teacher Education and Special Education, 18* (3), 147–155.

Burstein, N., Cabello, B., & Hamann, J. (1993). Teacher preparation for culturally and linguistically diverse urban students: Infusing competencies across the curriculum. *Teacher Education and Special Education, 16* (1), 1–13.

Burstein, N., & Sears, S. (1998). Preparing on-the-job teachers for urban schools. Implications for teacher training. *Teacher Education and Special Education, 21* (1), 47–62.

Bynoe, P.F. (1998). Rethinking and retooling teacher preparation to prevent perpetual failure by our children. *The Journal of Special Education, 32* (1), 37–40.

Cardinal, D.N., & Drew, D.E. (1993). Institutional and faculty influences on the reputation of doctorate-granting programs in special education. *The Journal of Special Education, 27* (1), 52–65.

Cartledge, G., Gardner, R., & Tillman, L. (1995). African Americans in higher education special education: Issues in recruitment and retention. *Teacher Education and Special Education, 18,* 166–178.

Cook, L.H., & Boe, E.E. (1995). Who is teaching students with disabilities? *Teaching Exceptional Children, 28* (1), 70–72.

Ewing, N.J. (1995). Restructured teacher education for inclusiveness: A dream deferred for African American children. In B.A. Ford, F.E. Obiakor, & J.M. Patton (Eds.), *Effective education of African American learners: New perspectives* (pp. 189–207). Austin, TX: Pro-Ed.

Ford, B.A., Obiakor, F.E., & Patton, J.M. (1995). *Effective education of African-American learners: New perspectives.* Austin, TX: Pro-Ed.

Futrell, M.H., & Witty, E.P. (1997). Preparation and professional development of teachers for culturally diverse schools: Perspectives from the standards movement. In J.J. Irvine (Ed.), *Critical knowledge for diverse teachers and learners* (pp. 189–216). Washington, DC: American Association of Colleges for Teacher Education.

Garcia, S., & Dominguez, L. (1997). Cultural contexts that influence learning and academic performance. *Child and Adolescent Psychiatric Clinics of North America, 6* (3), 621–655.

Gay, G. (1997). Multicultural infusion in teacher education: Foundations and applications. In A.I. Morey & M.K. Kitano (Eds.), *Multicultural course transformation in higher education: A broader truth* (pp. 192–210). Needham Heights, MA: Allyn & Bacon.

Gilmore, R.J., Marsh, S.M., & Garza, S. (1997). *Leadership grants funded from 1990–1999.* Washington, DC: U.S. Office of Special Education Programs, Division of Leadership to Practice, United States Department of Education.

Goodlad, J.J. (1984). *A place called school.* New York: McGraw-Hill.

Goodlad, J.J. (1991). Why we need a complete redesign of teacher education. *Educational Leadership, 49,* 4–6.

Grant, C.A. (1997). Critical knowledge, skills, and experiences for the instruction of culturally diverse students: A perspective for the preparation of preservice teachers. In J.J. Irvine (Ed.), *Critical knowledge for diverse teachers and learners* (pp. 1–26). Washington, DC: American Association of Colleges for Teacher Education.

Hilliard, A.G. (1995). Culture, assessment, and valid teaching for the African American student. In B.A. Ford, F.E. Obiakor, & J.M. Patton (Eds.), *Effective education of African American learners: New perspectives* (pp. ix–xvi). Austin, TX: Pro-Ed.

Kea, C., & Utley, C.A. (1998). To teach me is to know me. *The Journal of Special Education, 32* (1), 44-47.

Kitano, M.K. (1997). What a course will look like after multicultural change. In A.I. Morey & M.K. Kitano (Eds.), *Multicultural course transformation in higher education: A broader truth* (pp. 18–34). Needham Heights, MA: Allyn & Bacon.

Kozol, J. (1991). *Savage inequalities: Children in America's schools.* New York: Crown.

Ladson-Billings, G. (1990). Culturally relevant teaching. *College Board Review, 155,* 2025.

Lenz, B., & Deshler, D.D. (1990). Principles of strategies instruction as a basis of effective preservice teacher education. *Teacher Education and Special Education, 13* (2), 82–95.

Maheady, L. (1997). Preparing teachers for instructing multiple ability groups. *Teacher education and Special Education, 20* (4), 322–339.

National Center for Education Statistics (1995). *The condition of education.* Washington, DC: Author.

Obiakor, F.E. (1994). *The eight-step multicultural approach: Learning and teaching with a smile.* Dubuque, IA: Kendall/Hunt.

Obiakor, F.E. (1993). Multiculturalism: Critical issue facing teacher education programs. In *Bueno Center for Multicultural Education Monograph Series* (Vol. 9, No. 1) (pp. 1–16). Boulder, CO: University of Colorado.

Obiakor, F.E., Algozzine, B., & Ford, B.A. (1994). Education reform and service delivery to African-American students. In S.B. Garcia (Ed.), *Addressing cultural and linguistic diversity in special education: Issues and trends* (pp. 1–9). Reston, VA: Council for Exceptional Children.

Obiakor, F.E., & Utley, C.A. (1997). Rethinking preservice preparation for teachers in the learning disabilities field: Workable Multicultural Strategies. *Learning Disabilities Research & Practice, 12* (2), 92–106.

Office of Special Education Programs (1997). *Building partnerships: Preparing special education teachers for the 21st century.* Washington, DC: Office of Special Education Programs, U.S. Department of Education.

Reitz, A.L., & Kerr, M.M. (1991). Training effective teachers for tomorrow's students: Issues and recommendations. *Education and Treatment of Children, 14* (4), 361–370.

Reynolds, M.C. (1991). Educating teachers for special education. In W.R. Houston (Ed.), *Handbook of research on teacher education* (pp. 423–436). New York: Macmillan.

Rodriguez, F. (1982). Mainstreaming a multicultural concept into special education: Guidelines for teacher trainers. *Exceptional Children, 49* (3), 220–227.

Sindelar, P.T., & Schloss, P.J. (1987). A citation analysis of doctoral-granting programs in special education and relationships among measures of program quality. *Remedial and Special Education, 8* (5), 58–62.

Smith, D.D., & Salzberg, C. (1994). The shortage of special education faculty: Toward a better understanding. *Teacher Education and Special Education, 17* (1), 52–61.

Smith, D.D., & Tyler, N.C. (1994). Pipeline data for doctoral students from historically underrepresented groups attending HECSE colleges and universities. *HECSE Report, 1,* 1-15.

Smith, G.P. (1998). *Common sense about uncommon knowledge: The knowledge bases for diversity.* Washington, DC: American Association of Colleges for Teacher Education.

Trent, S. (1995). Teacher preparation: The missing link in behavior management. In F.E. Obiakor & B. Algozzine (Eds.), *Managing problem behaviors: Perspectives for general and special education* (pp. 207-239). Dubuque, IA: Kendall/Hunt.

Tyler, N.C., & Smith, D.D. (1999). Career decisions of doctoral graduates in special education. *Teacher Education and Special Education, 22*(1), 1-13.

Utley, C.A. (1995). Culturally and linguistically diverse students with mild disabilities. In C.A. Grant (Ed.), *Educating for diversity: An anthology of multicultural voices* (pp. 301-326). Needham Heights, MA: Allyn & Bacon.

Utley, C.A., & Mortweet, S.L. (1999). The challenge of diversity. In M.J. Coutinho & A.C. Repp (Eds.), *Inclusion: The integration of students with disabilities* (pp. 59-90). Belmont, CA: Wadsworth.

Voltz, D.L., & Dooley, E.A. (1999). Culturally responsive curricula for learners in a diverse society. In F.E. Obiakor, J.O. Schwenn, & A.F. Rotatori (Eds.), *Advances in Special Educators: Multicultural education for learners with exceptionalities* (Vol. 12, pp. 133-148). Stamford, CT: JAI Press.

Voltz, D.L., Dooley, E.A., & Jefferies, P. (1999). Preparing special educators for cultural diversity: How far have we come? *Teacher Education and Special Education, 22* (1), 66-77.

Wald, J.L. (1996). *Culturally and linguistically diverse professionals in special education: A demographic analysis.* Reston, VA: National Clearinghouse for Professions in Special Education, The Council for Exceptional Children.

Welch, M., & Sheridan, S.M. (1993). Educational partnerships in teacher education: Reconceptualizing how teacher candidates are prepared for teaching students with disabilities. *Action in Teacher Education, 15* (3), 35-46.

Wisnieski, R. (1995, November). Three futures of colleges of education. *Education Week,* pp. 41 & 52.

Chapter 11

CONNECTING WITH COMMUNITY RESOURCES: OPTIMIZING THE POTENTIAL OF MULTICULTURAL LEARNERS WITH MILD DISABILITIES

BRIDGIE ALEXIS FORD AND CYNTHIA REYNOLDS

Higher standards, quality, accountability, equity, and inclusiveness are terms used by general and special education reformists and the public at-large to chart the restructuring of public schooling in this new millennium. These concepts focus attention on both the nature of services afforded within the nation's public school system and the quality of teacher preparation programs. Undergirding these concepts is the identification of programmatic strategies that enhance the provision of quality services to all America's youth, including the growing population of youth from multicultural backgrounds (e.g., African American, Hispanic, Asian/Pacific Islander, and American Indian). The establishment of productive school and community partnerships has been strongly recommended by general and special educators at all levels as an essential element in any strategic model or framework designed to promote equitable,

quality educational opportunities (Banks, 1997; Comer, 1989; Deslandes, Royer, Potvin, & Leclerc, 1999; Educational Research Services, 1997; Ford, 1998; Giles, 1998; Hatch, 1998; Telesford, 1994). Research has documented that collaborative school and community initiatives are important components of schools that make a difference; and those that optimize the educational service delivery for youth and their families (Comer, 1989; Cummins, 1986; Ford Foundation and John D. & C.T. MacArthur Foundation, 1989; Hatch, 1998).

Collaborative initiatives between schools and *significant resources* from local communities (e.g., organizations, agencies, and individuals) are beneficial to all students, especially when the relationship may be advantageous in enhancing the schooling process for multicultural youth. *"Significant Community Resources" (SCRs)* often operate as friendly domains for multicultural families to acquire vital information, develop and practice empowering skills, and to express opinions (Banks, 1997; Ford, 1995, 1998; Rueda, 1997; Telesford, 1994). In spite of this evidence, the public school system has failed to systematically acknowledge and therefore capitalize on the reservoir of resources operating within many multicultural communities, especially urban, lower socioeconomic class communities. One reason for this exclusion has been the negative framework in which schools typically operate when it comes to empowering poor multicultural communities.

NATIONAL POLICIES AND REFORM AGENDAS FOR EQUITABLE OPPORTUNITIES

Several legislative mandates to reform and restructure educational policies and practices have been promulgated for all students' benefits, in particular those who historically were rendered inequitable opportunities. The 1964 Office of Civil Rights Act, the Indian Education Act of 1972, the 1973 Section 504 of the Vocational Rehabilitation Act, the 1975 Education of All Handicapped Children Act, the 1990 Americans with Disabilities Act, the 1990 Individuals with Disabilities Education Act, the 1994 Goals 2000 Educate America Act, and the recent 1997 amendment to the Individuals with Disabilities Education Act were enacted to help optimize equitable learning opportunities. Spearheaded by the publication of *A Nation at Risk* by the National Commission on Excellence in Education in 1983, varied reform groups put forth literature during the mid-1980s on school reform to improve teacher preparation programs. Two of the more widely-known educational reform groups are (a) The Carnegie Forum on Education and the Economy's, *A Nation Prepared: Teachers for the 21 Century* (1986), and (b) The Holmes Group, that published *Tomorrow's Teachers* (1986).

In spite of the recommendations advocated within school reform documents and gains made from legislative mandates, the educational state of affairs for many multicultural learners (with and without disabilities) remains dismal. Nationwide, parents of multicultural learners witness the low performance reported by the local school districts. This alarming, persistent failure is most evident in poor urban areas. Multicultural youth remain disproportionately represented in special education programs for students with cognitive and/or behavioral difficulties while having limited access to services for learners with gifts and talents (Artiles & Trent, 1994, Artiles & Zamora-Duran, 1997; Chinn & Hughes, 1987; Ford, Obiakor, & Patton,1995; Harry, 1994; Obiakor, 1999). For instance, Obiakor noted that low and inappropriate teacher expectations toward multicultural learners remain problematic. Clearly, a reframing and restructuring of the school's traditional organizational structure, paradigms, and policies have become imperative for school districts where multicultural learners with disabilities and their families continue to be subjected to ineffective educational services.

The 1997 amendment to the Individuals with Disabilities Education Act (IDEA) mandates an increase in parental involvement. While this requirement is to be applauded, unfortunately, mandates do not automatically insure or guarantee that all parents are accorded equal opportunities to become involved. Many multicultural parents have a history of negative experiences with the school and consequentially are reluctant and/or intimidated to take advantage of their legal rights. For those multicultural parents, a "neutral" mechanism is needed to help them become knowledgeable about their rights and then exercise them. As discussed by Ford (1995, 1998), a defining attribute of many *SCRs* is participation by local residents (i.e., parents). These familiar resources have established mutually trusting relationships with residents and parents. To this end, *SCRs* possess the potential to help encourage and train parents to become empowered and more involved in the schooling process (Banks, 1997; Brant,1989, 1998; Deslandes et al., 1999; Educational Research Services,1997; Epperson, 1991; Rueda, 1997).

The importance of the school and community relationship on educational outcome for multicultural learners with (and without) disabilities demands that general and special educators respond to a pivotal question: How do we systemically refocus educational paradigms, policies, and practices to impact the professional development of preservice level trainees and practicing educators such that they are equipped with the necessary professional tools to *connect with and utilize* the strengths of the *significant* resources within multicultural communities' Most youth manifesting mild disabilities, with appropriate educational services, are able to become productive, contributing members of society. Therefore, it is vital that educators working with multicultural learners exhibiting mild disabilities possess a comprehensive repository of educational strategies and resources to optimize learning. *Significant resources* from these students communities should be included in the educator's storehouse of strategies. As Garcia (1991) pointed out, public schools are a community affair. They are made up of children from the community surrounding the school and, with minor exceptions reflect their human communities. He further elaborated that a school's community consists of varied social groups who interact with each other, developing cooperative (working together) and interdependent (using each other's strengths) networks of relationships. Regrettably, schools are more likely to extend and participate in the critical cooperative and interdependent networks with social groups who are not poor and/or from multicultural cultural backgrounds.

The 1996 Education Commission of the States third recommendation "make involving parents and the community a top priority" accentuates the importance of schools connecting with *SCRs* (Brant, 1998). Several questions and concerns surface pertaining to the formation of effective school and community relationships: (1) Who are the school personnel that must act in leadership roles? (2) What leadership roles should or must key school personnel undertake? (3) What school initiatives should be used to prepare school personnel and community constituencies for authentic relationships with multicultural community resources? (4) What does school and community collaboration mean in terms of the balance of power and decision-making processes? (5) Which multicultural community resources should be considered *significant* enough for inclusion in the school and community partnership? (6) Who makes this decision?

Special educators and school counselors are two key personnel who *must* take an active, ongoing role in helping schools to establish and maintain connections with *significant* local community resources. Three major reasons support this assertion. First, these two groups of professionals provide direct and indirect services to children and youth with disabilities and their families on a daily basis. Teachers are viewed as the most important link in home-school collaboration (Brand, 1996). Therefore, special educators and other certified and licensed school personnel (e.g., school counselor) who work directly and intensely with multicultural learners with disabilities can be considered invaluable professionals in extending the school linkage of home-school to community-school. Second, because of the complex problems confronted by youth with mild disabilities, the special educator and school counselor usually collaborate with each other, and with other professionals and agencies (e.g., social agencies, legal services, and mental health agencies). Also, with the present movement toward inclusion in the general classroom and access to the general education curriculum special educators are increasingly involved in co-teaching and in collaborative team arrangements with general educators (Cook & Friend, 1998; McLaughlin, 1999). In this capacity, special educators are required to provide more recommendations about intervention strategies for students with disabilities (and those not labeled, but manifesting academic and/or behavior difficulties). Hence, special educators must be knowledgeable about out-of-school resources that may be beneficial to students. And third, the special educator and school counselor team often serves on (or leads) the teacher intervention and assistance team within the school building. The team serves in the capacity of a problem-solving unit by providing support (e.g., prevention and intervention strategies) for classroom teachers. Consequently, the active participation of the special educator and school counselor in school and community initiatives is essential (Hobbs & Collison, 1995).

Atkinson and Juntenen (1994) used the term *school-home-community liaison* to describe school personnel role in school and community initiatives. Some school districts, particularly those in large urban areas, may have a designated individual who helps to connect the school with the community (e.g., *significant* member of the local community). Obviously, this is a move in a positive direction. However, in order to fully maximize the benefits of school and community linkages for youth with disabilities, it is important that key school personnel (e.g., special educators and school counselors) who make authoritative, daily decisions regarding educational services for these youth, assume leadership roles in connecting with *SCRs*. This, of course, is a purpose of this chapter.

SIGNIFICANT COMMUNITY RESOURCES: OPERATIONAL FRAMEWORKS

The term community is a multifaceted concept that includes all groups, individuals, and institutions that are touched by the school. It refers to groups, individuals, and institutions within communities of local schools (Mahan, Fortney, & Garcia, 1983). Garcia (1991) added that the school's community in a small, rural school district is easy to define but in some large cities, the school's community is not so easily defined. Due to reasons such as desegregation and busing, traditional changes and shifts in population, urban communities tend to change continuously. Presently, the population statistics for ethnic groups (multicultural groups) in America are changing rapidly. A condition that has been called the "browning of America" is occurring. The number of Americans commonly referred to as ethnic minority is rising in proportion to the number of White Americans. As the year 2000 begins, over one third of the students in the nation's schools are likely to be from multicultural backgrounds. The three fastest growing groups are Hispanic Americans, African Americans, and Southeast Asian Americans (Grossman, 1995). Presently, 23 of the 25 largest school systems in the United States are heavily composed of multicultural learners.

The professional literature (Obiakor, Mehring, & Schwenn, 1997) and the popular media highlight the daily and episodic crises plaguing the nation's public school systems and the detrimental impact on education in public schools. These crises include (a) increased identification of youth with severe social and emotional problems; (b) increased school violence; (c) persistent distrust between many parents and communities with local schools; (d) continued low school performances by certain populations of multicultural learners; and (e) widespread poverty and inadequate health care. Furthermore, despite recent changes in many teacher education programs to include issues of diversity and multicultural education, teacher candidates are still inadequately prepared and seldom choose to teach in multicultural schools, especially those with high rates of poverty (Ford & Bessent-Byrd, in press; Valli & Rennert-Ariev, 2000; Voltz, 1995). Another phenomenon is the significant decline in the number of teachers and administrators from multicultural backgrounds. The above issues impact school districts nationwide, but are more pronounced in large urban areas. The vastness and complexity of these crises vividly illustrate that schools alone *cannot* adequately address these multidimensional problems. There is a need for the involvement of others (outside of the school) who have a direct stake in what happens to these youth (i.e., parents and community). To this end, educational delivery models that include mechanisms to assist school personnel to reach out and collaboratively connect with primary stake holders (e.g., family members, guardians, and community resources) must be used. In other words, the institution of cooperative and interdependent networks between the school and multicultural communities must become actualized.

Although community-school involvement is presently being advocated as a priority factor in addressing the multidimensional problems faced by both general and special education, it is not a new remedy. The ideals and programmatic components embedded in the 1960s alternative social programs and community empowerment education approaches underscored the centrality of community involvement. The importance of school and community collaboration is explicitly described in Lewis and Morris's (1998) discussion of the *Communities in Schools* project (formerly known as Cities in Schools) founded in 1977. Given the current escalation of academic and social crises within schools, the mission of *Communities in Schools* "to champion the connection of needed community resources with schools to help young people successfully learn, stay in school, and prepare for life" (p. 34) is equally crucial today and for the near future.

As stated previously, a community can be defined as a group of people living under the same government in the same locale (Garcia, 1991). What determines community organizations or individuals as being *"significant resources"* varies and is dependent on several factors including economics, ethnic group, and geographic location (e.g., urban, rural, and suburban). For example, within many segments of the African American community, the African American church remains an important leadership institution (Billinsley & Caldwell, 1991). It extends a host of outreach programs to support educational levels ranging from early childhood to adulthood. Also, African American fraternities and sororities, professional organizations, civic and service organizations (e.g., National Association for the Advancement of Colored People, National Council of Negro Women, and 100 Black Men Club), numerous local social clubs, and grassroots organizations offer a multitude of community-based programs to foster the healthy development of African American youth, including those deemed as "at-risk" and those with mild disabilities. Community resources for certain ethnic/cultural groups may be limited. For instance, in many cities, community resources that target the needs of American Indians may be limited to a local or regional "Indian Center." Additionally, in certain geographic locations, for multicultural populations who are linguistically diverse and/or recent to the United States, a local or regional International Center or "sponsor organization" (i.e., churches) may be the *initial* community resource with whom school personnel should connect. These centers or "sponsor" organizations may in turn identify *significant* individuals or informal structures that are able to assist select populations of multicultural youth and their programs that have made efforts to enhance the quality of Latino parent participation includes (a) "Fiesta Educativa," (b) the Say "Yes" to a Youngster's Future, and (c) the Parent Empowerment Program-Students Included/ "Padres en Poder-Si" (Casas & Furlong, 1994; Rueda, 1997).

Involvement processes are cited as a main measurable feature of a community (Nettles 1991). Pertaining to schooling, community involvement is described as consisting of "the actions that organizations and individuals take to promote student development" (Nettles, p. 133). Involvement may center around four basic processes:

1. Conversion-Turning the [misguided] student around via powerful messages.

2. Mobilization-Complex activities, such as legal action, citizen participation, and neighborhood organizing that target change in institutions.

3. Allocation-Actions to increase students' access to resources, alter the incentive structure, and provide social support for students' efforts.

4. Instruction-Actions that support social learning and intellectual development.

Collectively, community involvement with the school can be viewed as an effective catalyst for improving the physical conditions and resources available, the attitudes and expectations within the school and the community, and the formal and informal learning opportunities for both children and adults (Hatch, 1998). Community leaders are viewed as valuable assets in helping to extend discussion about important educational issues and needed reforms into the community-at-large and generating support for the social action to effect needed educational reform (Banks 1997). With the need to educate the public about the status of multicultural learners with disabilities and other issues (i.e., inclusion), this becomes an important network. The growing population of multicultural learners in public schools and the continued failure of too many of these youth requires a restructuring of the educational system such that positive connections with *SCRs* from multicultural communities *become the rule* rather than the exception.

COMMUNITY NETWORKING AND LEADERSHIP:
NEW ROLES FOR SPECIAL EDUCATORS
AND COUNSELORS

A goal for both the special educator and school counselor is the overall well-being of students with disabilities. Specifically, the special educator is concerned with maximizing the learning experiences that address the individual needs of youth with disabilities (e.g., cognitive, academics, affective, social-emotional, verbal and nonverbal communication, daily living skills, motor skills, and vocational and career skills). Similarly, school counselors are committed to assisting all students to realize their full potential despite their disabilities (American School Counselor Association, 1998, 1999). In order to accomplish this, the roles of both the special educator and school counselor must undergo significant changes in this new millennium. Traditionally, both professionals have been responsible for providing direct services as a classroom teacher and/or counselor respectively. In the 1990s, the shift to more inclusive placement models in response to special education federal mandates and societal changing attitudes, requires special educators and school counselors to assume more collaborative roles with general educators and other school personnel (Cook & Friend, 1998; McLaughlin, 1999; Schmidt, 1999). To date, this collaboration has taken two primary forms:

1. Providing indirect services for youth with disabilities by providing the general teacher with strategies to optimize educational service to youth with disabilities who are included in the regular classroom.
2. Co-teaching and team teaching with the general educator in the regular classroom to deliver educational services to youth with disabilities.

While the move from the solely traditional (direct) service roles to more recent collaborative roles is helping to better address the needs of special needs youth and their families in general, this century requires the special educator and school counselor to place more overt attention on (a) their roles as an *advocate* for youth with disabilities, especially multicultural youth; and (b) their role in assuming *equal responsibility* (as other certified/licensed school personnel) in school and community initiatives that positively influence student outcomes (Downing, Pierce,

& Woodruff, 1993). Current and future school restructuring that supports more involvement from the community will result in special educators and school counselors working in more "site-based" managed schools whereby the locus of decision-making will shift from centralized bureaucracies to more local district and school levels. Consequently, under this organizational arrangement special educators and school counselors will be required to take on new leadership roles and make decisions that impact the entire school. Given the current priority of improving school/community relationships, this will be a major decision-making issue. No doubt the future roles of special educators and school counselors are mutually congruent with them assuming new leadership roles as schools attempt to productively connect with *SCRs*.

Special educators and school counselors in their new role must see themselves as advocates and community members in need. According to Compton and Galloway (1984), an advocate is a person who supports the rights of vulnerable populations to obtain benefits/services to which they are entitled. In their role as advocates, they must *rethink and respond* to the ways in which they can further enhance service delivery to multicultural children and youth with disabilities. *Six ways* that connecting with *significant resources* in multicultural communities can assist special educators and school counselors in their role as advocate are (a) the reinforcement of school-related skills, (b) improved sensitivity to culturally responsive programming and information needed by parents, (c) accessible adult role models and mentors and advocates, (d) increased parental involvement, (e) community and family-friendly school environments, and (f) dissemination and collection of information. In the next subheadings, each of the roles is meaningfully discussed.

The Reinforcement of School-Related Skills

At times, students with disabilities become unmotivated to complete school tasks that seem unrelated to the real world. They can be influenced by *significant* members of the community (e.g., accessible mentors from the youth's own multicultural group) who can demonstrate how a particular school skill can help a student achieve success outside the school setting. Community (and family) reinforcement of the school's mission helps to motivate reluctant learners. In order to connect multicultural youth with these accessible mentors, special educators and school counselors must be aware of their existence and how to connect with them. Thus, learning how to establish connections with *SCRs* will aid these professionals in their role as advocates for multicultural learners with mild disabilities. Furthermore, as discussed in a section below (i.e., accessible adult role models, mentors, and advocates), the serious decline in the number of teachers from multicultural populations means that many multicultural learners will experience a loss of role models, mediators,

and mentors from their own cultural/ethnic group. In addition, many *significant* community organizations sponsor youth programs to address various developmental needs of youth. Ford (1995, 1998) detailed examples of the programmatic topics and areas commonly addressed in youth programs sponsored by *SCRs* in many African American communities. Topics include, but are not limited to the following:

- Academic motivation, tutoring, and test-taking skills.
- Self-development/values/self-esteem and cultural group identity.
- Decision-making skills (e.g., school survival skills, drugs, alcohol teen pregnancy, and future planning).
- Goal setting.
- Information networks for parents regarding educational issues.

SCRs in other multicultural communities offer similar and/or other types of programming including topics about linguistic diversity.

Improved Sensitivity to Culturally Responsive Programming

As stated previously, some schools employ an individual in the role as the *home-school-community liaison.* One of the functions of the *home-school-community liaison* is to interpret the culture of the family to the school and the larger community, as well as interpreting the culture of the school and the larger community to the multicultural student, his or her family, and the multicultural community. Gentemann and Whitehead (1983) referred to this person as a cultural broker. While this individual is an integral part of the school and a paid employee, typically this paid position does not exist. For example, where there is no one in this position/function, the school coun-

selor and special educator may *with training* assume this role. Although this function can best be performed by a counselor or special education teacher who is a member of the multicultural/ethnic community, the preponderance of European-American counselors and teachers makes this unlikely. Therefore, it is essential that the special educator and school counselor become familiar with different cultures represented in their school, as well as the policies and legal standards of the larger community. The training would consist of the phases contained in the "multicultural-based training model" described in the implications section of this chapter. As certified and licensed school professionals who are most knowledgeable about student needs and existing community resources, the school counselor and special educator are the ideal people to push for the development of new programs to meet the needs of multicultural learners with disabilities and their families. By providing social networks both within the school and community that are supportive, the special educator and school counselor will automatically model respect for cultural, ethnic, and ability differences.

General and special educators continue to lack a comprehensive and ecological understanding of cultural nuances that affect multicultural children's ability to be successful. As aforementioned, despite the call for reform in teacher preparation programs, preservice level trainees continue to exit inadequately prepared to provide services for multicultural youth. For example, even when preservice trainees are exposed to multicultural education courses, direct instruction and experiences in the acquisition of English as a Second Language (ESL) is typically not a component. Also not available is the in-depth study of the influence of interpersonal communication patterns of multicultural populations on learning in the classroom. Apparently, concrete understanding of the

values and attitudes held by some multicultural parents and their impact on parental involvement in the school and learning is often restricted to "textbook" rather than actual face-to-face encounters or direct observation of multicultural families (Brand, 1996; Harry, Torguson, Katkavich, & Guerrero, 1993). *SCRs* may provide helpful feedback to aid in a more culturally responsive approach by the school to reach out to multicultural children and their families. School personnel who collaborate with *SCRs* could be permitted to directly observe multicultural parents in the role of "teacher" and/or other empowering role. This will help the school personnel to acknowledge the expertise of parents and to promote better collaboration. As discussed below, parental participation is an important feature of some community sponsored programming. The need for information is usually cited as a primary concern of many multicultural parents of youth with mild disabilities (Marion, 1980). Some *SCRs* are capable of either providing needed information or are able to connect families with appropriate individuals or organizations that can. Strategically, through school and community partnerships, schools are better able to link families with alternative, yet familiar sources of information or services.

Accessible Adult Role Models, Mentors, and Advocates

Varying degrees and systems of mentoring by adults (short- and/or long-term) are often offered by *SCRs*. Access to appropriate adult male and female role models may be built into programs sponsored by *SCRs* or extended to youth on an "as-need and/requested" basis by a caring adult. An unfortunate realism faced by many multicultural learners in urban areas is the recognition that the majority of teachers and administrators will not reside in the community of the multicultural learners they serve. Demographic school data

indicate a dramatic shift in the teaching force to White and female (Cook & Boe, 1995). Approximately 86% of the teaching force is White, with 68% female. It is predicated that the number of educators from multicultural backgrounds will drop to approximately 5% (National Clearing House for Professions in Special Education, 1998). This serious decline will occur at a time when projected data indicate over one third of the students in the public schools are likely to be from multicultural populations. Although, the projected shortage of multicultural teachers will be a tremendous loss to *all* students, the loss will be particularly detrimental for multicultural youth.

Historically, multicultural school personnel have served in important capacities (i.e., as leaders, role models, mediators, and mentors) for students. With the increase in the crises in the public schools, this loss becomes daily pronounced. Due to many political, economic, and social reasons, too many multicultural learners residing in poor urban areas find themselves at-risk for school failure. It is these youth who too often lack direct access to appropriate adult role models or mentors. Resilient survivors often sustain themselves by consciously enlisting support from accessible adults (Higgins, 1985). Researchers have noted that children's resistance to hardship or resilience is greater when they have access to one healthy caring parent or supportive adult outside the family (Karen, 1990; Kauffman, Grunebaum, Cohler, & Gamer, 1979; Rutter, 1983; Werner & Smith, 1983). Using their knowledge of contacts with *SCRs*, school counselors and special education teachers can facilitate students' opportunities to connect with appropriate adult role models, mentors, and advocates from the community.

Increased Parental Involvement

The school counselor and special education teacher have a responsibility to establish working relationships with parents and guardians of students in their school system. Both must cooperate with parents and guardians in designing educational programming for students, selecting helping processes and strategies, and making plans for future educational and career directions. In more ways than one, IDEA '97 emphasizes this role! It therefore becomes imperative that educators and counselors learn about families served by schools. In doing so, they must also determine the needs of the parents by assessing the role(s) that they (family) want to participate in (and/or can be encouraged or trained to undertake) in the schooling of their children. Parental involvement is typically a key element in the kinds of community sponsored programming described under the "Reinforcement of School-Related Skills" section above. The positive effects of parental involvement and academic outcomes for multicultural learners with and without disabilities has been documented (Banks, 1997; Brant, 1989; Croninger, 1990; Cummins, 1986; Epperson, 1991; Giles, 1998; Harry et al., 1993; Mannan & Blackwell, 1992). As stated previously, training parents to know how to enhance learning in the home may be an example of the kind of programs/services extended by *significant community organizations*. With the increased emphasis on parental involvement under IDEA '97, familiar and "neutral" structures that promote the involvement of multicultural families is needed. *SCRs* often are able to serve as (a) the neutral geographic location for a meeting between parents and the school, (b) the neutral location where empowered parents can pass on information and skills to less empowered parents, and (c) the neutral *significant* individual who helps parents feel more comfortable when communicating and conferencing with school personnel.

Community and Family-Friendly School Environments

Special educators and counselors can be instrumental in creating a school environment that is family-friendly. For example, one of the authors of this chapter collaborates with a local school district where an unused classroom was turned into a "Parent Room" that included comfortable furniture, a box full of toys, reading materials, refreshments, a TV/monitor/VCR. (Note: These were obtained from community donations and the local parent/teacher organization.) The school counselor was able to use the room for parent educational seminars, small support groups for parents, intervention assistance team (IAT) or individual education-al planning (IEP) meetings. In addition, parents with smaller children were able to bring them to meetings knowing the child could stay in the room playing with toys while the parents met with school personnel. Parents could also come and watch relevant videos from the video library. Professional organizations such as Educational Research Service (1997) offer similar activities that schools can do to create a family-friendly atmosphere.

Collection and Dissemination of Information

The American School Counselor Association (1989) in its position statement on cross-cultural and multicultural counseling recommended that school counselors "develop a resource list of educational and community support services to meet the needs of culturally diverse students and their families" (p. 322). A referral can be made to either enhance a student's development or to remediate a problem. Operating from a liaison role, the school counselor and special educator view community agencies and volunteer organizations as extensions of the school, as institutions sharing the common concern for the productive development of children (Heath & McLaughlin, 1987).

Referral in the school-home-community liaison role does not mean simply giving the student or parent a name and telephone number to call. Because multicultural learners and their families may feel disenfran-chised from community at-large support and lack the English-speaking or social skills needed to assert themselves, the school counselor and special educator must be prepared to assist with each stage of the referral. This may include (a) contacting the agency or organization, (b) arranging for a meeting with them, and (c) arranging for transportation to the agency on behalf of the multicultural learner and his/her family. A primary need often reported by multicultural parents and families of learners with disabilities is the need for information. When school personnel (e.g., special educators and school counselors) are able to provide parents with needed information, it may be a fundamental step in achieving more parental participation in the school and/or assisting a child at home. Communicating and sharing information with *SCRs* may be an initial method of getting families the information desired.

CAVEATS AND PROSPECTS IN COMMUNITY CONNECTIONS

Negative Attitudes

Collaboration between individuals can be a complex process, especially when the individuals are from different backgrounds (e.g., ethnic/cultural groups, linguistic diversity, socioeconomic status, and occupations). Characteristics of successful collaborative processes include caring among participants, joint-effort among participants, respect for each other, sharing of information and ideas, personal support, openmindedness, and reflectiveness (Goor, 1995). The process of collaboration between schools and *SCRs* in multicultural communities demands conscientious work. A conceptual framework that values inclusiveness of all stakeholders *and* school personnel who positively perceive the resources within local multicultural community as worthy partners is fundamental.

Genuine school and community partnerships require that each entity, the school and the (local) multicultural community is a willing participant. Each entity must (a) understand the need for the partnership; (b) be aware of the other's primary roles and responsibilities; (c) acknowledge what the other is capable of doing and is willing to do; and (d) be resolved to work together to achieve mutually established goals. One desired outcome of the partnership is quality educational services for multicultural youth with mild disabilities. Norris (1995) defined inclusiveness as "the act of encouraging belonging" (p. 5). He also added that "leaders of an inclusive organization do more than value diversity—they understand and aggressively eliminate barriers to performance that fall unevenly on different groups . . . they establish standards of behavior that affirm inclusiveness" (p. 5).

An examination of the historic relationship between public schools and multicultural communities reveals an *exclusionary* rather than inclusive one. The United States public school system operates from a distinct organizational culture. Organizational culture may be defined as "the particular set of policies, practices, values, and expectations that define [an organization] a workplace and guide the treatment of members or customers" (Norris, 1995, p.5). Traditionally, the organizational culture within the nation's educational institution has projected a "deficit and dysfunctional" mindset about multicultural communities. Most schools operate from the premise that multicultural communities (and families) have little or nothing constructive to offer to influence positive educational outcomes of their young (Barnes, 1991; Comer, 1985; Cummins, 1986; Jenkins, 1989; Ogbu, 1978; Slaughter & Epps, 1987). In spite of the progress made to eliminate this traditional dysfunctional frame-of-reference, too many school districts continue to deliver questionable educational services consistent with this negative perspective. Interestingly, these practices are more evident in economically depressed inner-city communities. The school's deficit mindset and paradigm about multicultural communities and families set the stage for the perpetuation of negative teacher attitudes and low expectations toward multicultural students with and without disabilities (Obiakor, 1999). By ascribing the principle cause of school difficulties of multicultural learners to external, out-of-school factors (e.g., family and community), school professionals are justifiably relieved of accountability and responsibility for equitable, quality educational services.

Lack of Training in "How To" Connect

In Cummins's (1986) examination of the variables associated with the empowerment of multicultural students, he concluded that "a major reason previous attempts at educational reform have been unsuccessful is that the relationships between teachers and students and between schools and communities have remained essentially unchanged" (p. 18). He emphasized that the required changes involve *personal redefinition* of the way classroom teachers interact with the children and the communities they serve. Outreach to and direct involvement of the community are deemed vital structural elements in the school's quest to empower multicultural learners (Comer, 1985; Hatch, 1998).

Teacher preparation programs and in-service training programs must provide educators with structured activities that help them examine and reshape negative attitudes about multicultural communities and children they serve. According to Valli and Rennert-Ariev (2000), multicultural competence (i.e., the ability to interact effectively with people of diverse cultural backgrounds) is perceived as an essential factor in the reforming and restructuring of teacher education programs. Their analysis of the components most agreed upon by the leading teacher education reform documents cited "multicultur-

al competence" as one of only two items that yielded the strongest level of agreement. Positive teacher attitudes and expectations reinforce students' motivation, persistence and beliefs in self. As indicated earlier, changing student and teacher demographics are influencing the resurgence of school and community partnerships. The student population is shifting to a significant rise in multicultural youth while the teaching population is becoming increasingly White and female. This White female teaching force may not possess knowledge about and access to *SCRs*. To prevent the existing *lack of connectedness between the school and the multicultural community of the children,* meaningful empowerment of the community in which multicultural learners reside is imperative.

A MULTICULTURAL-BASED TRAINING MODEL FOR SCHOOL COMMUNITY PARTNERSHIPS

The type of school and community partnership described throughout this chapter requires the support and commitment of all major stakeholders (e.g., school administrators, certified and licensed school personnel, and the targeted *SCRs*) and the adequate preparation of school personnel. Ford (1995, 1998) outlined a three-phase training model

designed to prepare preservice level trainees and/or practicing school personnel to productively connect and collaborate with *SCRs*. The three phases of the multicultural-based training model relative to the preparation of special educators and school counselors are discussed below (see Table 11.1).

Phase One

Phase One activities reshape and redefine personal attitudes and definitions of preservice trainees and practicing teachers (e.g., special educators and school counselors) about multicultural families and communities. This *core phase* is a prerequisite that conditions the mindset. Preservice level trainees and practicing special educators and school counselors are exposed to structured multicultural education classes or in-depth multi-

cultural workshops to obtain a better understanding of themselves and their beliefs about their own and other cultural/ethnic groups. Colleges and universities have an awesome role to play in preparing future special educators and school counselors to function effectively in school and community partnerships within *all* communities. Two major concerns surface: (a) the quality of the multicultural special education preservice

Table 11.1
TRAINING SPECIAL EDUCATION AND SCHOOL COUNSELORS TO CONNECT
SCHOOLS WITH SIGNIFICANT MULTICULTURAL COMMUNITY RESOURCES–
A THREE PHASE MODEL

Phase One:	Reshaping Attitudes and Personal Redefinition
Phase Two:	Development of an Accurate Knowledge Base
	a. Examination of Historic and Present School and Community Partnerships and Activities
	b. Creation of a Comprehensive and Inclusive Database of *SCRs*
Phase Three:	Productive School and Community Networks
	a. Establishment of Inclusive School and Community Connections
	b. Utilization of *SCRs* to Aid Multicultural Learners with Disabilities and Their Families

and/or in-service level training program; and (b) demonstration of competency in this area. Utley (1995) recommended the use of a multicultural perspective as a framework for special education programs. Earlier, Ford (1992) outlined the inclusion of four specific multicultural experiences in special education training programs:

- Engaging teachers in self-awareness activities to explore their attitudes and perceptions concerning their cultural group and beliefs-as well as the effects of their attitudes on students in terms of self-concept, academic abilities, and educational opportunities.
- Exposing teachers to accurate information about various cultural ethnic groups (e.g., historic and contemporary contributions and lifestyles, value systems, interpersonal-communication patterns, learning styles, and parental attitudes about education and disabilities).
- Helping educators explore the diversity that exists between, as well as within, cultural ethnic groups.
- Providing special education teachers with opportunities to manifest appropriate application of cultural information to create a healthy learning climate. (p. 108)

During this phase, specific emphasis must be placed on *performance-based assessment of pre-service trainees and practitioners* regarding their ability to apply acquired knowledge/skills into actual program planning and implementation with multicultural learners with disabilities and their families. Additionally, many school districts nationwide have Local Professional Development Committees (LPDC) to aid in the continued professional development of certified school personnel. Typically, the LPDC is responsible for recommending professional activities to school personnel and/or approving or disapproving activities submitted by school personnel. To assist school personnel in serving multicultural learners with disabilities, some vital questions that must be answered include: Are multicultural activities and topics included on the list of recommended professional development activities? What weight and priority are given to school personnel participating in multicultural education activities? If certified and licensed school personnel do not voluntarily select multicultural professional activities, what are the incentives for them to do so or consequences of not doing?

Clearly, if school districts are serious about improving the competency levels of school personnel to deliver equitable, quality service to multicultural learners with disabilities, then mechanisms must be incorporated for them to do so. In recognition of the need for a multicultural framework for special education training programs, one of the primary professional special education organizations, The Council for Exceptional Children (CEC) (1996) included specific multicultural-oriented items in the "CEC Common Core of Knowledge and Skills" essential for all beginning special education teachers. In addition, school counselors who are enrolled in CACREP accredited counselor education programs are required to have course work that addresses an understanding of issues and trends in a multicultural and diverse society. Monitoring activities and/or post-workshop assignments should be conducted to aid practicing special educators and school counselors in understanding how to incorporate the acquired knowledge base and skills.

Phase Two

In Phase Two, attention is focused on preservice trainees (a) developing an understanding of past and current local school and community partnerships; and (b) obtaining an accurate knowledge base about the varied local *SCRs*. If prospective special education teachers and school counselors are to become committed to the identification and inclusion of *SCRs,* meaningful structured community involvement activities must become a part of their entire preservice training experience. Community involvement activities must be explicitly emphasized in all course work rather than a brief assignment in one course. At a minimum, community involvement assignments must become essential components in all educational courses. Specific course objectives and the expected levels of performance should be precisely outlined in these courses. To address Part (a) of Phase Two, trainees could interview local principals, teachers, school counselors, and other school personnel.(i.e., school and community liaison) to learn about past and current local school and community involvement practices. As a class project, these practices could be critiqued regarding their inclusiveness (e.g., range of significant community resources) and productivity (e.g., nature and degree of use by school personnel and potential influence on student outcome). Next, as an in-class project (during Phase Three), trainees could outline ways to refine local school and community involvement policies and practices. As appropriate, these recommendations could be shared with local school personnel.

The compilation of local *SCRs* by preservice trainees and direct participation in the local programs are performed during phase two. For example, preservice trainees, in cooperative groups, could create a database of easily accessible human and published resources to help them gather information about local *SCRs*. Written and human resources such as, "informational resource" (i.e., Blackbook and Blackpages–a city or regional specific publications that lists Black-owned businesses, civic and social organizations, and churches), directors of community centers, members of fraternities and sororities, and informed parents. Next, trainees would select a community program and interview the program planner or other relevant staff to obtain more information. When learning about the local community and families the use of a "participation-observation" format is recommended (Garcia, 1991; Harry et al., 1993). Under this framework, the trainees would participate fully in cultural group experiences. To this end, teacher and school counselor trainees, with permission from program directors, perform systematic observations. This observational experience would be designed to allow the trainees the opportunity to interact with paid and volunteer community staff. From observations and interviews, the trainees obtain answers that aid them to understand the program's offerings. Finally, the trainees could construct a user-friendly practical product such as a Thematic Community Resource Calendar (Ford, 1995). Each month would be assigned a theme or topic (e.g., education month, nutrition and health month, self-awareness month, and family month). Community-based resources, extracted from the trainees' databases that provide services would be depicted. For instance, the education month would briefly describe programs and resources that offer tutoring or other academic-oriented activities; and self-awareness and family month may include resources providing cultural enrichment programs, and family togetherness activities.

Congruent with the goals of phase two *practicing* teachers would (a) acquire information about past and present partnership efforts within their school building (and local school district), and (b) identify and make contact with *SCRs*. Similar to preservice trainees, practicing teachers and school counselors can obtain an understanding of the nature of the collaboration activities from building personnel (e.g., principal, school, and community liaison) and possible effectiveness. When critiquing current school and community partnerships, questions to be considered could include the following:

- Are present linkages and partnerships inclusive? Are *all SCRs* included (e.g., multicultural resources, both formal and informal grassroots)? Who determined who should be included? In the linkages, who initiates cooperative activities?
- How often are the linkages used? When?
- Does the partnership help enhance educational outcomes for *all* students (e.g., including multicultural learners with disabilities and gifts and talents)? In what ways?

- What modifications in the partnership arrangements need further modification such that student outcome is positively impacted?

As indicated in the next section, these same or similar questions can be addressed by both the school and *SCRs* in order to refine the school and community relationship. During Phase Two, the examination of current practices could serve as the springboard to discuss ways to expand the use of *SCRs* and/or rationale for the compilation of more comprehensive resources.

To help identify *SCRs*, as an initial activity, practicing teachers could work with the school's community outreach specialist/school-community liaison person to obtain information about local *SCRs* and corresponding contacts. In addition, a [school] survival kit prepared by the Educational Research Service (1997) in cooperation with the National Association of Elementary School Principals that outline specific strategies to help schools identify and tap into local community resources, could be used. Earlier, Garcia (1991) noted that teachers must study the community of their students. For instance, they can join and develop friends in non-school-related community groups and survey the community to obtain understanding and appreciation of it.

To increase the probability of school personnel capitalizing on the expertise of *SCRs* contacts, a building-level team (BL-Team) approach could be instituted. The special educator and school counselor could lead the formation of the team to help facilitate objectives. During Phase Three, The BL-Team, along with selected *significant* community representatives could comprise the School and Community Team (SCT). The SCT could (a) examine present school and community involvement policies and practices, and (b) restructure ways they could better work together by using each other's strengths to improve educational outcomes for multicultural learners with disabilities. The special educator, school counselor, and building administrator could assume leadership in instituting this process in Phase Three. For instance, they could orchestrate the compilation of the SCT (i.e., BL-Team and community representatives) using processes that ensure representation from traditional community organizations, local businesses, and those previously *untapped SCRs.* The BL-Team could take responsibility for sharing information about the SCT with certified and non-certified personnel throughout the school building. In addition, the BL-Team could encourage the active involvement of certified/licensed school personnel in local community-based programs and illustrate how to connect multicultural youth with services offered by *SCRs.*

Phase Three

Phase Three concentrates on the facilitation of school and community collaborative activities to influence student outcomes. As discussed in Phase Two, practitioners, with representation from local multicultural community resources are encouraged to institute mechanisms that provide a systematic way to refine as needed current school and community partnerships. Efforts may encompass several formats such as (a) bringing human and published community resources into the school and classrooms; (b) school personnel helping connect individual students and their families to needed *SCRs;* and (c) school and community combining resources to combat issues that limit students' opportunities to maximum performance (e.g., deteriorating physical school structure, overrepresentation of multicultural learners in special education programming, school violence, and inadequate materials).

CONCLUSION

Public schools that make a decisive difference in educational outcomes of multicultural youth with disabilities, employ productive school and community partnerships. The information presented in this chapter discussed the rationale for school and community collaboration, challenges and benefits to students, school personnel, and parents when efforts are used to connect and collaborate with *SCRs. SCRs* within multicultural communities have traditionally been devalued and ignored. Recent crises in education, however, demand the authentic inclusion of these valuable assets. *SCRs* have the potential to provide varied services to help schools improve educational attainment for youth with mild disabilities and their families. We strongly believe special training is needed to help school personnel to work collaboratively with *SCRs* in multicultural communities. Culturally-based models can equip school personnel with the needed attitudes, knowledge base, and skills as they interact with community members.

REFERENCES

American School Counselor Association (1999). American School Counselor Association statement: Cross/multicultural counseling. *Elementary School Guidance and Counseling, 23,* 322–323.

Artiles, A.J., & Trent, S.C. (1994). Overrepresentation of minority students in special education: A continuing debate. *The Journal of Special Education, 27,* 410–437.

Artiles, A.J., & Zamora-Duran, G. (1997). *Reducing disproportionate representation of culturally diverse students in special and gifted education.* Reston, VA: The Council for Exceptional Children.

Atkinson, D.R., & Juntenen, C.L. (1994). School counselors and school psychologists as school-home-community liaisons in ethically diverse schools. In P. Pedersen & J.C. Carey (Eds.), *Multicultural counseling in the school: A practical handbook* (pp. 103–120). Needham Heights, MA: Allyn & Bacon.

Banks, C.A.M. (1997). Parents and teachers: Partners in school reform. In J.A. Banks & C.A.M. Banks (Eds.), *Multicultural education: Issues and perspectives.* Boston, MA: Allyn & Bacon.

Barnes, E.J. (1991). The Black community as a source of positive self concept for Black children: A theoretical perspective. In R.L. Jones (Ed.), *Black psychology* (pp. 667–692). Berkeley, CA: Cobbs & Henry.

Billinsley, A., & Caldwell, C.H. (1991). The church, the family and school in the African-American community. *Journal of Negro Education, 60* (3), 427–440.

Brand, S. (1996). Making parent involvement a reality: Helping teachers develop partnerships with parents. *National Association for the Education of Young Children, 51* (2), 76–81.

Brant, R. (1989). On parents and schools: A conversation with Joyce Epstein. *Educational Leadership,* 24–27.

Brant, R. (1998). Listen first. *Educational Leadership,* 25–30.

Casas, J.M., & Furlong, M.J. (1994). School counselors as advocates for increased Hispanic parent participation in the schools. In P. Pedersen & J.C. Carey (Eds.), *Multicultural counseling in the school: A Practical Handbook* (pp. 121–150). Needham Heights, MA: Allyn & Bacon.

Chinn, P.C., & Hughes, S. (1987). Representation of minority students in special education classes. *Remedial and Special Education, 8* (4), 41–46.

Comer, J.P. (1985). Empowering Black children's educational environments. In H.P. McAdoo & J.L. McAdoo (Eds.), *Black children: Social, educational and parental environments* (pp. 123–138). Newbury Park, CA: Sage.

Comer, J.P. (1989). The school development program: A psychosocial model of school intervention. In G.L. Berry & J.K. Asaman (Eds.), *Black students: Psychosocial issues and academic achievement* (pp. 264–285). Newbury Park, CA: Corwin Press.

Compton, B., & Galloway, B. (1984). *Social work processes* (3rd ed.). Homewood, IL: Dorsey Press.

Cook, L.H., & Boe, E.E. (1995). Who is teaching students with disabilities? *Teaching Exceptional Children, 28* (1), 70–72.

Cook, L., & Friend, M. (1998). Co-Teaching: Guidelines for creating effective practices. In E. Meyen, G. Vergason, & R. Whelan (Eds.), *Educating students: Strategies and methods for students with mild disabilities* (pp. 453–479). Denver, CO: Love.

Council for Exceptional Children. (1996). *What every special educator must know: The International Standards for the preparation and certification of special education teachers* (2nd ed.). Reston, VA: Author.

Croninger, B. (1990). African-American parents... Seeing them as colleagues, neighbors, and friends? *Equity Coalition for Race, Gender and National Origin, 1* (2), 8–9.

Cummins, J. (1986). Empowering minority students: A framework for intervention. *Harvard Educational Review, 56* (1), 18–35.

Deslandes, R., Royer, E., Potvin, P., & Leclerc, D. (1999, Summer). Patterns of home and school partnership for general and special education students at the secondary level. *Exceptional Children, 65* (4), 496–506.

Downing, J., Pierce, K.A., & Woodruff, P. (1993). A community network for helping families. *School Counselor, 25,* 242–246.

Educational Research Services (1997). *Getting parents meaningfully involved.* Arlington, VA: Author.

Epperson, A.I. (1991). The community partnership: Operation rescue. *Journal of Negro Education, 60* (3), 454–458.

Ford, B.A. (1992). Multicultural education training for special educators working with African-American youth. *Exceptional Children, 59* (2), 107–114.

Ford, B.A. (1995). African American community involvement processes and special education: Essential networks for effective education. In B.A. Ford, F.E. Obiakor, & J.M. Patton (Eds.), *Effective education of African American exceptional learners: New perspectives* (pp. 235–272). Austin, TX: Pro-Ed.

Ford, B.A. (1998). Productive school and community partnerships: Essentials to improve educational outcomes for ethnic minority students. In A. Freeman, H. Bessent-Byrd, & C. Morris (Eds.), *Enfranchising urban learners for the twenty-first century* (pp. 91–113). Kearney, NE: Morris.

Ford, B.A., & Bessent-Byrd, H. (in press). Reconceptualization of the learning disabilities paradigm: Multicultural imperatives. In L. Denti (Ed.), *New ways of looking at learning disabilities*. Denver, CO: Love.

Ford, B.A., Obiakor, F.E., & Patton, J.M. (1995). *Effective education of African American exceptional learners: New perspectives*. Austin, TX: Pro-Ed.

Ford Foundation and John D. & C.T. MacArthur Foundation. (1989). *Visions of a better way: A Black appraisal of public schooling*. Washington, DC: Joint Center for Political Studies. (ERIC Document Reproduction Service No. ED 312 320).

Garcia, R.L. (1991). *Teaching in a pluralistic society: Concepts, models, strategies*. New York: Harper Collins.

Gentemann, K.M., & Whitehead, T.L. (1983). The cultural broker concept in bicultural education. *Journal of Negro Education, 52*, 118–129.

Giles, H.C. (1998). *Parent engagement as a school reform strategy*. New York: ERIC Publications.

Goor, M.B. (1995). *Leadership for special education administration: A case-based approach*. Fort Worth, TX: Harcourt Brace.

Grossman, H. (1995). *Special education in a diverse society*. Boston, MA: Allyn & Bacon.

Harry, B. (1994). *The disproportionate representation of minority students in special education: Theories and recommendations*. Alexandria, VA: National Association of State Directors of Special Education.

Harry, B., Torguson, C., Katkavich, J. & Guerrero, M. (1993, Fall). Crossing social class and cultural barriers in working with families: Implications for teacher training. *Teaching Exceptional Children*, 48–51.

Hatch, T. (1998). How community contributes to achievement. *Educational Leadership*, 16–19.

Heath, S.B., & McLaughlin, M.W. (1987). A child resource policy: Moving beyond dependence on school and family. *Phi Delta Kappan, 70*, 205–209.

Higgins, R. (1985). Psychological resilience and the capacity for intimacy: How the wounded might "love well," *Dissertations Abstracts International, 46, 11b*. (University Microfilm International).

Hobbs, B.B., & Collison, B.B. (1995). School community agency collaboration: Implications for school counselors. *School Counselor, 43*.

Jenkins, L.E. (1989). The Black family and academic achievement. In G.L. Berry & J.K. Asaman (Eds.), *Black students: Psychosocial issues and academic achievement* (pp. 138–152). Newbury Park, CA: Corwin Press.

Karen, R. (1990). Becoming attached. *Atlantic Monthly*, 49–74.

Kaufman, C., Grunebaum, H., Cohler, B., & Gamer, E. (1979). Superkids: Competent children of psychotic mothers. *American Journal of Psychiatry, 136*, 1398–1402.

Lewis, R., & Morris, J. (1998). Communities for children. *Educational Leadership*, 34–36.

Mahan, J.M., Fortney, M., & Garcia, J. (1983). Linking the community to teacher education: Toward a more analytical approach. *Action in Teacher Education, 5* (1–2), 1–10.

Mannan, G. & Blackwell, J. (1992). Parent involvement: Barriers and opportunities. *The Urban Review, 24* (3), 219–226.

Marion, R.L. (1980). Communicating with parents of diverse exceptional children. *Exceptional Children, 46* (8), 616–623.

McLaughlin, M.J. (1999). Access to the general education curriculum: Paperwork and procedure or redefining "special education." *Journal of Special Education Leadership, 12*, 9–14.

National Clearinghouse for Professionals in Special Education (1988). *Information on personnel supply and demand: The supply of minority teachers in the United States.* Reston, VA: The Council for Exceptional Children.

Nettles, S.M. (1991). Community contributions to school outcomes of African-American students. *Education and Urban Society, 24* (1), 132–147.

Norris, D. (1995). *Winning with diversity: A practical handbook for creating inclusive meetings, events, and organizations.* Washington, DC: American Society of Associate Executives.

Obiakor, F.E. (1999, Fall). Teacher expectations of minority exceptional learners: Impact on "accuracy" of self-concepts. *Exceptional Children, 66* (1), 39–53.

Obiakor, F.E., Mehring, T.A., & Schwenn, J.O. (1996). *Disruption, disaster, and death: Helping students deal with crises.* Reston, VA: The Council for Exceptional Children.

Ogbu, J.U. (1978). *Minority education and caste.* San Francisco, CA: Academic Press.

Rueda, R. (1997, January). *Fiesta Educativa: A community-based organization.* Paper presented at the Council for Exceptional Children Multicultural Symposium, New Orleans, LA.

Rutter, M. (1983). Stress, coping, and development: Some issues and some questions. In N. Garmezy & M. Rutter (Eds.), *Stress, coping, and development in children* (pp. 49–74). New York: McGraw Hill.

Schmidt, J.J. (1999). *Counseling in schools: Essential services and comprehensive programs* (3rd ed.). Needham Heights: MA: Allyn & Bacon.

Slaughter, D.T., & Epps, E. (1987). The home environment and academic achievement of Black American children and youth: An overview. *Journal of Negro Education, 56* (1), 3–20.

The American School Counseling Association. (1997). *National standards for school counseling programs.* Alexandria, VA: Author.

Telesford, M.C. (1994, Summer). Tips for accessing and involving families of color in a significant way. *Focal Point,* 11.

Utley, C.A. (1995). Culturally and linguistically diverse students with mild disabilities. In C.A. Grant (Ed.), *Educating for diversity: An anthology of multicultural voices* (pp. 301–324). Boston, MA: Allyn & Bacon.

Valli, L. & Rennert-Ariev, P.L. (2000, January/February). Identifying consensus in teacher education reform documents: A proposed framework and action implications. *Journal of Teacher Education, 51* (1), 5–17.

Voltz, D.L. (1995). Learning and cultural diversities in general and special education classes: Frameworks for success. *Multiple Voices For Ethnically Diverse Exceptional Learners, 1* (1), 1–11.

Werner, E., & Smith, R. (1983). Vulnerable but invincible. In N. Garmezy & M. Rutter (Eds.), *Stress, coping, and development in children* (pp. 69–82). New York: McGraw Hill.

Chapter 12

RACE, CLASS, SOCIAL INEQUALITY, AND SPECIAL EDUCATION: SUMMARY COMMENTS

Edgar G. Epps

Justice requires both equality in the treatment of all members of the society and the protection of the least advantaged members of the society. Equal treatment is generally endorsed by the majority of American citizens. However, Gordon (1999) noted that educators and stakeholders must make a distinction between *equality* and *equity*. As he pointed out, "*equity* requires that treatments be appropriate *and* sufficient to the characteristics and needs of those treated" (p. xiv). But as Ogbu (1995) observed, "There are three ways in which minorities are denied equal educational opportunity. One is the denial [of] equal access to desirable jobs and positions in adult life . . . A second way is to deny minorities equal access to good education. . . . A third way is to lower expectations and limit support within classroom settings" (p. 91). This chapter presents an overview of research and pedagogy concerned with issues of equality of opportunity for learners from multicultural and low socioeconomic backgrounds who have special needs. By doing so, it also provides summary comments for this entire book.

HISTORICAL CONTEXTS

Race and class have been consistently associated with access to educational resources, including both material and sociopsychological resources (Epps, 1995). Sociological and psychological research and theory have not adequately appreciated the importance of variations in environmental circumstances (family social status, race/ethnic status) and their impact on family life-styles and child-rearing practices. Because racial/ethnic

228

groups and social classes inhabit different cultural niches, they face different subsistence demands, provide different role models, and different conceptions of adult success. The notion of a universal pattern of human development does not pass the test of human experience, even within the boundaries of a single diverse nation such as the United States. Unfortunately, the social and behavioral sciences and the education and other helping professions have been slow to take into account this diversity in their conceptualizations of human development and the educational process. For instance, Carter and Goodwin (1994) described three paradigms that have defined educational research on African Americans and members of other racial/ethnic groups in this country: "the inferiority, cultural deprivation, and cultural difference paradigms" (p. 294). The educational proposals supported by the inferiority paradigm are based on the assumption that African Americans (and by extension, other stigmatized groups) are biologically incapable of learning complex abstract subject matter. The cultural deprivation paradigm gave rise to compensatory education programs such as Head Start and Title I of the Elementary and Secondary Education Act that are designed to supplement "deficiencies" in the culture and socialization practices of African Americans, Latinos, American Indians, and poor people of all racial and ethnic groups. A considerable amount of research and commentary has been done on the *problems* of low income families and multicultural communities. Whether the studies focused on historical subjugation, institutional racism (reflected in segregated housing, concentrated poverty and social isolation, problems of substance abuse, crime and violence, welfare dependency, and teenage parenthood), or low reading scores, there was a tendency to "blame the victim." Only the cultural difference perspective has looked for positive strengths in diverse communities. This paradigm has formed the basis for the promising work on culturally responsive or culturally responsible pedagogy in general and special education programs (Ladson-Billings, 1995).

SCHOOL REFORM: MORE THAN LIP SERVICE

This book, as a whole, provides a welcome change from the monocultural stance of much previous work on special education. Utley and Obiakor, and their contributors provide compelling evidence that low socioeconomic status and minority status students (multicultural learners) do not receive either equal or equitable education in general and special education programs. According to Utley and Obiakor, in this volume, multicultural education attempts to increase respect for diversity, reduce prejudice, improve intergroup relations, enhance the understanding of intraindividual and interindividual differences, and resolve incompatibilities between students' styles of learning and behavior and educators' styles of instruction. *Some common themes appear throughout the volume. One such theme is inclusiveness. Another focuses on high expectations. A third is appropriateness of instruction and/or treatment.* Utley and Obiakor clearly emphasize that educational reforms that do not embrace these themes are not likely to improve the outcomes of education for multicultural learners who are classified into the categories of mild mental retardation, learning disabilities, and seriously emotionally disturbed.

Whether the school reform movement will embrace the themes of inclusiveness, high expectations, and appropriate instruction is problematic. As I have written elsewhere

(Epps, 1994), the reforms of the 1980s emphasized the increasing role of the states in determining curricula, monitoring achievement, evaluating and certifying teachers, and setting goals and standards. A second strand of reform efforts used the language of school restructuring, with an emphasis on reducing the isolation of teachers, increasing the role of teachers in formulating and implementing school policy, sharing decision-making at the local school level, and devolving authority from the central bureaucracy to the local school. Some reformers have emphasized empowering the major actors at the school-site—teachers, principals, and *parents and communities*. None of these reforms, however, did more than pay lip service to the goals of inclusion that are central to the philosophy of multicultural education.

The goals of multicultural education are not compatible with the first type of reform cited above (state level standard setting). The movement to increase state control of education implies a standardization of curricula, teacher certification, and student evaluation, and relies on the standardized norm-referenced achievement test as a universal assessment tool. There is little room for flexibility of the sort that would be required to serve adequately the needs of a diverse student population with special needs. The goals of both multicultural education and special education emphasize flexibility and adaptability; a willingness to respond to the needs of individual children as well as the needs of students classified as needing special attention because of linguistic, cultural, or economic diversity. Utley and Obiakor are correct in concluding that the heavy reliance on testing, tailoring "accountability" assessment to suit students from privileged backgrounds, and the proliferation of choice and voucher reforms mitigate against effective infusion of multicultural education into public schools.

The national reform effort symbolized by *Goals 2000* equates high expectations with raising standards (and standards are typically equated with achievement test scores). It also includes a plea for making high quality education available to all children irrespective of social circumstances, academic abilities, and cultural backgrounds. In order for high quality education to be available to all children, attention would have to be paid to "opportunity to learn standards" as well as content standards (Stevens, 1993). The concept of opportunity to learn encompasses issues related to availability of curriculum offerings, resource allocation, as well as quality and appropriateness of instruction. However, the federal government has little direct control over local education agencies. It can only use persuasion or enticement in matters not covered by civil rights law (including the special education laws). This leaves the fates of multicultural learners in general and special education up to state and local governments which are guided by local values, customs, and traditions that are loaded with vestiges of attitudes and behaviors carried over from the historical period of "separate but equal education" (e.g., the battle in South Carolina over the Confederate Flag as we enter the new century). According to Grant (1985), "schooling experience, for the most part, seems to contribute to socialization of each race-gender group in a manner consistent with prevailing societal norms about appropriate roles for adults of each ascribed-status group" (p. 73). The contributors to this volume provide striking data on the relationship between family social status and educational outcomes. Schools reflect the social system of which they are a part. Therefore, it should not be surprising that children whose families are positioned at the bottom of the status hierarchy, whether because of income or race/ethnic status, are overrepresented in special education and low ability groups or tracks in elementary and secondary schools, but underrepresented in gifted programs, honors programs, and advanced placement classes.

It is even more troubling that general and special educators and helping professionals justify their actions by claiming that they are acting in the best interests of children.

BEYOND TRADITION: OLD DREAMS AND NEW STEPS

Obiakor (1999) summarized that "when teachers fail to respond to intraindividual and interindividual differences, processes of identification, assessment, classification, placement, and instruction become loaded with inappropriate assumptions, prejudicial expectations, negative stereotypes, and illusory conclusions" (p. 41). Some general and special educators appear to believe that to present multicultural learners with challenging academic work or complex subject matter would lead to frustration and loss of self-esteem. For such teachers, the task of the school is to convince children (and their parents) that they are getting the quality of education they "deserve." It does not seem to occur to these professionals that children cannot learn what they are not taught (and I would add, "taught appropriately"). Denying children access to a rich and challenging curriculum forecloses their opportunity to learn. Rather than excluding students from high quality instruction, the effort should be made to provide the types of social, emotional, and cognitive supports each multicultural child needs.

The tension between serving the needs of special education children in segregated environments and the goals of inclusion highlights two themes. On the one hand, some special educators sincerely believe that the interests of children are best served in restricted environments, while others believe that providing services in the least restrictive environment provides children with optimal developmental opportunities. Those in the second camp appear to have the law on their side. However, the goals of test-driven standards–based reforms seem to encourage segregation because they force general and special education teachers and administrators to adopt strategies that will maximize test scores. The effort to raise test scores may lead to exclusion of multicultural learners with special needs from classrooms that will be tested. Test-driven standards also encourage ability grouping and tracking which tend to segregate multicultural learners in the general education program. Hilliard (1999) emphasized *quality of service.* In his view, that is where the problem lies. In which environment and with what services can general and special educators make it possible for all children to succeed? "There's nothing wrong with the kids! There's something wrong with the services that [go] to the kids. There's not a single recipe. It's a bad way of thinking about how to improve schools" (Hilliard, 1999, p. 83). He explained that there are many schools that are successful with multicultural learners, but this fact is ignored by both the research community and federal and state education agencies. If the problem is not lack of knowledge about how to make schools successful, there is a serious lack of interest in this body of knowledge, according to Hilliard.

Entwistle and Alexander (1993) reviewed how out-of-school social structural influences complicate early school adjustment. Poverty, ethnicity, and family type are called "risk factors" that affect educators' decisions about ability group placement and retention. "At-risk" children have benefitted from participation in high quality early childhood education programs. However, children from low-income families are less likely to attend preschool than those from more affluent families. The same pattern applies to multicultural learners; they are less likely to be enrolled in preschool than White children. Recently, Entwistle and Alexander (1999) argued that "the transition into full-time schooling—entry into first grade—constitutes a 'critical period' for children's academic development" (p. 404). They also contended that "this transition experience may be key for the prospects of 'at-risk' children. For children brought up outside the middle-class mainstream, differences between home and school are dramatic" (p. 405). This suggests that developmental researchers and special education researchers should be aware that "conditions outside the individual are important as well as those within the individual" (p. 405). Understanding the social contexts in which multicultural children develop is essential to the provision of developmentally appropriate education for children who do not come from backgrounds described by Entwistle and Alexander as the middle-class mainstream. Differences in out-of-school learning opportunities are reflected in children's grades and test scores (see, for example, research on summer learning loss [Cooper, Nye, Charlton, Lindsay, & Greathouse, 1996; Entwistle & Alexander, 1992; Heyns, 1978]).

In their study of 790 children who began first grade in the fall of 1988 in 20 Baltimore City public schools, Entwistle and Alexander (1992) found small or negligible race differences in standardized test scores in reading and math. However, they found substantial differences across socioeconomic status (SES) levels. They concluded that, "SES, not race/ethnicity, is the main divide" (p. 407). Among the school adjustment factors cited are the following: being identified by kindergarten teachers as being at risk for serious academic or adjustment problems; more frequent absences in first grade; and lower teacher ratings on "interest/participation" and "attention span/restlessness." The students identified as having problems in first

grade typically continue to have difficulty in school in later grades and are more likely to drop out of school before graduating from high school. As an example, the plight of African American males in the education system has been a persisting area of concern. It has been observed consistently that males are severely overrepresented in special education and that they are at greater risk than females for being retained in grade. The difficulties of African American males in the education system extend throughout the elementary and secondary years and are reflected in higher education and adult roles and statuses (Epps, 1992; Garibaldi, 1992; Hare & Castenell, 1985). Schools play a major role in allocating people to different adult roles through grades, retention, assignment to ability groups and tracks, and the provision of information and encouragement to pursue higher education. There is a need for general and special educators and policymakers to design strategies that will lead to the improvement of educational performance, persistence, and participation in higher education by African Americans. This will require initiatives that will circumvent limitations of the opportunity structure to help low income children from multicultural families and communities succeed in school and ultimately attain jobs in the primary employment sector.

Are there any promising strategies for weakening the link between SES and overrepresentation in low ability groups and special education? As noted above, Hilliard (1999) identified many schools that are successful in raising the achievement levels of African American and Latino students from "worst to first." A case study of one such school by Sizemore (1988) provided detailed information on the strategies used by an elementary school principal to turn a low achieving school serving an inner-city student body into one of the highest performing schools in Pittsburgh. However, as Hilliard pointed out, general and special educators and researchers largely ignore this type of evidence. This suggests to me that the message may be ignored because an African American educator who has a reputation for advocacy delivers it. Would the message be better received if it came from members of the "establishment"? The response of educators and researchers to Brookover, Beamer, Efthin, Hathaway, Lezotte, Miller, Passalaqua, and Tornatzky's (1979) research on effective schools suggested that even when the lead researcher is a well-respected member of the academic fraternity the message will be ignored if heeding it would require drastic changes in belief systems and school organizational structures. A case in point, is the struggle to "detrack" schools; too many individuals and groups have vested interests in maintaining the status quo (Oakes & Lipton, 1992).

The difficulty parents have in getting school personnel to be flexible is dramatically described in Hudak's (1996) account of the struggle he and his wife went through in their efforts to obtain appropriate placement for their son with special needs. The fact that the child could read at grade level and was quiet and well behaved did not sway the classroom teacher or the panel of experts who made decisions on placement. Hudak was convinced that "control" and a belief the each child can be labeled and put in his/her designated slot guided the actions of school personnel. Even these well-educated middle-class White parents had to fight constantly to have their child included in the regular classroom with adequate support. The school personnel considered the request unreasonable because they provided services for children with special needs children in segregated classrooms. The general education classroom teacher and the special education personnel attempted to convince the parents that the child would be served more effectively in a segregated setting. However, others have demonstrated that children with special needs can be integrated into general education classrooms with adequate support. Fisher, Sax, and Grove (2000) presented evidence that teachers and administrators can create an inclusive environment for all students. They investigated how one school changed its method of delivery service and "sustained inclusion in the face of internal and external challenges and opportunities" (p. 214). They reported that "students with special needs . . . were not simply assigned to general education classes but rather were *educated* in these classes" (p. 224, emphasis added). They also concluded that one strategy "for schools attempting to become inclusive, resilient places is to *provide students with appropriate support in their classes*" (p. 224, authors' emphasis). However, it is not an easy task. Change of the kind described by Hudak requires strong principal leadership, appropriate staff development, teachers who believe in the goals of inclusion, adequate resources, and enough local school autonomy for teachers to adopt flexible strategies and learn to work together cooperatively to implement and maintain the program.

CONCLUSION

Research suggests that schools are implicated in the educational inequities faced by low-income children from diverse backgrounds. Among the factors that should become the focus of educational reform are school climates, academic expectations of educators, disciplinary policies, ability group and track assignments, preparation of preservice teachers and staff development for continuing teachers. In addition, there is evidence that parental involvement, when supported and encouraged by school personnel, can be a major resource for improving children's achievement (Haynes, Comer, & Hamilton-Lee, 1988).

The climate for educational policy as we enter the new century appears not very promising. Schuman and Krysan (1999), in a review of white Americans' beliefs about racial inequality, reported that "the most striking finding over the years . . . is the high percentage of white Americans (47 percent in 1998, the most recent year available) who agree with the statement that. . . . blacks just don't have the motivation to pull themselves out of poverty" (p. 848). In addition, the majority of Whites tend to deny the existence of job discrimination. They added that responses to questions about financial aid to African Americans and affirmative action "generally reveal low support for policies intended to reduce inequality between Blacks and whites along socioeconomic lines" (p. 854). They also reported that support for federal efforts to achieve school desegregation has declined since the 1960s. Apparently, while African Americans perceive high levels of racial discrimination in many areas of life, racial discrimination is not seen by most Whites as the major factor in racial inequalities. Whites increasingly believe discrimination has virtually disappeared in the United States, or has been reversed and now favors African Americans. This leads to the attribution of all types of inequality to failures of the African American family and community. On the other hand, the majority of African Americans believe discrimination is still a major factor impeding their efforts to obtain decent housing, good jobs, and high quality education. For many Whites, it appears that the myth of equality overshadows all evidence. Many White Americans have developed an ideology that defends the status quo of racial inequality and rejects social responsibility as it relates to race.

If the attitudes described above guide the selection of political leaders and educational policymakers during the next decade, it is not likely that the lingering vestiges of racism and discrimination—the poor quality of preschool, elementary school, and high school education available to low income children from multicultural families—will be addressed with effective government supported programs. The most popular current strategies—charter schools, vouchers, neighborhood schools, statewide standards and testing—tend to encourage resegregation of multicultural learners.

Utley and Obiakor, and their contributors to this book have made a strong case for comprehensive reforms that infuse multicultural education into both general and special education. Because the proportion of children in special education who come from multicultural backgrounds is increasing rapidly while the teaching force remains largely White, it is imperative that schools/colleges of education infuse multicultural education into all aspects of teacher preparation. Both general and special educators should be provided with a thorough grounding in multicultural knowledge and sensitivity. In addition, these teachers need to learn effective instructional strategies for multicultural student populations, become familiar with appropriate assessment tools and effective instructional materials. They must also be aware that children bring a variety of learning and communication styles, and that teachers must acquire the skills needed to adapt instruction to the needs of multicultural learners. Finally, general and special educators must learn how to develop trusting relationships with children, parents, and communities.

There is no doubt that Utley and Obiakor have made an important contribution to our awareness of the issues involved in providing effective education to multicultural learners with and without disabilities. This book should be an asset to teacher educators who are trying to prepare prospective teachers to be effective with all children, irrespective of racial, linguistic, or disability status. However, the likelihood that substantial changes will be made in the way we prepare teachers and organize instruction appears not promising. I end my summary comments with a call for all concerned: general and special educators and policymakers to urge their constituencies to bring whatever influence they can to bear on those who have the power to implement programs and strategies that will help to address issues raised within this book.

REFERENCES

Brookover, W.B., Beamer, L., Efthin, H., Hathaway, D., Lezotte, L., Miller, S., Passalaqua, J., & Tornatzky, L. (1979). *School social systems and student achievement.* New York: Praeger.

Carter, R.T., & Goodwin, A.L. (1994). Racial identity and education. In L. Darling-Hammond (Ed.), *Review of Research in Education, 20,* 291–336.

Cooper, H., Nye, B., Charleton, K., Lindsay, J., & Greathouse, S. (1996). The effects of summer vacation on achievement test scores: A narrative and meta-analytic review. *Review of Educational Research, 66,* 227–268.

Entwistle, D.R., & Alexander, K.L. (1992). Summer setback: Race, poverty, school composition and mathematical achievement in the first two years of school. *American Sociological Review, 57,* 72–84.

Entwistle, D.R, & Alexander, K.L. (1993). Entry into school: The beginning school transition and educational stratification in the United States. *Annual Review of Sociology, 19,* 401–423.

Epps, E.G. (1992). Education of African Americans. In M. Alkin (Ed.), *Encyclopedia of Educational Research* (6th ed.) (Vol. 2, pp. 49–60). New York: Macmillan.

Epps, E.G. (1994). Radical school reform in Chicago: How is it working? In C. Finn & H. Walberg (Eds.), *Radical education reforms* (pp. 10–21). Berkeley, CA: McCutchan.

Epps, E.G. (1995). Race, class, and educational opportunity: Trends in the sociology of education. *Sociological Forum, 10,* 593–608.

Fisher, D., Sax, C., & Grove, K. (2000). The resilience of changes promoting inclusiveness in an urban elementary school. *The Elementary School Journal, 100,* 213–227.

Garibaldi, A.M. (1992). Educating and motivating African American males to succeed. *Journal of Negro Education, 61,* 4–11.

Gordon, E.W. (1999). *Education and justice: A view from the back of the bus.* New York: Teachers College Press.

Grant, L. (1995). *Uneasy alliances: Black males, teachers, and peers in desegregated classrooms.* Paper presented at the Annual Meeting of the American Educational Research Association, Chicago, IL.

Hare, B.R., & Castenell, L.A. (1995). No place to run, no place to hide: Comparative status and future prospects of black boys. In M.B. Spencer, G.K. Brookins, & W.R. Allen (Eds.), *Beginnings: The social and affective development of black children* (pp. 201–214). Hillsdale, NJ: Lawrence Erlbaum.

Heyns, B. (1978). *Summer learning and the effects of schooling.* New York: Academic Press.

Hilliard, A. (1999, April). Colloquium on student achievement in multicultural school districts. *Equity & Excellence in Education, 32,* 79–86.

Hudak, G.M. (1996). A suburban tale: Representation and segregation in special needs education. In J.L. Kincheloe, S.R. Steinberg, & A.D. Gresson (Eds.), *Measures lies: The bell curve examined* (pp. 315–329). New York: St. Martin's Press.

Ladson-Billings, G. (1995). *The dream keepers.* San Francisco, CA: Jossey Bass.

Oakes, J. & Lipton, M. (1992). Detracking schools: Early lessons from the field. *Phi Delta Kappan, 74,* 448–454.

Obiakor, F.E. (1999). Teacher expectations of minority exceptional learners: Impact on "accuracy" of self-concepts. *Exceptional Children, 66,* 39–53.

Ogbu, J.U. (1995). Literacy and black Americans: Comparative perspectives. In V.L. Gadsden & D.A. Wagner (Eds.), *Literacy among African-American youth: Issues in learning, teaching, and schooling* (pp. 83–101). Cresskill, NJ: Hampton Press.

Schuman, H., & Krysan, M. (1999. A historical note on whites' beliefs about racial inequality. *American Sociological Review, 64,* 847–855.

Sizemore, B.A. (1988). The Madison Elementary School: A turnaround case. *Journal of Negro Education, 57,* 243–266.

Stevens, F.I. (1993). *Opportunity to learn: Issues of equity for poor and minority students.* Washington, DC: National Center for Education Statistics.

AUTHOR INDEX

A

Abbott, R. D., 94
Abedi, J., 10, 85
Aber, J. L., 9
Abraham, S. Y., 10
Adams, C. R., 30
Adelman, H. S., 99
Adler, S., 98
Aguirre-Munoz, Z., 10, 85, 189
Ahearn, E. M., 160
Alexander, C. M., 179, 180
Alexander, K. L., 231, 232
Algozzine, B., 3, 11, 21, 32, 118, 128, 155, 162, 168, 189, 190
Algozzine, R., 91
Allen, J., 31, 32
Alley, R., 151
Allington, R. L., 31, 32
Alter, M., 8–10, 68
Amati, C., 79
Anderson, M., 10
Anderson, M. G., 69, 70
Anderson, P. P., 13, 15
Aponte, J. F., 5
Apple, M. W., 40
Aramburo, D., 142
Arnold, N., 144
Arreaga-Mayer, C., 104–106
Arter, J. A., 77
Arthur, B., 14
Artiles, A. J., 3, 9–11, 30, 53, 85, 119, 165, 166, 189, 209
Asante, M. K., 35
Asha, K., 76
Atkinson, D. R., 21, 181, 211

Atwater, J., 105
Ayers, W., 37
Azmitia, M., 80

B

Babcock, N. L., 176
Baca, L., 20, 21, 142
Bahr, M. W., 68
Baker, E. L., 165
Baker, J., 31
Baker, L., 144
Baker-Sennett, J., 80
Bakewell, D., 105
Ball, E. W., 20
Balow, I. H., 61
Banks, C. A. M., 18, 208–210, 213, 217
Banks, J. A., 3, 4, 16, 18, 32, 42, 141, 146, 147, 174
Barnard, K. E., 8
Barnes, E. J., 219
Barton, L., 31
Baruth, L. G., 19, 147
Baumeister, A. A., 8
Bazron, B., 132
Beamer, L., 233
Bebout, L., 14
Bell, D. A., 31
Belmont, J. M., 76, 79
Bender, W. N., 94
Benson, P. L., 35
Bercovici, S. M., 84
Berends, M., 33
Bergan, 178
Berktold, J., 165
Berliner, D. C., 33, 39
Berninger, V. W., 94

237

SUBJECT INDEX

A

Academic expectation
  linguistic differences, 4
  multicultural learners, 4, 140
  recommendations for full school participation,
    41–43, 131–136
  socioeconomic status, 31–34, 140–141
Acalculia, 93
Access to services, 4, 166
Accessible adult role model, mentor, advocate,
    209–211, 216–217
Accountability, 156–162, 230
  access focus with results-based emphasis,
    157–158, 230
    hazards, 165–166, 230
    hopes, 166–167
  assessment bias, 108, 155–156, 162–165, 230,
    231
  disabled students' performance, 157–162, 230,
    231
  educational goals and outcomes, 158–165
    commonalities and differences, 160–162
    national goals, 158
    NCEO goals, 160
    State goals, 159
  Individuals With Disabilities Education Act
    (IDEA), 54, 90, 119, 155, 157–158, 209
    disciplinary provisions, 125–126
    disabled students, 126
  multicultural disabled students, 157
    assessment of outcomes, 162–165
  results-based hazards, 165–166
    accountability and exclusion, 165, 166, 230
    diversity downplayed, 165
    outcomes narrowed, 165

results-based hopes, 166, 230
    diversity drives outcomes, 166
    inclusive systems for all, 166
    outcomes open opportunities, 166
  school accountability system components,
    158, 230
  States, inclusive accountability reports, 158
  systematic collection of data 158
Achievement outcomes, 3, 31, 33
  recommendations for full school participation,
    41–43
African American English (AAE), 16, 40, 98
  teacher attitudes, 98
African Americans
  achievement discrepancies, 10, 35, 232
  behavior and interpretation, 16, 119, 125
  Black English, 16, 40, 98
  demographics, 9–10, 211
  educational placement, 10, 31, 35, 57–66, 140,
    142, 232
  educational punishment imbalances, 125, 232
  emotional disturbance, sociocultural charac-
    teristics, 122–123
  HIV and child development, 8
  independent Black institutions, enrollment, 35
  LD and environmental risk factors 10
  LD and ethnic representation, 57–66
  MMR and environmental risk factors, 8–9
  MMR and ethnic representation, 57–66, 140
  perception of disabled child, 12
  poverty and MMR, 8
  poverty and special education placement, 10,
    31, 233
  predictor variables for LD, 10
  prenatal, perinatal, postnatal environment,
    7–9, 36, 231